LION OF THE LEAGUE

Copyrighted 1895 By
The Calvert · Litho. Co.
Detroit, Mich.

LION OF THE LEAGUE

Bob Emslie and the Evolution of the Baseball Umpire

LARRY R. GERLACH

University of Nebraska Press
LINCOLN

Frontispiece: Chromolithograph showing a batter standing at home plate with catcher and umpire awaiting the pitch, 1895. Library of Congress Prints and Photographs Division, Washington DC 20540 USA.

Acknowledgments for the use of copyrighted material appear on pages xxi–xxii, which constitute an extension of the copyright page.

The University of Nebraska Press is part of a land-grant institution with campuses and programs on the past, present, and future homelands of the Pawnee, Ponca, Otoe-Missouria, Omaha, Dakota, Lakota, Kaw, Cheyenne, and Arapaho Peoples, as well as those of the relocated Ho-Chunk, Sac and Fox, and Iowa Peoples.

♾

Library of Congress Cataloging-in-Publication Data
Names: Gerlach, Larry R., author.
Title: Lion of the league: Bob Emslie and the evolution of the baseball umpire / Larry R. Gerlach.
Description: Lincoln: University of Nebraska Press, [2024] | Includes bibliographical references and index.
Identifiers: LCCN 2023048985
ISBN 9781496237651 (hardback)
ISBN 9781496239983 (epub)
ISBN 9781496239990 (pdf)
Subjects: LCSH: Emslie, Robert Daniel, 1859-1943. | Baseball umpires—United States—Biography. | Baseball umpires—Canada—Biography. | BISAC: SPORTS & RECREATION / Baseball / History | BIOGRAPHY & AUTOBIOGRAPHY / Sports
Classification: LCC GV865.E56 G47 2024 | DDC 796.357092 [B]—dc23/eng/20231117
LC record available at https://lccn.loc.gov/2023048985

Set in Whitman by A. Shahan.

For my umpiring friends Dennis Bingham and Perry Barber on behalf of all the dedicated men and women who, by "calling 'em as they see 'em," allow baseball from youth leagues to the majors to be played in a fair and orderly manner.

Here exist the oldest words the hand of man has written,
"Umpire's bum decision lost the game."
Shortstops may have booted six or seven easy chances,
Batsmen may have popped to first or whiffed in dull-eyed trances,
But the next day in the public prints this line meets angry glances—
"Umpire's bum decision cost the game."
Fielders kick the ball about from season unto season,
Pitchers tear off passes in a style that smacks of treason,
But when the bally scrap is lost, you know the final reason—
"Umpire's bum decision cost the game."

—Grantland Rice, "The Cause Eternal," *Songs of the Stalwart*

Mother, may I slug the umpire?
May I slug him right away?
So he cannot be here, Mother
When the clubs begin to play?
Let me clasp his throat, dear mother,
In a dear delightful grip
With one hand and with the other
Bat him several in the lip.
Let me climb his frame, dear mother,
While the happy people shout;
I'll not kill him, dearest mother,
I will only knock him out.
Let men mop the ground up, Mother,
With his person, dearest do;
If the ground can stand it, Mother,
I don't see why you can't too.
Mother, may I slug the umpire,
Slug him right between the eyes?
If you let me do it, Mother
You shall have the champion prize.

—Anonymous, "Mother May I Slug Him,"
Chicago Tribune, August 15, 1886

Contents

Illustrations

Preface

The umpire is a lonely man
Whose calls are known to every fan
Yet none will call him Dick or Dan
In all the season's games.
They'll never call him Al or Ed
Or Bill or Phil or Frank or Fred
Or Jim or Tim or Tom or Ted
They'll simply call him names.

—Milton Bracker, "The Umpire,"
New York Times, April 8, 1962

Jacques Barzun's famous adage, "Whoever wants to know the heart and mind of America had better learn baseball," is overwrought, but to know "the rules and rhythms" of the game you need to know umpiring, the decision on every play influencing the course, even outcome, of games. Despite their central role, umpires are nameless, faceless figures; fans know little about their work and profession, let alone off-field identities. That is not surprising. Although embedded in record books far more than officials in other sports and the only ones listed in newspaper box scores, umpires are conspicuous by omission in baseball histories.[1] There are a few recent as-told-to autobiographies, but only Bill McGowan (1925–54) has received an authoritative biography; the lone history is James Kahn's 1953 informal survey.[2]

This book is about Bob Emslie, the least-known famous umpire in baseball history. On September 19, 1896, the *New York Clipper* wrote, "Few men are better known in baseball circles than Robert D. Emslie," but today he is virtually unknown to baseball constituencies, including those interested in umpires. Aside from two brief sketches he is only occasionally mentioned for a few diamond disorders, notably the (in) famous 1908 Merkle game.[3] He is absent from biographical encyclopedias and is not to be found among the fifty-two umpires in a three-volume baseball dictionary or a compendium of "the 2,000 most significant and influential people in baseball history."[4] Even a Montreal newspaper in 1974 said Paul Runge and Jim McKean were the first Canadian regular Major League umpires, a claim later corrected in column titled "Emslie was first—by 83 years!"[5]

This is a book I did not intend to write. Just as Emslie got into umpiring by happenstance, I unwittingly became involved in researching his career. In March 2019 two friends, Bob Barney, sport historian at Western University, and Andrew North, organizer of an upcoming Canadian baseball history symposium, cajoled me first into a twenty-minute talk, then a keynote address, on Emslie. I had no interest in him and knew little about his career, but agreed to talk about the difficult times umpires faced during the tumultuous 1890s. Preliminary research revealed sportswriters regarded Emslie as one of the finest umpires of his day, indeed of baseball history, and believed "the story of his career makes remarkable reading" and would "fill a very large book" without which "the baseball public will have missed something."[6] I also learned he was an international champion in the sports of trapshooting and curling. Clearly Emslie deserved a full-blown biography, but researching a professional playing and umpiring career spanning six decades, from 1880 to 1935, seemed a task both more arduous and less important than other projects already underway. Then came a historian's epiphany: an Emslie biography would not only address a void in baseball literature but also personify baseball's evolution into the modern game and umpiring's transition from a contentious temporary job to an esteemed professional career.

On a personal level, the project touched a lifelong interest. As a youth I was taken with sports officials. The first autographed baseball I ever had the nerve to request came in 1956 from Max Stone, Western League umpire at Sherman Field, where I watched many a Lincoln Chiefs game. I later tried umpiring amateur baseball and fast-pitch softball only to learn that just as I couldn't throw or hit a good curveball as a player, I couldn't call one, either. Then, impressed by umpires enduring the histrionics of managers like Earl Weaver, Billy Martin, and Bobby Cox, I set about writing a history of Major League umpiring, but, daunted by the magnitude of the project, settled for a collection of umpire autobiographies.[7]

So, setting other projects aside, I embarked on researching the life and times of a forgotten man in blue. It was a task far more ambitious, difficult, and time-consuming than I had imagined, owing to enormity of the research as well as travel lockdowns and archival and library closings during the COVID-19 pandemic. And I again had to face the problems inherent in biographies; having written two, I knew them well.

Procuring sufficient documentary material was challenging. Umpires are ignored by the press save for controversies and, like others in the world of sport, rarely save correspondence or keep a diary or journal. There are no Emslie papers, only a brief, three-page memoir written late in life and devoted overwhelmingly to his playing career. His son and daughter were childless, so there are no relatives to pass along family lore and remembrances. Fortunately the Elgin County Museum in St. Thomas, Ontario, has a collection of Emslie's baseball memorabilia as well as pictures, documentary ephemera, and a scrapbook containing mostly undated and unattributed newspaper clippings.

Despite the absence of personal papers, abundant information is available to construct a comprehensive portrait of Emslie's baseball career. Annual issues of the Reach and Spalding guides and record books provided rules, league information, and commentaries on umpires. For season and career records of Major League teams and individuals, I drew heavily from Baseball-Reference.com and Retrosheet,org. For Minor League team and individual statistics I drew from StatsCrew.org. The national baseball weeklies, *Sporting Life* and *Sporting News*, as well as Canadian and American newspapers, provided the principal paper trail. Spotty, partisan, and considerably varied reporting made it necessary to consult multiple home and visiting team dailies, and online compilations of digitized newspapers greatly facilitated research despite frequently failing to call up names and subjects covered in issues.

While newspapers provided a wealth of information about Emslie's umpiring, it consisted overwhelmingly of player confrontations, fan disturbances, and criticism of decisions. Rarely mentioned were basic issues such as travel and accommodation arrangements, salaries, ballpark dressing rooms, or instructions from league officials. We know a great deal about Emslie on the field, but almost nothing of him off it. A reserved, private man who eschewed interviews, he preferred to let his deeds speak for themselves; on the rare occasions he spoke to the press, I quote him at length to accord him his voice.

Because historical context is crucial for understanding a life, this biography takes note of the proximate and broader circumstances of the times and places in which Emslie grew up and lived. A Canadian whose life's work was in the United States, Emslie's thinking and behaviors were affected by the social and economic transformation of life in North America as well as by World Wars I and II, the viral pandemic of 1918–19, and the Great Depression. And the baseball field in and around which he spent most of his adult life was then a very different place. He experienced pitchers throwing the ball underhanded at ground level fifty feet from home plate to hitters holding a flat-sided bat asking for a high or low pitch; a lone umpire calling pitches behind the plate, then moving behind the pitcher with a man on base; spectators sitting on the field during the game, often interfering with play; and umpires getting into fistfights with players and being escorted from the field by police after games.

Every biographer tries to capture the private person behind the public persona, with varying degrees of success. If I've come to know a great deal about Bob Emslie as a pitcher and umpire, the inner man remains elusive save for the personality traits evident in a competitive sportsman and his manner of umpiring. Given the absence of personal papers virtually nothing is known about his parents, siblings, wife, or children, let alone his childhood or familial experiences. We know he was a hunter, trapshooter, and curler and that he liked dogs, horses, and cigars, but nothing about his personal likes, dislikes, values, and beliefs, or what he thought about the extraordinary transformations and events occurring without the ballpark during his lifetime.

It helps to understand a life when it has a through line. For Bob Emslie baseball is an unbroken thread in what seems like a well-plotted story progressing seamlessly from batboy to pitcher to umpire. He was, quite literally, a lifelong baseball person, the game the all-consuming central feature of his life. My words describe in detail what Emslie saw and did, but only hint at what he thought and how he felt about things. While it is not appropriate to read between nonexistent lines, known facts point to the possible and probable, so I have occasionally engaged in cautious and appropriate speculation. As it is irresponsible if not dangerous to delve too deeply into the psychology of a historical person, I have let Emslie be known by his words and deeds.

In the end, biography is an art of research, analysis, and exposition, and a conceit given the impossibility of the task. It is presumptuous to attempt to retrieve a life that has slipped away, foolish to think you can capture fully the thoughts, deeds, and personality of another human being. Notwithstanding mounds of material, there is no arguing with Mark Twain: "What a wee little part of a person's life are his acts and his words! His real life is led in his head, and is known to none but himself. His acts and his words are merely the visible thin crust of his world . . . a mere skin enveloping it. Biographies are but the clothes and buttons of the man—the biography of the man himself cannot be written."[8]

That said, if biographies fail to capture fully a life, they speak intimately about the uniqueness of the individual as well as the commonalities of human experience. Bob Emslie's experiences as a player and umpire were sui generis, but they were also representative of all who threw and called pitches. This biography of an umpire is really about umpires and umpiring, the routines and rhubarbs, techniques and equipment, travel and loneliness. My hope is that readers will derive appreciation both for the work of umpires and for a man who played a significant role in the development of the profession.

In recounting Emslie's umpiring career, of a recital of game time experiences there seems to be no end, not because they are interesting (though most are) but because it is nigh impossible to convey the life and times of an umpire without what might appear to be a surfeit of repetition. Umpires perform the same duties and encounter similar incidents game after game, but no two games are alike, and recurring game-time encounters, differing in nature and detail, demonstrate various ways of handling the realities of the workplace. Along with player confrontations and controversies, press condemnation and commendation—all of which speak to the trials and tribulations of umpiring—there are recurring examples of the exhilaration and transcendent joy of umpiring. That's what it was, and had to be, for Emslie to handle the indicator for thirty-six years.

A note on details major and minor. To avoid excessive reiteration of home and away newspapers, I have not provided citations for games identified by date and place; as Casey Stengel famously said, "You could look it up." I have read extensively with profit and pleasure on baseball and beyond, but since most titles are well known, I have cited only those less common or specific to Emslie. To avoid undue repetition, statistics drawn from the websites Retrosheet, Baseball Reference, and Stats Crew are without attribution. I have quoted extensively partly because it is my wont but principally to convey a flavor of the times and give press and players voice, however stilted and hyperbolic. After all, Emslie and fans read what reporters wrote. Following convention I have silently corrected obvious typos and modernized haphazard punctuation and capitalization; I have also used the closed compound *baseball*, even in direct quotations, although until World War I it was usually written as two words; *foul tip* for a hit ball that goes backward when by definition it is a ball caught by the catcher (the others are simply *fouls*); and Pittsburgh, although from 1891 to 1911 it was commonly spelled without the *h*. While Emslie was widely heralded as a champion trapshooter and curler, I have not extensively chronicled his participation in those sports as they are peripheral to his baseball career.

Bob Emslie has been on my mind for four years. While admiring his dedication and achievements I have tried to be dispassionate and objective in discussing his actions, career, and place in baseball history, offering neither praise nor criticism beyond what the facts allow. However, I do realize the enormous responsibility of a biographer. Looking at the mannequin in the Elgin County Museum in St. Thomas, Ontario, bedecked in Emslie's umpiring uniform, underscored I was not exhuming documentary remains but describing a human being. That imparts the obligation to get the facts straight, to be empathetic, and to be fair in judgment.

Herewith, then, is *a* life, not *the* life, of Bob Emslie. The redivivus is what Henry James called a "partial portrait," an assemblage of stories, scenelets, and statistics of Emslie's career as a player and umpire in the context of extraordinary times in the development of both professional baseball and North America.[9] The old saw that umpiring is the only job where you are expected to be perfect the first day and improve every day thereafter is nonsensical; umpires, like players, are prone to human error. If Bob Emslie, who surely missed countless calls over the years, was not perfect, neither is this book. I know there are ambiguities and loose ends, gaps and probably gaffes, but I hope Bob would say I was fair and called 'em like I saw 'em.

Acknowledgments

Historical writing is an obsessive and lonely undertaking, but many people facilitated my research and made the project the more enjoyable. First and foremost, thanks to Bob Barney and Andrew North, without whose initiative and encouragement this book would never have been written. And a heartfelt thanks to Bob and Ashleigh Barney, the latter a superlative chef, for graciously providing room and board during research trips to Canada.

The work of a historian relies on the unsung heroes of research, the archivists and librarians who preserve and provide the documents and material objects that are the stuff of history. I especially appreciate the assistance of Gina Dewaele at the Elgin County Archives and Michael Baker at the Elgin County Museum in St. Thomas, Sophia Grande-Lawlor of the Wellington County Archives in Fergus, and the staff of the London Room of the London Public Library. South of the border, impersonal but heartfelt gratitude to the archival staffs of the Cleveland Public Library Center for Local and Global History for document scans; the Giamatti Research Center at the National Baseball Hall of Fame and Museum in Cooperstown, New York, for access to the individual files of umpires, managers, and players; the Family History Library of the Church of Jesus Christ of Latter-day Saints in Salt Lake City, Utah, for guidance in mining its treasure trove of genealogical records, public documents, and obscure local histories; and the Special Collections Department of the University of Utah Marriott Library for graciously accommodating my repeated rummaging through forty-three boxes of photocopied umpire material stored in my collection of papers. And for promptly processing myriad requests I owe an incalculable debt to the University of Utah's interlibrary loan staff, notably Gregory Burbank, coordinator of borrowing.

Thanks to Glen Curnoe, retired librarian of the London Room of the London Public Library, for providing unflagging encouragement and copies of documents; Riley Nowakowski of Western University in London for assistance with last-minute newspaper research; Pete Sheridan, former president of the St. Thomas Historical Society, for a guided tour of Emslie's home environs and for checking newspaper citations; Benson Taylor of the *Sporting News* for photographs from the Charles Conlon Collection; David Stinson, Baltimore Orioles historian, for the rare 1884 scorecard from the Ted Patterson collection; Sean Holz, for a poem from baseball-almanac.com; and Lee Lowenfish for the 1959 Pony League poem.

I am deeply indebted to the historians whose galaxy of baseball books and articles provided both information and inspiration. Special recognition to members of the Society for American Baseball Research for biographical sketches of players, managers, administrators, and even some umpires available online via the SABR Baseball Biography Project; David W. Smith, biology professor cum baseball researcher extraordinaire and founder of Retrosheet, the most important statistical database for Major League games, teams, and individual careers; and Sean Lahman, whose index of baseball guides allowed ready access to annual guides.

Through their unqualified love and support my sons, T.J. and Jonathan (Jona), and daughter-in law Jennifer, ardent baseball fans, contributed profoundly to the preparation of this book. I hope Bob Emslie's story adds to their appreciation and understanding of umpiring and the game we all so enjoy.

Larry Gerlach
Salt Lake City

LION OF THE LEAGUE

Prologue

From Gentleman Arbiter to Folk Villain

> Ideally, the umpire should combine the integrity of a Supreme Court justice, the physical agility of an acrobat, the endurance of Job and the imperturbability of Buddha.
>
> —"Villains in Blue," *Time*, August 25, 1961

"What's past is prologue." William Shakespeare's famous line speaks to history as context for understanding the present. Current Major League Baseball Rule 8.01(a) stipulates, "The umpires shall be responsible for the conduct of the game in accordance with these official rules and for maintaining discipline and order on the playing field during the game." It has ever been so. A chapter in a pioneering baseball history book is entitled "The Troubles of an Umpire: A Public Individual Who Has Few Joys and Many Sorrows." That, too, has always been so.[1] When Bob Emslie began umpiring in 1887 he probably never thought about the origin or development of the vocation he chose to pursue. While umpiring had changed dramatically over the previous four decades, mirroring the distinctive eras of baseball itself, past conditions and attitudes still influenced how he worked and was perceived.

The umpire—the function borrowed from cricket and the word derived from the French *noumpere*, meaning a peerless or impartial arbitrator who decides disputes between equals—has been a part of baseball since it evolved from youthful play to adult competition.[2] The umpire played a secondary role from the 1830s through the Civil War, when baseball was a recreational activity for social clubs. The earliest extant written rules, from Philadelphia's Olympic Ball Club in 1837, appointed a member as an umpire to record the action of intraclub games and adjudicate disputes between team captains, and declared "from his decision there shall be no appeal."[3] The expanded 1845 rules of the New York Knickerbockers instructed the umpire to fine players for disregarding rules, arguing his decisions, or displaying ungenteel behavior; on October 6, D. O'Brien was fined "for Swearing" and in a subsequent game Ebenezer Dupignac Jr. was dunned six cents "for saying s—t."[4]

For match games between clubs whose rules often varied, there were typically three officials: two team umpires and a neutral "referee" chosen to resolve disagreements The proliferation of clubs in 1857 led to the expansion and standardization of umpire duties. With two team umpires being redundant and increasingly causing disputes, the National Association of Base Ball Players in 1858 sanctioned a single umpire chosen by the home team with the consent of the rival captain. Most umpires lacked experience, qualifications, or both, their only credentials being a respected member of the community (often a lawyer), a former player, or simply an interested spectator. There was no dress code, but contemporary illustrations and photographs depict an idealized gentleman arbiter resplendent in top hat and long frock coat who stood or sat a distance from home plate in foul territory along the first base line. The now-independent official still had a passive role, rendering decisions only on appeal by players who disagreed about the application of rules.

As pitchers transitioned from a "feeder" tossing balls batters could easily hit into play to altering pitches to get batters out, the umpire became a more active participant, authorized to call strikes in 1858 and balls in 1863. Calling pitches required moving behind home plate, but the umpire, lacking protective gear, to avoid being hit with pitched or backward batted balls stood erect some distance behind the gloveless catcher, also positioned well behind home plate. No longer able to rely on the sportsmanship of gentlemen to maintain order as games became increasingly competitive, he had to know the playing rules. By 1862 umpires, still chosen by the captains of the contending teams, were required to be a member of a ball club, but few were familiar with an arbiter's duties. That year *Beadle's Dime Base-Ball Player*, the game's initial guidebook, provided an extensive description of the umpire's responsibilities, noting "the position of an Umpire is an honorable one, but its duties are anything but agreeable, as it is next to an impossibility to give entire satisfaction to all parties concerned in a match."[5]

With the organization of the National Association of Professional Base Ball Players (NABBP) in 1871, the umpire, now less formally attired, became an essential component of the play-for-pay game: without someone to enforce rules and decide every bit of the action, competitive contentiousness would rule the day.[6] While given greater authority by limiting appeals of decisions to rules interpretations, not judgments, the umpire, picked by the home team from a list of names submitted by the visitors, continued to receive for their services nothing other than the honor of being chosen to judge fair and unfair play. As NABBP games became more competitive, teams began paying competent umpires respected for their knowledge and impartiality. Henry Chadwick, the day's foremost baseball writer, feared that by paying the arbiters "impartial umpiring will become a thing of the past," but by 1875 umpires were "privileged to accept such compensation for his services as the competing clubs shall deem advisable, provided he receives from each club the same amount of compensation, but not otherwise."[7] Nonetheless, a multiplicity of arbiters inevitably produced inconsistent umpiring; in 1875, the last year of the NABBP, only six of ninety umpires called more than ten games.

The professionalization of baseball eventually led to professional umpires. A second "major league," the National League, in 1876 allowed the home team to choose an umpire from a list of five members drawn from three or more clubs "known as acknowledged and competent men for the position" telegraphed by the visiting team at least ten days in advance of a game. But to avoid suspicion of "homer umps" and to streamline the process, the league in 1878 took selection of umpires away from clubs, creating an official league roster. Each team submitted to the league secretary the names of "persons of good repute and considered competent to act as umpires," none residing in the club's city. Those with the greatest number of nominations constituted the list of authorized umpires. From five names submitted by the visiting team not less than three days before a game, the home team selected an umpire, the visitors paying the official's $5 fee and all travel expenses. To promote orderly play, the "master of the field" was authorized to fine players from $10 to $20 for violating rules or using "abusive, threatening or improper language to the umpire, audience or other player."[8] While umpires were often unable or unwilling to leave their regular jobs and travel to a distant city for games, there was better work from fewer arbiters: of sixty-one umpires in 1876 only nine worked more than ten games; of thirty-three umpires in 1877 six worked more than nine games. In 1878 five of nineteen umpires called 70 percent of games.

In 1882 the new Major League, the American Association (AA), created the first professional umpire staff. The six-team circuit began its inaugural season having the home team pay the umpire chosen by the visiting club from three or more local umpires, but in the face of "alleged partiality in umpiring" and perhaps fear of crookedness signaled by the termination of Richard Higham in June, the owners in July decided to hire, pay, and assign umpires. Six umpires, paid $75 per month with on-road expenses covered by the visiting team with whom they traveled and lodged, were required to wear blue caps and coats accented by gold cord and buttons, the distinctive uniforms symbolizing authority.[9] That December the National League (NL) followed suit with a uniformed four-man staff paid $1,000 per season. The NL also underscored umpires' authority by allowing fines of $5 to $50 and their independence by paying their rail and hotel expenses (but not per diem) and prohibiting them from traveling with or staying at the same hotels as players. NL umps initially were not uniformed identically: George "Watch" Burnham wore black pants, a blue shirt, and a white hat and belt, but all soon wore blue suits. A proposed "umpire school" for the staff held by Secretary Nick Young in Washington to ensure consistent interpretations of rules never materialized, likely because owners were unwilling to cover the additional cost.[10] The AA in 1883 also paid travel expenses, as did the upstart Union Association in 1884. The latter not only paid three regular umpires $140 per month but also uniquely required each umpire to sign an oath to "faithfully, honestly and impartially discharge" his duties, "not be influenced by any personal feelings," and "abstain from all forms of gambling."[11]

Full-time professional staffs increased umpires' competence and uniform application of rules, but did not free umpires from suspicion of favoring the home team or colluding with gamblers. With gambling rampant in the game, umpires, meagerly compensated and required to cover travel expenses and purchase their own equipment, were tempting targets for bookies and gamblers.[12] It would have been easy for a single arbiter to fix a game, but Higham, a former player, remains the only umpire ever banished for allegedly advising gamblers how to bet on games he worked, a decision eventually shrouded in uncertainty. Following Higham's expulsion, the leagues in 1883 provided for the permanent disqualification of any umpire convicted of "selling, or offering to sell" a game and inserted into the playing rules the most extensive account of umpiring duties and responsibilities.[13]

Umpiring was a stressful occupation. Official complaints from two, then four clubs could lead to termination. Given the difficulty of applying the often revised and haphazardly written regulations, it was suggested in 1884 an interleague committee revise the entire code since many of the rules, "anything but models of pure or ordinary good English," were "ambiguous, improperly worded and capable of widely different constructions."[14] In 1886 the NL and AA compiled a common set of regulations, but frequent revisions and innovations in playing techniques continued to complicate the umpire's job.[15] Applying the ill-defined strike zone—"over the Home Base, not higher than the Batsman's shoulder, nor lower than his knee"—became more difficult with the advent of "curved pitching" in 1876–77, the umpire now having to determine "whether a ball is an inch over the corner of the plate."[16] Standing closer to the catcher behind home plate, the better to call pitches, led to battering from pitches or foul balls. Following catchers' lead, by 1882 umpires had begun donning masks and chest protectors and using indicators to keep track of balls and strikes; some felt the mask obscured their vision and others shunned padding, but by decade's end the use of protective gear was common.[17] But it was the persistent verbal abuse and threat of physical violence from fans and players that made an umpire's life so difficult.

With the advent of professional baseball, which transformed the sport into an entertainment spectacle, players and spectators soon began contravening the traditions of good sportsmanship and fair play. Players, motivated by an emphasis on winning and hope for higher salaries, were increasingly given to disrespectful, even disgraceful behavior. Beleaguered umpires were routinely baited, bullied, badgered, and sometimes beaten as well as spiked, sworn at, and spit on. With baseball alone allowing players and coaches to argue decisions it was difficult to maintain discipline and decorum on the field. Despite being able to impose fines for "abusive, threatening or improper language" and disorderly conduct, the cussing and criticizing continued unabated since umpires could not remove players from the game until 1889 (and then only for repetition of a finable offense).[18]

Fans, predictably imitating players, became more partisan rooters than sporting spectators. Although the 1876 National League rules declared umpires were "entitled to the respect of the spectators, and any person hissing or hooting at, or offering any insult or indignity to him, must be promptly ejected from the grounds," fans, then called "cranks" or "kranks," whether actuated by civic boosterism, emotional frustrations, opposition to authority, or simply the heightened competitiveness of games, breached behavioral norms, hurling vituperation, bottles, and all manner of debris at umpires as well as threatening physical harm. Postgame mobbings were commonplace, police escorts familiar and welcome sights to the men in blue. The National League was prescient in requiring each club to provide "sufficient police force upon its own grounds to preserve order," although few clubs did so.[19]

The adversarial attitude toward and de rigueur criticism of umpires, denouncing their decisions, ridiculing their competence, questioning their honesty, and blaming them for defeat was a remarkable development in the annals of sport. And the umpire's transformation from esteemed arbitrator to despised folk villain was largely deliberate. Newspapers, eager to attract readers, increasingly fingered umpires for defeats. Club owners and league officials, believing that berating and baiting the arbiters boosted attendance, refused to support umpires' decisions, paid players' fines, and even joined sportswriters in depicting umpires as scoundrels and scapegoats.[20]

While much of the vilification of umpires was gratuitous and partisan, criticism was often justified. With no systematic method of selection, training, or supervision, many umpires were unprepared for the pressures of the job. The leagues admitted "it is a difficult task to secure men for the position who are fully competent for the service."[21] Consequently, umpire staffs were notoriously unstable, many arbiters having tenures as short as a single game; some were released for incompetence or failing to show up for games, while others quit because of abuse, paltry pay, and intolerable working conditions. There is no gainsaying *Sporting Life*: "If the official umpires don't earn their salaries, there is not a class of men on the face of the globe who do."[22]

The root problem, apparent since the designation of a single umpire in 1858, was the inability of a lone arbiter from behind home plate to unerringly call decisions on the distant bases and balls hit down the foul lines. The 1876 proviso that the umpire "shall not enter the infield while the ball is in play" was removed, but even when racing from behind the bat onto the field it was impossible to see clearly sliding runners and "phantom" tags, follow multiple base runners who frequently cut in front of bases or were hindered by fielders, determine if fly balls to the outfield were caught or trapped, and judge whether balls hit near the lines were fair or foul. That umpires were authorized to ask spectators for advice about outfield catches illustrates the problem.[23] In 1888 John Gaffney caused "no end of comment among the spectators" by moving from back of the plate to behind the pitcher with a runner on base. Some umpires followed Gaffney's lead, but if switching positions facilitated base decisions, it made judging pitches and plays at home plate more difficult. Given the central importance of calling pitches, umpires remained behind the plate.[24]

It took the first "World's Series" between the National League and American Association champions in 1886 to experiment with the double umpire system—sort of. The Chicago White Stockings and St. Louis Browns agreed upon a Board of Umpires, two from each league, to be on hand each day with the game's umpire, chosen by lot, to be paid $25 by the winning club. A single umpire called the first game, on October 18, in Chicago, but for the next two games the teams adopted a proposal, concocted by James Walter Spalding, to have two umpires alternating behind the plate, a National umpire when St. Louis was at bat, an Association arbiter for Chicago, and a referee to decide disagreements or, more cynically, "check any dishonesty or over-partiality." A single umpire worked the final game in Chicago and the first one in St. Louis; on October 22 the system of two umpires and a referee was used again; then a lone umpire worked the final game. Reviews of the two umpire system (basically a modern version of what had been used before 1858) were mixed. *Sporting Life* thought it "seems to be a good one" but the *Chicago Tribune* believed it looked "fairly well on paper" but "resulted in a circus" when applied, so should be "tried some time when there is less at stake" than in a championship series.[25]

The leagues went back to using a single umpire for regular-season games, but at the insistence of Frederick Stearns, owner of the Detroit club, two umpires called the 1887 postseason championship series between his Wolverines and the Browns. The teams selected former umpires who had been managers in 1887, John Gaffney of the Washington Nationals and "Honest John" Kelly of the Association's Louisville Colonels, and again had them alternate plate and field assignments, each calling pitches when the other league's team batted. Their compensation is unknown, but their attire signaled league affiliation, Gaffney wearing matching blue jacket and cap and Kelly in dark suit and white cap. Everyone was "delighted with the smooth working" of the double-umpire system giving "eminent satisfaction" throughout the series. The *Detroit Free Press* agreed the system "proved so satisfactory that it's liable to become a fixture in baseball," but since hiring two umpires would be "very expensive," proposed using a spectator or extra player to umpire the bases. But it was not to be. National League president Nick Young flatly declared, "The double system will not be adopted," and parsimonious team owners were not willing to finance two umpires for regular-season games despite the system's obvious merit. Two umpires continued to be used in subsequent World's Series, 1888–90, but they were paid from gate receipts, not league funds.[26]

The travails of the single umpire and high turnover rate notwithstanding, umpiring's pioneering era produced several outstanding men of the cloth. Three made history: John Lensor Boake umpired the first professional game on May 4, 1871, in Fort Wayne, Indiana; William "Billy" McLean called the first National League game in Philadelphia on April

22, 1876; and Charles "Pop" Smith worked the first World Series game, on October 6, 1882, in Cincinnati. Robert Ferguson and John Gaffney were principal exponents of the two basic styles of umpiring. Ferguson, known during his playing days as "Robert the Great" and "Death to Flying Things," ruled as an iron-fisted autocrat, while Gaffney, dubbed "The King of the Umpires," controlled the game through tact and diplomacy. "Honest John" Kelly worked more games and appeared in more World Series (five) than any other umpire of the day. In 1887 Benjamin Young, with prevision, drew up a proposal to improve umpiring that included a professional behavior code, the adoption of the double umpire system, forbidding any player from questioning decisions, umpires working in both major leagues, and giving umpires "absolute and sufficient police protection," carriage transport from game to hotel and a salary "equal to that of the players;" to maintain dignity, umpires would be forbidden to enter a saloon.[27]

During the forty years since William Wheaton umpired the first recorded Knickerbockers game in October 1845, the judicious enforcer of rules and fair play became an adversary, seen as hindering, if not robbing, players and teams of their rightful wins. The homicidal trope "Kill the umpire!" was so popular a Rochester newspaper in 1886 followed its declaration that "the reports of baseball riots, of a baseball umpire fleeing to the woods for safety afford welcome assurance that the harbingers of Spring are genuine and that the great National game is once more with us," with doggerel verse:

> The chilly winter's on the wane,
> The hopes of baseball men are high,
> And the umpire soon will be around again
> With a broken nose and a blackened eye.[28]

A single umpire, untrained, unsupervised, criticized by the press and subjected to vilification and violence from players and fans. Such was the state of umpiring when Bob Emslie began callin' 'em.

1
Grounding in Guelph

’Twas in Guelph that I first got my baseball lesson. As a kid I went to all the ballgames there.

—Robert Emslie, unpublished memoir

Guelph, Ontario, is famous for many things, among them the invention of the jockstrap, wire clothes hangers, and five-pin bowling; North America's first cable television system and first call-in radio program; and the oldest veterinary college in the Western Hemisphere. But it is best known, at least locally, as the birthplace of Robert Daniel Kean "Bob" Emslie, who made his planetary debut on January 27, 1859, the fourth son and seventh of eight children born to Alexander and Mary (née Graye) Emslie.[1]

Bob's ancestry is to be found not in Scotland but in England, in the ancient market and parish town of Helmsley in Yorkshire. After the Norman conquest of 1066 many Anglo-Saxons whose Old English name was Elmeslac fled to Ireland, Scandinavia, and Scotland. The diasporic clan, found predominately in Aberdeenshire, a county in the northeast corner of Scotland bordered on the north and east by the North Sea, adopted a variety of phonetically based surnames: Elmslie, Elmsley, Emsley, and most commonly Emslie, meaning "woodland," derived from Old English *elm* (the tree) and *leah* (a wood or forest).[2]

Bob's immediate lineage is traceable to grandparents John Emslie (b. January 18, 1794) of Strathdon and Barbara Callum (b. May 15, 1796) of Tillylodge, Aberdeenshire. After marrying on November 9, 1815, they settled in Strathdon on the Don river in the eastern Highlands some forty-five miles west of Aberdeen city, where they raised eleven children, one every two years from 1816 to 1835.[3] Like other Scottish immigrants, who typically came self-financed in families or kinship groups together or at intervals, the John Emslie family joined the exodus of 10,409 Scots between 1831 and 1854 who settled primarily in southwestern Canada, a region whose burgeoning population included immigrants from all parts of Great Britain as well as Loyalist refugees and fugitive slaves from the United States.[4]

The circumstances of the Emslie family in Scotland and their motivations for emigrating are unknown, although the great Scottish immigration to Canada corresponded with a time of increased agricultural famine and general economic depression. Many emigrants from the Highlands were crofters (tenant farmers) evicted during the Highland Clearances from 1815 to 1850; Lowland emigrants were typically from artisan and middle-class backgrounds. The Emslies, members of the Church of Scotland, may have been victims of the evangelical schism culminating in the Disruption of 1843.[5]

Whatever their situation, why emigrate? They may have been lured by Adam Fergusson's promotional tract touting the economic prospects in Canada. Perhaps they had been encouraged by Bob's great-grandfather, John Emslie, a member of the Queen's 83rd Regiment who had served in Canada. Or they may have received enticing letters from George Elmslie, an immigrant merchant from Aberdeen who in 1834 opened the Bon Accord Settlement near Elora. What pushed the Emslies to emigrate is unknown, but the pull is obvious: with plentiful land and abundant jobs, untold opportunities for life improvement awaited in Canada West, known since 1867 as Ontario.[6]

Whatever their reason(s) for emigrating, Bob's grandparents and most of the family in 1836 or 1838 came to the village of Guelph, a stronghold of Scottish settlement on the river Speed, just south of Elora and some sixty miles west of Toronto.[7] Guelph, subsequently called the Royal City, as the first town named after the British royal family (Guelph was the Hanoverian surname), was founded on April 23, 1827, by John Galt, Scottish novelist, businessman, and land speculator who was the first superintendent of the Canada Company, incorporated in 1826 to facilitate the colonization of a large part of Upper Canada, territory of the Iroquois Six Nations.[8]

The Emslie family quickly became contributing members of the nascent community. John took up farming, perhaps his vocation in Scotland, but his sons sought different employment. Peter became a schoolteacher, while John, James, and Robert, perhaps familiar with the stone industry in Aberdeenshire, a principal area of limestone and granite production in Great Britain, were drawn to the abundant dolomite limestone deposits on the outskirts of town and became stone masons. Robert eventually became a prominent stonecutter and owner of a major quarry, his kilns producing the uniquely amber-beige magnesium-laced limestone that graced buildings throughout the province and in much of Guelph, often called the Limestone City.[9]

In late 1843 the Emslies' eldest son, Alexander (b. July 12, 1816), and his wife, Mary (b. 1817), arrived in Guelph with their infant daughter, Barbara. They had remained behind so Alexander could complete his guild apprenticeship in tailoring, a prestigious craft in Scotland. By 1850 factory-made clothes were increasingly common in Britain, but in a developing community like Guelph there was great demand for custom-made clothing. One of thirteen tailors in Guelph in 1847, Alexander hoped advertising "moderate charges, punctuality, and good workmanship" would entice customers. Quality and performance won out. In 1851 there were only three tailors in town: Nathaniel Croft and Robert Martin, both merchant tailors, meaning they also sold cloth, and Alexander, a "tailor and clothier," which meant he offered custom tailoring as well as manufactured clothing. From his shop on Market Street, he was "always prepared to execute orders in every department of his business, in the latest and most approved style, upon moderate terms, and with accuracy and dispatch."[10]

Making garments by hand required long hours of slow, meticulous work, so his workshop likely included the usual two craftsmen: a hired cutter who measured clients and cut patterns from selected cloth, and a tailor, the shop owner, who sewed the finished garments.[11]

Owner of a "handsome double-seated buggy—back seat made to fold up—with iron axels, shafts and pole," Alexander prospered, as did Guelph.[12] The village, thanks to Scottish and Irish immigration, grew steadily, if slowly, from approximately 800 residents in 1831, to 1,240 in 1846, to 2,000 in 1853. It experienced rapid economic and population growth after the arrival of the Grand Turk Railroad in 1856, reaching a population of 4,500 in 1858.[13] By 1857 Alexander was doing well enough to expand beyond tailoring, also becoming "a dealer in dry goods, groceries and clothing" on Guelph's main business street, Wyndham. Although a prominent member of the Guelph commercial community, he had a low profile in public affairs. Other than being elected to one term as a school board trustee for the East Ward, there is no record of service in either public office or civic organizations. His defeat in 1851 as a candidate for Tavern Inspector, part of the pro-temperance Reform Party's campaign to crack down on "disreputable drunkeries," signaled not only sobriety, morality, and frugality but also the industrious, work-over-frivolity mindset that had led to his economic success.[14]

Alexander produced children in addition to clothing. He and Mary were a remarkably fecund couple. Immigrating with their firstborn in 1843, they welcomed in Guelph in rapid succession a second daughter, Margaret (1845), and three sons, John Alexander (1846), Alexander (1848), and William George (1850). Another girl, Mary, arrived in 1854, followed by James Arthur (1857), Robert Daniel (1859), and, finally, Alberta (1862). All the children were born at home, likely with the aid of a midwife, as there was no hospital in Guelph.

Of the growing Emslie family virtually nothing is known. Bob's childhood is shrouded in obscurity save that we know he grew up in a commodious two-story house constructed of local limestone on Kent Street at the intersection with Norfolk. The unpretentious house, befitting a middle-class artisan family, had no electricity, running water, or indoor plumbing; meals were prepared on a wood-burning stove, and fireplaces provided warmth during cold Ontario winters. To escape the crowded, noisy household, the nine children for privacy and pleasure spent most of their time outdoors except during inclement weather. Young Bob attended one of the town's two one-room private schools for students five to sixteen years of age and, thanks largely to the influence of his mother who was active in the Upper Canada Bible Society, went with the family to services at St. Andrew's Presbyterian Church, an affiliate of the Church of Scotland in Canada.[15]

Since Bob's brief memoir, written after he retired in 1935, contains no mention of his family or childhood, unknown are the influences of his parents, siblings, circle of friends, or youthful activities on the development of his character, temperament, and personality. He likely received little individual attention from his parents, neither of whom had much leisure time. His father worked long, tiresome hours in the tailoring shop, while his mother had her hands full doing household chores and tending to nine children. Fortunately Alexander was financially able to hire two domestic helpers, Margaret McBride and Mary Stephen, both thirty-one years old, who were immigrants from Ireland and Scotland, respectively.

Sports were important recreational activities in Guelph from early on. Formal clubs for the traditional games of cricket, curling, and lacrosse were organized in the 1830s. Bob's father and older brothers were curlers, but at an early age he caught baseball fever. It is not surprising that Bob was drawn to the diamond, as Ontario was the crucible of Canadian baseball.[16] A game that closely resembled baseball was played in Beachville on June 4, 1838; thereafter "the Canadian Game," featuring five bases and eleven players like cricket, spread rapidly throughout the province. Was it an omen that Bob Emslie was born the same year that American baseball—the New York Game—came to Canada? With faster play and emphasis on fielding, baseball quickly outstripped cricket in popularity among spectators and players alike; fueled by civic pride, every whistle-stop along the rail lines in Middlesex and Wellington counties fielded a team.[17]

The Maple Leafs, founded in 1863 by George Sleeman, owner of the Silver Creek Brewery, became the exemplar of baseball in Guelph, "one of the most enthusiastic baseball centres in all North America."[18] That "Guelphites never neglect to learn how to play the game—in fact they are taught from childhood up" applied to Bob Emslie, whose only mention of childhood in his memoir was about baseball. It was at the newly constructed grounds near the Great Western railroad station, featuring two large stands for spectators and "other necessary conveniences," he recalled, "I first got my baseball lesson. As a kid I went to all the ballgames there." It was an understatement. His brother, Alexander, played for the Maple Leafs, and Bob, who skipped school to go to games, at age six was the team's mascot and batboy.[19]

Guelph's baseball success far outlasted its wave of prosperity. The economic bust that followed railroad speculative growth negatively affected the Emslie family. Faced with declining business, Alexander by 1862 had abandoned his mercantile store, becoming once again only a tailor and clothier. As the hard times continued, he downsized in 1864 to a "merchant tailor," relocated to St. George's Square, and tried to earn money as an agent for sewing machines. The economic recession continued and by 1866 "hundreds of lots in Guelph's new subdivision were sold for delinquent taxes."[20]

Amid the economic downturn the Emslie family split over the future in Guelph. Bob's uncles James and Robert decided stay in the stone business, but others sought fortunes elsewhere. Peter moved to Eramosa, where he unexpectedly died, from consumption, on June 17, 1862, at age thirty-six. But it was John's move south of the border, to Kansas, that had long-term consequences for the family. After attaining statehood in 1861 Kansas experienced explosive economic growth fueled by farmers lured by the 1862 Homestead Act's promise of 160 acres of free land, immigrants from southern Europe drawn by coal mines, and others attracted to the employment opportunities afforded by the expansion of railroads throughout the west.

Sensing a limited future in the crowded stone industry in Guelph, John and his wife, Jane Sim, who never had children, moved in 1862 to Leavenworth, a boomtown located on the western bank of the Missouri River.[21] An experienced stone worker, John quickly became a highly successful contractor, quarrying limestone and providing masonry work for railroad bridges. In 1871 he followed rail lines west to Cottonwood Falls where, impressed by the extent and quality of limestone in the Flint Hills, he became an entrepreneur of the first order, owning five quarries and raising cattle and growing crops on a three-hundred-acre estate east of town where he hosted baseball games at "Emslie's park" and interments at "Emslie's cemetery." When the town was incorporated as a city in 1881, "so great was his reputation and influence" as founder of the quarrying industry and leading employer that residents petitioned to have it named Emslie. But the legislature, kowtowing to the influence of railroads, named it Strong in honor of W. B. Strong, recently elected president of the Santa Fe Railroad. John settled for a street named in his honor.[22]

Migrations within families are usually inspired by those who have gone before, and so it was that Bob's oldest brother, John Alexander (called

J.A.), impressed by Uncle John's reports of opportunities in the Sunflower State, relocated in the late 1860s to Atchison, another burgeoning railroad hub. On November 23, 1870, he married Anna A. Crookham, and through her father, a prominent building contractor and undertaker, learned of a business opportunity in Waterville, a hundred miles west. When A. J. Simis, who in 1870 had established the first drugstore in Waterville, decided to move to New York, J.A. bought the business. By January 1874 he had made City Drug Store "as popular as when our old friend Simis there held forth."[23]

Soon another brother, William George, familiarly Will, also headed to Kansas in 1875 to work with his uncle John. He went partly seeking better employment than his intermittent work as a salesman and railroad baggage handler, but also hoping the milder winters would ease his lifelong respiratory affliction. His decision was undoubtedly affirmed upon learning in 1879 his brother James had died in Canada of a respiratory disease, consumption (tuberculosis).

Benefiting from the association with his famous uncle, Will quickly rose to prominence in the community. He and Mary C. Stuart of Cottonwood married on October 7, 1880, then moved to Strong. After welcoming their firstborn, William Alexander, on November 27, 1881, Will was elected city clerk from 1880 to 1882 and in 1883 became a member of the city council and delegate to the Republican county convention. Just as the couple's future looked bright, Will's health began deteriorating. In July 1884 he went to Hot Springs, Arkansas, hoping the supposed healing properties of the thermal waters would ameliorate his failing health. But he continued to decline, and in November 1886 Will Emslie died of consumption (tuberculosis) at age thirty-five.

What of the rest of Bob's immediate family? Far horizons did not beckon Alexander. Unlike his brother and two sons, single or married laborers without children, he was a craftsman with a family of nine. So in 1868 he packed up and moved some seventy-five miles southwest to London, hoping better financial opportunities awaited the tailoring business in a much larger city with a thriving economy.[24]

For nine-year-old Bob, the move initially was disruptive and disappointing. It cut short his career as a batboy, and he missed watching the

Maple Leafs' rise to baseball glory. Thrice, from1869 to 1871, Guelph received the Silver Ball, emblematic of Canadian baseball supremacy, and in 1874 claimed the "non-professional championship of the world" by winning three straight games in the seven-team tournament in Watertown, New York, including a 13–4 trouncing of the Ku Klux Klan team from Oneida Castle, New York.[25] But Bob's baseball passion was rekindled anon in London, soon reputedly "the best baseball city of its size in all of North America."[26]

2

Coming of Age in London

> After moving to London, I still had my mind on baseball, and my parents had their own troubles keeping me at school in the summertime. All I thought about was baseball.
>
> —Robert Emslie, unpublished memoir

Located at the confluence of the two branches of the Thames River, London was a dramatic contrast to Guelph. The Middlesex county seat was twice the size, with a population of about eighteen thousand, and streets laid out in a grid instead of circuitously arranged around hills. It was very British; street names—Queen, Regent, Piccadilly, St. James, Grosvenor, Trafalgar, and Blackfriars—replicated those in its English namesake. And its economy was booming, as evidenced by three railroads, two daily newspapers, offices of the major Canadian banks, and a plethora of industries including oil refineries, foundries, flour mills, and breweries (notably Labatt and Carling). The Emslie family, the household now including Bob's grandmother Margaret, initially settled on Fleet Street, but soon established permanent residence between King and York streets at 360 Ridout, a block east of the south branch of the Thames.[1]

It takes a flight of imagination to conjure up Bob coming of age, but living adjacent to the hustle and bustle of downtown London offered numerous youthful excitements. In addition to adventurous roaming, there was a prescribed regimen. He faithfully attended Sunday school and church with the family, sitting in pew eighty at nearby St. Andrew's Presbyterian, and on weekdays dutifully went less than a block from home to school, where the principal, Archibald J. Campbell, and senior teacher, Miss Isabella Mearns, supervised the education of their young charges. (In 1871 Ontario became the first province to institute free and compulsory public education for youngsters ages eight through twelve, the goal being an educated citizenry the better to deal with burgeoning social issues, notably immigration, and the economic transformations wrought by technology and industrialization.) But as in Guelph, Bob, not a studious lad, saw less of the classroom than of the London ball park located at the Fair Ground about six blocks northwest of home, frequently skipping classes to watch ballgames. He later mused about the course of his life, "If I had stayed in school more, perhaps it would have been a different story."[2]

Organized baseball came to London in 1856, but cricket, thanks to the presence of a large contingent of soldiers stationed there after the Mackenzie Rebellion of 1837, remained the most popular sport in town until supplanted by baseball following the removal of the garrison in 1869. Spurred by intertown rivalries, the widely reported exploits of the Cincinnati Red Stockings, the first fully professional team, and numerous exhibition games played by teams from the National Association of Professional Base Ball Players, the first professional circuit, interest in baseball exploded.

Young Bob was particularly caught up with the diamond exploits of the Tecumsehs. Organized in 1868, the independent amateur team was named after both the American Shawnee chief Tecumseh, a hero to Canadians for helping repel a United States invasion of Canada during the War of 1812, and the team's chief sponsor, the Tecumseh House, the finest hotel in town. At every opportunity, often at the expense of class attendance, Bob hied over to the fairgrounds to watch afternoon team practices and games.[3] The ten-year-old was likely among the fans who in 1869 watched Guelph win the three-day championship of Canada tournament, defeating the local club 43–20 in the deciding match. And in three summers between 1872 and 1873 he surely joined the throngs who watched the touring Boston Red Stockings, whose team featured future Hall of Famers Harry and George Wright, Al Spalding, Deacon White, and Jim O'Rourke. The American professionals had a major impact on the development of baseball in Canada, demonstrating playing skills and fueling an explosion in the popularity of the game. By the early 1870s London, called by *Canadian Illustrated News* "the best baseball city of its size in all of North America,"[4] boasted numerous games between amateur clubs whose names mimicked those of prominent National Association teams—Athletics, Atlantics, Eckfords, and Mutuals—as well as countless informal interoccupational contests—bankers versus lawyers, policemen versus firemen, cabinetmakers versus upholsterers.[5]

Young Bob did more than watch. He took to the field, learning to play the game on various sandlot and amateur teams, quickly developing a reputation as a fine outfielder. In 1873 the fourteen-year-old was skilled enough to earn a spot on the Tecumseh's second nine. During an intrasquad game on August 14 won by the second nine 12–11, Emslie batted third and made fly catches in the outfield that were "very much admired" by the spectators.[6]

In 1874 Bob Emslie left childhood. He was almost fifteen, past the age of compulsory education, when many boys and girls entered the workforce. The 1871 Ontario school law provided for two kinds of secondary education—high school for general studies and collegiate institutes for classical instruction—but schooling was the farthest thing from Bob's mind. An indifferent student with no apparent aptitude for or interest in either academic or technical education, he explained, "After moving to London, I still had my mind on baseball, and my parents had their own troubles keeping me at school in the summertime. All I thought about was baseball. Finally, the climax came in the summer of 1874, when my father took me from school and sent me to learn the drug business with my brother, who had a store in Waterville, Kansas." Actually, as he later more accurately recalled, he left town on January 19, a week before his fifteenth birthday.[7]

If Alexander was worried about Bob's obsession with baseball, the lack of academic interest was not a concern as he anticipated his sons following him into artisanal occupations. But why send Bob to Kansas to apprentice in J.A.'s drugstore instead of having him learn a trade in London? Perhaps Alexander thought exiling the undisciplined youngster to an unfamiliar distant environment would be a maturational experience. Family finances may have played a role. The move to London had not improved family fortunes as Alexander found it difficult to compete with numerous tailoring shops clustered together, Old World style, at least seven others in the two blocks around his; in all, there were fifteen tailors and sixteen clothiers in the city. In the face of formidable competition and the increasing availability of factory-made clothes reducing the demand for custom clothing, Alexander, in 1874, at age fifty-eight, found himself no longer self-employed but instead working as a cutter in a tailoring shop.[8] The family became modest contributors to their church, indicating their shrinking financial resources.[9] Since Bob's older brother, James Arthur (called Jimmy), age seventeen, also went to Waterville, downsizing the family may have been a way to make ends meet, there now being two fewer mouths to feed.

Whatever the case, the two Emslie teens headed two blocks from home to the Great Western depot to board a train to Kansas. Traveling some nine hundred miles to Waterville via a circuitous rail route was alternately exhilarating and tedious. Given family finances, they rode in coach, sleeping on wooden benches, instead of in more expensive sleeping cars. Upon disembarking after the arduous journey, they faced a culture gap wider than the miles between London and Waterville. They were away from home for the first time, at great distance and in a foreign county. Common language eased the transition, but socially and environmentally it was literally a new world.

Incorporated in 1870, Waterville, the western terminus of the central branch of the Union Pacific railroad, was a small but burgeoning frontier town located along the Blue River in the northeast quadrant of Kansas. It was far enough east to be spared the danger of Indian incursions, but the Canadian lads promptly heard about the sporadic fights, skirmishes, and raids in northwest Kansas during the 1860s and 1870s as local indigenous peoples and Northern Plains tribes tried in vain to preserve their way of life against ranchers and nesters encroaching on their territory and hunting grounds, hunters exterminating once-vast buffalo herds, blue-coated soldiers bent on relocating them to federal reservations, and the fire-breathing railroads that transformed the landscape and provided rapid transportation for the invaders. It was recent history—Bob and Jimmy were in Waterville during the Red River War of 1874–75 and the conflicts that continued in western Kansas until 1878.

They heard, too, of the day of the cowboy. Waterville was initially a cowtown, its stockyards filled with longhorns driven from Texas awaiting shipment eastward. Supplanted by other towns as the railroads extended west, it was no longer overrun with saloons, dancehalls, and bordellos or populated by itinerants, but the cowboy mystique remained. "Home on the Range" had been penned two years before their arrival in nearby Smith County.[10]

While soaking up local lore, Bob and Jimmy help run J.A.'s drugstore. Despite a massive grasshopper infestation in 1874 and the rapid growth of nearby Marysville and Topeka, which drew away population and commercial enterprises, his business prospered. The few surviving issues of the Waterville newspaper from 1874 point to a thriving operation. To entice customers, J.A. advertised, "Go to J. A. Emslie's for Drugs and medicines of all kinds, toilet soaps, hair brushes, tooth brushes, mirrors, cigars, imported and domestic, school books, account books, wall paper, note paper and stationeries of all kinds, hair oils, and in fact everything that can be found in a first-class drug store." After visiting the store, a resident of Atchison reported "the prominent druggist" was "comfortably situated and enjoying a large share of the public patronage in his line. His store is one of the neatest and most complete of any we have seen west of Atchison." While J.A. tended to filling physicians' prescriptions with "none other than the very best drugs and medicines," Bob and Jimmy stocked shelves and served customers. They were especially busy during the Christmas season as J.A. had acquired a "select stock" of special gifts. A customer's son became enchanted when Bob wound up a racially insensitive music box, the lad "wrapped in glee" as "one darkey plays the banjo, another the fiddle, and the third dances in the middle."[11]

It was not all work and no play for Bob and Jimmy. Bringing with them their love of baseball, they promptly took to the field. Organized baseball had come to Kansas in 1867 and new towns like Waterville were quick to form clubs for recreation, entertainment, and publicity. In April 1872 young men formed a town team called the Pacifics after the branch of the Central Pacific railroad that connected towns in the region. Baseball being a new activity, the players evidenced a lack of skill, losing the first recorded game on June 11 to neighboring Irving 19–3. They improved with practice but dropped a pair in July to Blue Rapids 19–3 and 28–23. But there were no further reports of games, the paper reporting croquet, a "pleasant outdoor game[,] has taken the place of baseball in this place."[12]

A team was again organized the next year, but without Waterville newspapers for the summers of 1873–75 it impossible to ascertain the level or extent of ballplaying. However, it is clear from papers in other cities that the team, fielding five formidable players—the pitcher Lansdell and two pairs of brothers, the Emslies and Finchs—played area clubs and traveled to games in Atchison and St. Joseph, Missouri. It was unusual for teenagers to play with adults on a formal town team, but experienced ballplayers were scarce in rural towns like Waterville and the Emslie boys had advanced abilities and understanding of the game. Jimmy, the first baseman, was the best player on the team, and Bob, playing left field, further developed his ballplaying skills.[13]

In June 1875 Bob accompanied Jimmy when he and Lansdell joined the Atchison club for a game in St. Joseph, Missouri. Although given "a terrible drubbing" 20–4 by the semi-pro Pastimes, Jimmy "did well" playing first base and was described as "a good baseball player," one of three Atchison players who "evidently understand the game well." On August 2 he started at first, but in the third inning moved to catcher. The newspaper reported he made "some beautiful catches of swift balls as though they were paper. Emslie's playing throughout was grand, and the ease and grace with which he did his work, and his exceedingly modest demeanor made him a general favorite, while the ladies were wild with enthusiasm over the young gentleman, and manifested their approval by waving their delicately perfumed handkerchiefs with remarkable vigor and bestowing their favors by plaudits that were very flattering to the bashful youth."[14]

The young ladies were not the only ones impressed with Jimmy. The St. Joseph Pastimes brought him up to catch against the Quicksteps of Council Bluffs, Iowa, on August 19; on August 30, playing against the barnstorming St. Louis Brown Stockings, he "did extremely well behind the bat" in his first encounter with a fully professional team. After the game he boarded a train, probably with the Brown Stockings, for a game in Atchison on August 31. Tired from catching the previous day, Jimmy played second base, got a hit that drove in the first run against the Brown Stockings since leaving St. Louis, and had five put-outs and five assists.[15]

Save for Jimmy's out-of-town excursions, the Emslie brothers spent the summer starring on the Waterville nine. Their most satisfying game came on September 4 in St. Joseph when Waterville beat the haughty Pastimes 9–8 by scoring five runs in the ninth inning. In commenting about the play of the "Nameless" team from "the little town of Waterville," the St. Joseph *Herald* allowed "we have never met a better set" and "equals for the Finch brothers and Emslies can seldom be found in the west, [Bob] Emslie's fly catch in the ninth inning was the prettiest of the game." (Bob's subsequent fame as a National League umpire led to misinformation about his Kansas ballplaying.)[16]

Baseball enthusiasm tempered when J.A., soon after celebrating the arrival of a son, William Alexander, on May 21, 1875, began experiencing difficulty breathing. He went to Atchison seeking medical treatment, but his malady worsened, and on March 28, 1876, at his father-in-law's home in Atchison, James Alexander Emslie died at age thirty of tuberculosis. In reporting his passing, the local newspaper noted he was "a favorite with everybody, not only for his many good qualities but for his straight forward manliness, and his well-known uprightness and integrity." Funeral services were held on March 30, and on April 4 the Sutton Lodge No. 85, A. F. and A. M. in Waterville offered memorial resolutions of respect to his memory. His widow sold the drugstore at auction on April 25 and relocated with her ten-month-old son, Will, to her parents' home in Atchison.[17]

After J.A.'s death Bob and Jimmy went to Atchison to live with their aunt, but soon went their separate ways. In May Jimmy contracted to play second base with the now professional St. Joseph Pastimes. After suffering two humiliating defeats in a St. Louis tournament in June, Jimmy, despite being "spoken of very complementary" in newspapers, left the team to work with his uncle John in Cottonwood Falls. When the town organized a baseball club in March 1877, three Emslies were on the nine; John pitched, Jimmy caught, and Will played first base. Jimmy remained with the team at least through May, then, perhaps because of the dearth of organized clubs in the area and the poor quality of play, headed to Wellington, Ontario, where he died of consumption on January 30, 1879, at the age of twenty-two.[18]

When James left Atchison to play ball, Bob, whether homesick, summoned home, or simply not interested in whatever Kansas had to offer, headed back to London. While in Waterville for just over two years he had broadened his social and cultural experiences, helped run the drugstore, and improved his baseball skills. Witnessing his brother's fatal illness surely prompted reflection on life's vicissitudes. J.A.'s death so troubled him that years later he said he left Kansas because "the grass-hopper plague of 1875 put my brother out of business in the Fall of 1876." Bob had gone to Kansas fresh from school; now, boarding the train alone, he faced an uncertain future. He had gained no more than a cursory introduction to the drugstore business, which seems not to have interested him anyway—his memoir mentions nothing about the experience in Kansas other than being there "did not break me from playing baseball." If anything, playing on the town team and traveling with Jimmy only solidified his obsession with the game.[19]

Upon returning to London, Bob learned Canadian baseball had entered a new era. On April 17, 1876, barely two months after the formation on February 2 of the first "major league" in the United States, a group of Ontario businessmen founded Canada's counterpart, the Canadian Association of Base Ball Players (CABBP). Unlike the National League, a centrally administered consortium of privately owned clubs, the CABBP was modeled after the NAPBBP. There was then no set schedule, the ten teams playing mostly arranged games against other clubs, with four—Dundas, Guelph, London, and Toronto—vying in championship competition. Catching the baseball fever sweeping London, Bob rushed to William Bryce's Ontario Game Emporion on Richmond, the lone store in town offering a complete array of baseball equipment, and pored over *Bryce's Base Ball Guide* for 1876, which contained the CABBP constitution, playing rules, instructions for playing each position, diagrams of ball fields, and commentary on the duties and qualifications of umpires. It was the first and only Canadian counterpart to three American guidebooks.

Of particular interest to Bob was the reorganization of the Tecumsehs. With baseball no longer just a game or amusement for spectators but a signifier of community identity and pride, London civic leaders were no longer willing to be runners-up to Guelph, whose Maple Leafs' three-year dominance was due to hiring some American professional players. The British concept of amateur sport was pervasive in Canada, but the growing popularity of the game, the ever-increasing skill level of players, and developments in American baseball made commercialization and professionalization inevitable. The Tecumsehs, headed by president and principal owner Jacob L. Englehart, a wealthy oil refiner, and managing director Harry Gorman, newsman with the *London Advertiser*, became as the city's first professional club.[20] Gorman immediately acquired American professionals. His initial signee was first baseman and manager George Warren "Juice" Latham of Utica, New York, who had briefly played for London near the end of the 1875 season. It was a brilliant choice as Latham was instrumental in helping Gorman attract outstanding young talent, most notably Fred Goldsmith, a pioneer of the innovative "skew ball" (curveball), who signed for $100 in gold each month.[21] Boasting strong hitting and outstanding pitching, the Tecumsehs cruised to the 1876 CABBP title with a 22-0 record in championship competition. Overall, they won forty of forty-five games, outscoring opponents 683–169. In thirty-six games Goldsmith gave up 23 earned runs and struck out 205. (They lost one game by forfeit and two to the eventual National League champion Chicago White Stockings.)

Bob Emslie, at the age of seventeen, initially played a role in the team's success. The Tecumsehs, remembering his performance in outfield before leaving for Kansas, sent him to replace Latham in a game on July 3 against the Michigan champion Jackson Mutuals. In keeping with the Chicago White Stockings' recent innovation of players wearing different colored hats according to their positions, he took right field in an orange and brown cap. He did not wear a glove—most fielders, like cricketeers, played barehanded until the late 1870s. His debut with London's professional nine was auspicious: "Emslie made his first appearance after an absence of about two years, and contributed two good base hits as his share of the game, though he was unable to reap the benefit of them in runs, having the hard luck to get caught both times at third—once on an erroneous decision by the umpire."[22] He then went with the Tecumsehs for a four-team tournament in Syracuse, New York. In the first game, a 24–1 rout of Utica, on July 12, Bob played center field, made one put-out, got two hits in five at bats, and scored a run. He did not see action in the next two games; the Tecumsehs lost one to finish second and take home $400 in prize money.

After returning to London, Bob, judged not mature or experienced enough to play regularly, joined the amateur Atlantics, essentially the Tecumseh's reserve squad. The name, calling to mind the success of the Brooklyn Atlantics, the dominant team of the 1860s, was apt, the team having won the Canadian amateur title the past two years. The 1876 team was also a good one, and Emslie took great pleasure in the Atlantics' defeat of the Tecumsehs 7–5 in a practice game on July 28.

However much Bob enjoyed playing baseball, it was a recreational pastime. He needed a job, so at his father's insistence began to learn the jewelry business as an apprentice with his brother-in-law, William Henry Phillips. Phillips, who had married Bob's sister Mary on February 28, 1876, operated a jewelry shop near the Emslie home at 32 Richmond. It was seemingly a good move, as Phillips was a familial connection and crafting items for personal adornment from precious metals and gemstones was a flourishing industry in the Victorian Era. Besides, it provided a job during the height of unemployment in the "Great Depression" of 1873–79.[23] But for Bob, throwing and hitting baseballs was much more interesting and enjoyable than making rings, pins, pendants, earrings, bracelets, and necklaces. By his admission, the apprenticeship was short-lived: "I never finished my trade, owing to too much thought of baseball."[24]

Bob was not the only Londoner afflicted with baseball fever in the spring of 1877. The *London Advertiser* on April 9 declared, "The baseball epidemic has broken out this spring with renewed virulence. The excitement is up to the highest pitch and it appears to be catching." The symptoms manifested in three pivotal events. First, the Tecumsehs and Guelph joined a new professional league, the International Association of Base Ball Players (IA), created to rival the National League. As the name implies, it was an alliance of some two dozen independent clubs with no set schedule; some teams were also members of other associations, and only the two Canadian and five American teams participated in championship play. Second, the Tecumsehs built a state-of-the-art ballpark. Tecumseh Park, the finest grounds in Canada, featured an enclosed six-hundred-seat grandstand; dressing rooms for players; refreshment stands; a press box for scorers, newspaper reporters, and telegraph operators; and a novel piped-in water system for maintaining the grass. (Just ten years younger than the Dominion of Canada, the facility, acquired by the city of London and renamed Labatt Memorial Park in 1936, is the oldest baseball grounds in continuous use in its original location).[25] Third, the Tecumsehs, with a legion of young American talent from National League teams, won the IA's first pennant with a 14-4-2 record in championship play. Historian Bill Humber, noting the quality of IA team rosters and the Tecumsehs' success against National League teams, has argued "in fact, the International Association was a major league" and the Tecumsehs were "probably one of the top three teams in all of North America."[26]

While Bob was a faithful fan at Tecumseh games, he continued honing his playing skills with the Atlantics. London's top amateur club. Comprising promising youngsters and older London players squeezed out of the Tecumseh lineup by American imports, the Atlantics was the third-best team in Canada behind the Guelph and London professionals. The formidable squad won most of the reported games against teams throughout Ontario by a large margin, ending the season by winning another title, finishing 5–0 in the championship tournament.

With public and press attention focused on the Tecumsehs, spotty and incomplete game reports make it impossible to reconstruct the Atlantics' season or Emslie's performance in 1877. He did not play in practice games against the Tecumsehs in the old grounds on April 21 or in the inaugural contest in Tecumseh Park on May 3, both won by the professionals, 8–2 and 5–1. His first mention came on July 3 in right field as the Atlantics won the Dominion Day tournament in Waterford, beating the hometown Blue Stockings 21–3 to capture the $20 prize. During the subsequent seven-day tour through the league, he mostly held down center field, the key outfield position, his fielding clear of errors. Although he hit last, he was also proficient at bat. In the six game reports that mention his batting performance, he went 8-25 (.320), but without the first and last outings, 0-4 and 1-5 respectively, he was 7-16 (.438). His best performance came on July 10 in a 19–0 drubbing of the Bowmanville Royal Oaks, when he went 2-5, including a rare triple, and scored three runs. In a losing 11–4 effort on July 24 against the Tecumsehs, Emslie had one hit and scored a run.

Though Bob had been an outfielder from the time he began playing baseball, his thoughts now gravitated toward learning a new position:

pitcher. What prompted his desire to move to the center of the diamond? It was not that, as a center fielder, he had few opportunities to catch balls on the fly and wanted a more active role in the game. Late in life he said, "It was through Mr. Goldsmith that I took up the game of baseball." Specifically, the eighteen-year-old was impressed by Fred's curveballing artistry and taken with the accolades and attention given the pitcher, the most important player in the game. Goldsmith was not only the star player on the Tecumsehs but also London's first bona fide sports hero. Bob Emslie wanted to be a pitcher.[27]

He faced a steep learning curve. Since 1874 pitchers had to face the hitter while standing on a flat surface with both feet in a six-foot square box, the front edge forty-five feet from the center of home plate, and deliver the ball in an underhand motion, the arm passing below the hip, nearly perpendicular to the side of the body, much like a modern softball pitcher. Learning to throw the now-standard curve, to make the ball break downward to the left or right with a sharp twist of the wrist inward or outward at the point of release, was challenging. Moreover, as batters could wield a bat flat on one side like a cricket bat and request pitches high (between belt and shoulders) or low (between knees and belt), the pitcher's effectiveness depended on guile, adjusting to each batter's strengths by delivering the ball from various places in the box and altering its speed and placement. On the other hand, pitchers had an important advantage: a single ball used unless it was damaged or lost became softer, harder to hit with force and for distance as the game progressed.

While few were able to master the art of pitching, Emslie made such progress during the winter that when the Atlantics gathered in March to prepare for the 1878 season, the right-hander was designated as the team's principal pitcher. On April 13 he made his debut—against his idol, no less—as the Atlantics, "all young boys from London, all amateurs," took on the Tecumsehs, "all noted professionals," in the first game of the season. The defending International Association champs, with a powerful lineup and Goldsmith's "old-time deceivers" working well, won 4–3 by scoring two runs in the top of the ninth inning, Emslie recalling "the winning run was scored on an error of our second baseman, with two men outs." Bob pitched impressively, yielding but two runs through the first eight innings, the press noting he "gave every promise of being a good one. He throws a very swift, deceptive ball, and if he continues to practice hard, and is not spoiled by overdue flattery, will make a name for himself on the ball-field."[28]

That summer Emslie and the Atlantics again played in anonymity as the London papers, focusing on the Tecumsehs and other professional teams, mentioned games played, but provided no account of the action—often not even the result, let alone a box score. Still, fragmentary accounts reveal the essential course of Emslie's first season as a pitcher.

While ignored in the press, the Atlantics enjoyed considerable popular support. In May a large group of Londoners accompanied the team to Cleveland for a May 23 game against the professional Forest Citys. For the team and fans who paid the $3 round-trip fare from Port Stanley across Lake Erie it was not a pleasant excursion. Although bursting with confidence and ahead in the betting pool, the Atlantics got only six hits and committed seventeen errors in a humiliating 16–2 defeat. Emslie was embarrassed. Cleveland "hammered his balls terribly," scoring in each of the first six innings, so in the seventh he went to the outfield, replaced in the box by captain James Ross. There was no solace in the *Cleveland Leader* on May 24 saying the Canadian contingent "conducted themselves with dignity and gentlemanly demeanor."

After returning to London the chastened Atlantics headed to Listowel for a July 1 game. Feted as the champions of Canada, they were escorted from the train to their hotel and treated to an "excellent dinner" followed by a band concert before heading to the ballpark. Emslie "pitched exceedingly well," yielding five hits and striking out fourteen in the 16–4 victory. He also had a good day at bat, going 2–5 and scoring twice. But when the Atlantics returned to Cleveland on July 4, Emslie was again "battered so badly" he had to be replaced by Ross, the 9–4 loss assuaged by team having "done well financially" from its share of the gate receipts.

Come August both the Atlantics and the Tecumsehs underwent major changes. Goldsmith's declaration that he would leave after the season, combined with poor play, took a toll at the turnstiles, and on August 21 the Tecumsehs' board of directors disbanded the club due to debt from "insufficient patronage from the public." As for the Atlantics, Emslie, hit hard and often, was consigned to right field, the pitching duties given to newcomer James "Jim" Devlin. Devlin, who with the Louisville in 1877 recorded thirty-five wins and a 2.25 ERA, had been one of four Grays players banned from the National League for conspiring with gamblers to throw games. Signing with the amateur Canadian club to remain in baseball and perhaps repair his reputation, Devlin in his first outing "pitched exceedingly well" in a 5–2 win on August 13 in Woodstock. For his part, Emslie, no doubt in something of a funk, went 0–5 at bat. He was again in the outfield for games against Seaforth and Woodstock, in the latter game going hitless in four attempts.

On August 24 the Atlantics routed Guelf at Tecumseh Park, 12–2, to capture their fourth Canadian championship, but for Bob Emslie, the season that had started so well ended in disappointment, even humiliation. After brief initial success, his pitching became increasingly inconsistent, then utterly ineffective, whether due to inexperience in sizing up batters' weaknesses, inability to control pitches, failure to master the curveball, or growing mental frustration. Undeterred by being removed from the box and exiled to the outer pastures, he set out during the winter to master the elusive breaking pitch.

3

Pitching for Pay

> The pitcher is the most important player on the field, and on his skills and judgement depends half the battle in a match.
>
> —Henry Chadwick

During the winter of 1878–79 Emslie worked on pitching. His confidence grew as his curve broke sharper and he threw faster and with greater accuracy. He also learned to pitch with guile. With the pitcher's box reduced from a six-foot square to a rectangle six feet deep, he practiced delivering pitches from various places and angles behind the front line to confuse batters. Come spring he was ready to prove himself. But with the popularity of baseball waning in London after the demise of the Tecumsehs, Bob, in keeping with family tradition, looked elsewhere for greater opportunity. As he later recalled, "I pitched around London until the 30th of June 1879 when I decided to go out into the world for myself. I landed in a small town, Harriston, Ontario. I had heard that they had a ball club there, and I was conceited enough to think that I could help them."[1] Whether he initiated contact or was recruited, it was a momentous decision, for at age twenty-one Bob Emslie began pitching for pay.

HARRISTON BROWN STOCKINGS

Like so many small towns experiencing an economic boom after the arrival of railroads, Harriston, located at the headwaters of the Maitland River, in Minto Township, forty-nine miles northwest of London, grew from a sleepy village of five hundred people to an incorporated town of two thousand by 1879. Town fathers, bursting with community pride, were anxious to field a baseball team to contest with other towns in the region, so in 1880 the Brown Stockings, or Browns, joined five other Ontario clubs in the newly formed Canadian Amateur Association of Base Ball Players (CAABBP). With "the largest bachelor population of any town of its size in Western Ontario," it was easy to find players. The difficulty was obtaining a quality pitcher. Flushed with confidence, the Browns directors made extensive preparations for the upcoming season, including purchasing a cup to be awarded to the league champions. The reason for optimism was their new pitcher, Bob Emslie.[2]

The CAABBP was an amateur circuit, but some teams, Harriston and Woodstock among them, paid players, and the pitcher, the most important, was usually the best compensated. The lone pitcher on the ten-man team, Emslie received board and room as the head clerk of the Royal Inn, the leading hotel in town, and $1.50 to $1.75 per game. Looking considerably younger than his mostly mustachioed teammates, Bob, with an arm so strong he could throw a ball from the Royal Inn on the corner of Elora and Arthur to the corner of Elora and Maitland, demonstrated his ability before some three thousand enthusiastic Harristonians at a preseason exhibition game with Guelph. The Browns lost 2–1, but his pitching was "greatly admired" and the team impressed spectators as "a good strong one" that "will give a good account of itself." Emslie reportedly was the first curveball pitcher in the league, and "the manner in which he could bend a baseball around a batter's neck filled the natives as well as the opposing batsmen with utter amazement." With Emslie "fast becoming a great star," the Browns were one of "the fastest going bunch in all the country around them."[3]

Owing to the absence of newspapers, Emslie's pitching and the team's season record are unknown save for four championship games against Guelph.[4] On May 24 the Browns beat the Leafs 2–1 in Harriston behind Emslie's masterful pitching. Before the game on June 14 in Guelph the Maple Leafs entered a protest with the league against the Harriston for using paid players, but won 4–0, Emslie giving up nine hits. The Browns lost again 6–4 on July 26, Bob giving up only six hits, but in the final contest on August 27, the Browns won 3–2, with Bob throwing a splendid two-hitter, only one Leafs player reaching first base until the ninth inning.[5] With the teams having split four games, the title was in doubt pending the results of Guelph's protest against the Browns for paying players.

On September 3 the league's judiciary committee met in Guelph to adjudicate the Maple Leafs' claim the Browns had a professional club.

Harriston was dubious of the outcome as two of the four committee members represented the Maple Leafs, President George Sleeman and Secretary John Hewer. Hewer charged that Emslie was paid, catcher Thompson left a London job paying $12 per month to get $1 per day in Harriston, and the Browns paid rail fare for two players acquired from Listowel. The meeting deadlocked when the Galt and Woodstock representatives thought the title should go to Harriston for want of evidence Browns players were paid, but in October the championship was awarded to Guelph. Meanwhile, Emslie played exhibition games for and against the touring Empire club of Shortsville, New York. On September 16 he and two other Browns joined the New Yorkers for a game in Guelph, Emslie going 2–4, but pounded for ten hits in a 10–4 loss. He pitched much better on September 22 in Harriston, the Browns beating the visitors 22–2.

TORONTO CLIPPERS

In early July 1881 Emslie and two other Browns stars, the catcher and second baseman, joined the Toronto Clippers. Their defection destroyed the Browns, who promptly folded. Bob, receiving $40 per month plus board and $1.50 per game, was the first professional player in Toronto.[6] In his debut on July 16 "Elmslie"—it took several games for the newspapers to spell his name correctly—coasted as the Clippers beat the reorganized Tecumsehs 30–4. On July 24 he gave up four hits and struck out six in defeating the strong Woodstock nine 9–8, the Actives benefiting from fifteen Toronto errors. The Clippers then took to the road, losing 5–4 in Guelph on July 28. The Maple Leafs touched Emslie for only seven hits, but thanks to Clippers miscues scored three runs in the second inning. The next day's game in Woodstock ended in a tie when Bob suffered a leg injury in the eighth inning—it turned out to be "badly sprained" instead of broken—and was unable to continue.

Toronto's hope the Harriston trio, "men of great excellence," would produce a winning team, thereby increasing interest in baseball, was modestly fulfilled. While upward of two thousand spectators attended a cricket match with Montreal on August 1, the press declared residents who "thought the interest taken in baseball was about dead would have been greatly surprised" to see about six hundred people attend the game against Guelph, the fans leaving pleased as Emslie—his name now spelled correctly—struck out seven in beating Guelph 7–3. On August 6 Bob fanned eight Woodstock Actives but lost 10–3 as the weak-fielding Clippers committed ten errors. In Guelph on August 12 he "pitched in remarkably fine form," yielding two hits and striking out eight in winning 5–1. After the game he left for London, having learned his sister was on her deathbed.

While in London Bob played one game with the Tecumsehs against St. Thomas. Inasmuch as competitive baseball in London had declined precipitously and the Atlantics had won the Ontario championship, after the game he "made arrangement to remain and play with St. Thomas."[7] Just has he had left the Browns for more money, he abandoned the Clippers for a better team, and as had Harrison, Toronto disbanded after the loss of their star pitcher.[8]

ST. THOMAS ATLANTICS

With the rapid spread of baseball's popularity across North America after the Civil War, St. Thomas, Ontario, was among many rapidly growing communities to use the game as both a prominent civic activity and promotional enterprise. Some fifteen miles south of London, St. Thomas grew slowly until the arrival of railroads in 1872. With its location near the northern edge of Lake Erie and halfway between Detroit and Buffalo providing cheaper, faster train linkage with major northern American cities, the seat of Elgin County became a major railroad hub, designated a city in 1881 with a population of ten thousand.[9] Since first organizing a team in 1868, St. Thomas fielded nines made up of local players, but to enhance its reputation in the barnstorming world of intercity Ontario baseball hired William "Bill" Watkins, Guelph player-manager of the 1881 Ontario champion Atlantics.

Preparations for the 1882 season proceeded apace. In March the club's board of directors, headed by president Elijah Moore, a founder of the St. Thomas Street Railway, allocated $100 for grounds behind the Horton market, but then, taken by grandiose visions, decided instead to build a playing facility with a grandstand worthy of a championship team near the Great Western railroad station at the sizable cost of $700. To fund construction and cover team expenses, the club innovatively reorganized as a joint stock company, issuing $1,000 worth of shares, thirty percent coming from team members. The directors also deviated from fashion by outfitting the team in gray Halifax tweed uniforms accented by red stockings and belts instead of traditional flannel jerseys and woolen pants.

Watkins wasted no time recruiting "a first class nine," signing by early April seven players, including Emslie as the team's pitcher. Bob pitched well in the home opener on May 7 against the London Tecumsehs, a 2–2 tie called after nine innings. He gave up only three hits, but the Atlantics having not yet practiced, committed seven errors, including a game-tying miscue in the ninth inning. On May 24 Bob and the Atlantics tested their mettle against Major League competition. Agreeing at the last minute to replace the scheduled Cleveland Blues, the National League's Detroit Wolverines took a special train to St. Thomas, dressed for the game en route, and raced to the ballpark, which was jammed with more than 1,600 fans. Despite the hurried trip, they thoroughly outclassed the home team, winning 6–1. Emslie pitched well, yielding only six hits to the Major Leaguers, but George Derby flummoxed Atlantics batters, allowing only one hit and striking out thirteen. Bob, taking a break from pitching, caught two flies in the outfield during a 7–3 win over Hamilton on May 20, but was back in the box on June 6 when the Tecumsehs came to St. Thomas to make up the aborted May game. It was a disaster. After three scoreless innings, the Londoners "battered Emslie all over the field," piling up seven runs in the fifth, six in the sixth, and four in the eighth for a 20–3 rout. Things were not much better on the June 8 return game in London, which the Tecumsehs decisively won 13–3.

With the lineup bolstered in late June by new players, the Atlantics won three games straight, Emslie pitching effectively until succumbing to overuse on July 4 in London. He struck out eight, but after hurling six scoreless innings gave up one run in the seventh and eighth innings and five in the ninth to lose 7–6. The *St. Thomas Times* noted a pattern—"as the game approaches completion the effectiveness of his delivery dissipates"—and suggested the Atlantics change pitchers in the sixth or seventh innings. But since Bob was the team's only pitcher, it was up to him to develop more consistency either by pacing himself or by developing greater arm strength.[10]

The Atlantics then went on the road and won six games in five days from July 9 to 14, outscoring opponents 85–43. Back home, a tired Emslie gave up ten hits in an 18–9 win over the Tecumsehs on July 15, then, rested, coasted to two victories over Hamilton on July 20 and July 21, 10–1 and 14–7. Riding high, the Atlantics now faced a scheduling and therefore also a financial problem. The semiprofessional team depended on raising money by playing games for a share of gate receipts, but now had difficulty scheduling games. With only London and Hamilton fielding competitive nines, Watkins decided to seek more and better competition with semipro and professional clubs south of the border in New York.

Early Sunday morning, July 23, Emslie and his teammates boarded a train for games against Rochester, Syracuse, and Auburn. The trip began auspiciously on July 24 as the Atlantics, described as "a champion professional team," administered a 15–4 shellacking to the Rochesters. Emslie had a fine day, giving up just six hits, striking out seven, getting a single and double in four at-bats, and scoring a run. But success was short-lived as they dropped the next three games. By the end of the scheduled tour, exhausted from playing four games in a row, the Atlantics were ready to go home. Emslie, expecting the trip would last about a week, had his uniform hastily "done up in newspapers" instead of luggage and packed only "one shirt and one pair of socks."[11] But Watkins, hoping for a lucrative grand tour, had telegraphed inquiries to other American clubs, hoping to find teams whose schedules could accommodate games with the Atlantics for a share of gate receipts sufficient to cover travel expenses and to pay the players. The result was a grueling five-week barnstorming tour with twenty-six games in New York, New Jersey, and Pennsylvania.[12]

Rejuvenated and excited about playing more experienced American teams, the Atlantics ran off a string of eight straight victories—mostly lopsided—in upstate New York, then, emboldened by success, headed to New York City for a date with the professional Metropolitans, splitting two games en route in Newark.[13] We can imagine what went on in Bob's mind on August 9 as he gaped in amazement at the awe-inspiring urban scene before him while ferrying across the busy Hudson River to

Manhattan and then wending uptown through the teeming streets of the largest metropolis in North America, population just over a million. His jaw likely dropped even further upon entering the Polo Grounds, an expansive elliptical polo field reconfigured for baseball in 1880 as the home grounds of the Metropolitans.

Managed by Jim Mutrie, the Metropolitans, eventual champions of the League Alliance, was a topflight independent professional squad, Major League in all but name. (They won the 1882 title, then in 1883 joined the Major League American Association.) The Atlantics knew they faced a formidable challenge in taking on a team whose roster included two native-born Canadians, both future Major Leaguers, John "Jack" Doyle from Halifax, Nova Scotia, and James "Tip" O'Neill from Springfield, Ontario. Although blanked 5–0, Emslie pitched effectively, holding the Mets scoreless for the first four innings before yielding one in the fifth, three in the seventh, and one in the eighth, none earned. The Atlantics batting was "very weak," getting only two hits, but the team was complimented on having "a good battery" and received "well deserved" applause for "sharp fielding" and making "quite an interesting fight of it."[14] Both teams regarded the rematch on August 10 as an exhibition game, the Mets resting their regular pitcher and catcher for the next day's league game and the Atlantics moving Emslie to center field. The Canadians got off to a good start, scoring three runs in the top of the first, but when the Mets plated eight in the bottom of the inning, Bob returned to the box for the rest of the game and gave up no more than one hit in an inning. The Atlantics came out losers, 15–5, but despite two defeats left New York satisfied, having given a prominent professional club a good tussle.

On the way to Philadelphia to take on another top Alliance club, they stopped in Camden, New Jersey, for a two-game set with the Merritt. The arrival of the Canadians created great enthusiasm, the games reported on the front pages of both daily newspapers. For the game on Friday, August 11, labeled "Jersey vs. Canada," a thousand fans came to watch the home team's 5–2 victory over the "Canucks"—the first time that term had been applied to the Atlantics. Emslie played right field, recording no hits but catching two flies and firing a throw to second base for double play. The next day, with Emslie pitching "very effectively," giving up but four hits and striking out ten in addition to posting three singles and scoring a run, the Atlantics defeated the Merritt 6–4. It was a life-changing performance, not because "a lady admirer" gave Bob a bouquet of flowers after the game, but because his sharp-breaking curveball so impressed Merritt management they offered him his first professional contract. Flattered, he promptly signed an agreement to join the team when the Atlantics tour ended.

After six games in as many days, the Atlantics rested on Sunday, leisurely crossing the Delaware River, then catching a train to Reading. On Monday they beat the Actives 8–5. Emslie struggled in the box, fanning none and yielding ten hits, but held the Actives scoreless after the fifth inning. The next day the Actives downed the visitors 6–0. Emslie, in right field, went hitless but made "a splendid" fielding play.[15]

It was then on to historic Philadelphia, a bustling seaport of 850,000 on the Delaware River. That America's second-largest city was also where the Declaration of Independence was adopted in 1776 and the Federal Constitution drafted in 1787 may not have been of interest to the Atlantics, but the appearance of the first "foreign" team was much anticipated. Newspapers printed accounts complete with box score of Atlantics games with Camden and Reading, noting the Canadians' "pitcher, catcher and third baseman are spoken of as more than ordinarily expert."[16]

The Atlantics' opponent was the League Alliance Philadelphia Phillies, managed by Billy Barnie, Emslie's future manager with Baltimore. (Major League quality like the Mets, the Phillies would join the National League in 1883 as the Quakers.) *Philadelphia* in Greek means "city of brotherly love," but the home team proved ungracious hosts on August 16, handing their guests a 7–4 beating. Emslie walked five but allowed only four hits. The *Philadelphia Inquirer* reported the "heavy batsmen of the home nine were completely outwitted" by his "very peculiar and puzzling delivery" and the Phillies probably would not have scored a run were it not for eight Atlantics errors. The next day's game featured a first-rate pitching duel between Emslie and Hardie Henderson, future Baltimore Orioles teammates, Philadelphia scoring twice in the second inning to post a 2–0 victory. Emslie continued to baffle batters with his "puzzling curves," again yielding only four hits. The umpire for both games was Wes Curry, who inadvertently launched Bob's umpiring career five years later.

Unhappy about dropping two in Philadelphia, but buoyed by better performance in the second game, the Atlantics sped across New Jersey to Atlantic City. Throngs of people hoping to beat summer's heat flocked to the shore and the entertainments along the famous boardwalk, but the Atlantics had come to play ball against Ferguson "Fergy" Malone's Atlantic City nine, self-proclaimed champions of the Garden State. It was not a pleasant stay, the Canadians losing 8–1 and 2–1, the latter game well pitched by Emslie. Undoubtedly tired after again playing six days in a row, dispirited by five consecutive defeats, and weary of a trip that had extended far beyond initial expectations, the Atlantics headed home. On the way they stopped in Reading, dropping the rubber game of the series 18–3, the Actives pounding Emslie for nineteen hits—the most he had ever given up. On August 25 in Syracuse he lost again, 9–5, to the Stars, another League Alliance team.

When they arrived back in St. Thomas on Sunday, August 27, Emslie and his teammates had completed the most extensive tour undertaken by a Canadian baseball club. With Bob pitching all but three games, they had won twelve of twenty-six games against far more experienced and skilled American teams, including four against two clubs of Major League caliber. But there were only a few days of rest for the weary "champion club of Canada." On August 29 the Atlantics hosted Port Huron, Michigan. Emslie, now well rested, yielded but one run for the first six innings, but in the bottom of the sixth he sprained an ankle while running the bases; although "practically disabled," Bob gamely returned to the box for the seventh, whereupon the Hurons scored six runs, adding two more in the eighth to win 9–3. The next day the teams played in London and the Atlantics defeated Port Huron 20–7. Then, on September 2, the Atlantics finished the season by defeating Hamilton 8–6.

Producing "a heap of fame but a paucity of cash," the glorious tour of 1882, which brought inestimable pride and publicity to St. Thomas while introducing Americans to the growing proficiency of baseball players north of the border, had an inglorious ending.[17] After the Huron series, the widely hailed "Canadian champions" disbanded. Bill Watkins jumped to Port Huron, leading his hometown club as player-manager to the 1883 Michigan State League championship. Billy Hunter, Chub Collins, Jay Faatz, and Jim Tray also left to play Minor League ball in the United States, each eventually reaching the Major Leagues in 1884 (as did Watkins). On September 4 Bob, too, left town for more baseball, this time in Camden, New Jersey. If his recollection of the tour late in life was mistaken in several respects, he was correct saying it was "a lucky trip for me" as it led to his first professional contract.[18]

CAMDEN MERRITT

For the Albert Merritt Base Ball Club—the first team named after a person and the first instance of naming rights in sports history—to sign a pitcher after only one game and to delay his appearance until an undetermined future time was unusual, but understandable.[19] The Merritt fielded a solid team, but with pitching a chronic problem, the club was willing to wait for the Canadian right-hander with a sharply breaking curveball.

Just why Emslie decided to throw in his lot with the Merritt is unknown. Now twenty-three, he was past the age when an adult male should have obtained a respectable and secure occupation. As a professional ballplayer he would draw a salary, but baseball was a seasonal job. He may simply have been impressed with the caliber of ball played in the United States and taken the first opportunity to join an American club. Besides, signing a professional contract was a big deal for a ballplayer, evidence of his skill on the diamond, and he was undoubtedly flattered by the Merritt's offer after only one game. Still, Camden, New Jersey, was a long way from his home and the baseball world he knew so well, and his parents, like most first-generation immigrants, may not have appreciated the game's place in North American culture, and, if they did, knew ballplayers had a reputation as a foul-mouthed lot given to hard drinking, gambling, and womanizing. If Bob had any misgivings about joining the Merritt after returning home, they disappeared when his Atlantics teammates began dispersing and the demise of the Tecumsehs left no other competitive team in the province.

Quite a change lay ahead. Bob's former teammates had been overwhelmingly fellow Ontarians, but now would be exclusively Americans of diverse personalities, backgrounds, and experiences. And he would be residing in a foreign city markedly different from the small town of Waterville, Kansas. Located directly across the Delaware River from Philadelphia, Camden was a thriving port and industrial city, its population increasing from 20,045 in 1870 to 41,659 in 1880 (108 percent). Its most illustrious resident was the poet Walt Whitman, a baseball fan who wrote several revisions of his most famous poem, "Leaves of Grass," after moving there in 1873. Whitman exhorted in 1888 and 1889, "Baseball is our game: the American game" and "the hurrah of the republic."[20]

The Merritt's new pitcher arrived in town at 11 a.m. on September 6. Although tired from three days of travel, he was inserted into the lineup that afternoon against an amateur team, the Defiance of Philadelphia. Wearing Camden's new uniforms—white pants, shirt and cap trimmed in cardinal red, cardinal red belt and stockings—he played center field and batted second; he had no put-outs, but got two "clean hits" and scored twice in a 9–2 victory. The next day Bob debuted in the box against, the ironically named Atlantics of Philadelphia. Under the front-page headline "The New Pitcher" it was reported, "Emslie, the Canadian, plays a splendid game." The Philadelphians, "unable to hit him," struck out seven times and managed only two hits, not scoring until tallying two in the bottom of the eighth when Bob tired. He also got two hits and scored run in the 12–2 victory.[21]

The auspicious beginning was no fluke. On September 15 Bob allowed one hit in a 3–2 victory over the Major League Baltimore Orioles of the American Association. He may have celebrated too much that night, as the next day in center field he got no hits and "played poorly, missing an easy fly and making a bad throw" in the 8–1 loss to the Orioles. The *Camden Post* generously commented that "Emslie, like any other good player, has a bad day occasionally." The next day in Trenton he pitched superbly, striking out thirteen and yielding one hit in a 3–0 win. He again blanked the Trentonians 1–0 two days later, fanning seven and yielding two hits.

Of the late-season signee, the *Post* proclaimed on September 22, "In Emslie the Merritts have one of the best pitchers in the profession. We doubt if any of the great teams could hit him badly." But during a five-game tour through Pennsylvania, he tired and gave up eleven hits in a 9–1 drubbing in Harrisburg. He recovered after returning to Camden, on October 4 yielding only four hits to the Philadelphia Athletics, the second-place team in the American Association. The Major League club won 5–2, but after scoring five in the first inning failed to score again. Emslie's pitching was "the feature of the game." The two teams played again the next day, the Merritt beating the Athletics for the first time, 6–5. For the second straight day Emslie pitched splendidly, again yielding but four hits while striking out seven and walking one. As the *Post* summed up, "They could not hit Emslie, and that tells the story." Eventually, the strain of six months of pitching took its toll. On October 16 in Philadelphia the Athletics pounded him for thirteen hits in a 9–1 victory, and two days later, against the against the Philadelphia Quakers, the last-place club in the National League, he was "batted freely," giving up ten hits in a 5–1 loss.

Albeit brief and ending on a negative note, Emslie's first foray into the world of professional baseball was successful, boding well for the future. Irregular newspaper accounts and box scores make it impossible to tabulate his pitching statistics, but by all accounts he usually pitched superbly. At a season-ending celebratory dinner for the team that went "to a late hour," Bob, who had made many friends since coming to Camden, "put himself on record as a good after-dinner speaker, he expressing himself as much pleased with the treatment he and the other players have received in this city."[22]

As Emslie headed home to St. Thomas, the Merritt directors, heady with the success of 1882, hoped for even greater success next year as a Major League club. In early August it was rumored the six-team American Association would expand to ten teams for the 1883 season, adding the Merritt and New York Metropolitans as eastern clubs and Indianapolis and Milwaukee in the west. But Camden's application in October for admission failed, the circuit admitting only two new regional teams, the Metropolitans and the Columbus Buckeyes. Upon returning from the association meeting, Gus Richter, the Merritt's secretary and treasurer, said, "Western clubs favored our candidacy, but some Eastern ones opposed us, but I will not give the names at present."[23] He didn't need to.

A team in the country's largest city was sine qua non, but Philadelphia and Baltimore did not want another franchise in the immediate area.

With the major leagues not an option, the Merritt opted in November to join the Inter-State Association, a four-state federation of seven teams, New Jersey's Merritts and Trenton Trentonians; Delaware's Wilmington Quicksteps; Pennsylvania's Harrisburg Olympics, Pottsville Anthracites, and Reading Actives; and New York's Brooklyn Greys.[24] In December the Inter-State and Northwest League clubs were admitted to the American Base Ball Association, a cooperative agreement meaning their player contracts would be as binding as those in the two Major Leagues.[25]

That provision was particularly important for the Merritt, which had already engaged the nucleus of the 1883 team. Immediately after season's end the Merritt signed the four most important players from the previous year's team: pitchers Emslie and Sam Kimber, third baseman Fred Warner, and outfielder Frank "Gid" Gardner. In December they inked John "Jack" Corcoran and Francis "Frank" Fennelly of the Philadelphia Phillies of the League Alliance, and four American Association Major Leaguers: William "Bill" Greenwood and William "Bill" Kienzel of the Philadelphia Athletics, first baseman Charles W. "Charlie" Householder from Baltimore, and John J. "Rooney" Sweeney, who had signed with Pittsburgh Allegheny. The 1883 Merritt was a juggernaut, fielding a Major League caliber player at every position. (By season's end, each Merritt player was on a Major League team.)

By mid-March the players were engaged in formal practices except the team's star pitcher, who topped the payroll at $150 per month. Bob, who had been working out all winter in a gym, said he was in "excellent health" and, anxious for the season to start, would arrive about April 1. But he did not arrive until around noon on April 9, too late to pitch in the first game of the season. Having missed spring workouts, he was eased into shape against two Philadelphia amateur clubs. Despite not pitching since October, he was sharp on April 10 against the Archer, yielding four hits and fanning eight in an 18–3 rout that was rained out after six innings. The next day he returned to the box, again giving up just four hits in blanking Hartville 6–0. He had yet to issue a base on balls. The Merritt then took a southern tour, Bob hurling winning games in Baltimore, Washington DC, and Alexandria, Virginia. Upon returning home on April 15 fans saw "the worst game of ball that was ever played in Camden, or anywhere else." With Emslie striking out ten and giving up only three hits, the Merritts scored in every inning en route to a 36–0 humiliation of the Alaska club of New York City. (In 1883 rules now allowed pitching above the waist, the hand below the shoulder, a sidearm motion that brought a sharper vertical break to Bob's curve.) Bob's first serious test came on April 19 in an exhibition against Major League Philadelphia. The Athletics, who had scored in the top of the first inning, plated two unearned runs in the sixth and seventh to win 5–1 as the Merritts "muffed flys, fumbled balls and threw wildly," playing, as one player put it, "like a lot of old women" in committing eight errors. Emslie pitched well but was made "a trifle nervous" by the fielding debacle and ultimately gave up eight hits.

Following the announcement of the Inter-State Association's season schedule, Emslie alternated games with Kimber before championship play began at home on May 4. Bob pitched on April 22 in Manayunk against the amateur Ashland team. It was another mismatch, some of the Merritts amusing themselves, but certainly not their opponents, by batting left-handed in the 15–3 rout. Better and more valuable competition came in a pair of games with the Philadelphia Athletics. On April 25 Emslie threw "very effectively" until the Athletics scored twice in the sixth, once in the seventh, and five times in the eighth on "little 'pop hits' just out of reach of the infielders" to win 9–3. When the Athletics came to Camden for a rematch two days later, Emslie, in left field, caught three fly balls, had one base hit, and endured a memorable stint at the plate in the fourth inning. In the course of taking six called balls, he fouled off four pitches, then hit a foul tip that injured catcher Jack O'Brien's fingers. Bob then struck several more fouls before another foul tip hit the luckless Athletics backstop in the mouth, causing a halt to the game for several minutes. When the game resumed, Emslie took a seventh ball and headed to first base.

As the Merritt's lead pitcher Bob was in the box for the season opener on May 4, yielding eight hits while coasting to a 21–7 victory over the Pottsville Anthracites. Two days later he pitched "an elegant game," yielding four hits in a 6–1 win over Harrisburg. His reputation was such that when Philadelphia's pitcher, Fred Corey, got hurt, the Athletics asked the Merritt to loan Bob to pitch for them against Major League Baltimore on May 9. Camden agreed, and Emslie headed to Baltimore, only to learn that the Orioles, citing Association rules against non-league players, refused to allow him to pitch. The Merritt then went on a winning tear, Emslie and Kimber pitching superbly.

With the team on a roll, good news and bad news greeted Merritt fans in early June, as Camden newspapers reported both Bob had pitched "an excellent game" in beating the Actives 13–3 in Reading and talk that the club would disband for financial reasons. The papers termed the rumors "all nonsense," assuring fans that the club was "never in a healthier condition financially or otherwise."[26] But declining attendance was a concern despite the team's winning ways. Fewer than eight hundred spectators showed up to see the back-to-back 12–1 and 15–5 thrashings of the Columbus Buckeyes of the American Association and Emslie's four-hit, 5–0 whipping of Pottsville, in which he surprised himself by catching a hot line drive in his bare left hand. Bob followed with a resounding performance on June 16 when the Merritt crossed the Delaware to knock the conceit out of the Major League Athletics with a resounding 21–10 victory. When Emslie, bored by a 14–1 lead, tossed "dew drops," Philadelphia plated eight in the sixth, to which the Merritt responded with five to put the game out of reach. After the seventh inning the teams agreed to end the fiasco. The Merritt was so dominant that when they suffered a rare defeat, a 5–4 loss to third-place Trenton in an away game on July 16 in which Emslie gave up the winning run in the bottom of the tenth inning, the hometown fans "rushed onto the field and cheered till they were hoarse, threw up their hats, umbrellas and canes, and made every demonstration of joy they could think of." Unfazed by the extra-inning loss, Bob pitched "almost perfectly" in beating Brooklyn's Greys 6–3 on July 18.

After the Brooklyn game the Merritt went on the road amid increasing rumors they would soon disband. Wilmington, Delaware, fans were delighted "almost beyond bounds" as the Quicksteps on July 19 beat the Merritt for the first time, 2–1, a shutout averted when Emslie, playing left field, tripled in the eighth inning and subsequently scored on a sacrifice fly. In the sixth inning Kimber retired the side on three pitches, each batter flying out, reportedly "the first time in the history of baseball that such a thing happened."[27] The next day in Reading the Merritt players received word the club was indeed about to fold. Not surprisingly, they lost to the Actives 11–9, both teams of "demoralized players" turning in a sloppy game, the Merritt committing ten of the nineteen errors. Neither Emslie, who struck out only one, nor his opponent pitched well, each giving up twelve hits. After the game the dispirited squad headed to Wilmington, where they lost 5–2 to the Quicksteps the next day, Bob in left field catching three flys for outs and going 0–4 at bat. It was his last game for the Merritt; that night the club's management disbanded the club.

The Camden Merritt, arguably the best team outside the Major Leagues in the nineteenth century, was history.[28] Despite losing their last three games, they left in first place with a 27-7 record (79 percent). Prior to the three losses they were 27-4 (87 percent). A successful team featuring highly accomplished players at every position, each of whom advanced to the Major Leagues, had fallen victim to the financial plague that did in many Minor League clubs. Faced with $2,000 in debt, and losing about $200 a month, Albert Merritt, who had suffered substantial financial losses from a fire to his business, decided not to be "the chief loser" any longer, and the other stockholders were willing only to liquidate the debt and pay the players. (The Merritt was the only Inter-State team to fold during the season, but the circuit did not survive its inaugural year.)

If Camden losing the team was, as the *Courier* termed it, "a public calamity," it was a bonanza for the players. Representatives of Major League and other Inter-State clubs, wallets bulging, descended on Camden. Brooklyn, first on the scene, signed five players at more than double their previous salaries, a haul sufficient to carry the Greys from fourth place to the league pennant; the National League Philadelphia Quakers signed Fred Warner, raising his $100 salary to $425 plus "other considerations." Baltimore manager Billy Barnie, desperately in need of an outfielder and battery, was zealous in pursuing Gardner, Emslie, and Sweeney, the Merritt's best players. He signed Gardner for $300, but Emslie and Sweeney rejected his "liberal offers." Pitchers and catchers are the most important players on any team, and the Merritt duo had received offers from "a dozen or more" clubs. Barnie would not be denied, finally signing the battery mates for $350, a monthly increase of $200.[29]

Bob Emslie, who in his first full if abbreviated professional season started seventeen league games, finishing 14-3 (.824) with a 0.82 ERA, had finally realized his youthful dream of becoming a Major League pitcher—quite an achievement for a second-generation Scottish immigrant from Canada, whose forebears certainly never anticipated baseball might be a well-paying occupation.

4

Curveball Artist

There ain't much to being a ballplayer—if you're a ballplayer.

—Honus Wagner

For Bob Emslie, having enjoyed "great pleasure at the way he had been treated" in Camden, new experiences awaited on and off the field with the Baltimore Orioles. The team was a charter member of the American Association, organized in 1882 to rival the National League. Comprising six "river cities," the "Beer and Whiskey League" broke new ground in catering to working-class patrons by charging lower admission prices, playing on Sundays in cities without blue laws, and selling beer and liquor at ballparks.[1]

Baltimore, located on a harbor connected to Chesapeake Bay, was the largest city Bob had lived in and the farthest south he had been. A thriving shipping and manufacturing center second only to New York City as a port of entry for immigrants, Baltimore hosted a polyglot population. Nearly a quarter of its of 350,000 residents, the country's seventh largest, was of German ancestry, including the parents of George Herman "Babe" Ruth. Maryland, founded in 1762 partly as a haven for persecuted Catholics, became a slave state, and its postbellum legacy was strict racial segregation imposed on the largest Black population of any northern state, including separate seating at Orioles games. Summers brought disease, the city annually enduring the highest rate of typhoid fever in the country.[2]

The ballclub also called for an adjustment. It was not that Bob and English-born Tim Manning were the only non-Americans on the team but that the Orioles were only marginally Major League caliber. The 1882 Orioles were a dreadful outfit, finishing in last place with a 19-54 (.260) record, statistically last in batting, pitching, and fielding. A new manager, William H. "Billy" Barnie, a former National Association catcher, and owner Henry "Harry" Von Der Horst, proprietor of the Eagle Brewery, were determined to provide a better brand of baseball in 1883. Barnie revamped the roster and Von Der Horst provided better funding and a new playing facility, Oriole Park, located outside the city limits at York Road and Huntington Avenue. They even tried to present a new look: the 1883 squad donned white uniforms with blue pinstriped stockings and blue caps at home and "blueish-gray" outfits on the road.[3]

1883

Alas, the 1883 Orioles were again a woeful bunch. Starting the season on May 1, they won five of the first nine games, then from May 15 to June 28 won only four of twenty-nine in a rapid descent to the cellar. Their pitching, ever the key to success, was miserable. And with his catcher and an outfielder faltering badly with glove and bat, Barnie's desperate need for a new battery and a competent outfielder explains his zealous pursuit of the Merritt three.

Gardner and Sweeney were quality additions, but Emslie, the key acquisition, was the answer to the Orioles' pitching woes as he and James Harding "Hardie" Henderson alternated pitching the rest of the season. (Each had a special backstop: Sweeney caught for Emslie, Phil Baker for Henderson.) With pitchers in 1883 allowed to throw with an arm raised below the shoulder, Emslie now threw with greater velocity and a sharper break on his trademark curve. Spencer Thomas Oldham, a famous American cricket player attending his first baseball game in August, was amazed by Emslie's devastating curveball: "I was sitting just in a line with the pitcher and catcher. That fellow Emslie was a terror. I saw the balls break in the air—start straight, shoot down—without touching the ground. They just curved around and fooled the batters." Years later it was believed "any expert critics of the period named Emslie as the greatest curve ball pitcher in the game."[4]

The lowly Orioles were firmly in last place with a 14-40 record on July 25 when the Camden trio celebrated their first game with a 13–9 win in Baltimore over Pittsburgh. Gardner's errorless play was "a relief," and Sweeney, besides throwing "wonderfully well to second base," turned in the "prettiest play of the game" by catching a "hot foul tip" in his bare hand and firing the ball to first base to double up the runner. Emslie, undoubtedly nervous, gave up nine hits but only two earned runs. Bob was in the box two days later, this time as "effective as possible," yielding one earned run and striking out five in a 21–8 trouncing of the Allegheny. He also had a fine day at bat with three hits, one a double, scoring twice.

That night the Orioles embarked on a disastrous trip, winning only two of eleven games. On August 13 the *Baltimore Sun* called the team "an eleemosynary institution, traveling around giving games to poor, but deserving teams." Emslie pitched well, but lost his next three starts due to errant fielding support. He lost twice at the Polo Grounds, first 8–2, with nine Mets reaching first base on errors, and then 5–3, in which he gave up only six hits and two earned runs while his teammates committed seven miscues. It was on to Philadelphia for four games against the league-leading Athletics. On August 4 Bob was "very effective," yielding six hits but losing 5–4 in ten innings; the winning run was scored on the last of four Sweeney passed balls. Two days later the Orioles broke their five-game losing streak by beating Philadelphia 14–9, Emslie striking out five and allowing only four hits.

Hopes were high for the four-game set in Pittsburgh as the Allegheny were only marginally better than the Orioles, but Baltimore dropped three games. Emslie pitched three of the four games, suffering two losses: 4–2 in the opener, in which he pitched well, and 6–4 two days later, when the error-prone Orioles committed eight miscues. The trip ended on a positive note on August 13 with an 11–3 Baltimore victory; despite Bob pitching a second game in a row, Pittsburgh, "unable to do anything with Emslie's delivery," tallied no earned runs.

The weary road warriors welcomed three days of respite before beginning a sixteen-game home stand. Despite the losses Emslie and Henderson had stabilized the Orioles' pitching staff, engendering optimism as five thousand fans, the largest crowd in some time, watched on August 17 as the Orioles beat St. Louis for the first time, 6–4. Emslie, in the box for the third straight game, recorded his second consecutive win. He scattered eight hits and allowed no earned runs, the Browns tallies owing to seven Orioles errors. He then suffered heartbreaking losses on August 21 and August 22, 3–0 and 1–0, giving up five hits and no earned runs in the first loss and only four hits in the second, holding the Browns scoreless after the first inning. In the bottom of the eighth, after Sweeney tripled with two out, Emslie came to bat with a chance to drive in the tying run, but after his thumb was badly split by a pitch he was replaced by Henderson, who flew out to retire the side. (At that time no base was given when hit by a pitch.)

The first serious injury of his playing career kept Emslie out of action until August 30. During his absence Henderson threw five consecutive games, giving up lots of runs but still winning four games at home against the mediocre Louisville Eclipse. Emslie then gave his pitching partner a well-deserved rest by pitching two games against Cincinnati on August 30 and 31, striking out eight in the 7–5 victory on August 30 but the next day losing 5–3, the Reds aided by eight Baltimore errors and Sweeney's four passed balls.

A visit from the Columbus Buckeyes ended the home stand. It started on September 3 with a sloppy win, 12–9. It was indeed a "queer game," as the *Sun* aptly put it. Emslie struck out eight and walked one, but gave up eleven hits, "hit quite freely, more so, indeed, than in any game for the past week or two." The next day the Orioles suffered the most humiliating defeat to date, a 21–4 thrashing, the Buckeyes racking up twenty-five hits and scoring in every inning but the second. Henderson started the game, but after three innings was replaced by Gardner after Columbus scored nine. Gardner fared no better, in one inning giving up two hits, one a home run, and throwing two wild pitches. Emslie, who in center field had committed two errors, came in to pitch the final five innings and was "hit freely," giving up thirteen hits and eight runs. That Oriole fielders were "unable to stop a double-barreled watermelon" was a slight exaggeration as they muffed their way to twelve errors. The lead sentence in the *Sun*'s report said it all: "The home nine were manifestly in no condition to play base-ball yesterday, and the Columbus made an exhibition of them."

What on earth had happened? Barney was not on hand to witness the debacle, having gone to New York to work out a deal for Sweeney, who was increasingly error-prone and given to excessive drinking and hosting late-night poker games during road trips. Taking advantage of Barnie's absence, several Orioles, including Emslie, went for a night on the town. Organized by Sweeney and Gardner, both unduly fond of intoxicating liquids, the high-spirited outing ended at Kernan's Monumental Theatre with the players crashing the Bal Masque and Fancy Dress Carnival held in honor of the Oriole, the upcoming weeklong civic celebration. The unwelcome and intoxicated guests caused a disturbance. When Henderson got into a "wrangle" over a girl, police were called and Hardie wound up in jail. Upon returning to Baltimore, Barnie admonished the players "to keep straight" or he would blacklist them so they could never play for other clubs, then fined Sweeney $150 and Gardner $100 for drunkenness; Henderson $50 plus the "station-house fine"; and Emslie, Kelly, Manning, and Stearns each $10 for the after-midnight misadventure.[5]

The Orioles responded to the chastising by going into a funk. They lost the next two games to lowly Columbus, Emslie pitching ineffectively in a 9–2 loss and Henderson doing likewise in an 11–7 drubbing. After the dispiriting defeats, the *Baltimore Sun on September 8* announced, "The little *bal masque* escapade has relegated them finally, it seems, to last place." Three days off en route to St. Louis did not alter the team's mood. After Henderson lost the first game 9–2, Emslie and Sweeney put on miserable performances on September 10 as the Browns "slaughtered" the Orioles 15–4. Sweeney had three errors and three passed balls, and the Browns "knocked the life right out of Emslie," pounding him "in every direction" for twenty-three hits. Recovering from the humiliation, Emslie ended the Orioles' six-game losing streak in the series finale with a sterling 3–0 three-hit shutout on September 13, striking out six while walking only one.

Then, in the first of three games in Louisville, the Eclipse routed the Orioles 16–8. Emslie and Sweeney again "failed miserably," raising suspicion that they had been out carousing the night before. Baltimore scored four in the top of the first, but when the Eclipse responded with five in the bottom of the inning thanks to several errors and passed balls, Emslie, discouraged by his teammates playing "like a lot of school-boys," pitched ineffectively the rest of the game. The Eclipse scored in all but two innings, getting sixteen hits off Emslie and benefiting from ten Orioles errors and Sweeney's astonishing twelve passed balls. Whatever was wrong with Sweeney, hungover or disgruntled, it was obvious, as the Louisville paper observed, that the Orioles were "greatly in need of a good catcher."[6]

Emslie, continuing his good game–bad game pattern, concluded the Louisville series on September 17 by losing a thrilling pitcher's duel 2–1. He pitched the next game in Cincinnati on September 20, but with Cecil "Cal" Broughton, recently signed after being released by the National League's Cleveland Blues behind the plate instead of Sweeney, Emslie was not himself. He got through the first inning, but started the second by walking the batter on seven straight balls. (The number for a walk was reduced to five in 1885 and to four in 1889.) Barnie, sensing Emslie's negative attitude, brought in Henderson to pitch, sending Bob to right field.[7] Having pitched only one inning, Emslie pitched the next day. It was a disaster. He was racked for thirteen hits in a 10–2 loss, and the Orioles again reverted to sloppy fielding, committing eight errors. Emslie was back in the box for the final game of the series on September 23. With Sweeney catching again, he pitched very well, giving up but two hits, until torrents of rain ended the game in the fifth inning. Bob did not pitch again until the season-ending game in Columbus on September 27. He was again "wild" and poorly supported by Sweeney, but the Orioles ended on a successful note, beating the Buckeyes 6–4.

With the second-lowest team batting average (.246) and second-highest ERA (4.08), the Orioles again wound up last with a 28-68 record (.292). From August 31 to the final game on September 27, the Orioles won four and lost fifteen, two losing streaks of five and six games stopped by an Emslie win. There was truth to the belief the Orioles' lack of success was because "they drink occasionally," but the more significant was the wear and tear on Emslie and Henderson, who were unaccustomed to such a heavy workload, and the poor fielding that often "paralyzed their efforts." Henderson, age twenty, simply ran out of gas, winning only one game in the final month and finishing 10-32 with a 4.02 ERA.[8]

Bob Emslie's first two months in the Major Leagues were both exhilarating and frustrating as he adjusted to professional play and pitching. Despite a losing record of 9-13 (.409), he had pitched fairly well, completing twenty-one of twenty-three games, posting a 3.17 ERA in 201.1

innings and striking out sixty-seven while walking forty-one. He suffered four losses by one run and four others by two. As the team's workhorse, from July 25 to August 21 he pitched twelve of fifteen games—twice two in a row, once three straight, and six of the last nine games. From the five games he played in the outfield, two in center and three in right, it was evident he was a pitcher as he committed fourteen errors (.827) and got just sixteen hits (.165).

After the season Baltimore played exhibition games against five National League teams who came to Oriole Park for two-game series to generate additional revenue for players and the club. The games, poorly attended and played with a "lack of vim and earnestness," were not well covered in the press. The last mention of Emslie pitching was on October 5, a "disagreeably cold" day when he was "invulnerable," yielding four hits in beating Detroit 10–5.[9]

Notwithstanding a physically and emotionally taxing five months, Emslie was not sated with baseball. When Andy Piercy, California baseball enthusiast and game broker, came to town looking for players to come to San Francisco to play winter ball, Bob signed up. But when the financial backer failed to provide the funds, Emslie went home to St. Thomas.

1884

Despite finishing last the Orioles did well financially, their $30,000 in earnings ranking fourth in the league. But in 1884 they faced increased competition with the league expanding to twelve teams and an intracity attendance threat from the Baltimore Monumentals of the new Union Association, named in recognition of Baltimore's status as "the monument city," the first to erect a civic monument to honor George Washington. The Unions scheduled home games the same day as the Orioles, and with club finances dependent on gate receipts, Baltimore's ability to support two clubs was in question.[10]

Well aware of their precarious situation, Barnie and general manager Alphonse T. Houck lost no time strengthening the team. Barnie signed catcher Bill Traffley, shortstop Jimmy Macullar, and third baseman Joe Sommer before Cincinnati had reserved the players, and acquired veteran Cleveland outfielder Tom York as team captain to impose discipline and provide leadership. With Sweeney gone the Orioles were "the most improved nine" in the league. Houck, with consummate braggadocio, declared they would be "the best nine in the American Association."[11]

To better accommodate the expected throng of spectators, year-old Oriole Park was reconfigured and improved. The bleachers were moved from the right side of the field to the left and partially roofed to shield the sun, and the grandstand, moved back to accommodate 2,500 chair seats, was fitted with a "ladies' retiring room" and a "refreshment booth." To "bring the boys into trim," the club hired S. W. Kimball, Baltimore Police Academy gymnasium instructor and professional Greco-Roman wrestler, to install a training facility in the ballpark clubhouse. Under his watchful eye the team would "enhance their playing qualities greatly" by regular "intelligent and systematic training" with dumbbells, Indian clubs, and wands, along with skipping rope, running, and jumping exercises. To complement the pioneering effort to increase conditioning and build muscle, players would follow "a careful regimen of diet and temperance" and after games be "cleansed, well dried and thoroughly rubbed." Moreover, Houck and Barnie, believing the team's shortcomings in 1883 were "largely due to the drunkenness of the men," devised ten draconian commandments directing players to abide by a curfew at home and away, not gamble or use "profane or obscene language," and abstain from "malt and spirituous liquors."[12]

Emslie, who prepared for the season during the winter by working out with a quartet of other major leaguers, including Tip O'Neill, and running competitive foot races, one for a $50 side bet, arrived in game-ready shape. Despite "blustery and uncomfortable weather" on April 7 in the first preseason exhibition game against a National League team, he outpitched Buffalo's ace, James "Pud" Galvin. With "near perfect control," Bob gave up only three hits, struck out five, and walked none, but lost 1–0. The *Sun* enthused if the Orioles "continue to play up to the standard of yesterday's game it is odds on them against any club in the American Association, bar none." Emslie thereafter pitched erratically, sometimes evidently "saving himself," other times suffering from a cold or, alarmingly, "showing signs of soreness." On April 18 he was wild and ineffective, losing to Cleveland 10–1; then on April 21 he beat the same

Blues 5–3, holding them scoreless in the first six innings. As the exhibition season progressed Bob rounded into form, throwing easier, faster, and with greater effect.[13]

During the last week of preseason Emslie was one of five pitchers timed without their knowledge to determine the velocity of pitches. In the first known effort to calculate pitch speed, a Longines chronograph machine (i.e., stopwatch) several times recorded "when men were on the bases, and the pitcher apparently exerted himself to foil the batsman, and when, of course, in all cases the catcher was playing close behind the bat, the space of time elapsing from the time the ball left the hand in delivering until it entered the catcher's hands." The fastest was Henderson at one-fifth of a second. Tied for second were Emslie, Galvin, and Philadelphia's Charlie Ferguson at two-fifths of a second; third was Buffalo's Art Hagan at three-fifths of a second. Emslie may actually have had the fastest delivery, as the pitchers were timed in their first outing, except Bob, who had the disadvantage of being timed in the second of two successive games.[14] (Today a 95 MPH Major League fastball reaches the plate in .425 seconds.)

To complement his curve Bob developed a variety of deceptive motions before releasing the ball. The most effective was "holding the ball in both hands over his head, and then, with a graceful but quick corkscrew motion of both body and arms, delivering." His sharply breaking pitches caused fits for catchers as well as batters. When the catcher played back of the plate, Emslie's "very swift in-curve" was "seldom batted effectively," but when the catcher moved up with runners on base, Bob's effectiveness was "marred owing to his great speed and the difficulty of handling his in-shoots." He also now exhibited a competitiveness that drew comment in the press: "Emslie glances at the ump with the full-blown Conkling sarcasm in his eyes, as much as to say 'What's the matter with you, you half parboiled mummy? You don't want to stand there rolling up your eyes like a sick codfish and call strikes on me; I know when I get a good ball, you four-quarter idiotic imbecile.' And then he punches at the ball viciously."[15]

On May 1 the Orioles opened season against the presumptive title favorite, Mutrie's New York Metropolitans. Reportedly ten thousand spectators jammed Oriole Park, some fifteen hundred on the field along both foul lines, to watch the home town lads, resplendent in new uniforms—white pants and shirts accented by maroon stockings, belts, and caps—behind Henderson best the Mets 5–3. The next day Emslie, on a very windy day, gave up five hits in winning 8–3. The Mets beat Henderson to take the final game of the series, but Emslie won the next game against the visiting Philadelphia Athletics, again 8–3, striking out nine. After yielding two runs on three hits and in the first inning, he scattered three hits over the remaining eight. In Philadelphia's home opener on May 9, Bob suffered his first loss, 5–4 in twelve innings; the Athletics were scoreless after the third inning until plating the winning run on Emslie's third wild pitch of the game.

Bob, now sporting a moustache, the de rigueur masculine fashion of the day, then posted a remarkable record through June. He won sixteen of twenty games, had a thirteen-inning tie on June 12, and during that span won eleven of twelve games at home. Highlights were a four-hit 3–0 shutout of Brooklyn on May 23; a two-hit 3–0 whitewash of Cincinnati on May 29; and a two-hit, ten-strike-out 8–0 win over Toledo on June 4, followed the next day by a three-hit, ten-strike-out 4–1 defeat of the Blue Stockings. After donning the Oriole's new "purplish gray" road uniform, Emslie twice defeated the St. Louis Browns and ace hurler George "Jumbo" McGinnis 5–1 on June 16 and 6–1 on June 18, and finished the month on June 26 and June 28 with a pair of 3–1 wins over the Hoosiers in Indianapolis.

Eventually Bob encountered the pitcher's bane, arm trouble. His third consecutive day in the box resulted in a 4–2 loss to Toledo on June 6; three days later, in his lone bad outing during the first two months, he gave up sixteen hits in an 11–10 win against Indianapolis. The *Sun* thought he pitched "way below his usual standard and seemed to make no effort to prevent the visitors hitting his delivery, except occasionally, when he would settle down to work and strike out the batters with ease." In fact, he was suffering from "a very sore arm" that worsened as the game wore on. He finally told York about it in the seventh inning, but with no other pitcher available, Bob carried on. In the ninth inning, after the Hoosiers got four runs on five hits and had the tying run on third with only one out, he buckled down and struck out the next two batters—a remarkably gutsy performance that demonstrated both his pitching skill and his competitive fortitude.

Three days later, rested, he was "in splendid form," yielding but five hits and fanning ten in a thirteen-inning 4–4 tie in Baltimore that was marred by riotous fans. At the end of the tenth inning a "disorderly mob" jumped onto the field, one man pointing a "huge revolver" at first-year umpire John "Jack" Brennan. Players from both teams, bats in hand, defended the umpire while police cleared the field so the game could resume. When, after three more scoreless innings, Brennan called the game on account of darkness, police and Orioles players escorted him off the field, but he was struck in the back of the neck by an outraged fan and "slugged to the ground" unconscious by another. One wonders what Emslie thought of the frightful encounter—a preview of the kind of dangerous assault he would face as an umpire in a few years. As a result of the "disgraceful" episode Brennan did not return for 1885, and Baltimore management installed a double line of barbed wire above the railings in front of the bleachers to prevent fans from swarming the field, posted signs prohibiting "rowdy behavior and abusive language," and hired a security force to preserve order.[16]

Following the debacle the Orioles took two of three from St. Louis, then embarked on a month-long six-city road trip. After taking the series in Toledo and sweeping hapless Indianapolis, Emslie posting four wins, they headed to St. Louis to take on the red-hot Browns, who were in a virtual tie for first place with Louisville and riding a six-game winning streak. Anticipation was high for the July 1 matchup between the teams' aces, "phenomenal" Bob Emslie and Jumbo McGinnis. The fans at Sportsman's Park were delighted with the Browns' eighth consecutive win, 11–5, but disappointed by the "careless and spiritless" play of the visitors. Orioles fielders committed ten errors and Emslie had "a way-off day" pitching, suffering his first loss in eight games. "Badly rattled" by the "wretched fielding," he gave up seven runs in second inning and contributed to the defeat with two wild pitches and errant throws to bases.

The game was an embarrassment, but the worst was yet to come. That evening the Browns' Tip O'Neill and Fred Lewis met Emslie, Gardner, and Henderson at the Lindell Hotel, where the Orioles were staying, for a festive night out—something of a jamboree for the two Canadians, it being Dominion Day. About two o'clock in the morning, the quintet, "pretty badly loaded," wound up at Maude Abbey's house of ill repute. As they registered in the parlor one of the women made "a sharp retort" to O'Neill and was ordered out of the room by Abbey. As she was leaving, Tip threw a spittoon at her, the missile hitting the wall and spraying her with its vile contents. The irate madame then attacked O'Neill and in the ensuing melee fell to the floor, reportedly sat on by three players who "beat her." During the fracas someone blew the police whistle, whereupon O'Neill and Emslie beat a hasty retreat into the night, Bob surreptitiously returning to his hotel room. Just as Henderson and Lewis were leaving, carrying a spittoon between them, they were arrested, driven to jail in a patrol car, and locked up in a cell. Lewis. becoming "very obstreperous" in resisting being searched, was "clubbed into submission."

Gardner, who was not arrested, perhaps because he was not involved in the assault on Abbey, went with her to the jail and tried to persuade Maude not to bring charges against the players, whereupon she "struck him a hard blow in the face." Gid then returned to the hotel about 3 a.m. and woke up Barnie, who had just retired after waiting in the lobby "for the return of the prodigals," pleading in vain for him to bail out Henderson and Lewis. As far as the irate Barnie was concerned, Henderson could remain in jail "as long as the authorities want to keep him there."

At 10:30 that morning, Henderson and Lewis, accompanied by P. W. Fauntleroy, "attorney and base-ball enthusiast," appeared in the First District Police Court to face charges of disturbing the peace. Looking "weary and worn out," they stood before the bench "meek as lambs" in disheveled clothes, Lewis's collar stained with blood. When Maude Abbey failed to appear to press charges, the case was postponed until the next day and the prisoners went back to their cells. About noon "a friend" bailed them out of jail.[17]

That afternoon the game between the Browns and the Orioles took place as scheduled, but team chemistry, the togetherness that allows players to focus on the game, was noticeably absent. St. Louis players, "very indignant" over Lewis's behavior, favored expelling him from the team. Captain York and the Orioles were "highly mortified" by their teammates' behavior. The result was a game that probably should not have been played—indeed, in some senses it wasn't, as neither team showed "any spirit or vim" in "one of the worst exhibitions of the national game ever witnessed at Sportsman's Park." The teams combined for twenty-four hits and twenty-five errors, the Orioles outlasting the Browns 15–12. O'Neill, who replaced Lewis in center field for the Browns, was no worse for the evening out, getting three hits and scoring twice in addition to pitching very effectively for six innings in relief. Gardner didn't play, but Emslie, forced to pitch the second day in a row, pitched "a weak and weary game." He was not "sulking" in "an exhibition of ill-temper," but "sick and physically incapable of pitching a swift or effective ball. His efforts were painful to observe, and at one stage of the game he got so weak that he had to stop." After the game the Orioles, "badly broken up" over the disgraceful conduct of Henderson and Gardner, left for Columbus "pretty badly discouraged."[18]

The disgraceful affair never reached a conclusion. With the Orioles off to Ohio and the Browns to New York, Abbey did not press charges and the St. Louis papers made no more mention of the incident. The players escaped criminal conviction, but were punished by their teams. Perhaps because of his value to the Browns, O'Neill, who started the incident by throwing a spittoon but falsely claimed that reports about his involvement were "unfounded" as he had "no connection" with the fracas, was neither fined nor publicly chastised. Lewis, on the other hand, was suspended for drunkenness and insubordination, but was reactivated a week later when he pledged to "severely abstain from all fermented, vinous or alcoholic liquors" for the rest of the season. Barnie, tired of recurring problems with untoward player behavior, fined Henderson $150 plus the $35 bail cost and Emslie $100, warning them another incident would bring dismissal. And he expelled Gardner, "the disturbing element," a persistent disciplinary problem who in June had been jailed for beating a woman, Effie Frank, in Baltimore.[19]

Gardner was gone and Emslie and Henderson were reportedly penitent for their misbehavior, but the St. Louis ruckus had a lingering effect. Even if Orioles players were fed up with Gardner's disregard for team rules and off-field behavior, they wanted him back, knowing the outstanding fielder with a strong arm and solid bat was key component of their success. The Orioles, who had not lost more than two games in a row, now went into a funk, dropping twelve of the next thirteen. Henderson pitched well, losing several close games, but Emslie, upset by the dismissal of his friend and long-time teammate, lost five in a row and seven of eight. He pitched poorly in all except the fifteen-inning 5–4 loss in Louisville on July 10.

Emslie and the Orioles were suffering from a bad attitude. Rumors spread that Bob said he would not win another game until Gardner was reinstated. The Baltimore press accused unnamed players of "playing for their release," hoping Barnie would cut them so they could sign with another team. That seemed to be the case on July 22, when fans at Oriole Park witnessed a "miserable" and "thoroughly disgusting" performance as Philadelphia punished the Orioles in a 14–4 loss. Emslie pitched fairly well, giving up nine hits and one earned run, but his teammates committed sixteen errors and struck out ten times. Things were so bad an exasperated York left the team, replaced as captain by shortstop Jimmy Macullar.[20]

If Emslie's subpar performance was due partly to petulance, he was also having arm trouble. On the western trip Barnie, ever pursuing a dollar, at every opportunity made the team play exhibition games—at least five on that tour. By the time they reached Cincinnati the players were overworked, several were hurt, and both pitchers were crippled. Although not in shape to play, Bob gamely pitched on July 13, struggling with "a very lame shoulder" in a 9–2 loss to the Reds. After a rainout the next day, both pitchers' arms were still so sore that outfielder Jim McLaughlin was sent to the box. Bob, his arm still aching, lost to Brooklyn 6–1 on July 19 and to Philadelphia 14–4 on July 22. He beat lowly Washington 13–8 on July 28 for his first win in six outings, but gave up fourteen hits.

While still complaining of soreness in early August, Bob kept pitching. He got "battered rather freely" in a loss to Brooklyn on August 2, and although "not hit very hard" in beating Pittsburg 4–3 in ten innings on August 12, "did not show anything like his real form" due to "soreness in his back and right arm." Henderson pitched two games in a row to give

Bob a break, but the *Baltimore Sun* correctly believed he needed a longer rest. Returning to the box on August 14, he won 14–4 in Pittsburg, but the next outing, on August 18 in Philadelphia, was the low point of the season for Bob and the Orioles. In a game hauntingly reminiscent of Emslie's humiliation in the Quaker City with the Atlantics in 1882, the Athletics administered a 22-hit, 20–1 whipping. Bob, never before so punished, was pummeled in the eighth inning "like a country amateur": thirteen batters came to the plate and all but one got a hit as the Athletics scored eleven times, ten earned, with six runs plated before the first out.

Word among ballists on the streets of Baltimore was that Barnie was either about to accede to his players' request to reinstate Gardner or dump Emslie. Barnie was not foolish enough to do either. Instead he began a wholesale restructuring of the team, bringing in a stream of new blood in hope of bolstering weak positions and creating a new frame of mind. The most important move was acquiring veteran pitcher Fred Goldsmith on August 9 from the Chicago White Stockings. Goldsmith would pitch only four games with Baltimore, but he provided rest for the weary Emslie and Henderson and, more importantly, gave encouragement and advice to his protégé. After Goldsmith's arrival Bob and the Orioles came out of the doldrums, winning twelve of fourteen games between August 19 and September 9, including six straight. Emslie won all six starts, capped by a ten-inning, six-hit victory in St. Louis. He retained his form the rest of the year with only one subpar performance, on September 21 in Cincinnati, an 11–10 loss in ten innings. The final score was misleading. Effective for the first six innings, he injured his pitching hand in the seventh, and his inability to grip the ball resulted in seven Reds runs.

Emslie did not pitch the next two games, but on September 25 set the tone for a fifteen-game home stand to end the season in beating the second-place Louisville Eclipse and the league's best pitcher, Guy Hecker, in the process of turning in the most remarkable season in baseball history.[21] It was Bob's best all-around game of the season. In addition to limiting the Eclipse to seven singles while striking out six, he put on a slugging performance at bat, going 3-4, including a triple, and scoring two runs. The Orioles won eleven of the next twelve games, nine in a row, then lost three, but capped off the season on October 15 "in glorious style" with twenty-five hits in a 13–0 trouncing of St. Louis. The rout was mercifully halted when, after Baltimore scored two in the sixth, the Browns walked off the field, refusing to play any longer, the score reverting to the fifth inning.

Though games in October were meaningless for the standings, Emslie bore down. In shutting out Cincinnati 3–0 on October 1, he demonstrated the grit that marked his pitching. No Reds runner got as far as third base. In the fourth inning, after throwing six straight balls to Bid McPhee, Bob struck him out on three pitches. On October 6, with Baltimore leading 7–6 in the bottom of the ninth inning, it looked as if Louisville, with runners on second and third and no outs, might win. Bob then "braced up," striking out the next three batters.

As the season wound to a close, the Orioles showed their appreciation to Barnie, who had worked so hard and endured so much to achieve a successful season. On October 6, in Baltimore, after the Orioles jumped to a 3–0 lead in the first inning, Barnie was called from the ticket office to home plate. Surrounded by Orioles players, the manager was given a $300 solitaire diamond ring and a letter signed by the players "expressing their high appreciation of his kindness and care for their interests." Apropos the occasion, Emslie pitched a 7–6 victory.

It was a resounding end to Baltimore's best Major League season. The Orioles, much improved, finished not in the basement, as they had in 1882 and 1883, but in the middle of the twelve-team circuit, finishing 63-43-2 (.594). The sixth-place finish, bolstered by a 42-13 home field record, was due partly to the poor performance of the expansion teams, none of which finished higher than eighth, but owed more to the pitching of Emslie and Henderson. The two workhorse hurlers started 102 of the team's 106 games and earned fifty-nine of the team's sixty-three victories. Fireballing Hardie, 27-23 with a .262 ERA, was erratic, striking out 346 but throwing 43 wild pitches. Bob started and completed fifty games, winning seventeen of his first twenty-one appearances and finished 32-17 (.653) with a 2.75 ERA in 455.1 innings, striking out 264 while walking only 88. In over half his losses he gave up six hits or fewer. He was dominant at home (20-5) and thrice won six games in a row and once four straight. Although Bob was plagued off and on by a sore arm for the first time in his pitching career, 1884 was, as he later called it, "my most successful year," a brilliant season in which he recorded the most Major League games ever won by a Canadian-born pitcher. In two games in the outfield Bob fielded a woeful .833 and hit a meager .190.[22]

It was also a memorable season in personal respects. It was a pleasure to be Goldsmith's teammate in his idol's last year and to impress his former Atlantics skipper, Bill Watkins, now player-manager for Indianapolis, by winning three games against the Hoosiers. He also witnessed the debut of the first Black players in Major League history, catcher Moses Fleetwood Walker and his outfielder brother, Welday, of the Toledo Blue Stockings.[23] Bob never faced Welday, but he played against Fleet when Toledo came to Baltimore in early June. Segregation was the custom of the day in the city, but there were no editorial comments about Walker's arrival, and game advertisements announced "Walker the wonderful Colored Catcher will play."[24] Walker did not play on June 3, but the next day was behind the bat when Emslie shut out the Blue Stockings 8–0. "Utterly unable to do anything with Emslie's peculiar curves," Toledo was "at his mercy" as he gave up but three weak singles while striking out ten. Walker went 0–4 and had three errors and three passed balls. He did not play the next day, when Bob, again in the box because Henderson's arm was "quite sore," showed no sign of fatigue in fanning ten and yielding three hits to win 4–1.

The end of the season was not the end of Emslie's ball playing in 1884. On October 20 the Orioles divided into two teams to play a benefit game to augment their income, the Hendersons defeating the Emslies 5–4. The Orioles then went to Norfolk, Virginia, for two games. Emslie was "batted freely" for ten hits but won 5–4 on October 21. Upon returning home they played a benefit game on October 24 against the Picked Nine, professional players from Baltimore, to raise money for Annie Smiley, mother of William "Bill" Smiley, a popular Baltimore ballplayer who had died after a brief illness on July 11. Emslie, playing third base for the only time in his career, recorded one hit and run, two putouts, three assists, and no errors in the 5–4 win.[25]

On a personal note, Bob was smitten with a girlfriend. In late October, as players were preparing to head home, the "gallant Canadian" who was “so modest and tender hearted” spoke of his recent affliction with “domestic felicity”: “Canada is a cold country, but it will have to freeze out all the fervor of an unusually red-hot affection if I get left this winter.” Eventually one party was left in the cold, there being no further mention of a relationship, but instead of heading north to St. Thomas, Bob went south to New Orleans.[26]

NEW ORLEANS

Whether attracted by additional income, exciting life in the Crescent City, or simply more baseball, he agreed to play on a team made up of Major Leaguers organized and managed by Cincinnati’s Warren “Hick” Carpenter. When it was announced Bob would replace Guy Hecker, the American Association’s leading pitcher, the *New Orleans Daily Picayune* proclaimed him “a better pitcher than Hecker.” Emslie’s team, aptly called the Expositions, was the home team for games against visiting professional teams and picked nines during the World’s Industrial and Cotton Centennial Exposition. Open from December 16, 1884, to June 2, 1885, the sprawling 249-acre complex, highlighted by the largest roofed building ever constructed in America and illuminated with five thousand electric lights, offered attendees a wide array of entertainments and domestic and international exhibits.[27]

For Emslie it promised to be an interesting and pleasurable venture. The Expositions lineup was filled with familiar faces, seven from American Association teams; the only Nationals were Detroit Wolverines batterymates pitcher George “Stump” Weidman and catcher Charlie Bennett. Bob would receive a monthly salary and play in the new ballpark on Canal Street that reportedly could seat 33,000. Since the Expositions played only once a week in order to accommodate the schedules of the local five-team amateur league, he would have ample time to enjoy the city. Emslie had never before been to America’s Deep South, and New Orleans, a city of some 220,000 with distinctive architecture and unique blends of French, Spanish, and African cultures—Creole and Cajun—offered new and exciting social life, food, drink, and music.[28]

The first Expositions first game on November 2 was against a local amateur club since the scheduled Louisville Eclipse failed to show up.

It was no contest, the professionals winning 6–1 as Weidman struck out twelve and yielded only two hits. Bob played right field, making one put-out and going 0-4 at bat. On November 9 Wiedman pitched the Expositions by the Daytons, a picked nine from Ohio, 6–1. The visitors did not score until the ninth inning, when Emslie, in right field, muffed a fly ball in his only fielding opportunity of the game; he again went 0-4.

Bob's pitching debut on November 13 against the Daytons ended in a 5–5 tie. He "seemed to labor in his delivery," but struck out twelve and gave up just two hits, Dayton scoring thanks to six Exposition errors. He pitched again against the Daytons on November 16, striking out eleven in winning 7–3. On November 30 he pitched the Expos to a 9–8 win over the St. Louis Maroons, actually a picked Union Association team. Bob was again impressive, fanning eleven, but "lost his temper and became wild several times," perhaps owing to nine Expositions errors, including one of his own. He did have his finest day at bat, going 3-5 and driving in a run. On December 7 the Expos lost for the first time, St. Louis edging Weidman 2–1. Emslie, in right field, had no put-outs and failed to get a hit in three attempts.[29]

Although the Expositions had won five of six games, the team and the ballplaying enterprise were in trouble. After 2,5000 fans showed up for the first game, attendance dropped dramatically, sometimes to merely several hundred spectators. The *Daily Picayune* initially blamed "inclement weather," but then acknowledged "the public here seldom finds time to patronize week day games, even when professionals play." The low attendance, which meant visiting teams were losing money, also affected the quality of play: "There can be no exciting game without a crowd. It requires public interest to interest the players." A number of Expositions players began to think about leaving. Bennett and Wiedman departed on December 8, and three days later a "clever trio," including Bob Emslie, headed home.[30]

Citing growing monetary losses, the managers of the baseball program decided on December 12 to suspend operations until January, optimistically saying the Expositions would then field "nearly the same nine" and open with a series against the Baltimore Orioles. It didn't happen. None of the players had any intention of returning, especially Bob Emslie, for whom the junket was costly. Having had arm trouble during the 1884 season, he should have gone home to rest instead of heading to New Orleans. As he later recalled of his time with the Expositions, "While playing in one of those games, I hurt my arm, back of the shoulder. I felt it go at the time. I tried everything, but it never got right."[31]

1885

For Emslie and the Orioles, optimism marked the arrival of the 1885 season. His shoulder and arm seemingly recovered after three months' rest, Bob looked forward to another successful season in the box. Baltimore strengthened the club by adding third baseman Mike Muldoon, multitalented twenty-year old rookie outfielder Thomas "Oyster" Burns, and catchers Phil Powers and Vincent "Sandy" Nava, the first Mexican American player in the Major Leagues. Anticipating public enthusiasm, Barnie hired a photographer to take team pictures, one in "civilian dress," the other in the new home uniform—white pants, red stockings, and pink-striped caps and jerseys—that had "a novelty about them, even if they are not very pretty."[32]

During spring exhibition games Emslie appeared to have recovered from the injury suffered in New Orleans. He didn't exert himself in an easy 10–3 win over Brown University in his first outing on April 2, but pitched "a splendid game" in beating the National League's Buffalo on April 6. But he seemed "tired and out of condition," striking out only two in losing to the Bisons on April 10; pitching against Providence four days later, he complained of a sore arm as his "slow balls were batted well" by the Grays in a 13–7 victory. Although losing the last preseason game on April 18 to Boston 7–3, he pitched a "strong game" except for the fourth inning, when the Beaneaters scored six runs.

Orioles had opened 1884 with a win at home, but in 1885 lost to Brooklyn, an omen of things to come. The team did not play with the spirit or confidence exhibited in the preseason, and Emslie, his arm now bothering him, did not pitch until the fourth game, on April 23. In beating the defending champions, the New York Metropolitans, 6–4, he pitched "a steady game," but with "a very sore arm" was hit "rather hard," for the first time in his career recording no strikeouts. Two days later, his arm still hurting, he was "hit hard and often" during a 9–2 loss in Brooklyn. He sat out the next seven games, hoping to recover by resting. Returning to the box on May 9, he was hammered for fourteen hits, losing 9–1 to Louisville.

There followed the worst run of his career: seven consecutive losses. After being idle for four days, he was "very wild" on May 14, losing 6–5 in St. Louis, only Traffley's "great work" behind the plate saving him from numerous wild pitches. Emslie pitched another "miserable game" in Cincinnati on May 20 and was removed after yielding six runs in the fifth inning; the *Baltimore American* proclaimed, "Emslie is Played Out," and the reporter declared himself "reluctantly compelled to admit that Emslie has lost his power a pitcher." Gamely trying to pitch on May 23, Emslie lost 5–0 in Pittsburgh, throwing three wild pitches and fanning none. Three days later he lost again to the Alleghenys. It was a close game, 2–1, but he had only one strikeout and gave up eleven "batted hard" hits.

It was not only Bob who failed to meet expectations. From May 12 to June 1, the Orioles dropped eleven of thirteen games. Barnie blamed "indifferent playing on the part of several members" who were more concerned with "drawing their salaries rather than the winning of games." Emslie, however, he thought "has been playing good ball, and is expected to do some good pitching." If, given Bob's subpar performance for the previous five weeks, the manager's complimentary remarks were intended to encourage his struggling pitcher, they didn't work.[33]

After the May 26 loss in Pittsburgh, Henderson pitched two consecutive games to rest Emslie's ailing arm. On June 1 in St. Louis Bob was weak, tossing three wild pitches and hitting a batter, the Browns battering him for twelve hits in a 10–4 rout. Two days later he showed "great improvement," scattering ten hits and giving up one earned run in losing to the Browns 6–5. But he fanned only one, indicating arm weakness.

Then, on June 6, Emslie and the Orioles erupted in the finest game of the season for both, thrashing the Cincinnati Reds 21–5. The Orioles pounded out twenty-two hits and committed only two errors while Emslie, switching from overhand to underhand pitching, won his first game since April 25, giving up eight hits, fanning a season high of four batters, and for the first time in several games throwing no wild pitches. Moreover, he had a career day at bat with five hits, including a double and a triple, and scored four runs. In the fifth inning he left the box because of pain in his stomach, but returned the next inning and finished the game. All in all, a terrific performance that seemed to bode well for the rest of the season.

It was not to be. He rested for two days after his superb outing, but then was hit hard, losing to Pittsburgh 12–8 on June 11. He was again rested until June 18 in Louisville, when he pitched efficiently and won his third game 11–2, giving up just eight hits and striking out a season high of nine. He left the diamond in good spirits, unaware it would be his last Major League victory.

Prior to the Philadelphia Athletics' arrival in Baltimore, Barnie arranged an exhibition game with the Westminster, Maryland, club on their home grounds on June 22. More than a few Orioles players resented playing on an off day; some, Emslie included, failed to show up, and those who did played sloppily, committing seven errors as the amateurs won 9–7. To add insult to injury, after the game Barnie signed Westminster's Ed Greer as Baltimore's catcher. When Greer took the field on June 24 against Philadelphia, the Orioles protested his acquisition by "playing like a lot of old women," committing eleven errors, "many of them of the grossest character," in losing 10–4. Many spectators, who initially "laughed and hissed alternately" at the "disgraceful exhibition," eventually left the grounds "disgusted." While the entire team was at fault, Emslie, who gave up nine hits, "acted like a sulky school boy." After the game, in response to "bad and indifferent playing," an irate Billy Barnie released Emslie and Manning, saying Manning, hitting .204, was "weak" and Emslie "is about played out." He was right about Emslie, whose arm kept giving him trouble. Bob later recalled, "It kept getting worse all the time. From an over-hand pitcher, I tried under-hand, as it did not hurt me so much with that delivery, but I was not successful with it and Baltimore let me go."[34]

The Orioles, like Emslie, regressed badly in 1885. (Perhaps metaphorically representative of the ups and downs of the season was the appearance that year of the country's first modern roller coaster at Coney Island in Brooklyn.) Losing sixteen of the last twenty-one games, Baltimore, with the league's lowest team batting average (.219), second highest ERA (3.90) and third worst fielding average (.909), returned to last place at

41-68 (.376). Emslie had contributed substantially to the team's demise, compiling a 3-10 (.231) record with a 4.29 ERA in 107 innings. Symptomatic of his arm problems were persistent wildness and dramatic decrease in strikeouts (27).

PHILADELPHIA

Emslie was done with Baltimore, but his Major League career was not finished. After the ten-day mandatory waiting period required before signing with another American Association club, he joined Philadelphia. The Athletics' fortunes declined after winning the pennant in 1883, their first year in the league, unable to find a reliable pitcher to complement their ace, Bobby Mathews. Despite Emslie's ineffective outing against Philadelphia on June 24, player-manager Harry Stovey, recalling Bob's effectiveness in 1884, signed him to replace Tom Lovett, who had been out with a sore arm since June 26.[35]

On July 6 Emslie joined the Athletics in Pittsburgh, watching his new teammates, behind Mathews, shut out the Allegheny 8–0. The next day, when his release from Baltimore became official, Bob pitched against the Allegheny. Perhaps in part from trying too hard to impress his new teammates, he was very wild, but struck out five in losing 5–1. In his next outing, on July 10 to Cincinnati, he was reached for twelve hits but allowed only one earned run as the Athletics staged "the vilest exhibition" of fielding with eleven errors and lost 10–4. Two days later he pitched a good, steady game; in the first eight innings the Reds got only five hits and two runs. But he weakened in the ninth, Cincinnati plating four runs on five hits to win 6–5. After an outing that pointed to possible success, Bob had a meltdown in St. Louis on July 16. In the first inning he walked the first two batters, escaping trouble thanks to an inning-ending double play. But in the second, after the Browns "pounded the life out of Emslie" in scoring six times, he was sent to right field, then to the bench after the inning. With Lovett reactivated on July 15, Emslie, having ineffectively served his purpose, was released on July 25. In nine days with the Athletics he lost all four starts, posting a 6.28 ERA in 28.2 innings. Indicative of arm weariness, he struck out only nine batters. He was equally deficient at bat with a lone single (.083).

Bob Emslie's once promising Major League career was seemingly over. Serious arm troubles in 1885 ruined his statistical career profile. In two partial and one full Major League seasons he started ninety games and finished eighty-five; in 792.1 innings he yielded 775 hits and 507 runs (281 earned), walked 165, struck out 362, threw seventeen wild pitches and hit nineteen batters in posting a 44-44 record and 3.19 ERA. His fielding record as an outfielder in nine games (.750) was below average but on par for a pitcher (.826). He came to bat 355 times, recording sixty-six hits—eight doubles, six triples, no homers, and four RBI for a paltry .186 average.

What had happened? While later umpiring in the National League he used his own experience to comment on the recurring arm problems with pitchers:

> If the pain is in the shoulder, it's all up with a player. If it is anywhere else, one can recover the use of his arm in time. When I was pitching in the American Association, I suddenly felt a stinging sensation in my shoulder. It didn't prevent my pitching at first, although I had to practice for fully a half hour before each game in order to limber up. But after the game my arm always became so stiff that I couldn't raise it. Finally, I found that I could pitch fast balls without any pain but the curve balls caused me to suffer agony. Then, in a week or so, it was just the reverse. The fast balls hurt and the curved ones didn't. This thing went on for some time, until no matter what kind of a ball I threw, it gave me great pain, and then I knew my arm was dead.[36]

The injury might have been either a torn rotator cuff or a SLAP tear, but Bob's description suggests recurrent transient subluxation of the shoulder, commonly known as dead arm syndrome, caused by excessive rotation of the humeral head.[37] With a rotator cuff or SLAP tear, both requiring surgery to repair, Emslie would not have been able to pitch effectively at all. With a dead arm, the sharp pain abates with rest, but the resumption of throwing results in recurrent shoulder instability, erratic control, and decreased velocity.

Emslie's injury obviously resulted from the forceful movement of the arm above shoulder level (overhand pitching), but the specific cause is uncertain. Overuse is most commonly cited for pitchers' arm injuries, and while Emslie's professional pitching career lasted less than six years, he pitched a lot of ball in that short time since he threw complete games and alternated with just one other pitcher. Emslie certainly worked very hard in 1884, pitching 455 innings in completing fifty games. But a two-man staff was not unusual—Philadelphia was alone in using a trio—and a heavy workload does not necessarily lead to arm problems. In 1884 Louisville's Guy Hecker pitched 670.2 innings with a 1.80 ERA; in 1885 he threw 480 innings with a 2.17 ERA. On the other hand, Hardie Henderson, a one-man staff after Emslie left, pitched sixty-one games for an astonishing 539.1 innings and was soon out of the game.

Emslie's injury most likely resulted from altering his delivery. He started pitching underhand, then sidearm in 1883. Coincidentally or not, his arm troubles began immediately after all restrictions on the pitcher's delivery were removed in June 1884. Releasing the ball from above the head brought even sharper breaks to Bob's curveball and greater velocity to his fastball, but the overhand motion also transferred tremendous kinetic energy to his shoulder joint and muscles (the subscapularis and, especially, the latissimus dorsi), precisely where he first felt discomfort. The new rule in 1885 requiring pitchers to keep both feet on the ground while releasing the ball might have caused him to alter awkwardly his pitching motion, thereby adding additional strain to his shoulder. Whatever the cause, persistent shoulder and arm soreness seemed to have brought an end to Bob Emslie's promising pitching career.[38]

5

Comeback Trail

I remember ignoring the sore arm
I remember the sting of my fingertips
  when I let one go just right
I remember the best pitch I ever threw
I remember having nothing left
I remember how sad I felt
Now I can only remember pitching.
  —Andrew Peters, "I'm a Pitcher"

Although faced with the end of his Major League career, Emslie was reluctant to give up the game, his passion since childhood. After leaving Philadelphia he went to Newark, hoping to catch on with manager Charlie Hackett's Domestics of the Eastern League, a haven for former Major Leaguers. With pitcher Levi Hickman out with a lame arm, Hackett invited Bob to join the team near the end of a southern road trip. On August 3 he pitched against the eventual league champion Washington Nationals. It did not go well. He uncorked five wild pitches and gave up ten hits in losing 5–0. After the game Bob said that, having pitched with the Reach ball in Baltimore, he was "unaccustomed to the Shibe ball and could not control it." Upon returning to Newark, Bob was slated to play left field against the independent Baltimore Mutuals, which hoped to replace the recently disbanded Pennsylvania Lancasters. That, too, didn't go well. The Mutuals had only five players for the August 6 game—the others failed to catch the train from Baltimore—so Hackett loaned them four Domestics, including Emslie, who went hitless in left field as Newark easily won 9–1. On the basis of the embarrassing game the league rebuffed the Mutuals and Hackett sent Emslie packing.[1]

SYRACUSE

En route to St. Thomas Bob stopped in Syracuse. Whether owing to happenstance or prior contact, Stars manager Henry Ormsbee gave him a trial. Stocked with eleven former Major Leaguers, Syracuse was in first place and would go on to win the championship in the first and only year of the seven-team New York State League, but at the moment Ormsbee needed a third pitcher to spell Jim Devine and Mac MacArthur. It was old home week, the roster dotted with familiar faces. Bob had played with Devine on the London Atlantics and Jay Faatz on the St. Thomas Atlantics, and knew well three former AA opponents, including Fred Lewis, his house of assignation companion in St. Louis. And three teammates were Ontario Canadians: John "Jack" Humphries, Jimmy Reardon, and Bob Casey.

On August 29 Emslie took the box for the first time with the Stars in what probably was a "make good" game. Displaying a "quick delivery" that made runners "hug their bases," he pitched "a credible game" in defeating an unidentified amateur team. Two days later he pitched superbly in a league game against Rochester, shutting out the Flour Cities for seven innings on three hits before yielding a run in the eighth. With the Stars leading 5–1 in the bottom of the ninth, Rochester, aided by sloppy Stars fielding, scored five to win 6–5. If disappointed by the loss, Emslie was pleased with the local newspaper describing him "a master of the profession," a pitcher rather than a thrower: "He is not a mere machine for delivering the ball but a strategist. His pitching is hard work throughout. He has thorough command of the ball and knows almost every time just where it is going. He does not throw swift and his curves are not wide. But he exercises the best judgment in guessing which time a batsman is going to bat and when he will let a good ball past him."[2]

Despite the strong outing that won him place on the roster, Emslie was relegated to playing the outfield and pitching non-league games. He won a second game 5–4 against an unidentified opponent on September 11. On September 16, given an eight-run lead after the first inning, he pitched the first and only no-hitter of his career, a 21–0 whitewash of a semipro team from Oneida. Getting two hits and scoring a run added to his pleasure.

When Ormsbee resigned on September 16, Jack Humphries, taking over as manager, lost no time in signing veteran John "Daisy" Davis, lately of the Boston Beaneaters, thereby giving the Stars a quartet of pitchers and further reducing Emslie's work. In the Syracuse paper's haphazard reporting of games, Bob's next mention is in a 16–8 loss to Binghamton on September 29 at Stars Park. When Devine was removed after six innings, Emslie, who had dropped two routine fly balls in centerfield, took over. He gave up four runs in the seventh before finding his groove, blanking the Bingos in the last two frames.

Besides giving Bob a chance to pitch, Syracuse afforded him another baseball first. Novelty contests, including games on ice, were popular from the 1860s to the 1890s, and the Stars and a local picked nine played a game on roller skates at the Empire rink on October 5 to raise money for Syracuse players. Davis and Devine played for the picked nine; Emslie likely donned a pair of "treacherous rollers" for the Stars. When the Providence Grays came to town for an exhibition game on October 13, Bob played first base and batted cleanup, going 0–2 but scoring a run in the 2–2 tie game called after six innings. The season over, Bob went home to assess his future.

TORONTO

Back in home in St. Thomas Bob Emslie had all winter to think about life without baseball. What lay ahead? Since as an adult he had known nothing but pitching, and his modest success in Syracuse absent arm problems got him thinking about trying to continue pitching at the Minor League level and, should his arm recover, perhaps even returning to the Majors. Comeback prospects were bleak, but the opportunity came thanks to the grandiose plans of the directors of the Toronto club.

Undeterred by an unsuccessful attempt to join the New York State League, Toronto officials in early 1886 fancied becoming a Major League team. With the departure of Buffalo and Providence, the National League needed two teams—one in the east and another in the west. Washington quickly joined, leaving Toronto among four cities under consideration as the western addition. The idea of adding a Canadian team struck some as odd, but *Sporting Life* thought Toronto's prospects were good considering it had solid financial backing, a strong club already signed, plans underway for a new ballpark, a sizeable population of 123,000, and "sporting enthusiasm none of the other cities can approach." The only downside was climate: persistent wintry conditions might prevent spring competition. That was not a problem for Albert Spalding, president and co-owner of the Chicago White Stockings, who in January consulted with team officials and, after tobogganing with great delight on several park slopes, promised to support their application. But Toronto declined to apply for admission since club chairman Lemuel Felcher thought joining the National League was "premature." Instead, the Canucks and Hamilton joined the New York State league, renamed the International Association (IA) given its transborder composition.[3]

To capitalize on burgeoning enthusiasm for baseball, the only professional sport in town, Toronto's directors built a new stadium commensurate with the city's prominence as the provincial capital and major commercial center.[4] They also hired Jack Humphries to assemble players strong enough to win the pennant. He did so by signing virtually the entire champion 1885 Syracuse Stars, among them Bob Emslie, who, if no longer able flummox hitters with fastballs or sharp-breaking curves, had demonstrated an ability to confound batters with guts and guile. With Emslie, Daisy Davis, and newcomer William "Peek-A-Boo" Veach, the Canucks had a formidable trio of hurlers. If Bob's manager and the majority of his teammates were familiar, a new team in a new league playing in a new facility and wearing new uniforms—maroon pants, jerseys, and caps accented by old gold belts and stockings—seemed the harbinger of a new beginning.

Emslie's preseason preparation, which began by pitching the last four innings against the University of Toronto team on April 23, was interrupted when George Sleeman, president of the Guelph club and the Canadian League, sued Hamilton and Toronto for violation of contract and requested an injunction to prevent them joining the International. It was a nuisance suit, since the CL constitution provided for club withdrawal; besides, should Sleeman win, the Canucks and Clippers could assemble an alternate uncompetitive team to play in the league.

To avoid being called as a witness in the case, Humphries fled across the Niagara River into the United States, then summoned his team, taking them to Ithaca, New York, where he had secured permission to train mornings in the Cornell gym and afternoons on the school's diamond until the IA season began. When the chancellor of the High Court of Justice of the Province of Ontario ruled against Sleeman's injunction, saying the suit over breach of contract would likely not be resolved until fall, the Canucks headed to Rochester, where they opened the season on May 8 on a sand field as the new Culver Park grounds had not yet been sodded. A large delegation from Toronto, including club officials, were so confident in the team that they wagered $5,000 the Canucks would start the season with a victory; they did, defeating the Maroons 6–4.

Emslie's comeback attempt began on May 12 in the second game in Rochester in right field, going 0–3 with one put-out and no errors in a 6–0 loss. After two more losses Humphries decided to give Bob his first start on May 14 in Buffalo. He got off to a shaky start, giving up three runs in the first inning, but then settled down, striking out the side in the fourth and yielding but two runs the rest of the game in pitching the team's second win of the season, 6–5. In his next outing, in Toronto on May 19, he again began slowly, the Bisons scoring four runs in the first inning and three in the second before Bob "settled down to good work," his eight strikeouts countered by ten Canuck errors in the 9–8 loss. It seemed Bob's arm had recovered with the winter's rest as he won his next four starts; then, after losing three, he won seven straight for a 12-4 record through July 13. No longer a dominating pitcher, he was hit often and hard. He gave up nine or fewer hits only five times and more typically allowed double-digit safeties (averaging thirteen per game), but was able to scatter the hits and bear down when necessary. His best outing came on June 25, when he beat Utica 3–1 on only four hits.

Then, with the return of arm and shoulder problems, he became ineffective. Although beating Rochester 12–11 on July 13, he was wild, throwing 114 balls, including four wild pitches, against thirty-nine strikes. Rest did not help his aching arm. Hit hard in a 10–4 loss to Utica on July 29, he did not pitch again until August 3, when the cellar-dwelling Oswego Starchboxes battered him for nineteen hits in a 12–10 loss.

With Daisy Davis's season ended by arm injury and Emslie struggling, it was obvious by mid-August that Toronto needed another pitcher. But Bob soldiered on, grimacing as his "slow drop-curves" were "pounded heavily" game after game. He beat lowly Oswego 7–5 on August 14, but on September 7 was again "in poor form, hit frequently and hard," yielding sixteen hits in a 15–6 loss to seventh-place Binghamton. The *Toronto Mail* asserted that, "given the familiarity established between Emslie and the visiting batsmen," Emslie would soon be released. It was indeed his last outing; having "palpably panned out," Bob was replaced in the box on September 11 by James McKinley, lately of the New England League.[5] Along with his declining performance on the field, he faced two unsettling real-world problems.

RACE

Not only players had reported to the Canuck's preseason camp. Humphries had summoned Syracuse's 1885 mascot, "a chubby little 'coon,'" who reportedly "walked from Brooklyn to Ithaca to meet his old friends." (The term *coon* derived from *barracoon*, "the term for the depot holding African slaves awaiting transit to the Americas.") This was Willie Hume, an adult male disparagingly described as "a very small and very fat coloured boy," who would accompany the Canucks as "their Mascotte" to bring good luck to the team. The "little darky mascot" was to entertain spectators in addition to serving as a batboy. On away games Hume wore a red uniform with old gold stockings, like the players, but for home games he dressed in a blue uniform accented with inch-wide gold lamé. Racism was not restricted to Humphries. To offset the presumed good luck of Toronto's "colored cupid," Bufffalo manager Jack Chapman hired "a young coloured boy" to sit on the Bisons' bench during games with the Canucks.[6]

Humphries believed the "little fellow's presence helps his men to win games," but Emslie could testify to the unreliability of Hume's supposed preternatural powers. During the Canucks' first game in their new stadium, on May 22, he cavorted around in his gaudy new suit to no avail as

Rochester won 7–5. With Bob pitching a "weak game" on June 11, Willie sprinted across the diamond, spit on home plate and menacingly bared his teeth to the umpire, but Toronto lost to lowly Oswego 7–3. Hume was absent on July 13 as Emslie, pitching wildly and hit freely, trailed 7–1 after four innings. Willie finally showed up out of uniform in the fifth and after "the fat little fellow stood on the plate and shook hands with his favorite batter," the Canucks, reportedly actuated "by good luck rather than good play," scored in three of the final four stanzas to win 12–11.

While nothing is known about Hume's pay, he augmented his income as a vaudeville entertainer. After a game in Buffalo on May 16, his harmonica playing at the Adelphi Theatre so delighted the patrons he was summoned back to the stage for four encores. Eventually alcohol, "the enemy of baseball players and mankind," ended his tenure with Toronto. He disappeared for several days while the team was on an unsuccessful road trip in New York, and when he reacted "too awfully fresh" to being reprimanded after showing up in Binghamton on July 17, Humphries sent him packing for "insubordination and tardiness." Hume defiantly said he was not to blame for the team's poor showing since he had "spit on their bats until he is weary." Whether Hume did not regard performing as a mascot demeaning or just saw it as an easy way to earn money, he subsequently advertised in newspapers he was available for hire to any team "wanting a first-class Mascot."[7]

There were, of course, negative consequences beyond the racially insensitive employment of young Black males for nonsensical ends. As the *Toronto Mail* noted, "Without prejudices against the coloured race, it may here be said that if the Torontos cannot find any other kind of a mascot they should do without one at all. It's so easy, you know, in case of defeat, to raise talk about 'a little nigger on the fence.'" Black mascots like Hume perpetuated demeaning stereotypes, underscoring notions of racial superiority by contrasting the Black mascots' "unmanly" behavior with the athletic "manliness" of the white ballplayers.[8]

The pervasive racism also arose on the field. When the Bisons signed Ulysses Franklin "Frank" Grant in July, the *Buffalo Times* described the "wonderful fielding" African American as "a tawney colored Spaniard," and noted manager Chapman happily hummed "there's a new coon in town." He was humming the ex-Confederate army captain J. S. Putnam's 1883 hit "New Coon in Town," one of numerous "coon songs," some written by Black composers, that were popular on the minstrel and vaudeville circuits well into the early twentieth century. The songs, along with related racist images in cartoons in newspapers and magazines, stereotyped "coons" as urban counterparts to rural "Jim Crows," Black "city-slickers" who wore ostentatious clothes and were prone to stealing, drinking, gambling, and violence.[9]

DEATH

Emslie's thoughts about race, Hume, and Black players—he did not pitch against Grant—are unknown, but he was deeply affected by the death of William Smith, the team's third baseman and second-leading hitter (.316). On August 8, there being no Sunday games in Toronto, Smith and some friends took the ferry to Centre Island, the largest and outermost of the islands located south of the mainland in Lake Ontario for an afternoon of swimming at Hanlon's Point, "Canada's Coney Island." While playing "leap frog" in about three feet of water, Smith's head struck bottom, breaking his neck. Pulled from the water, he was conscious but could not speak and was paralyzed save for slight movement in his left foot. Transported on a stretcher to Toronto, William Smith, age twenty-one, died at 3 a.m. on August 9.

Bob was among the steady flow of players, friends, and admirers who paid respects to the popular player later that day, passing silently by his coffin in Humphrey's funeral parlor. On August 10, with the game with Buffalo canceled, a parade of carriages containing Toronto club officials, players, and friends followed the hearse to Union Station. Smith's casket was then taken to Cleveland, where his mother and sister lived. Smith's death was a blow to Emslie and the Canucks and especially to his mother, who was heartbroken at the loss of a second son within a year and dependent on William as her sole source of support. The Toronto club covered Smith's medical and funeral expenses and provided his salary through August 15 plus $300 donated by the club's directors and stockholders. To further assist the near-destitute family Toronto held a benefit game on September 8 against a picked nine of volunteers from three teams in the Western Amateur League, who came at their own expense. Gate receipts were not great; either 500 or "not more than 150" attendees paid to see the Canucks win 20–6. The inscription on the verso of the $1 souvenir ticket with Smith's picture on the front urged the purchaser to keep it "in memory of the honest player, for the benefit of whose Mother it is issued."[10]

DEMISE

With the tragic death of the young player with a promising future hanging over the club, the Canucks went into a tailspin. Beset by a decline in offensive production, erratic pitching, atrocious fielding, and "a lack of harmony and good feeling," they finished third, 53-41 (.563), eight games behind the champion Utica Pentups.[11] For Humphries and Emslie the season ended on a particularly sour note. A Toronto scribe blamed Humphries for "the sorry experience," charging he had "the material with which he could easily have won the pennant," but had "his eyes closed to dissipations that were plainly visible to all." Noting that every club has a black sheep, the scribe asserted Toronto suffered severely from "a red sheep."[12] The target was a player, but the inference is unclear. "Dissipation" usually meant alcohol abuse, a common problem in ball clubs, but since red sheep—actually reddish brown—do not produce wool, the charge may have been a lack of productivity. Given the club's reserve list for 1887, the finger may have been pointing at a pitcher who failed to live up to expectations: auburn-haired Bob Emslie.[13]

Whatever the validity of the allegations, Humphries and Emslie and were done with Toronto. Humphries, frustrated by his relationship with club officials and press criticism as well as with being savaged for his lack of diligence in paying bills and sending money to Smith's mother—he admitted being "culpably slow in settling this matter" and that "the wrong I may have done is this matter is an affair of my own conscience"—obtained his release and in October signed to manage league rival Rochester in 1887.[14] While Emslie's ineffectiveness was only partially to blame for the Canuck's decline, he wrote years later in his memoir he had had "only fair success" with Toronto, "my arm getting weaker all the time."[15] Regularly hit hard and often pitching wildly, he posted in 239 innings an impressive 2.30

ERA but a mediocre 14-12 (.538) record. In three games in the outfield he batted .246. When the club in September announced the players reserved for 1887, Bob Emslie was absent; he was free to sign with another club.[16]

SAVANNAH

Bob Emslie pondered his future for a second winter. At twenty-eight, with limited education and no experience other than throwing baseballs, the options for making a living were not great. Owing to persistent shoulder and arm pain, his pitching ability had demonstrably declined, but like every pitcher who becomes less effective, Emslie remembered how successful he had been and hoped, however fervidly, to recover enough to continue pitching as long as he could. He was not alone. As the popularity of baseball swept the country like wildfire in the 1880s, new leagues popped up every year; the decade filled with "career" Minor Leaguers who hung on from team to team, trying to remain in the game despite diminished skills.

Emslie, too, refusing to let his baseball dreams die, hoped to try again in 1887. It was rumored in late 1886 he would sign with Buffalo, then in March 1887 that he would join the Hastings Hustlers of the Western League managed by Fred Corey, his 1885 Philadelphia teammate. Neither happened. But just as it seemed his playing days were over, he signed with Savannah, Georgia, in the Southern League.

How on earth did Emslie catch on with far-off Savannah? William Veach, his Toronto pitching partner who had pitched in the Southern in 1885 with Macon, might have suggested the lower-level circuit as a place Bob might resurrect his pitching career. He may have heard about Savannah from Gid Gardner, who had started the 1886 Southern season with the Charleston Seagulls before joining the International Association. He may have been recommended by two of his New Orleans Expositions teammates, Mac McArthur and John Peltz, currently on the Savannah roster. Whatever the case, Savannah manager Charlie Morton, desperately needing a pitcher and recalling Emslie's curveballing success from his time as manager of the 1884 Toledo Blue Stockings, offered him a contract. Only too glad to accept, Bob headed down south in April 1887.

What went through Emslie's mind on the long, multipart train ride from St. Thomas to Savannah? Did he really think "the hot southern weather might bring my arm around?" Was he afraid of failure, that his career might finally end? However slight the odds of regaining his pitching prowess, he had nothing to lose, so was determined to give it a go. Savannah was his *pis aller*.[17]

Bob now headed to a strikingly different geographical and cultural part of the United States. Located along the Savannah River approximately twenty miles from the Atlantic Ocean, Savannah, founded in 1733, exuded Southern history and culture; the Georgia Historical Society, established in 1839, was the oldest continually operating historical society in the South. The only city spared during Sherman's march to the sea in 1864 featured elegant antebellum mansions surrounding twenty-two squares filled with fountains, monuments, and trees draped in Spanish moss. Unlike polyglot Baltimore or cosmopolitan New Orleans, Savannah was a provincial community marked by a languorous lifestyle and the harsh legacies of Atlantic slavery. Emslie encountered, in addition to hot and humid subtropical weather, a city rigidly divided racially by law and custom. He was no stranger to racist attitudes or segregation, but the discriminatory practices of post-Reconstruction apartheid, along with newspaper reports of racist incidents including lynchings he encountered in Savannah and throughout the league must have been disconcerting, as it was for Morton, whose Toledo team included the Walkers.

On the field he again found himself on a weak team in a fragile league. Founded in 1885, the Southern League had struggled financially the past two seasons; three teams dropped out in the initial year, and four of the 1886 teams failed to reup for 1887. The newly organized and geographically expanded circuit, comprising six cities of disparately sized populations in five states extending from South Carolina to Louisiana, was known as a haven for Northern ball-playing carpetbaggers trying to eke out a living on the diamond. It also had a reputation for widespread gambling and "disgusting kicking and wrangling on the ballfield." The league's new president, John Morrow, of Nashville, was determined to crack down on gambling and eliminate "profanity and vulgarity on the diamond" by imposing heavy fines. Moreover, as the *National Baseball Gazette* observed, Southern audiences had a well-deserved reputation as front-runners: "When the home club is winning the attendance is always large. Let it strike a losing streak, the way it falls off is wonderful to behold. No city has any use for a losing club." Emslie and the Savannahs would experience league woes firsthand.[18]

The Savannah club, which finished second in 1886, underwent reorganization. The extensive turnover in rosters common on lower-level Minor League teams was writ large; no player from 1886 returned for 1887. The club's directors, who never came up with a team nickname, tried an innovative experiment to generate enthusiasm for attendance at home games: they telegraphed play-by-play game reports of the opening series in Memphis to a downtown theater, where "every convenience will be provided for the comfort of those who attend," including ushers and the "front rows of the dress circle reserved for ladies." Alas, with telegraph lines broken by a heavy storm in Tennessee, the fans who gathered at the theater on April 16 had to wait from 3:30 to nearly 5 p.m. before reports began to come in, and even then the transmissions were "so disconnected" it was impossible to tell anything except the score at the end of each inning, and they stopped after the seventh inning. It was just as well; the Browns shelled McArthur 17–3. Savannah won the next day 9–8, but the fans who went to the theater found it closed as the previous day's storm had so seriously damaged telegraph lines that it was impossible to get satisfactory transmission. It was an omen.[19]

It was evident that the team was not very good, losing all six preseason exhibition games to Charleston. The directors decided on a "general cutting off of heads."[20] While the team headed to Memphis to open the season, Morton, who had managed the team in 1886, remained in Savannah, loading the telegraph wires with solicitations for new players. Pitching was problematic as neither MacArthur nor Joseph Summers had performed well in the preseason, hence the wire to St. Thomas.

Immediately after arriving in Savannah on April 19, Emslie headed with Morton to Memphis. What must Bob have thought the next afternoon watching his new teammates routed 25–3? The team left that night for Nashville, where Bob debuted on April 21 in right field, going 1–4 at bat and recording three put-outs and one assist. On April 23 he took to the box for the first time, pitching Savannah to its second win of the season, 6–5 over the Blues. The *Savannah Morning News* reported Emslie was "very effective and had good control of the ball" and Nashville hitters had "hard work to find his delivery," getting but eight hits and one earned run. The *Nashville Daily American* likewise noted Emslie's curves were "a puzzler"; only three Blues were able to get hits—his ex-Orioles teammate Jimmy Clinton managed four, two on walks. (In 1887 walks counted as hits, resulting in unusually high batting averages.)

Bob was back in right field the next day, April 24, called by the Nashville *Daily American* "an eventful day in the history of baseball playing in this city." That was not because his "magnificent catch" was the "feature of the game"; because the umpire, Burbidge, was released after the game for refusing to preserve order and prevent profanity; or because Nashville won 15–12. Rather, it was because the first game ever played on a Sunday in the Southern League violated the prohibition of playing baseball on the Christian Sabbath in Tennessee.[21]

Sabbatarian legislation, intended to promote observance of the Lord's Day by restricting or prohibiting work, the sale of alcohol, commercial and amusement activities, and organized recreation, was commonplace in the largely Protestant United States prior to the Civil War, and had been in place in Bible Belt Tennessee since 1803. "Blue laws," the term denoting strict adherence to a moral code, increasingly came under attack in the late nineteenth century due to waves of European immigration (largely German and Catholic) and the secularization of an increasingly urban-industrial society. After an attempt in the Tennessee legislature in March to repeal the act prohibiting playing baseball on Sunday failed in committee by a close vote, 15–12, the directors of the Nashville club, knowing there was substantial public support for Sunday ball, decided to force the issue by scheduling the game with Savannah on April 24.

Their motivation was less to remove restrictive religious legislation than to increase gate receipts, and the experiment was a success. The largest crowd of the season, jamming the stands and overflowing onto the playing field, contained "many ladies" and "a very large number of new faces," including "workmen, carpenters, clerks, laborers in mills and factories and the like, who never have an opportunity during the week for amusement" because they worked ten to twelve hours per day six days per week. The behavior of the throng—no drinking, no rowdiness—drew support from law enforcement officials, the police chief saying it was "the quietest and most orderly Sunday that he had seen for months." After the next day's game, Emslie back in right field going 1–4 in an embarrassing 18–5 defeat, both teams left town amid a seething controversy between the sectarian and secular voices in the community reflected in the opposing stances of the city's two newspapers. The *Nashville Banner* condemned the game as "a premeditated, prearranged and deliberately bold violation of the law," while the *Nashville Daily American* enthusiastically supported Sunday baseball.[22]

Savannah headed to Mobile, Alabama, Emslie taking the box on April 29 after the team had lost the first two games. He lost 6–2 but pitched well, giving up five runs in the second inning and one in the third, then shutting out the Swamp Angels the rest of the way. The only Mobile player to reach him was their new left fielder, Fred Lewis, a compatriot in the infamous St. Louis row, who got two hits and scored a run. In right field the next day, as Savannah lost its fourth straight game to Mobile, Bob toed the rubber in New Orleans on May 1 after only one day's rest. It was a disaster for Emslie but a delight for the six thousand fans present, the largest crowd in Crescent City history. In losing 13–1 Bob, "battered left and right," gave up seventeen hits, walked four, and had no strikeouts; in the (un)lucky seventh inning the Pelicans scored seven runs on seven hits. He faced the Pelicans again on May 4, losing 9–4 as New Orleans pounded out sixteen hits and scored in each of five innings. With Emslie's arm again aching, Morton decided to give him a rest.

Having lost their tenth game in a row the next day 11–1, the team, firmly ensconced in last place at 2-14, headed to Savannah hoping for improvement in the season's first home stand. Upon arriving they learned a Nashville grand jury, following Criminal Court judge Granville Sumner Ridley's instructions, on May 2 had indicted all the players who participated in the April 24 game as well as the officers and directors of both clubs for violating the Tennessee law against playing baseball on Sunday. The next time Bob and his teammates appeared in Nashville, they would be charged with a misdemeanor fine of not less than \$25 or more than \$50. (The *cause célèbre* passed without conclusion, although Sunday baseball was not allowed in Tennessee until 1919.)[23]

Savannah's immediate concern was the May 7 home opener against the Charleston Seagulls. Hoping for a big crowd, the directors proclaimed it "ladies' day," with women admitted free to the grounds and grandstand. But only seven hundred people passed through the turnstiles. The Savannahs, wearing their new uniforms for the first time, "probably the handsomest uniform in the league"—white shirts and caps, blue pants trimmed in maroon, and maroon stockings—looked great but played badly and were trounced 25–2. "A good many" spectators left the grounds disgusted by Savannah's atrocious fielding, one of thirteen errors by Emslie, who was driven from the box in the third inning and went to right field. The *Savannah Morning News* said most of the people who went to the game "expected to see Savannah beaten, and they were not disappointed." Most disappointed was Charlie Morton. Taking responsibility for the team's miserable showing and its 2–15 record, he headed home to Ohio.

The Charleston debacle had a pronounced impact on future attendance. Fewer than three hundred people showed up the next day to watch Savannah behind the team's new pitcher, the veteran Fred "Tricky" Nichols, atone for the lousy performance by giving Jack Peltz his first win as player-manager, erupting for thirteen hits in defeating Charleston 13–8. While the win was welcome, acquiring Nichols, age thirty-six, who had not pitched since 1882, was an act of desperation, as future events would demonstrate.

On May 9 Emslie was not in the box or in right field. Instead, he stood behind the catchers, called on to umpire the game when the scheduled arbiter, Joe Diestel, failed to appear after becoming ill. Umpiring in his street clothes—not the league's prescribed white shirt, blue pants, and black cap—Bob must have done well, the visiting Seagulls allowing they were "better treated" than they had been by the regular umpires. In right field the next day he enjoyed his best day at bat, 2–5, as Savannah beat Charleston 12–6 to end the homestand.

In Charleston on May 12 the Seagulls sent their best pitcher, Fred Smith, to the box for their first home game of the season. Nichols was scheduled to pitch for Savannah, but Peltz decided to start Emslie instead, probably to save Nichols for a less formidable opponent. During the first five innings, played in light rain, the Seagulls had "sort of a baseball picnic," scoring thirteen runs en route to a 21–2 rout. The humiliating defeat, in which Bob gave up twenty-one hits, walked two, hit a batter, and struck out none, would be his last appearance in the box for Savannah. His arm obviously gone, Bob later recalled Peltz "tried to make an outfielder out of me, as I was a pretty fair hitter."[24] He was correct in that he had been assigned to the outfield, but mistaken in claiming to be a decent hitter. During the rest of the three games in Charleston, all decisive wins for the Seagulls, he went 2–11.

Upon returning to Savannah the club looked forward to a three-game series against the cellar-dwelling Mobile team, but learned the 5–18 Swamp Angels had folded owing to poor play and fan support. So for three days Savannah took the field in uniform, defeating by default an absent opponent 9–0 after MacArthur threw nine pitches, all called strikes. They then lost three games to formidable New Orleans, Emslie in the outfield unable to contribute much at the bat, going 3–18 (.167) in the series. When the Pelicans left, Memphis arrived. On May 27 the Browns shelled Nichols 14–5 in the first game of the series while Emslie, replaced in right field, watched from the bench. After the game he was released.

It was not unexpected, as Bob's attempted comeback had not worked out. The trip to Savanah, instead of enabling him to reclaim his pitching prowess, resulted in the worst performance of his career. Starting and completing five games, he posted a 1-4 (.200) record and a 4.60 ERA; in forty-five innings, he struck out only five while walking ten and giving up fifty-four runs on sixty-eight hits. Bob pitched so poorly he was dispatched to the outfield, where he played twelve games in right field and one in left; he also failed at bat, 14–73 (.219), getting more than one hit in only one game and none for extra bases.[25]

Emslie was the first to go but not the last. The night he was released Bob joined several teammates in the Marshall House, the players home-away-from-home, to discuss growing rumors the club was about to disband. Some engaged in "sort of desperate humor about the way they pictured the pleasures of walking home."[26] Rumor became reality the next day. After a 16–12 loss to Memphis, the Savannah directors, facing an expensive western road trip, decided to fold. According to the club president the reason for the demise was simple: "The people of Savannah have signified by their attendance, or rather their non-attendance, that they do not care for baseball. Savannah would not support the team and it had to go under."[27] He did not mention the cause of paltry attendance was management's failure to put a competitive team on the field. Savannah finished 9-26-1, three wins by forfeit, a record commensurate with the league's second-lowest team batting average (.290) and worst fielding percentage (.835) and ERA (4.46). Savannah was not the last to disband; Nashville left on August 2, leaving the other three of the original six and newcomer Birmingham to finish the season. (In the financially volatile world of Minor League baseball, the Southern League was not alone in facing defections; of nine organized leagues, only two finished intact.)[28]

Some players, likely Emslie among them, had drawn their pay in advance, but others had "not got a cent," so an exhibition game was played on May 30 between the team and an amateur club to raise money to pay the remaining salaries. After the game, which netted $100, the six best Savannah players joined other Southern League teams and Bob Emslie went home. The rumor that he would be given a trial by Cincinnati, looking for a pitcher after Tony Mullane's departure, was just that—a rumor.

It was a long, sorrowful train ride back to St. Thomas. The attempt to resurrect his pitching career was a disaster. The South's insalubrious climate and cultural environment was oppressive to the Canadian, and he again experienced the financial instability of lower-level Minor League baseball. Worse, he had come to the painful realization that his playing career was over: if he couldn't make it in Savannah, he couldn't make it anywhere. It was especially distressing—galling really—for a pitcher who had achieved great success with a devastating curveball to be removed from the box and exiled to the outer pastures. And as his career had begun, it ended on a miserable team. In his professional career he played on two teams that failed to finish the season and in three Major League seasons twice played on a team that finished last. Perhaps fittingly for Bob's misbegotten Savannah venture, recaps of his baseball career and obituaries years later had him playing in 1887 with Memphis, not Savannah.[29]

6

Learning to Call 'Em

> Umpiring . . . is the most important and far-reaching of any one factor that enters into the successful conduct of professional baseball. It is by far the most exacting position on the diamond to fill to the satisfaction of the manager, the player, the public and the regularly constituted baseball authorities. The umpire, clothed as he is with unlimited and autocratic power under the playing rules, must exercise the utmost discretion and judgment in the application of that power. He must be a man of good physique, strong mind, clear eyes, even temperament, quick judgment and forceful enough in character to command the respect and acquiescence of all concerned in his rulings and decisions. He must so conduct himself at all times as to inspire confidence in his honesty and ability, and be able to impart to all observers his evident desire and intention to treat everybody with the utmost consideration and impartiality.
>
> —Address given by Harry "Steamboat" Johnson at the National Association of Professional Baseball Leagues meeting, 1922

Bob returned to St. Thomas on June 6 unheralded, the local newspaper simply noting, "Bob Emslie who has been pitching for Savannah returned last night." The bland comment was apt. The comeback trail had ended in Georgia, and with no backup plan, no job awaiting him after ball playing, he was again at life's crossroads, the future uncertain. From youth to his twenty-eighth year his mind had been filled with thoughts of baseball. For the last thirteen years he had been a professional pitcher. For two years he had tried gamely to overcome arm and shoulder problems, but there was no denying he was finished on the diamond. What now?

There was money to be had in the booming economy of North America, but for Bob, who had no interest in tailoring, running a drugstore, or learning the jewelry business, entrepreneurship was not a calling. With limited education, no skills other than throwing a baseball, and no influential familial connections, the options were limited. Needing time to unwind and assess, he "just layed around for a week or two." But a man has to eat. Bob started pitching for pay as a hotel clerk and, coming full circle at the end of his playing days, joined friend Peter McNulty as comanager of the Elgin House hotel in St. Thomas.[1]

He still had baseball on the brain. If he was unable to continue in the game as a pitcher, could he stay in it by umpiring? Many a former player had unsuccessfully tried umpiring, but the two games Bob had called as a substitute, most recently in Savannah, had gone well. Deciding to take a flyer, he wrote in late June to Charles White, president and secretary of the International Association, about a position. It was a long shot. The league had a full staff, but turnover was common. While waiting for White's response he went to Toronto with McNulty, thinking the June 30 International Association morning-afternoon doubleheader, a feature of the civic holiday celebrating Queen Victoria's golden Jubilee, "would be interesting to watch." He was especially interested in the first game between the Canucks and the Hamilton Hams, since there was "always bad blood" between the teams. Little did he know that within a few hours his life would forever change.[2]

Everyone needs a break, and Bob got one. When the scheduled umpire, Wesley "Wes" Curry, who had called several of Emslie's games in 1882 and 1885, failed to show for the morning game because of illness, several players spotted Bob in the stands and suggested him as the substitute umpire. The rival managers, Toronto's Charlie Cushman and Hamilton's William Stroud, agreed, assuming the former Major Leaguer knew enough about the game to make judicious decisions. Initially taken aback by the request, Bob recalled years later, "After much deliberation, I consented to tackle it" despite being "nervous as a cat."[3] Lacking proper equipment and uniform, be borrowed a catcher's mask, positioned himself behind home plate, and called, "Play!"

It must have felt strange calling pitches on several former Canucks, Orioles, and Atlantics teammates. Although there was "some kicking over one or two close decisions" at first base, which was typical when umpiring behind the plate, both sides were satisfied with his work, so asked him to stick around for the four o'clock game if needed. With Curry still absent, Bob again umpired, the press reporting he "did well." He did better than that. After the game both Cushman and Buffalo manager Jack Chapman asked Bob if he wanted to umpire for the rest of the season; if so, they would recommend him to White. He initially responded, "I might," but recognizing that umpiring was a reputable livelihood, one that would put him front and center in the game he loved and, given the popularity of baseball, provide an appreciable dose of respect, even envy, it didn't take him long to decide. At ten o'clock that night Robert Emslie became an umpire in the premier Minor League.[4]

Timing, as usual, was everything. "It was purely a matter of accident how I came to follow umpiring as a means of livelihood," Emslie later recalled.[5] The impromptu decision to go to Toronto to watch ball games was fortuitous, as was illness sidelining the scheduled umpire. What, one wonders, might have been Bob Emslie's future had Curry umpired that day? If Charlie White hadn't needed an umpire? Finding—and keeping—good umpires in the Minor Leagues was even more difficult than in the Majors, and the IA staff had undergone extensive turnover; most recently, Larry Sutton had been released for wagering on games. With positive recommendations from two respected managers, White didn't hesitate to offer Emslie a contract.

Bob hustled back to St. Thomas, grabbed an old hotel register for protection, and returned to Toronto for his debut as a professional umpire on July 1. It was déjà vu as he again umpired a twin bill that was part of a festive and patriotic event: Dominion Day (renamed Canada Day in 1982), the national holiday commemorating the federation of Canada as a nation in 1867. Bob, again wearing street clothes, borrowed a catcher's mask, stuffed the hotel register inside his shirt, and kept track of balls and strikes with his fingers. (Emslie was not alone in improvising; chest protectors were then commonplace for catchers, not umpires.)[6]

1887

When Bob Emslie began umpiring, it was the best and worst of times for umpires. The proliferation of independent and organized professional leagues increased the demand for umpires, but the emphasis on team victories and player statistics increased kicking from players and criticism from press and fans. Moreover, without systematic evaluation or supervision and with the renewal of one-year contracts resting more on the approval of league presidents and the whims of owners than on actual performance, few umpires lasted more than a couple years. And with four to six umpires per league, the odds against advancing to the Major Leagues were far greater for umpires than for players. Still, it meant being in baseball. Enough said.

White first sent him to Rochester for a game on July 2, where, as throughout the league, his reputation as a player preceded him. The Rochester paper noted, "'Bob' Emslie, the old-time pitcher, walked out upon the field and called out play." He was pleased to be back in baseball, but soon found life as an umpire was far more difficult than as a pitcher. His playing experiences gave him a sense of what to do but not how to do it, and seeing players give umpires grief and witnessing a few fan mobbings did not prepare him for the pressures of the job. Whatever he thought about umpires and umpiring during his playing days, his views now certainly changed.

First there were the practicalities. He immediately encountered the grueling travel required in a league consisting of ten cities in Ontario, New York, New Jersey, and Pennsylvania. He was constantly on the road, scurrying from city to city: in fourteen days, from August 4 to 17, he went from Syracuse to Wilkes-Barre, then to Jersey City and Newark, next to Binghamton, and thence to Scranton. And the money went fast. He initially received $200 per month; two weeks later staff salaries increased to $250, but he had to purchase a mask, padded chest protector, and ball-strike-out indicator as well as the mandatory cap and coat (perhaps gray, as the league followed the National League's rules and procedures). And as he had to pay his own expenses on the road, he looked for the cheapest railroad fares, bargain lodging, and inexpensive restaurants.

It was one thing to look like an umpire; it was another to perform like one. Bob's love of the game and a desire to stay in it as an umpire did not guarantee success. His accomplishments as a ballplayer turned on physical skills, but umpiring required intangibles—visual judgment, yes, but also instinct, dedication, the proper temperament, and courage. But first he had to master three things: the rules, making accurate decisions, and "running" the game.

Emslie knew the playing rules, but had to learn the "book rules" and how to apply the unwritten rules, the traditions and expectations of play. Bob immediately had difficulty enforcing the instructions White issued just as he began umpiring. It was easy to ensure pitchers faced the batter with the ball in plain sight before delivering it, but how, when standing behind the catcher, was he to determine that "the left foot [was] enough to the left of the right foot so as to allow daylight to be seen between them, and both feet [were] squarely on the ground" with neither "his heel or toe in the air?" How to decide whether infielders, wearing thin fingerless gloves, "accidently muffed" a pop fly or intentionally dropped it to facilitate a double play? Bob also found that even calling the apparently obvious was harder than he anticipated. In 1887 the high and low strike zones were collapsed, but judging pitches precisely was difficult when standing upwards of ten feet behind home plate and looking around—not over—catchers who stooped, not crouched. And from behind the plate, he suffered from angle and distance in making close calls on the bases.

Ultimately, he learned that what was most important for success was style—how he "ran" the game, ensuring play continued in an orderly, efficient, and fair manner in the face of disputatious player behavior and unforeseen special circumstances. The Minors comprised a volatile mix of eager young bucks trying to advance in the game and wizened former Major Leaguers hoping to stay in it, both given to blaming the umpire for their shortcomings. In order to endure the seemingly unending, often vicious and personal criticism from players and spectators, Emslie had to develop a thickly calloused epidermis.

Working alone, bereft of personal contact with other league umpires or White, he developed a trademark style of umpiring. He understood that as a new, inexperienced umpire it was best to maintain a low profile until he had established a reputation, and knew from his playing days there were two primary methods of controlling games, one personified by two recent league hires: William "Billy" McLean, coaxed out of retirement, and Grayson "Gracie" Pierce, released by the National League for alleged "crooked umpiring," were "tough cops" who led the staff in fining players; McLean fined ten players on September 12 in Toronto for "finding fault with his decisions." That players could unleash their anger on Emslie while not daring to assault McLean, a former bare-knuckle prize fighter, was expressed poetically:

> Step down as you like
> On Bob Emslie's neck,
> Or batter his frame
> All into a wreck,
> But I am just goin' ter
> Give you a pointer—
> Billy McLean is loaded.[7]

Emslie personified McLean's antithesis and was soon noted for his patience with kicking and reluctance to reach into a player's pocket. By mid-August, after more than six weeks of umpiring, he had yet to impose a fine. Word was that his forbearance was owing to understanding, as a former player, the competitive spirit that invariably led to disputes and to knowing fines were no deterrent as they were routinely paid by the club. But he also knew from experience that the umpire was an absolute autocrat on the diamond; his word, right or wrong, was final, and the best way to handle disputes was not to let them start. A tactful, conciliatory approach to defusing flare-ups would be the hallmark of his umpiring career.

While slightly above average in stature, 185 pounds on a five-foot-eleven-inch frame resting on size eight shoes, he did not look like an umpire, his face radiating boyish innocence. But somewhere along the line he developed the self-esteem and determination required of an umpire. Initially naïve in the ways of umpiring and with no formal training or even an instructional manual, he learned to call 'em through trial and error on the job. He learned quickly, "giving good satisfaction" in passing the various tests presented to a would-be umpire. Turns out, Bob Emslie was a born umpire. After only two weeks he was reported to be "doing well as an International League umpire."[8]

Over the course of three months he traveled to all ten league cities and received far less criticism than other umpires. No doubt his reputation as a Major League ballplayer initially brought a modicum of respect, even deference, but primarily it was the result of doing a good job. Reports of kicking by players or hissing from spectators were absent save for in Rochester, where he played with the 1886 Canucks, and Scranton, a mining town in the heart of the anthracite coal region in northeastern Pennsylvania.

Fans in Scranton, experiencing their first year of professional ball, had a reputation for being especially hard on umpires: "It's a cold day when Scranton can't figure out that it is all the umpire's fault."[9] During his first visit, on July 19, the local newspaper personalized its criticism: "somewhat of a pitcher himself," Emslie "should be more able to judge 'Doc' Oberland's drop balls, and not do him the injustice he did." The next day the fans gave him grief when Syracuse routed the Miners 12–1. Bob had "given the best of satisfaction" through three innings, the score tied 1–1, but in the fourth the fans howled at his controversial but probably correct double play call against Scranton, their anger increasing when the Stars then scored seven runs. Bob was getting used to catcalls and boos, but the prospect of bodily harm was new. He did not see the next morning's newspaper headline, "Rotten Bob Emslie," as he had left town after the game "without his supper" on account of threats from a number of coal miners, led by "Red Mike," who thought he had not treated Scranton fairly.[10]

It was smooth sailing thereafter until on August 23 in Rochester, when he had the most contentious game of his young career. The crowd, on Bob from the outset for "showing plainly several times that he did not know the difference between a ball and a strike," erupted in the fourth inning due to his handling, however proper, of an unusual occurrence. After the Toronto shortstop overthrew first base, the ball going over the fence into the spectators, the fans erupted in frustration as the game was delayed "about ten minutes" while the Maroons fetched the ball. Since Rochester had provided only one ball instead of the two required by the rules, Emslie decided to let the game continue, but said if the lone ball went over the fence or grandstand, the game would be forfeited to Toronto. As luck would have it, the next inning a Canucks batsman lofted a foul that lodged in a grandstand eave, whereupon Emslie declared, "I will give you just five minutes to get that ball. If you don't have it in that time, I will give the game to Toronto." The Rochester catcher saved the day by throwing a bat "a half-dozen times" to dislodge the ball. Meanwhile, Maroons manager John Humphries, Bob's 1886 Toronto skipper, drove to town to get a supply of balls; while they were regulation in size and weight, Emslie, following the letter of the rules, judged them unusable as they lacked White's signature. The crowd's frustration with Emslie came to a head in the eighth inning. With the score tied 2–2, Toronto scored the winning run from second after Bob ruled fair a hit "without going within five feet of third base." The angry crowd "hissed and groaned at the rank decision" and the newspaper railed at the "most unsatisfactory umpiring that has been done here in a long time."[11]

While Emslie's attention was focused on umpiring, league officials were concerned about another issue: Black players. The number of African Americans in previously all-white professional leagues had grown steadily, if slowly, from two in 1883 to eleven in 1887. When the National Colored League, which debuted on May 6, suddenly disbanded on May 23 because of low attendance, seven Black players joined five International clubs. Association teams and players had played against Black teams and players, but having them as teammates was objectionable to some. Nine Binghamton Bingoes threatened to strike if John "Bud" Fowler and William Renfroe were not released, and on July 14 league owners ordered White not to approve any more contracts for "colored men" on the grounds that "many of the best players in the League were anxious to leave on account of the colored element." (The most famous racial incident in baseball history occurred on the same day, when Cap Anson and his Chicago White Stockings refused to take the field in an exhibition game against Newark if the latter team used their Black battery, Stovey and Walker.)[12] Players and club owners were not the only ones opposed to Black players. Umpire Billy Hoover and Toronto manager Charlie Cushman were among the ardent segregationists who "waged a relentless battle for the color line."[13]

Bob Emslie's views on racial integration are unknown, but it likely was not an issue for him as he had played without concern against Fleet

Walker in 1884 and Frank Grant in 1886. As an umpire in 1887 he called eight games against Newark, six in which either George Stovey pitched or Fleet Walker caught, four when they were the battery. He also worked nine games involving Grant and a game in which Robert Higgins pitched for Syracuse. Newspaper reports of those games contain no mention of game incidents, racial or otherwise.

As the season progressed Emslie's schedule reflected his growing reputation. Aware of Bob's ties to his native Ontario and as a player for the 1886 Canucks, White assigned him to only seven games involving the two Canadian teams, three in Canada, prior to August 29. Then, confident of Emslie's impartiality, essentially sent him home for the last three weeks of the season, Bob working seventeen of last the twenty-one games in Ontario, six in Toronto and eleven in Hamilton. The respite from travel was welcome, and the return to his old stomping grounds initially brought compliments on his umpiring from the press. After two games in Toronto on September 2 and 3, both won by the Canucks, the *Toronto Globe* said he had "umpired satisfactorily" and the *Mail*, while thinking he "gave several doubtful decisions," allowed that he "discharged his duties conscientiously, each team experiencing exactly the same treatment." The gratification was fleeting.

Whether Emslie was tiring from the unaccustomed daily grind of umpiring or old animosities were coming to the fore, criticism of his work became frequent. On September 18 in Hamilton the Hams beat Jersey City 7–6, but his umpiring was reported "not very satisfactory," base calls favoring the Skeeters. When Jersey City visited Toronto two days later, both teams "severely criticized" his work in a doubleheader. Emslie, after resorting to levying fines "with scanty success," in exasperation asked, "What do you fellows want—the earth?" According to the *Toronto Daily Mail*, his "rank umpiring" was "bad enough" in the morning game, but in the afternoon "it paralyzed anything seen in Toronto this year." The paper contended he lost track of ball-strike counts, called pitches "erratically," and missed a tag at third base, "the most glaring unjust decision that can be imagined." Some fans thought Bob deliberately made bad calls against the Canucks because he was upset Toronto had released him last year, while others "could not believe he was dishonest but thought that he was incompetent." And when he called the afternoon game with the Canucks leading 6–2 after "intermittent drizzle" turned into "a steady down-pour," both teams charged he had allowed the game to go too long. The Canucks manager, Charlie Cushman, even telegrammed White asking that Emslie not be allowed to umpire another game.[14]

After umpiring his season-ending game on September 26 in Hamilton, Bob headed to London, where he boarded with his parents, now living at 633 Queen Street, to assess his umpiring experience and contemplate the future. Late-season criticisms aside, Bob later said of his first year, "I got along fine."[15] He did better than that. He proved to be a competent umpire and staff stalwart; Emslie, McLean, and initial hire William "Billy" Hoover alone of a dozen umpires finished the season. Still, being often recognized as a former pitcher rekindled memories, and he had frequently worked out with players before games. Deciding his arm was "again all right," he considered "trying it in the box again next season," but by December stopped talking about resuming pitching. Finding officiating to his liking and having earned his stripes, he decided instead to apply to umpire a full season in the International Association. White, having received positive reports from managers and club officials, wanted him back.[16]

1888

When the league directors met on March 20, Emslie and Hoover were reappointed. The four-man regular staff was completed by Jeremiah "Jerry" Sullivan, who had umpired briefly in the Majors in 1887, and John "Jack" Sheridan, a highly respected umpire in the California League. When Sheridan decided not to leave California, White hired Wes Curry, whose absence had launched Emslie's umpiring career. The magnates also made travel easier by dropping the three New Jersey and Pennsylvania teams and adding two New York clubs (Albany and Troy) and the London Tecumsehs to form a compact eight-team circuit.

Emslie opened his first full season umpiring on April 28 in Rochester. An aura of nostalgia obtained as the opponent for the team, now named the Jingoes, was the London Tecumsehs, making their first appearance in Rochester in three years. Led by the 54th Regiment, the two teams paraded as customary for home openers through the streets in carriages to

Culver Park where, following opening ceremonies, Emsie called the game at 4:00. Just as Rochester got off to a great start with a pair of victories, it was a fine beginning for Bob, who received a rare compliment from the notoriously critical Rochester press: "Umpire Emslie gave very prompt and to all satisfactory decisions in both games he has officiated in."[17]

Bob again faced the inherently difficult task of working alone and enforcing imprecise rules. The league did not follow the American Association's adoption in 1888 of Gaffney's innovative proposal to move umpires from behind home plate to behind the pitcher with runners on base, but White's "earnest recommendation" was that his umpires shift positions. Emslie found it easier to make correct pitch calls from behind the pitcher than to make close base decisions from behind the catcher, but switching positions created another problem. By rule any foul tip caught by the catcher was an out, but from behind the pitcher he could not hear the "tip," thereby erroneously voiding an out and placing base runners—also unable to detect the sound—in jeopardy of being thrown out when attempting to advance. (The foul tip rule was eliminated after the season so that backward hit balls not rising above the catcher's head were simply fouls whether caught or not).[18]

With the battle between pitcher and catcher being the heart of the game and pitch calls the source of most complaints, White then ordered umpires to work only behind the plate and stand close behind the catcher to judge pitches better. That made it easier for Bob to call pitches but more difficult to enforce the pop fly rule, which was intended to prevent infielders from deliberately dropping the ball with runners on base to create a double play. White's instruction to declare the batter out if the ball touched a fielder's hands before reaching the ground failed to resolve the problem, so he subsequently ordered umpires to rule the batter out only on "short pop flies" that seemed "very easy" to catch. (In 1895 the infield fly rule made the batter out automatically out on a fly catchable by an infielder with runners on first and second base and fewer than two outs.) Bob also found the new rule stipulating a single base coach "must direct his coaching to the base-runner only" troublesome, it being easy ensure only one coach was on the lines but impossible to prevent him passing along advice to batters.[19]

What made Emslie's job most difficult was "the infernal nuisance of kicking." Henry Chadwick, the nation's most esteemed baseball writer, claimed umpires "could never reach the point of satisfactory work in the position as long as players are allowed to kick against decisions as they are now." Challenges, invariably heated and often personal, escalated despite Rule 60, which stated, "The umpire is the sole and absolute judge of play. In no instance shall any person be allowed to question the correctness of any decision," and Rule 58, which stipulated, "The captain only may address the umpire, and then only upon a question of interpretation of the rules." White instructed the staff to impose a fine, the amount to be at the umpire's discretion, "whenever a player indulges in back talk." (Fines, remitted to White, were a source of league income. Gaffney's suggestion that umpires keep the fines they imposed, while unfeasible, would surely have increased fines and perhaps reduced kicking.) But Emslie knew strict enforcement was impractical given the inevitable competitive flare-ups and that fines not only increased animosity toward the arbiter but also were ineffective, as clubs paid them, not players.[20]

Eventually kicking took a toll on Bob's colleagues. Veteran Billy Hoover, a good umpire, was the first driven away by constant arguing. Resigning in early June, he opened a beer hall in Rochester, which did a booming business under the sign proclaiming, "You're out. Come in." Jack Remsen, a former Bison ballplayer, debuted on July 20 in Buffalo, but resigned the next day after being belted with cushions and pop bottles during the game and afterward escorted off the field by police. James Bayne, a former Hamilton player, lasted a few weeks in July; in August two umpires with some Major League experience, James Devine and Ed Hengle, failed to last the month. Ben Young, son of a Cleveland clergyman, was released after White received formal protests from several clubs. His replacement, John Brady, who umpired a few Major League games in 1887, fared no better; he was hired in late July and dismissed in late August. The competent but short-fused Jerry Sullivan was released after five clubs submitted formal protests. All told, twelve umpires, the equivalent of three full staffs, umpired International Association games in 1888. Of the initial four only Emslie and Curry finished the season.

Amid the turmoil Bob thrived. On June 13 *Sporting Life* reported he was "doing the best umpiring" in the league. Umpires were typically identified only by surname in box scores, but Emslie was often listed as Robert Emslie, R. D. Emslie, R. Emslie or, most often, Bob Emslie. When the Baltimore Orioles of the American Association came to Syracuse for an exhibition game the Stars proposed a local umpire, but the Major League club held out for Emslie. He must have derived particular satisfaction when calling the game on June 4, won by Syracuse 5–4, behind the Black battery of Robert Higgins and Fleet Walker and against his old manager, Billy Barnie, and a couple of former Oriole teammates. (In a first for white professional baseball, that day two African Americans, Higgins and William Renfroe, pitched against each other.) Syracuse spoke to his reputation: "Much idle talk has been indulged in here in regard to umpire Bob Emslie, and there are many people who really believe that he is for some cause or other sore on Syracuse, and has given the home team the worst of it in all games. Anybody acquainted with Emslie knows that all these tales go for naught. Some folks may dislike him, but everybody seemed pleased when he stepped on to the field last Tuesday to umpire the Baltimore game."[21]

That the Buffalo press thought Emslie was a good umpire was due to his temperament and mode of umpiring. His trademarks were hustle—he once took "an involuntary sliding seat on the grass" while running to make a call on the bases—and tactful control of the game. While reluctant to impose fines, he rarely allowed back talk, and players generally honored his decisions when he conveyed unmistakably, by word or glare, that enough was enough. He imposed only three fines, all $5: he dunned Charles "Lefty" Marr of Syracuse for "talking back," Albany's Foreman Halpin for kicking "so vehemently," and London's Patrick "Patsy" Donovan for interfering with a baserunner. While always steadfastly in charge, he was too lenient at times. Syracuse's first baseman William "Mox" McQuery argued so contumeliously "the air became so blue that spectators could hardly see right field," but Emslie did not fine him. If words did not hurt Bob, the ball could, as it did on August 18 in Buffalo, when he was hit in the stomach by a foul tip. After rolling on the ground "about five minutes in great agony," Bob was applauded when he "pluckily resumed work."[22]

Running the game also required the improvisational ability to handle unusual situations, such as one Emslie faced in Buffalo on May 12. After giving up five runs on six hits, including two home runs in the first two innings, London's Emil Geiss stayed on the bench, saying he was too sick to pitch. Buffalo protested that Geiss wasn't sick and that London, trailing by two runs, was simply trying to insert "a heavy batter" into the lineup; the Tecumsehs responded that Geiss, from New Orleans, was sick with malaria. Emslie, unwilling to determine a health issue, called on two doctors who happened to be at the game to examine Geiss. They declared him fit to play, but when Emil still refused, Bob ordered him to take the field or he would forfeit the game to Buffalo. Reluctantly, Geiss went to first base, the crowed jeering him for a thirty-minute delay. The next inning Emil again said he couldn't play. Another delay ensued, Tecumseh manager Phil Powers finally telling Bob he had suspended Geiss so he was ineligible. With no formal rule covering suspension of a player during a game, Emslie ordered Geiss to the field. He remained recalcitrant, so London offered to continue the game with eight players. This Emslie refused and, pulling out his watch, told Emil, "I'll give you half a minute to get up and play before I declare the game forfeited." Geiss again went to first base and the game concluded without further incident, Buffalo winning 9–5, Emil recovering sufficiently by the ninth inning to drive in a run and subsequently score himself. Emslie's rendering a firm decision, absent applicable rules, solidified his reputation for integrity, decisiveness, and refusal to take any nonsense, which served him well the rest of the season.

As throughout the Minor Leagues, the International again faced two issues simmering beneath the surface. Controversy over racial integration carried over from 1887. When the IA reorganized in November 1887, Buffalo, Syracuse, Hamilton, and London were in favor of having Black players, but in January 1888 the owners came to a "general understanding" that no team should be able to sign "more than one Ethiopian." The effective message was exclusion, but since Buffalo already had Bud Grant and Syracuse had Robert Higgins and Fleet Walker under contract, they would be the only three "sun-burned players" in the league that year. No racial issues arose during the season and newspaper reports about the Black players were uniformly positive, but Higgins, tired of racial prejudice, quit Syracuse in August, leaving Grant and Walker as the only Black players.[23]

The other issue, Sunday baseball, came to a head in Rochester on July 29 and, as in Nashville, involved Emslie. Restrictions against league teams playing on the Christian Sabbath meant a day of rest for players and umpires but a loss of gate receipts for club owners and revenue for local entrepreneurs. Games had been played at Windsor Beach, one of several Rochester suburbs with a Lake Ontario beachfront amusement park, but they were contests between local amateur clubs. The owner of the Windsor Beach park, the Rome, Watertown and Ogdensburg Railroad, seeing the potential for Sunday ball, attempted to circumvent the prohibition of exhibition games between league clubs by arranging with the managers, not the owners, of Rochester and Syracuse to play a series of Sunday games for "the championship of New York" and a purse of $2,000. (The principal director of the Rochester team, Henry Brinker, was also a director of the RW&O railroad.) The inaugural game on July 29 was a resounding success; more than seven thousand people packed the small park. Syracuse won 6–5. Emslie, in town for the scheduled Rochester-Troy series, pocketed an undisclosed free for umpiring.

Opponents of Sunday baseball immediately protested, as did C. W. Cushman, president of the Buffalo Bisons. Whether because of Buffalo's exclusion from the series or the clear violation of the league's constitution, he summoned club representatives to Buffalo on August 2. Hamilton and London introduced a resolution censuring Rochester and Syracuse for violating the constitution and insisting the rule against intraleague exhibition games be strictly enforced. (No mention was made of Emslie having umpired.) After heated debate the three Ontario clubs and Buffalo supported the resolution; the two offending clubs, joined by Albany and Troy, both having scheduled later Sunday games at Windsor Park, opposed it. Given the deadlock, no action was taken and the Sunday games proceeded.[24] Emslie, still in town for the Albany series, umpired another Sunday game on August 4. Owing to mounting opposition to Sabbath games, "a light attendance" was on hand August 12 to see Rochester defeat Troy, Bob again umpiring.

To counter growing opposition to "Sunday Desecration," the organizers emphasized that no beer or liquor was allowed on the grounds and the newspaper promoted the contests, writing, "Many people have a very erroneous idea of these Sunday games. They, by no means, draw assemblages of roughs but exceedingly quiet and orderly audiences largely composed of ladies," and "those who work six days in the week are entitled to any recreation at all can find it in no more orderly or respectable place than the grand stand on the ball grounds at Windsor Beach." A large crowd was on hand on August 19, with Bob umpiring, but after the game the team managers "decided Sunday games were a mistake," saying they had "no idea and little warning of the depth and extent of public feeling against such games, and had no idea of shocking it or defying it when they undertook the series." The impetus came from the directors of the Rochester team, who, "as business men who depended for patronage on the people of Rochester, and have no desire to run counter to their expressed wishes, made up their minds to discontinue Sunday ball-playing, and stand the pecuniary loss that will doubtless ensue." Thereafter only local amateur nines took the field on Sundays in Rochester.[25]

Emslie's first full season went smoothly. He was rarely criticized by the press or subjected to crowds' disapproval save for occasional carping about ball-strike calls, and he was never threatened by fan mobbings or in need of police protection. He certainly made mistakes, misjudged pitches, and made wrong calls on the bases. On June 26 in Buffalo he was "hooted for the remainder of the game" after calling a Bison out at third base in the first inning, the "sheepish look" of the Rochester player intimating a blown call. And on August 18 in Buffalo he may well have misapplied the infield fly rule as alleged. But only once was his work protested to White: Hamilton manager Jack Fisher complained Emslie had not allowed a player to take first after being hit by a pitch; if Bob erred it was probably because he was umpiring behind the pitcher, not the plate, and did not see the ball hit the batter.[26]

He faced harsh criticism only in Rochester. Normally newspapers were critical of decisions during a home team's loss, but the Rochester baseball reporter, carrying over a dislike of Emslie's umpiring from 1887, was pointedly critical even in recounting Jingoes victories. When Rochester beat Troy 4–3 he claimed Emslie's umpiring "was not altogether what it might have been," criticizing his "sickening" ball-strike calls and "lunk-headed interpretation" of the infield fly rule. After Rochester defeated Albany he said, "Emslie didn't give the home team the benefits of many doubts," and following the Rochester win over Toronto he went ballistic over "the very bad umpiring of Emslie. His decisions on balls and strikes were questionable, those on bases were outrageously bad, and all were against Rochester." Asserting Rochester "ought not to consent to play tomorrow's game with Emslie [as] umpire," he concluded that unless Bob "does much better" his tenure in the league would be "very brief indeed."[27]

It was a wrongheaded comment. Emslie began the season still very much an unproven novice but became a highly respected umpire, the daily grind of sixty-six games a whetstone for honing his umpiring skills. He had learned to call games competently, let players and managers have their say while maintaining discipline and order, ignore critical press comments, and establish a reputation for integrity. Without a set season schedule his assignments often fluctuated wildly; in nine days, from August 22 to August 30, he umpired eight games in eight cities. But travel had been easier in the more compact league; no Sunday games afforded him a full day of leisure; and he worked only two twin bills, both on major national holidays: Canada's Dominion Day commemoration of confederation in London on July 2 and America's celebration of national independence in Buffalo on July 4.

When the season started Bob was eager to give umpiring a try as a means of staying in the game, but at some point came an epiphany: he enjoyed umpiring, was good at it, and wanted to pursue it as a career. Folks in St. Thomas, too, thought he had found his true calling, and would perhaps now be "brave enough to face matrimony" since he "earns a fat salary and could keep a wife comfortably." Umpiring provided a better-than-average salary, but it was also an unstable undertaking that meant being absent from hearth and home half the year. Bob, not yet prepared to settle down, was focused on the 1889 season, not domestic life.[28]

1889

Prior to the 1889 season league owners grappled with three issues. League instability was resolved by replacing Troy and Albany with the Toledo

White Stockings (in July renamed the Black Pirates) and the Detroit Wolverines, back in business after seven seasons in the National League. Fearful players might jump to the proposed Player's League in 1890, owners increased player salaries to $1,000, or $200 per month with expenses paid, but kept umpires at $250 a month without expenses covered. Race remained a troubling issue. Hamilton hired a Black mascot, "Man Morton, the Zulu giant"; London and Rochester proposed excluding Black players, but it was again decided that Grant could remain with Buffalo and Walker with Syracuse. Racism persisted as Canucks manager Charlie Cushman, who had lobbied to exclude Black players, started a petition to have them "fired out" of the league and even tried to organize a player strike were they not removed. Grant, fed up with teammates' racist behavior, signed with the all-Black Trenton Cuban Giants in the racially integrated Middle States League, leaving Walker as the lone Major League Black league player—and the last until Jackie Robinson in 1947.[29]

When Curry signed with the National League as a substitute and McLean retired, Bob Emslie, after one full season, became the chief umpire in the Minor League's top circuit. To fill the staff White reached agreements with Billy Hoover, James Gifford, and Albert Bauer, but the owners, after approving Emslie unanimously "without a word of dissent," rejected Hoover and Gifford, hiring instead William "Billy" Carlin, who was championed by Buffalo, and Edward West, Detroit's choice. Following "a vigorous discussion" Bauer was also approved with Hoover, Gifford, and John Henry "Herm" Doscher designated as substitutes. Save for Doscher, who had umpired in the NL in 1887 and AA in 1888, it was a shockingly inexperienced crew. Bauer had called thirty-five AA games in 1887, Gifford three in the NL in 188l, Carlin thirty five in the AA in 1886, and West seven in the NL in 1878,

On April 28, two days before the season opened, Bob Emslie headed to Utica, summoned by White for a staff meeting to go over assignments, regulations, and new rules. Eliminating the foul tip out and requiring the pitcher to stand with one foot in the center of the box made umpiring much easier. Also welcome were steps taken to increase umpires' authority and decrease kicking. Players coming in from the field had to go directly to the bench and stay there until called to bat, and, most important, umpires could now remove from the game a player who, once fined, continued to argue.

Bob opened the season on April 30 in Toledo, receiving the Toledo lineup before the game from manager Charlie Morton, his skipper in Savannah. He began the season alternating positions from behind the plate or pitcher depending on whether there was a base runner. When the National League, believing it difficult to determine foul and fair balls from behind the pitcher, directed umpires to work solely from behind home plate, the International Association followed suit as usual, but Bob continued switching positions, thinking it the best overall way to call the game, until White on July 27 instructed him to remain behind the plate.[30]

It was soon apparent the owners were mistaken in repudiating two of White's umpire recommendations and pressuring him to assign, or not assign, certain umpires for games. Almost immediately formal protests began pouring in about Carlin and West, and both were gone after three weeks. Bauer lasted barely a month. Replacements Herm Doscher, Joe Quest, and Phil Powers lasted but a few weeks. Emslie, who missed three games between July 17 and July 19 due to illness, was the only initial hire to finish the season.

Whether rumors in late May that the directors of the London Tecumsehs were interested in hiring Emslie to replace Phil Powers as manager were founded or not, Bob enjoyed a successful season umpiring, fulfilling the preseason prediction it would be "safe to presume that he will go through the forthcoming season without incurring the displeasure of the club managers—a difficult feat it must be confessed, for Emslie is capable and impartial in the discharge of his duties." With fewer cities and lengthier assignments, typically two series or six days in a city, he had less travel and more leisure time. Enjoying universal respect for his courage, he alone was deemed unafraid of "the Syracuse bullies" and was quick to silence unacceptable coaching, take "no chinning," and fine offenders: "When he says shut up, they shut up or get taxed a V."[31]

As a result Bob had a remarkably trouble-free season. There were no reports of fines or kicking. He undoubtedly took the few player rants with a grain of salt, any hurt feelings assuaged by praise in the press. The *Buffalo Courier* said Bob was "generally admired for his fair decisions," and even the Rochester press became complimentary, thinking his umpiring not only "very acceptable" but also "the best seen here this season." He was held in such high regard that scribes came to his defense. When fans criticized him for fining George "Orator" Shafer $80, the Detroit reporter said Emslie, "a conscientious umpire" who was "the most intelligent umpire in the International Association," had every right to fine Shafer, who "does too much talking and wrangling" and went on to lecture the "enthusiasts" that "good umpires in the International are a rare commodity. When found they should be cherished." And the Rochester reporter who regularly roasted Emslie in reporting the crowd's "united opinion" that his decision leading to the opponent scoring the winning run was "dead wrong," concluded, "The crowd was wrong, however, and Emslie right."[32]

Press criticism of Bob's umpiring was rare, with only two instances other than routine quibbles about pitch or base decisions. The Rochester baseball scribe creatively began his report of Buffalo's 6–5 victory on August 21 with a clever "book review" of *A DIAMOND Robbery: or, How I Roasted Rochester* by Robert Emslie. The review focused on the "expertness" of the "crime committed in the ninth inning, an erroneous out call at second base that prevented Rochester from tying the score," but also referred to "other minor robberies made on the same day." The reporter concluded the manual for felonious umpiring "should be sedulously kept" from other league umpires.[33] Less subtly the *Detroit Free Press* on August 14 blasted Emslie for allegedly missing a call that led to the Stars' 5–4 victory in the ninth inning as well as for making "palpably wrong" calls throughout the game and "more abominable decisions in the last few frames than a backwoods amateur umpire would in a month." He went on to term Bob's decisions throughout the homestand as "simply execrable," with "all his raw decisions against Detroit," and concluded, "One thing is certain. Detroit will tolerate no more of Mr. Emslie's peculiar decisions. He permitted the Rochester bulldozers to ride over him rough shod and gave them a game that did not belong to them. He has distributed 'yellow' decisions right and left in the path of the Detroits, and caps the climax by giving Syracuse a game to which it was not entitled. Mr. Emslie can rest assured that if he does any more umpiring here this season (and it is sincerely hoped he will not) and renders any more of the cross-eyed disgraceful decisions of the past few days he will regret it."[34]

Despite the roasting, and indicative of his stature, Bob was sent to Detroit to umpire the first-place Wolverines' final six games of the season. The only incident occurred on September 21, when he deprived Toronto's Eddie Burke of an inside-the-park home run, calling him out for not touching first base. After ejecting Burke, Bob initially summoned a policeman to escort the outraged player from the grounds, but then, understanding the player's emotion, allowed him to remain on the Canucks bench after he promised to keep quiet. The season ended with a laugher on September 23, the Tecumsehs playing as if "their fingers were full of oleomargarine and their optics clouded." At the end of eight innings, the Wolverines ahead 19–7, Bob, who thought the fans, "laughing continually" at London's sloppy play, had gotten enough fun for their money, called the game.[35]

At season's end, after umpiring 112 games—one more than any team played—Bob Emslie was heralded the league's "king umpire."[36] Having demonstrated that he had the talent and temperament to be a successful umpire, he was hopeful his performance warranted appointment next season to one of the Major Leagues.[37]

7

Reaching the Majors

> There is no position on the baseball field, the duties of which are more difficult to fill satisfactorily than that of the Umpire. Nor is there one which deserves higher pay for the work accomplished than that of this self-same arduous and unthankful position. To be a successful umpire is to be one man in a thousand. Both teams look upon him as the general enemy of each side. The majority of the crowd of spectators regard the Umpire as an especial target for abuse in every instance in which the home team is defeated. Last on the list of the Umpire's opponents are the betting class of reporters, who take especial delight in pitching into him, whenever his decisions go against their pet club, or the one they bet on.
>
> —*Spalding's Official Base Ball Guide*, 1890

In 1890 Bob Emslie found himself much in demand, able to choose where he would umpire. Charlie White tendered a contract, but returning to the International Association was not an attractive option. With four clubs bolting to the Major Leagues its viability was in doubt; indeed, the six-team circuit folded on July 7. He also received an offer from J. S. McCormick, president of the Western Association, the other top Minor League, but having proved his mettle, Bob eyed the three Major Leagues. It was widely rumored he would sign with the Players' League, sponsored and directed by the player's union, the Brotherhood of Professional Baseball Players. At first blush the new league seemed an attractive possibility. Besides needing to form an entire umpire staff from scratch, the PL was umpire-friendly, inaugurating a two-man system for all regular season games. (Owing to a scheduling snafu a four-man crew umpired in Brooklyn on July 14, 1890, the last arbiter quartet until the 1909 World Series.)[1] Also player-friendly in abolishing the reserve clause and allowing players to veto trades, the PL acquired many of the best players from the two established leagues but was less successful in attracting umpires. Only John Gaffney and Bob Ferguson, the American Association's best umpires, defected.[2]

With the success of the new PL uncertain, Emslie opted for one of the established leagues. Nicholas "Nick" Young, National League secretary-treasurer since 1876 and president since 1885, wanted him. His "liberal offer" to join the distinguished trio of Tom Lynch, Jack McQuaid, and Phil Powers in the senior circuit was tempting, but Bob preferred the American Association. As a former Oriole he was familiar with league cities, knew train connections and accommodations, and was personally acquainted with four team managers—Columbus's Al Buckenberger, Louisville's Jack Chapman, Philadelphia's Bill Sharsig, and Toledo's Charlie Morton. So Bob wrote to AA president Zach Phelps and secretary Harry Pulliam, "stating his terms and giving the Association an option on his services." Phelps, regarding Emslie as "one of the best umpires on the diamond" with "a happy faculty of commanding the respect of the crowd" that made him "a favorite wherever he goes," promptly accepted his terms, which included "a good salary" and monthly reimbursement of "all legitimate hotel and travelling expenses, viz: railroad fares, sleeping-car fares, price of meals en route, and hotel bills, not to exceed three dollars per day" ($100.78 in 2023 dollars). Bob Emslie was once again a Major Leaguer. (It may have been understood that IA umpires were reserved like players, as Emslie said White "kindly gave me permission" to join the AA.)[3]

Having lost last year's umpiring core, Phelps was delighted to have Emslie to anchor his staff. By the end of January he had received a plethora of applications, but the pool of qualified candidates was small. Finally joining Bob were John Hunt, an 1889 NL substitute, Terence "Terry" Connell, an occasional substitute arbiter from 1884 to 1889, and George W. Barnum, who had never umpired. Barnum, a New York City dramatic actor, hired after he came to Louisville as the manager of a touring company, admitted his appointment was "somewhat in the nature of a surprise," professing, "Next to my wife, I love baseball." Larry O'Dea, an employee of the A. J. Reach Company, who also had never umpired, was designated the substitute. The Louisville *Courier-Journal*, Phelps's hometown newspaper and the league's unofficial organ, declared that with Emslie, "one of the most valuable acquisitions yet," the AA would have "the best corps of umpires of any base-ball organization in existence."[4]

That was far from true. It was an embarrassingly inexperienced and incompetent staff. That may have been because Phelps hired on the cheap, save for Emslie. He had a limit of $6,000 to spend on a staff of four, which theoretically came to $1,500 per man, but with each umpire's salary left to the president's discretion, salary differentials, which often led to discontent, were the norm. Barnum, pointing out that last year Gaffney received $2,800 while Goldsmith got $1,200, argued each umpire should receive the same salary, no one being more important than the other. Point well taken, but the amount required to secure the service of a topflight umpire left less to pay the rest of the staff. Emslie's salary is unknown, but since he was regarded as "the most valuable acquisition" and had driven a hard bargain, he likely earned the most.[5]

Bob's delight in becoming a Major League umpire was soon tempered by two deaths in the family. On March 9 his mother, Mary, died at age seventy-four having "suffered for some time with bronchitis." The news was all the more distressing as his father, "dangerously ill from a paralytic stroke," had been given little hope for recovery; doctors and family were unsure who would die first. Bob, absent when his mother drew her last breath, hastened to London for the funeral at the Emslie home, then went to Guelph for the March 11 services and interment in the family plot at Union Cemetery. (His local celebrity was such that his mother's obituary mentioned as survivors two unnamed daughters and "Mr. Robert Emslie, the well-known base-ball umpire.") He must have been haunted by the specter of death. In addition to losing his mother, he recently had lost three brothers and two of his four sisters, and on March 7 a niece had died.[6] Bob's bereavement and time with his father and family were cut short. No sooner had interment services concluded than he headed to Syracuse for meeting with the AA's board of directors on March 15.

Instead of having umpires meet as usual with the league president to go over the interpretation and application of the rules old and new, club owners, now facing competition from two leagues, wanted to tell Phelps and the staff their plans for 1890 directly. First and foremost, they were determined to remedy the chronic problems of absenteeism and deportment. To remedy their frequent failure to show up for games, umpires were now required to notify the home team by 10:30 each morning that they would report. To avoid the league being "brought into disrepute," umpires visiting "houses of dissolute character" or "holding up the counter of a saloon" would be "severely dealt with." Neither directive was a concern for Emslie, but what caught his attention and no doubt brought a smile was the order that, to impart a sense of dignity and player respect during games, "the umpire must hereafter be addressed as Mr. Umpire." And to enhance their image, umpires were for the first time required to wear a standard blue uniform, the color of choice in the National League. (PL umpires wore white caps and suits, a symbol of purity rather than innocence?) More importantly, to lessen club interference in umpiring, instead of a committee of owners appointing the arbiters, the president was given exclusive hiring and supervising authority. Bob also perked up when the owners, believing that "people desire a change of umpires as well as ball teams," instructed Phelps to prepare a season-long schedule for each umpire that would ensure equal rotation among league cities and facilitate, by way of regional assignments, travel through the league, which was bordered by Brooklyn in the east and St. Louis in the west. Despite pervasive kicking the owners rejected the double-umpire system, primarily to avoid additional expense but also in deference to the National's preference for a single arbiter.[7]

Emslie's nationality had been frequently mentioned when he had reached the Majors as a player, but newspapers were silent about the arrival of the first Canadian-born career umpire.[8] At precisely 3:30 p.m. on April 17 in Philadelphia, Bob, attired in a new blue suit, stepped to the plate, threw out a new ball, and called "Play" to open the 1890 season. Despite twenty-five hits and ten walks it took exactly two hours for the Athletics to defeat the Rochester Broncos 11–8 and for him to umpire his first Major League game. One wonders about his reaction upon seeing, in the box score of his inaugural game, "Umpire Emslie." Unlike the players, who had five to seven preseason games, Bob began the year without umpiring for six months, but there were no complaints from either team. The *Philadelphia Inquirer* acknowledged, "Robert Emslie makes a good umpire." The rest of the four-game series also went smoothly, a harbinger of the rest of the season.

Bob was pleased with his schedule. At least at first. He worked his first twenty-eight games in the four eastern cities; after May 26 the next thirty-nine were in the west. To save money, for extended periods he traveled with and umpired games at home and away for a single team—seventeen with Philadelphia from April 17 to May 12, followed by thirty of the next thirty-six with Columbus. Because familiarity can breed contempt for umpires and players, Phelps decided umpires would switch cities and teams after two-series home stands. Emslie's schedule soon became frequently revised, occasionally to accommodate resignations and dismissals, but especially during the late-season pennant race to call games involving the four top teams in the league: pennant-winning Louisville followed by Columbus, St. Louis, and Toledo. Indicative of his respect by the league and players, he was assigned almost half of his games (49 percent) with the top three finishers; from August 1 to season's end on September 24, all but nine of sixty-two of his games involved those teams.

Unfortunately, Emslie's quality umpiring was not replicated by his cohort due to their incompetence and players' interminable, intemperate kicking. Hunt, unable to tolerate kicking in preseason exhibitions, resigned before the season opened. O'Dea, his replacement, who had two of his first four games officially protested, bailed on May 27; his replacement, Steve Toole, lasted thirty-eight games. Connell, who saw his first game officially protested and another end in a near riot, resigned on April 19; his replacement, Francis "Frank" O'Brien, lasted twelve games. George Barnum had enough after forty-seven games; his replacement, John Kerins, left after twenty. The *St. Louis Globe-Democrat* opined if the "wrangling" that marked the opening of the season continued, umpires would be "be justified in asking for permission to wear armor and carry a Roman battle-ax." The kicking epidemic was not confined to the American Association. By mid-June "at least twenty" umpires in the three Major Leagues had resigned. Finally, a modicum of stability obtained. Herm Doscher, hired May 7, and Wes Curry, hired July 13, continued to the end of the season. When Jimmy Peoples went home on September 1 after a forty-three game "siege" as an umpire, the local newspaper observed "he has lost his appetite and talks in his sleep, so shattered are his nerves." Truly, with kicking rampant, 1890 was "certainly not the season for umpires."[9]

Unlike his colleagues, Emslie survived the season relatively unscathed. He got off to a good start partly because his reputation preceded him. The only former player on the staff, he was usually referred to on his first appearance in a city as a former pitcher. The *Louisville Courier-Journal* reporter's recollection of Bob's superb fifteen-inning pitching duel in 1884 with the Colonels' Guy Hecker was still vivid six years later: "He was then one of the most graceful pitchers on the diamond. He possessed great speed, and, although he pitched without apparent exertion, sent the balls spinning across the plate at a lively rate." Toledo's baseball scribe remembered his umpiring: "Bob—excuse me, Mr. Umpire Emslie—is a great favorite in this city. There never has been a kick against him here, and his decisions, win or lose, have always been respected. Toledo will cheer him when he appears upon the diamond the latter part of June." The *St. Louis Globe-Democrat* called Bob "the best seen in St. Louis this season," declaring him "decidedly the best umpire in the American Association." The Louisville scribe agreed: "Emslie has a reputation as an umpire and it is well deserved, for he has no superiors in that capacity in either of the three major organizations."[10]

His reputation was such that reporters tempered their criticism of questionable decisions, noting "the best of umpires often have an off day." Aware that errors were inevitable in the single umpire system, scribes were occasionally forgiving, or at least provided perspective on controversial calls. After ruling a fly ball a hit instead of being caught just off the ground, the *Globe-Democrat* said "aside from this bad error Emslie's work has been first-class." When, in a game called on account of darkness, he missed seeing a Browns batter hit by a pitch, the paper allowed he was "conscientious in his judgment" and that the "bad mistake illustrates how uncertain at times is umpiring behind the pitcher. Had Emslie been at the plate he would have seen what occurred."[11]

Bob was held in high regard not only for his accuracy in making calls but also for his temperament and style of umpiring. First and foremost, he umpired with integrity, acknowledged even by the normally hostile Columbus paper, which noted that Phelps sent Emslie to work a crucial series with league-leading Louisville because "Bob is no home umpire." The Rochester paper agreed, with a backhanded compliment: "Emslie is undeniably honest. When he makes a bad break it is generally against the home club." And he didn't let criticism bother him. After being repeatedly "hissed" by fans for umpiring "a yellow game," the reporter noted, "He didn't mind a little thing like that and went on his way." The former player took a lot from players, too, understanding that kicking was part of the game, but relating to those who played the game contributed to excessive leniency. He occasionally fraternized with players off-field, violating umpires' customary behavioral norms. After a game in Columbus, Bob went with two Solons and a Louisville player to the Hustler vaudeville theater, where, enjoying the show in a private box, he "smiled audibly" at Flora Moore's rendition of "Down Went McGinty," the tragicomic song about the misadventures of a hapless Irishman jailed for "drinking whiskey fast and wild," which no doubt evoked memories of intemperate days with the Orioles.[12]

His tolerance was put to the test in mid-August when third-place Philadelphia, known for kicking, came to St. Louis for three games against the second-place Browns. Historically when those teams tangled the "baseball mercury begins to soar into the nineties," and in the opener on August 14 Emslie had "a very warm time of it," his decisions "kicked against viciously" by both teams. Enraged by a pitch call, Athletics pitcher Sadie McMahon approached Bob "in a threatening manner" and declared, "You are a robber and you know it." He was promptly ejected, but after pleading from team captain Curt Welch was fined and permitted to remain in the game, prompting the *Globe-Democrat* to comment, "Emslie is a good umpire, but he allows entirely too much arguing." Still, having had "one of the hardest games of the season to officiate in, and taking all things into consideration, he did well."[13]

Bob had an easy time of it the next day as the Browns played an exhibition game against their reserves, but on taking the field on August 16 the Athletics, despite having received "the most lenient consideration," like "roughs and blackguards" pushed Emslie to the limit, heaping "the vilest epithets upon him that it is possible for the human tongue to turn to." Bob took the "shocking profanity" until it became too insulting, then fined McMahon and William "Blondie" Purcell $5 each and hit Curt Welch with ejection and a $50 fine. Given that he had "a most difficult task," the press allowed he "did very well on the whole" but was again mistaken in allowing "too much back talk," thinking Philadelphia "deserved forfeiture" and the unruly trio should "apologize for their scandalous conduct and thank him for his forbearance."[14] Neither team was charitable in the final game on Sunday, and Emslie had to "discipline several" to maintain order. The *Philadelphia Inquirer*, musing that "the next time the teams meet brass knuckles and club will probably be a part of the uniform," summed it up: "Bob has just about earned his full month's salary in umpiring this Athletic series of three games." Of the contentiousness, Emslie said, "That kind of baseball was new to [me] this season."[15] More would come.

Like all umpires, Emslie made mistakes—more than he knew because he believed his calls were correct as he saw them. A perfectionist, but not perfect, Bob on occasion realized he had made the wrong call, but following the unwritten rule of umpiring, did not reverse himself, as admitting error often led to increased kicking. Still, it bothered him. In the eleventh inning of a thirteen-inning game on June 8 his "one mistake," calling a ball hit near the first base bag foul instead of fair, may have cost Louisville a victory. After the game he admitted to the errant call, and while he said it was "decided conscientiously and according to his judgment," he was so upset he hastily telegraphed his resignation to Phelps, who appropriately declined to accept it. The Louisville paper concurred: "There was no occasion for this, as he was perfectly sincere in his decision."[16]

On July 13 in St. Louis Bob experienced a rare instance of losing control. In the eighth inning the Browns' Tommy McCarthy on second base was hand signaling the catcher's signs to the batter. When Emslie ordered him to stop, McCarthy pointed out the rules prohibited only verbal signals. Bob got "very angry" and walked away. Moments later, McCarthy stole third base, reportedly "safe by a good big margin"—ten feet, said a Philadelphia paper—but to "the surprise of everybody" Emslie called him out and then threatened Tommy with ejection when he began to argue. The reporter attributed the apparent wrong call to "a fit of anger" and regretted that "Emslie so far forgot the dignity of his position as to show partisanship in the manner he did." After charging Bob with "the most open piece of spite work that has ever been seen on the St. Louis grounds," he conceded, "It is only fair to state Emslie was a very sick man throughout the game, and at one time had to suspend play for fifteen minutes while ice water was applied to his head, so near overcome was he by the heat. This physical infirmity may account in great measure for his exhibition of ill-temper."[17] Indeed, heat exhaustion may have contributed to his uncharacteristic umpiring. It was 98 degrees at game time and assuredly much hotter on the field. Whatever the case, Emslie surely regretted the incident.

His work was not immune to criticism, but it was infrequent and usually generic—"Emslie umpired poorly" and "Bob Emslie had an off day"—meant primarily for fans after a home team loss. Whether the criticism was warranted may have depended on the specificity of the account, but nineteenth-century reporters were unabashedly "homers," prone to praising hometown players and blaming losses partially or entirely to umpires' unfair or wrong decisions. Still, few faulted him until the dog days of August and September, when both the weather and the pennant race heated up. Then, in the highly competitive Major Leagues, he encountered critiques far more extensive and personal than experienced in the International Association. Bob understood partisan reportage and knew umpires had a more difficult relationship with the press in some cities. While Emslie was faithful to the umpire's credo of not carrying over feelings arising from disputes from one game to another, the adversarial attitude of baseball scribes in Columbus, Rochester, and St. Louis carried over from International Association days.

The Rochester reporter was especially given to personalizing criticism. When, on May 15, in the tenth inning, Emslie called a Columbus batter safe at first, negating a possible game-ending double play, after which the Solons scored to defeat Rochester 5–4. The loss dropped the Broncos from first place in what would be the city's only Major League season and the reporter, recalling past disputes with Bob, railed, "He has been here before, has Emslie, and Rochester people have known him to their sorrow, but yesterday he gave them a dose such as no other person in his position ever dealt out in this city. If larceny of a ball game were punishable by law Emslie would get about two hundred years at hard labor" for robbing Rochester "as coolly as a pickpocket relieves a farmer boy of his watch on circus day." On August 2, when the Browns beat the Broncos 5–4, the reporter proclaimed, "Bob Emslie went so blind a couple of times that he couldn't tell the difference between a base hit and a postponed game. Emslie was very bad, uncommonly bad in fact, and that means there was some very yellow umpiring done through the progress of the game. There is no possible, probable shadow of doubt, no possible doubt whatever but that Emslie has spells when he is the worst umpire that roams the good green earth." Only slightly less hyperbolic, the St. Louis scribe simply said, "Bob Emslie had an off day, and he was so far off that his work was simply painful."[18]

The personal antipathy of the *St. Louis Globe-Democrat* reporter was underscored in late August, when Emslie went to Baltimore for a four-game series with the Browns. It was something of a homecoming, the first time Bob had been in town since being released by the Orioles five years earlier. He still had friends in Baltimore and no doubt looked forward to demonstrating his success as an umpire to his former manager, Billy Barnie. It was also a special occasion for Baltimore: the August 27 game marked the Orioles' return to the American Association to replace the defunct Brooklyn Gladiators. Upon Bob's arrival in the Monument City the *Baltimore Sun* welcomed him with a capsule account of his career, but the *Globe-Democrat* writer threw water on the occasion, vehemently protesting that Emslie, as "the former Oriole pitcher could not, at his old home and with his old club, do otherwise than give the latter the best of every close decision." He alleged Phelps, who also co-owned Louisville, which was then in first place, six games ahead of St. Louis, assigned Emslie to the series to enhance the Colonels' chance of winning the championship; he even claimed that when Bob's name went up on the board in St Louis "base-ball exchanges" bettors said "the only way the Browns will win a game in Baltimore will be to outplay the home club at bat." When the Browns won the opener 11–10, the reporter snidely commented the victory was "most commendable" since they were playing against Emslie and Phelps as well as the Orioles.[19]

That particular reporter's partisanship—the *St. Louis Post-Dispatch* made no comment about Emslie umpiring the series—was manifestly unfair to Emslie and Phelps. There was nothing untoward about the assignment; Bob had just finished a series in Syracuse and was to have gone to Brooklyn, but instead went to Baltimore when the Gladiators disbanded. He must not have shown too much favoritism, as the Browns won the first game and two of the next three. Neither St. Louis paper made any negative comment about Bob's umpiring, but the *Baltimore Sun* reported "considerable wrath was unloaded upon the head of Emslie, who many persons in the crowd believed gave the visiting team benefit of nearly every close decision."[20]

Bob's worst criticism came in Columbus. "Emslie and Errors," screamed the headline of the newspaper report of the Solons' 15–14 loss to Philadelphia on June 1. Trailing 14–12 in the ninth, the Athletics staged a rally. When Sadie McMahon tried to score the tying run, Solons catcher Jack O'Connor tagged him out—by ten feet, said the Columbus paper, or five, according to Philadelphia's—but Emslie, making the call from the infield, called him safe. The crowd went "wild with anger," and when O'Connor, infuriated, grabbed Emslie by the collar and neck, it looked like Bob would engage in fisticuffs with a player for the first time in his career. But cooler heads prevented "a regular knockdown" and the inning continued, with Philadelphia eventually scoring the winning run. The Columbus paper claimed Emslie, with his "outrageous" decision, "lost all the good will the Columbus ball public ever entertained for him and created an enmity that he will not be able to remove with a season's good work."[21]

Emslie returned to Columbus later that month without incident, perhaps because the Solons won six of eight games. Then, with the Solons 2.5 games behind second-place St. Louis and four back of first-place Louisville, Phelps sent Emslie, his best umpire, to Columbus for three consecutive series (twelve straight games) from September 12 to September 21, the longest home stand he worked that season. After the Solons swept Louisville 3–0 and split the first two games with the Browns, the Columbus paper thought "the splendid work of umpire Emslie cannot be too highly commended," while the *St. Louis Globe-Democrat* claimed

Emslie had "shown his ill-will for McCarthy and the Browns." Then, whether owing to increased pressure of the drawn-out home stand or familiarity breeding contempt, the Columbus reporter skewered Bob during the doubleheader on September 17, claiming in the first game Emslie, who "stood out as the bright particular star" of league umpires "did much yesterday to destroy his heretofore splendid reputation." Derisively saying Bob lived up to his reputation of "giving no favors to the home team" and that "three-fourths of the close decisions" went to St. Louis, the writer asserted the "barefaced robbery" would have "brought the blush of shame to the hardened features of an Egyptian mummy." His anger carried over into his commentary on the second game even though Columbus won 6–1; he snidely commented the game was so one-sided "the umpire had no chance to make it close."[22]

Emslie couldn't win. During the final series with Baltimore, during which Columbus took three of five games, every game account contained claims of "very poor" umpiring and allegations of unfairness and "erroneous decisions." Barnie attributed the Orioles' poor showing in a 9–4 loss on September 19 "in a great measure to his former pitcher's partiality," while the Columbus papers alleged that "as usual [Emslie] gave every close decision to the visitors." The Columbus report of the doubleheader on September 20, in which the teams split victories, began, "The 5,000 people who saw the games yesterday will pass a resolution of thanks that Mr. Robert Emslie has made his last appearance in this city in the role of umpire, for the present season, at least." The reporter's animosity was so great that before the concluding home stand doubleheader on September 21 he snarled, "Bob Emslie leaves us after the game today. Ta ta Robert, and around the rosy glow of the winter fire at your baronial halls in St. Thomas [sic], Canada, may you think over the holy roast you gave Columbus in Wednesday's first St. Louis game. Tell your children how their father spoiled his reputation as a fair umpire on that exciting occasion."[23]

Emslie was relieved to leave the Columbus cauldron for two series in Toledo against second-division also-rans Baltimore and Philadelphia but found himself again under pressure, ending the season assigned twelve straight games with second-place St. Louis, nine at home. Fortunately for Bob the competitive fires banked as the Browns faded badly, losing the first three and ultimately eight of the nine in the home stand. After a peaceful game on October 14 in Louisville, the Colonels putting an exclamation point on the title with a 13–1 thumping of the Browns, Emslie packed his gear and headed to London, where after his mother's death he continued living with his father and sister.

In the friendly confines of home he could look back on his first Major League season with satisfaction. Reaching the Major Leagues was a huge step in handling both the quality of play and the emphasis on winning, and he had met the test with aplomb. Notwithstanding some harsh late-season press criticism, the thrashing from Columbus being especially hurtful, he had proved to be more than a competent big league umpire. The assignments, in the season's last two months, to the pressure-packed games between pennant contenders were indicative of his reputation. Before the season began, *Sporting Life* thought Emslie, who "has a good record, will, it is generally believed, be all that is expected of him." The prediction was accurate. In midseason he was thought to be "decidedly the best umpire in the American Association" and at season's end was regarded as "one of the best umpires in the country."[24]

In addition to making judicious decisions and demonstrating the ability to control games, he exhibited stamina and dedication. The only original member of the staff to finish the 140-game season, he worked 137 games, all but two behind home plate. Durable, he failed to complete only one game, which he had to leave in the third inning on July 17 in St. Louis after being "severely injured" when struck in the abdomen by a foul ball. With the next day a travel day, he was able to recuperate and take the field in Syracuse on July 19. He also missed two games when, on receiving word that his father was very ill, he left after the game in Toledo on July 1 to remain with the family for two days. There were no Association games on July 3, a travel day, but Bob was back in Toledo on July 4, too late to for the morning game of the holiday twin bill with Syracuse, but able to umpire home plate in the afternoon.

There were milestones along the way. Bob umpired back-to-back historic games. On August 25 in Syracuse he called the Gladiators' finale as the team, buried in last place, folded after the game. Then on August 27 he called the first game of the league's replacement team, the Baltimore Orioles. Bob left Baltimore with another first. The second game of the doubleheader on September 2 with Columbus ended in a 6–6 tie when he called it in the tenth inning because of darkness; the next day he again called the game because of darkness, this time after nine innings with the same teams tied 6–6.

What was next? The best umpire in the American Association decided not to reup for 1891. He was not alone: Kerins returned, but Curry, Doscher, Peoples, and Toole left. The unstable umpire staff was symptomatic of a league in decline. When hopes of merging with the Players' League ended with the Brotherhood circuit's collapse after the season, the financially troubled AA withdrew from the National Association to wage war for players with the National League and replaced three clubs with teams in more populous cities. For Bob the final blow may have been the ouster of his friend and supporter, Zach Phelps, as president.

The National League's Nick Young liked Bob, but his four-man staff of regulars was full with heralded newcomer Tim Hurst joining returnees Tom Lynch, Jack McQuaid, and Phil Powers. Bob might have signed as a substitute, but umpiring periodically as a short-term replacement was not appealing. His full-time options were the Eastern Association and the Western Association, the top Minor League circuits since the International Association disbanded after the 1890 season. With the Eastern and Western part of the National Agreement he would be in close contact with Young, who was in charge of hiring and supervising umpires in both leagues. The Eastern seemed the more likely choice given the geographical proximity to St. Thomas, his old friend Charlie White being the league president, and Bob's familiarity with most of the league cities save for three in New England.[25] But he decided to sign with the Western, the stronger of the two leagues and the one that afforded new experiences. Knowing he was Major League caliber, Bob was confident his return to the bush leagues would be brief.

SPORTING LIFE.

TRADEMARKED BY THE SPORTING LIFE PUB. CO. ENTERED AT PHILA. P.O. AS SECOND CLASS MATTER

VOLUME 24, NO. 24. PHILADELPHIA, MARCH 9, 1895. PRICE, TEN CENTS.

Fig. 1. The appointment of an umpire supervisor led to the first published depiction of an umpire staff. *Sporting Life*, March 9, 1895.

Fig. 2. Illustration of Emslie accompanying a biographical sketch in the *New York Clipper*, September 19, 1896.

Fig. 3. Emslie and his beloved terrier just before his eighty-fourth birthday. *St. Thomas Journal*, January 26, 1943.

Fig. 4. *Above:* Preseason publicity photo of Emslie for the 1886 Toronto Canucks. Courtesy of Elgin County Archives.

Fig. 5. *Right:* Emslie with an ever-present cigar. Courtesy of Elgin County Archives.

Fig. 6. Emslie portrait in 1916 taken at the time of the commemorative day at Ebbets Field honoring his twenty-five years umpiring in the National League on August 12, 1916.

Fig. 7. *Opposite top:* Emslie and William Jeremiah "Bill" Byron, known as Lord Byron and the "Singing Umpire" for making lyrical calls during his career in the National League (1913–19). Byron was a frequent visitor to St. Thomas and attended several World Series games with Emslie. Courtesy of Elgin County Archives.

Fig. 8. *Opposite bottom:* Emslie and John Heydler, National League president from 1918 to 1934, circa 1934. Heydler, who appointed Emslie the first umpire to serve as the league's supervisor of umpires, frequently visited Emslie in the off season to play golf. Courtesy of Elgin County Archives.

Fig. 9. *Above:* Opening game of the World Series at Navin Field at Briggs Stadium in Detroit, probably 1934. L-R first row: Emslie, Bobby Low, Frank Scheibeck, and Frank Bowerman. L-R back row: Tom Connolly, Bill Byron, Lou "Sport" McAllister. Connolly and Byron were retired umpires; Low, Scheibeck, Bowerman, and McAllister were former Detroit players who lived in the area. Courtesy of Elgin County Archives.

Fig. 10. *Above:* The champion 1880 Harriston Brown Stockings. A youthful looking Bob Emslie, in his first season as a professional pitcher, is third from the right, seated in a chair. Wellington County Museum and Archives.

Fig. 11. *Right:* Emslie in 1922, his final season as a regular field umpire; photo taken by photographer Charles Conlon. Courtesy of Benson Taylor, *Sporting News*.

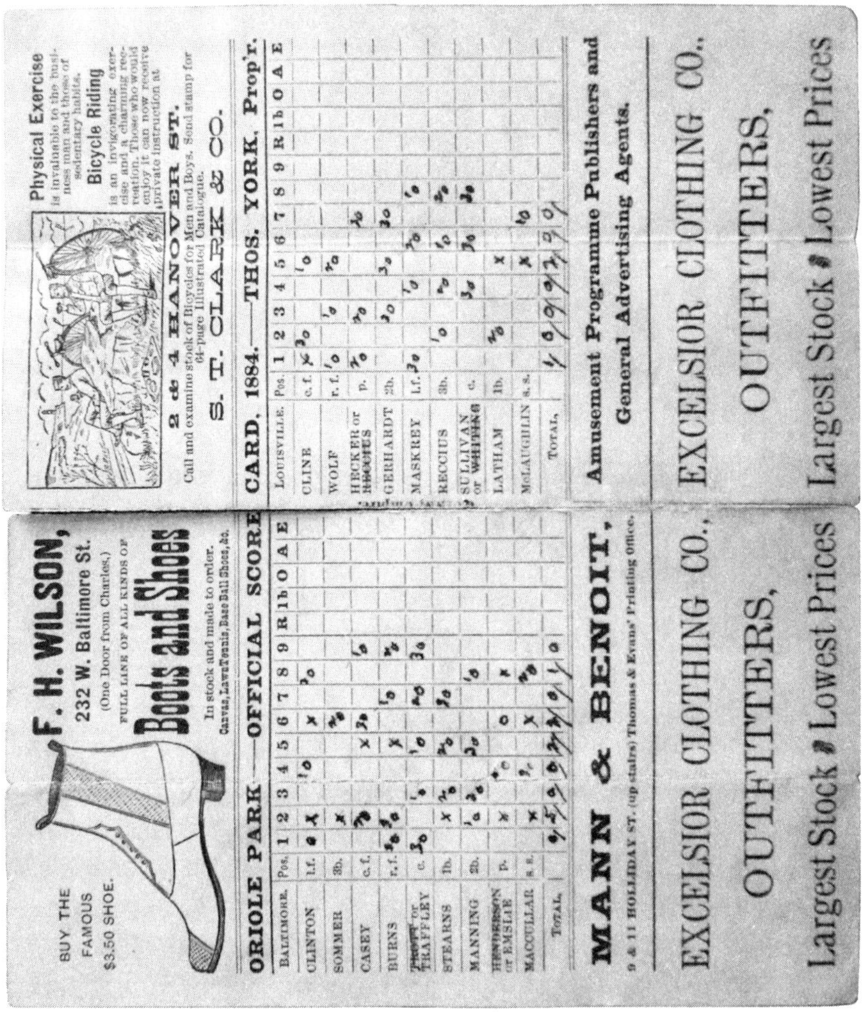

Fig. 12. Rare 1884 scorecard showing Emslie beating the Louisville Colonels and the league's ace pitcher, Guy Hecker, 10–3 on September 25. From the Ted Patterson Collection courtesy of David Stinson.

Fig. 13. *Above:* Preseason team picture of the 1885 Baltimore Orioles wearing new home uniforms. Emslie, mustachioed, is in the back row, second from the left. Back row: Tom York LF; Bob Emslie P; Dan Stearns 1B; Mike Muldoon 2B; Sam Trott C; Dennis Casey CF; Jake Evans, RF; Joe Sommer LF. Middle row seated: Billy Barnie manager; Tim Manning, 2B; Jimmy Macullar, SS. Front row: Vincent (Sandy) Nava, C; Tom (Oyster) Burns, 3B; Bill Traffley, C; James (Hardie) Henderson, P. Unattributed photo in James H. Bready, *Baseball in Baltimore: The First 100 Years* (Baltimore: Johns Hopkins University Press, 1998), 41.

Fig. 14. *Right:* Emslie and fellow National League umpire Charles "Cy" Rigler, who umpired in the NL 1906–35. In 1936 Rigler succeeded Emslie as supervisor of the league umpires but never served, as he died weeks after his appointment. Courtesy of Elgin County Archives.

Fig. 15. Emslie making an "out" call. Illustration from his essay "Ramblings of an Umpire," *Baseball Magazine*, November 1908.

Fig. 16. *Above:* The only extant picture of Emslie and his wife, Helena, date unknown. During his umpiring career they were able to celebrate their wedding anniversary together only once. Courtesy of Elgin County Archives.

Fig. 17. *Opposite:* As an indication of greater recognition of umpires, photographs of the 1912 National League staff appeared for the first time in the 1913 *Spalding's Official Base Ball Guide Book*, 33. In 1913 Byron, Guthrie, O'Day, and Quigley replaced Johnstone, Finneran, and Bush on the staff. Courtesy of the Baseball Hall of Fame.

1, Rigler: 2, Owens; 3, Orth; 4, Eason; 5, Johnstone; 6, Emslie; 7, Brennan; 8, Finneran; 9, Bush; 10. Klem.

GROUP OF NATIONAL LEAGUE UMPIRES, 1912.

Everybody Love
THE ALL AMERICAN

Figs. 18a and 18b. Bill Klem (*above*) behind the plate and Emslie (*opposite*) on the bases formed the best National League umpiring crew for six seasons, 1915–20. In 1953 Klem and Tommy Connolly became the first two umpires enshrined in Cooperstown. Library of Congress.

Fig. 19. *Above:* Hank O'Day and Emslie, close personal friends during and after their umpiring careers, pitched against each other in the American Association 1884–85 and umpired together in the National League 1895–1922. O'Day was elected to the National Baseball Hall of Fame in 2013. Courtesy of the Baseball Hall of Fame.

Fig. 20. *Right:* A former National League umpire (1888–1902), Thomas J. Lynch as league president (1909–13) strongly supported umpires, prevented an owner's cabal from ousting Emslie, and innovatively assigned umpires exclusively to field or plate duty to maximize individual talents. Courtesy of the Baseball Hall of Fame.

Fig. 21. Harry Clay Pulliam, responsible for Emslie's initial hiring as a National League umpire, during his tenure as league president (1903–9) increased the authority of the league president by creating the separate office of secretary-treasurer and supported umpires by imposing stiff fines and ejections as penalties on players for arguing decisions. He committed suicide on July 29, 1909. Courtesy of the Baseball Hall of Fame.

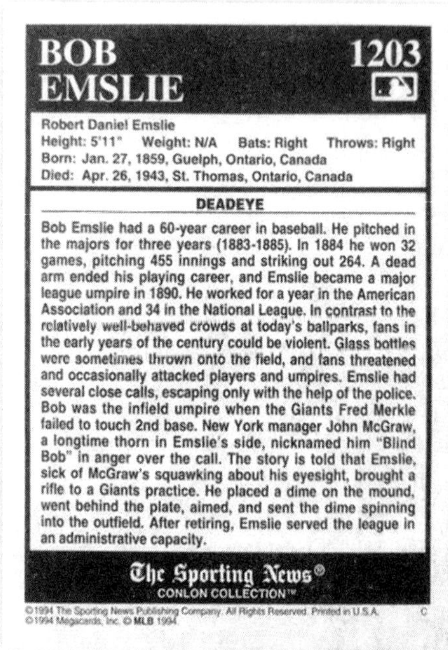

BOB EMSLIE 1203

Robert Daniel Emslie
Height: 5'11" Weight: N/A Bats: Right Throws: Right
Born: Jan. 27, 1859, Guelph, Ontario, Canada
Died: Apr. 26, 1943, St. Thomas, Ontario, Canada

DEADEYE

Bob Emslie had a 60-year career in baseball. He pitched in the majors for three years (1883-1885). In 1884 he won 32 games, pitching 455 innings and striking out 264. A dead arm ended his playing career, and Emslie became a major league umpire in 1890. He worked for a year in the American Association and 34 in the National League. In contrast to the relatively well-behaved crowds at today's ballparks, fans in the early years of the century could be violent. Glass bottles were sometimes thrown onto the field, and fans threatened and occasionally attacked players and umpires. Emslie had several close calls, escaping only with the help of the police. Bob was the infield umpire when the Giants Fred Merkle failed to touch 2nd base. New York manager John McGraw, a longtime thorn in Emslie's side, nicknamed him "Blind Bob" in anger over the call. The story is told that Emslie, sick of McGraw's squawking about his eyesight, brought a rifle to a Giants practice. He placed a dime on the mound, went behind the plate, aimed, and sent the dime spinning into the outfield. After retiring, Emslie served the league in an administrative capacity.

The Sporting News®
CONLON COLLECTION™

©1994 The Sporting News Publishing Company. All Rights Reserved. Printed in U.S.A. C
©1994 Megacards, Inc. © MLB 1994.

Figs. 22a and 22b. Emslie's 1922 photo, card No. 1203 in the *Sporting News* Conlon Collection issued by Megacards in 1994. Courtesy of Benson Taylor, *Sporting News*.

8

To the Bushes and Back

> Umpiring is a peculiar business and requires peculiar talents. One might almost say umpires are born, not made.
>
> —*Spalding's Official Base Ball Guide*, 1891

The 1890 Federal Census declared western expansion had ended frontier regions in the United States, a finding that inspired Frederick Jackson Turner's seminal 1893 thesis on the importance of the frontier in American history. But in 1891 Bob Emslie entered a new personal and umpiring frontier. St. Louis had been his western outpost, but his experiential horizon now extended from Wisconsin forests through Iowa farmlands and across Nebraska prairies to Colorado's Rocky Mountains. One thing remained the same: topflight baseball.

The Western Association (WA) was a product of the post–Civil War baseball boom. Until 1865 professional baseball, indeed the popularity of the game itself, was largely confined to the northeastern quadrant of the United States and Ontario, Canada, but after the war soldiers, miners, homesteaders, and railroaders carried the game west of the Mississippi River and an expansion of sports coverage and baseball guidebooks nationalized information and instruction. Most importantly, baseball rode the rails. The Cincinnati Red Stockings' trip to San Francisco via the transcontinental railroad, completed in 1869 at Promontory Summit, Utah Territory, was a metaphor for baseball's future. The expansion of a nationwide railroad system, which necessitated the establishment in 1883 of four standard time zones in North America, fueled the burgeoning economies and populations of Western towns along the rail lines sufficient to support professional baseball as a civic and promotional activity and made possible travel between geographically distant cities.

The Western Association, the only Minor League between New York and California that was part of the National Association, comprised the Milwaukee Brewers, Minneapolis Millers, St. Paul Apostles, Kansas City Blues, Sioux City Corn Huskers, Omaha Lambs, Lincoln Rustlers, and Denver Mountaineers.[1] It was organized in 1888, and by 1890 had not only supplanted the earlier Western League but also become the premier Minor League with the demise of the International Association. With wholesale signing of former AA, NL, and PL players, the circuit approached Major League quality. The pennant winner was scheduled to face the AA and NL runners-up in a postseason series. The league was so strong, Allen W. Thurman, chair of the National Board of Control, which managed the National Agreement, proposed it replace the defunct Players' League, thereby bringing Major League baseball beyond the Mississippi. Western's president, Louis C. Krauthoff, a wealthy Kansas City railroad and corporation lawyer, enthusiastically embraced the idea, as did Albert Spalding, the most influential figure in the National League, but the proposal came to naught due to the modest size of league cities, notably Lincoln and Sioux City.[2]

It fell to Nick Young, secretary of both the National League and the National Agreement's Board of Control, to select, assign, and supervise WA umpires. His first hire, on March 2, was Robert Emslie. There followed a pair of former PL umpires, Alonzo "Lon" Knight and John "Jack" Sheridan, and finally, on March 22, John Gaffney, the renown "autocrat of the diamond," enticed to come west from his home in Worcester, Massachusetts, by the "earnest efforts" of Krauthoff and Young. It was a superb quartet. The *Kansas City Star*, the major newspaper in the league's headquarter city, echoed praise found in the national press of the appointment of the "star umpires," the "superior staff of umpires of national reputation and unquestioned ability" recognized as "more efficient than even that of the National league." When Sheridan opted to return to California, a second Canadian, Charles "Chub" Collins of Dundas, Ontario—Emslie's Atlantics teammate who had ended his playing career in 1890 with the WA's Omaha Omahogs—joined the staff. Eschewing the American Association's "old fogy" system of using local substitutes, the WA hired George Strief as the league's official replacement arbiter.[3]

Preseason hyperbole aside, it was an impressive staff, a far cry from the aspiring umpires who usually made up Minor League rosters. The head of the "star force" was Gaffney, dubbed the "King of Umpires" and "Honest John," who was by far the most experienced, having umpired seven years in the Major Leagues from 1884 to 1890. Knight, famous for delivering the first pitch in the first National League game on April 22, 1876, had four years of Major League service (1887–90), most served in the Players' League. Emslie had one year of Major League experience after three years in the top Minor League circuit. Collins, the anomaly, had never umpired.

In early April Emslie headed to Kansas City for a staff meeting with Krauthoff to go over rules and their application. Bob was delighted to meet Gaffney, eager to solicit advice from the veteran arbiter. They were sympatico. Like Emslie, Gaffney signed with the Western Association because it gave him "an opportunity to see cities and people which I have not seen before," and Gaff's approach to umpiring matched Bob's perfectly. "I have studied the rules thoroughly," he said. "With the players I try to keep as even tempered as I can, always speaking to them gentlemanly yet firmly. I dislike to fine, and in all my experience have not inflicted more than $300 in fines, and I never found it necessary to order a player from the field. Pleasant words to players in passion will work far better than fines."[4]

At the conclusion of the meeting Bob received assignments for the entire season. Because of the time and cost of travel in the expansive circuit, especially to and from Denver, the norm was to have home stands of four series in each city followed by a league-wide travel day. To avoid undue familiarity, each umpire worked only two consecutive series. If the cities were new to Bob, he found the league peppered with familiar faces. Team rosters included numerous former teammates and opponents, and he knew five of the eight managers—Al Bruckenberger had left Columbus to pilot Sioux City; Charlie Cushman, his 1887 Toronto manager, led Milwaukee; his old St. Thomas skipper, Bill Watkins, managed St. Paul; Orioles teammate Dave Rowe headed Lincoln; and George Tebeau, who played for Toledo in 1890, guided Denver.

Emslie opened the season on April 16 in Lincoln, Nebraska. The league's smallest city, with a population of 55,164, the railroad hub and home of the University of Nebraska had more than tripled in size since being designated the state capital in 1869. With professional baseball returning last August after the transfer of the Des Moines Prohibitionists, excitement ran high for the city's first full-time entry in the league. Arriving in town the morning before the game, Emslie discovered a local newspaper had reprinted a biographical blurb from the *Kansas City Star*: "R. D. Emslie is a new man to the west, but has a reputation second only to Gaffney as an efficient umpire and is very popular in the east. He is a great admirer of the Western Association and writes the Star that he is glad to be with a live, progressive baseball association and hopes that he will be as successful in his official capacity in the west as he has been in the east."[5]

Without any preseason work he lived up to pregame billing with a splendid initial umpiring performance. Although 1,500 fans left M Street Park disappointed as the Rustlers lost a heartbreaker in which Minneapolis scored two in the bottom of the ninth to win 6–5, the local paper proclaimed, "Emslie's umpiring was the best ever witnessed in Lincoln. Not a decision was questioned throughout the game, nor was there ground for it." Though impartial, he may have smiled on April 17 when his former teammate Dell Darling pitched and hit a home run in the Millers' 8–7 victory, then grimaced three days later as Hank O'Day gave up fifteen hits and five walks in losing 12–0. With a voice echoing "like an Alpine call," Emslie continued to receive plaudits for "satisfactory decisions" in games with Minneapolis: "His decisions throughout the series have been uniformly impartial and if Lincoln is furnished as good a man during the season there will be no kick."[6]

When the series ended on April 23, Bob headed to Denver, population 107,000, the second-largest city west of Omaha, where trappings of the Old West were much in evidence.[7] The initial series with the Brewers went without a hitch, but controversy arose in the first game with the St. Paul Saints on May 1. With two on and two out in the bottom of the ninth, the score tied 3–3, the Mountaineers would have won the game had Emslie not ruled a hit down the left field line a foul ball. "Grand larceny" was the "mighty howl" of fans at Broadway Athletic Park who thought the ball fair. They were the more upset with Bob when the Saints scored a run in the tenth inning to win 4–3.

After the last game of the St. Paul series on May 3, Emslie and the Mountaineers boarded a Union Pacific train at 8:30 p.m. headed for Sioux City. The long and circuitous journey across the seemingly endless plains, by day hot and dusty with soot from coal-burning steam engines, finally ended fourteen hours later, at 10:30 p.m. on May 4. Weary from the trip, the next day he headed to Evans Park for the Corn Huskers home opener. Shortly before noon a brisk wind blew away the clouds and mist, the sun shining brightly as Emslie called "Play!" promptly at 3:30. The Huskers beat the Mountaineers 7–2 with players not disputing any of his decisions "to any considerable extent." With no complaints during the home stand, after the concluding series with Omaha on May 11, the Sioux City paper complimented him, writing, "Bob has done good umpiring here, and Nick Young shows that he knows an umpire if Bob is a sample."[8]

It was then off to Milwaukee, where, as in the previous year, his season was interrupted by a personal tragedy. His mother had died in March 1890, and on May 16, 1891, his father died at the age of seventy-five. It was not a surprise. When Bob left for the distant Western Association, he knew Alexander "had been very ill for some time, his mind being affected of late." After funeral services at the Emslie home in London on May 18, Alexander, like Mary, was taken to Guelph for interment. One wonders about Bob's state of mind, having lost both parents in slightly over a year. Not present when his mother and father passed, he had been away from London most of the time since 1880, and the once-large Emslie family he had known as a child was almost gone. After his mother's funeral Bob had quickly returned to work, which was for him both a job and a source of solace, but this time he stayed in London for several days with family, returning to Milwaukee on May 22. Tired from travel and in a distracted state of mind, he umpired bases in the doubleheader while Strief, who substituted during his absence, worked the plate. The next day Bob took over as the lone umpire.[9]

Emslie had a remarkably trouble-free season. For the first time there was staff stability; Emslie, Gaffney, and Knight formed a respected, dependable core. Inexperienced Collins was a bust, dismissed by the end of May; his replacement, Strief, who was no better, was gone by the end of July. But Joe Quest, a former National League player who had done some Major

League umpiring in 1886–87, proved a fine addition and worked to the end of the season. (Quest reportedly coined the term "Charley horse" for a muscle spasm or cramp, most commonly in the leg.)[10]

Travel in the expansive league was Bob's only persistent problem. With trains running infrequently between league cities, he was not alone in calling games short of nine innings to allow teams to catch a train. Arranging travel to Denver was especially difficult. He was not able to get to Denver from Sioux City in time for the game on June 18 or from Duluth for the June 27 game. He suffered no serious injuries—nothing like Gaffney, who disobeyed doctor's orders and continued to umpire after an errant pitch broke his collarbone on June 15, for a time working solely behind the pitcher. In the first game of a doubleheader in Sioux City on June 7, Bob was briefly disabled by a wild pitch and was replaced by a local substitute umpire while attended to by a doctor. Ever reluctant to have players call games, he worked in Denver while being "quite sick" for several days in June and under the weather in July, perhaps due to the mile-high altitude.[11]

Indicative of Bob's success was the absence of criticism such as he had endured in late 1890. He had been excoriated by the Columbus baseball reporter, but received no kicks from Bruckenbecker and his team. Indeed, newspapers were fulsome in complimenting his work. The Sioux City reporter consistently praised his "good umpiring," and the *Kansas City Star* scribe, calling him "an umpire of the first class," said "King Gaffney will have to look to his laurels." He was repeatedly commended for being "very fair in his decisions" to the extent that "no one who has ever looked him in the eye would impute willful partiality. He wouldn't give his grandmother an inch the best of it, knowingly."[12]

Indeed, local papers frequently came to his defense when fans criticized his decisions, noting the difficulty the single umpire had in determining whether a ball hit far down the lines was fair or foul, or seeing a runner cut a base. When fans in Sioux City hissed him for calling a Corn Husker runner out, the *Sioux City Journal* said, "From his position at the time Emslie could not have known whether he scuffed the inside of the bag or not" and reminded fans "players are not infallible, and maybe it is as well not to expect too much of an umpire who is trying to be just." His popularity stemmed from personality as well as performance: "Besides being a good umpire he is a pleasant gentleman." Known for mixing pleasure with business on travel days, he got to Sioux City early enough to attend the harness races, staying for all six heats despite the threat of rain and raw winds. And ever the pitcher, during pregame practices he frequently showed players "some of his old-time curves."[13]

Laudatory press coverage was the result of few kicks. Early in the season Bob let it be known that he would take no personal comments and stop excessive kicking by dunning players for money. He meant it. He fined Duluth's William "Bones" Ely $5 for saying "clean the sand out of your eyes" and Jack McMahon a like amount for saying his teammate was right. When Kansas City's John Pickett "registered a little kick just to keep up appearances," he, too, found himself $5 short. The strict approach worked. When Bob responded to St. Paul's Billy O'Brien's unsaintly objection to a call with "It's $5, if you don't keep quiet," O'Brien turned away with "a good-natured grin." He engendered such respect that he fined only eight players (three in one game) and ejected only two, the aptly nicknamed Chippy McGarr for saying Bob had "dirt in his eye" and the Husker's Frank Shiebeck for arguing pitches. Generally, he was forgiving. On one occasion he rescinded a fine and only once did he couple a fine with ejection. Bob brooked no nonsense from fans, either. He encountered "little kicking" from players during his first appearance in Minneapolis, but weary of the constant abuse from a fan who even "took exception to the way in which Emslie chewed gum," ordered the loudmouth from the grounds. He was appropriately chided by the press for his overreaction: "Technically Emslie was in the right; umpires are many times subjected to unnecessary abuse from the audience and must protect themselves," but he should have been "a trifle charitable."[14]

Special games relieved the tedium of daily routine. Bob relished the parades, festivities, and pageantry that attended season openers in four cities—Lincoln, Sioux City, Minneapolis, and Duluth—and had the distinction of calling historic games. He umpired the fastest game of the year, ninety minutes on May 29 in Milwaukee, and uniquely officiated games in different states on the same day. On July 26 Denver and Duluth played a postponed game at West Superior, Wisconsin, in the morning and the regularly scheduled game that afternoon in neighboring Duluth, Minnesota. And he umpired the only two games in the league that year featuring a triple play, unusual for the time and both exceedingly rare in execution. On June 11 St. Paul turned a 1-3-2 triple play in Sioux City, and later that month, on June 28, Denver pulled off a 5-2-1 triple play in Duluth. In mid-July in Lincoln he worked his easiest four-game series, receiving nary a kick and not even working up a sweat. Reminiscent of what he had experienced in Savannah, when financially troubled Omaha failed to show up for three games, Bob went to home plate at four o'clock each day, called "Play!" and after the Rustlers' Jack Roach threw one pitch, announced a 9–0 forfeit and left the grounds.

After not actually umpiring during the Omaha forfeits in Lincoln, Bob headed to Duluth for five consecutive series from July 22 to August 9. It was a memorable experience. The Duluth newspaper praised him for having "given excellent satisfaction" in all the games, and before the finale a fan presented him with "a mammoth floral baseball" to which was attached a card reading, "Umpire Emslie, with the compliments of Lakeside suburbanites who appreciate fair and conscientious work." After the presentation, the spectators in the bleachers and grandstand stood and applauded until Bob, both pleased and embarrassed, "raised his hat in appreciation." It was a bittersweet ending to the home stand as neither Duluth nor Bob Emslie would ever again appear on a Western Association field.[15]

For some weeks Bob had worried about suddenly being without a job given increasing talk the Western, financially troubled by the cost and logistics of travel as well as the unrealistic Major League–level salaries paid to key players, might fold. Signs were evident. St. Paul, languishing in the cellar at 13-30, transferred on June 6 to distant Duluth, a port town of only 33,000 at the southwestern tip of Lake Superior, the westernmost point of the Great Lakes chain. Omaha folded in mid-July but was reconstituted ten days later with new financing and players. Then, on August 20, Duluth, Lincoln, and Minneapolis disbanded. The actual denouement had come a week earlier when first-place Milwaukee bolted to the Major League American Association, replacing the defunct Cincinnati Porkers.

Emslie had firsthand knowledge of Milwaukee's departure. On August 14 in Sioux City, Brewers manager Charlie Cushman in the seventh inning asked him to stop the game. Cushman, who had just received a telegram from the Milwaukee club owner announcing he had bought the Cincinnati franchise, told the crowd he was forfeiting the game in order to catch the 7:15 train to St. Louis where tomorrow the Brewers would play the Browns. Timing aside, it was no surprise to Bob. He had recently received a telegram from Nick Young with the instruction, "When Milwaukee jumps to the American Association, you jump to Cincinnati in the National League." Immediately after the game he, too left the Western for the Majors. (He had an easier time than Milwaukee. The Brewers hurried to the station only to find no trains to St. Louis that night. They finally left on August 17, playing and defeating the Browns 7–2 on August 18.)[16]

The Western Association was on the verge of collapse, but four teams—Sioux City, Kansas City, Omaha, and Denver—remained until the league folded on September 14, shortly before the scheduled close of the season. With the league's demise Gaffney also joined the National League. As evidence of the Western's strength, Sioux City, which won the pennant by one game over Kansas City, in October won both postseason series with the second-place teams in each of the Major Leagues, the Corn Huskers defeating the National League's Chicago Colts four games to two and sweeping all five games with the St. Louis Browns of the American Association.

NATIONAL LEAGUE

Emslie probably thought he would be a substitute umpire, but Young wanted him to replace Phil Powers, released on August 18 after his decisions in the first game of Cleveland's series in Cincinnati prompted a fist-swinging, bat-throwing brawl that required a squadron of police to clear the field. The next day, August 19, Bob made his National League debut in the second game of the Cleveland series. To say he arrived, in more than one sense, would be an understatement.

More ominous circumstances cannot be imagined. Not only had players been through a disputatious game with the umpire and a violent free-for-all between the teams, but also, as the *Cincinnati Enquirer* observed, "a bitter feeling has long existed" between the two clubs. Fortunately, Bob experienced no "riot alarms" or "prize-fight embellishments" as Cleveland's Denton "Cy" Young in his first full season pitched six innings of two-hit ball in relief to preserve the Spiders' 4–3 victory. Actually, it was a smashing debut. The *Enquirer* reported, "Bob Emslie made his first appearance as a League umpire and it is likely he will prove a success. He made one or two mistakes against the Reds yesterday but seems to understand, for he will not allow the players to make stump-speeches and abuse him like a horse-thief."[17]

There followed four high-pressure games. The Reds lost again the next day by one run, then dropped three low-scoring games—2–0, 2–1, 2–1—to the last-place Pittsburgh Pirates. The tightly contested games increased "the usual clamor and uproar for the special benefit of the rookie umpire who, in addition was a 'Canuck,'" but Emslie "weathered the storm gallantly" with a "fearless spirit." The press reported on August 23, "Emslie's umpiring was very good." Indeed, the *Cincinnati Enquirer* thought he "seems destined to make a success equal to Gaffney, Lynch, McQuaid and the best of them. His rulings here in the Cleveland and Pittsburg series were of the best and though Cincinnati lost all four [actually three] of the games in which he officiated, by one run, still there was no kick coming against the umpire." Bob, too, was pleased with his return to the Majors. Interviewed in the *Enquirer* office, he said, "Yes, I like umpiring. I have not had the slightest trouble, and there is no reason why I should not like it." What a difference twenty-four hours can make in an umpire's life. Having survived baptism by fire in the first two sets, he was roasted on August 24. The *Enquirer* ran the headline "Umpire Emslie's Very Jesse James's Umpiring," blasting Bob for taking the game from the Reds "in the most bare-faced manner possible. He not only robbed the Reds, but he robbed patrons of the park. It was an outrage."[18]

What had happened? In the top of ninth the Reds scored a run to tie first-place New York 3–3 when it began to rain "at a very lively rate," the players and spectators heading for cover. After about twenty-five minutes, the rain turned to light mist, the sun came out, the grounds crew strewed sawdust on the base paths, players returned to the field, and fans took their seats. But when the delay reached precisely thirty minutes, Emslie, following the letter of the rule, called the game, the score reverting to the eighth inning for a 3–2 Giants victory. The crowd went berserk and the *Enquirer*, while acknowledging the decision was technically correct, said Bob had violated the spirit of the rule since there was no reason to call the game with the clouds clearing and the sun shining. The *New York Sun*, too, considered the Giants' win "an unexpected gift." The amount of precipitation sufficient to call the game was a matter of judgment, but Bob, overly eager to demonstrate his authority and command of the rule book, instead of using discretion had too strictly applied the rule.[19] There were no problems the next day, as Reds bats finally erupted in a 12–4 pasting of the Giants, or when the New Yorkers won the next two games, but when Bob left after the series ended on August 26, the *Enquirer* alleged Reds fans were "not a bit regretful about his departure. Bob may be a good umpire, but he is not up to Cincinnati's standards." Indeed, Queen City fans gave him a new nickname: "um-pirate."[20]

He had a much better time in Chicago. At the end of the three-game set with Philadelphia the *Tribune* reporter thought Bob "made a favorable impression" and the usually acerbic *Inter Ocean* sports editor Leonard Washburne agreed: "Emslie, the new umpire is doing quite well. Since he has been in town not one solitary man has driven his glove into the ground and walked in to tell Mr. Emslie that he was a chuckle-headed wen, and even the man on the house top across the street, who usually becomes angered at decisions on balls and strikes and lifts his voice through the drowsy afternoon to explain, is silent now. Emslie must be pretty good."[21]

From Chicago he went to Cleveland and then on an eastern swing with one series in New York, featuring his first back-to-back morning-afternoon doubleheader, and three series in Philadelphia. There was no comment in newspapers in either city about his work save for the New York *Sun* mentioning the "only excitement" in the afternoon game of a twin bill on September 11 was Cleveland questioning "nearly every decision" until things "grew quieter" after Bob threatened to eject Patsy Tebeau, Jake Virtue, and Ed McKean.

Smooth sailing continued until Bob returned to Cincinnati on September 21, when he again ran into a firestorm. Trouble began in the sixth inning when he called Chicago's Cap Anson safe at first because the Reds first baseman pulled his foot from the bag. The crowd roared its disagreement, one spectator "hallooing" so abusively that Emslie ordered him from the grounds. The sight of the chief of police and two officers, all of whom would have "preferred to chase the umpire," escorting a fan from the premises further angered the crowd. Things really got hot in the ninth inning. Trailing 4–3 with a runner at first, the Colts' "Pop" Schriver's pop fly bunt hit the third base foul line, then spun into foul territory, rolling all the way to the stands. Emslie correctly ruled it a fair ball because the rule stipulated that a batted ball that went into foul territory after first landing on the infield was fair. But Cincinnati pitcher Tony Mullane, arguing it was a foul, exploded like "an unfortunate canine who has swallowed a bunch of lighted fire crackers," stalking off the field in disgust. At the contemptuous display of one-upmanship, fans were "transformed into a howling mob of bloodthirsty cranks," the din increasing after the Colts scored twice to win 5–4. The *Enquirer* conceded Emslie was "not as unjust as the crowd thought," but in giving Chicago "all close decisions" was "about the worst excuse of an umpire that has visited Cincinnati this season. He is either wittingly biased against the Reds or is grossly incompetent."[22]

The Reds had no kicks the next day, but on September 23 Emslie was again vilified in the press in a way that revealed the unreliability of reports from away games. The *Chicago Tribune* stringer in Cincinnati said Emslie's umpiring "was as bad as any ever seen here" and the crowd "guyed him unmercifully" for giving Cincinnati "the worst of it all the way through." The Cincinnati reporter said he was "unfair to the pitcher in several decisions on balls and strikes" but "made a showing that no professional need be ashamed of." He did note the fans, still upset with Emslie's decision on September 21, "kept passing audible comments on his work all through the game."

Relieved to leave the Queen City, Bob headed with the Reds to Cleveland, where he encountered no problems in working the final three series of the season, in which the Spiders won seven of the nine games. After the finale on October 3 Emslie hurried to St. Thomas, having decided after his father's death to return to the city where he had launched his professional career.

Emslie could look back on the 1891 season with satisfaction. His success in the Western Association had led to his return to the Major Leagues, this time with the premier National League. In the Western he umpired far more games than any other member of the staff, then worked forty-three in the National, calling games with every team except the pennant-winning Boston Beaneaters. He called the most games involving the Reds (16) and Spiders (24). Assigned to games in the western portion of the league save for two series in New York followed by two in Philadelphia—sixteen games in all—he had not umpired in Boston, Brooklyn, or Pittsburgh; almost half his games were in Cincinnati (10) and Cleveland (14). He encountered little criticism of his work aside from late-season turmoil in Cincinnati, perhaps due to frustration as the inept Reds finished tied with the Pirates in last place. Having proven himself in the highest level of professional baseball, Bob Emslie knew he could be a career Major League umpire. He just had to endure, as he would for the next thirty-two years.

9

The Not-So-Gay Nineties

Whose virtues do we seldom sing?
At whom do we our curses fling?
Who gets the blame for everything?
The Ump!
Who never gets a word of praise,
Though right or wrong he calls the plays?
Who's sure to make our dander raise?
The Ump!

Who's always wrong and never right?
Whom do we hail without delight,
And kid whene'er he heaves in sight?
The Ump!
And if the game is twelve to two
Against us and the air is blue
With curses who gets blamed—O who?
The Ump!

But who, upon the other hand,
Before us comes and takes his stand,
The coolest gent in all the land?
The Ump!
And who's aloof from all of us?
Who smiles to hear us rave and fuss,
And doesn't care a tinker's cuss?
The Ump!

—C. P. McDonald, "The Ump," *Chicago Tribune*, April 24, 1910

For both the National League and Bob Emslie, 1892 was a historic milestone. Having absorbed four clubs from the defunct American Association, the National, dubbed "big league" by Francis Richter, editor of *Sporting Life*, reigned supreme as a twelve-team monopoly in Major League baseball. Emboldened by prospects of unprecedented profitability and stability, club owners expanded the playing schedule from 140 games to 154 and established a split-season format, the winner of each half competing for a postseason championship, a resumption of the popular 1884–90 "World Series." Emslie, "renown[ed] as an excellent umpire," joined Gaffney, Tim Hurst, Tom Lynch, Jack McQuaid, Jack Sheridan, and Charles "Pop" Snyder to form "the greatest star corps of umpires ever." He was also about to enter the worst decade in history for umpires, in which unprecedented vituperation and violence ruled the field of play. Even before the 1892 season began, newspapers in every city railed against players for dirty play and arguing, fans for ragging umpires and engaging in riotous behavior, owners for tolerating rowdyism, and umpires for not enforcing the rules against kicking. Throughout the inferno, the profane language and physical violence different in degree and kind than he had previously encountered, Emslie would prove his mettle with the skills and temperament that would sustain his career for the next thirty years.[1]

PROVING HIS METTLE

Bob opened the season on April 12 in Louisville. He received no criticism in the opener or during the following three series from Cleveland, Chicago, or Pittsburgh, teams known for kicking. When next to Cincinnati, where he had encountered considerable criticism in 1891, the police chief doubled his security force for the home opener game on April 24, fearing there remained "a cankering desire among Cincinnati canaille for Emslie's blood." It didn't happen. After three series in the Queen City, Reds fans regarded him as "a model umpire."[2] Veteran sportswriter Tim Murnane agreed, believing "if the league could get just about three more umpires of the Bob Emslie stripe all lovers of the game would rejoice."[3]

At season's end Bob was one of a quartet chosen to umpire the league's first Championship Series, a best-of-nine series between the first- and second-half winners, the Boston Beaneaters and Cleveland Spiders. For the first game, on October 17, Bob started behind the plate with Snyder on the bases, subsequently alternating positions each inning. Gaffney and McQuaid called games two and four, and Emslie umpired the plate in game three and the bases in the finale. Besides doing "the best work of the series," Bob, appointed "steward of the umpires," was responsible for handling local arrangements for the two crews.[4]

There was no postseason championship in 1893, but in 1894 the first- and second-place teams began competing in the best-of-seven games for the Temple Cup.[5] Emslie and Hurst were chosen to umpire the inaugural series between the champion Baltimore Orioles and runner-up New York Giants. It was an honor, but not a pleasant experience. With tensions already high before the first game on October 4 in Baltimore as John McGraw and the Orioles argued over the split of gate receipts, in the bottom of the ninth inning, the Giants leading 4–1, Emslie called out the Orioles' Hughie Jennings at first on "a very close play," thwarting a last-ditch rally. McGraw grabbed Bob by the shoulder and "gave him quite a shaking." After the game, disgruntled Baltimore fans surged onto the field, Emslie spared from assault by a dozen policemen who escorted him to the clubhouse. To keep order the next day some two hundred policemen patrolled the grounds; the Giants won 9–6 without incident. When the series moved to New York for game three on October 6, Emslie began behind the plate, but after several close base decisions by Hurst in the third inning, the crowd demanded a change in assignments, so Hurst and Emslie switched positions. When in the fourth Emslie ruled an Oriole batter hit by a pitch, the dead ball negating a run, he was called "such vile names" by McGraw that Bob rushed for "the young pug," restrained by Giants catcher Duke Farrell from punching the foul-mouthed Oriole. Tension broke momentarily in the seventh inning when one of the horses tethered in the carriage shed behind center field, frightened by the noise, bolted out, galloping across the field until captured by police. There was no game on Sunday, which allowed everyone to cool off, and Bob worked behind the plate on Monday without a problem as the Giants won 16–3 to sweep the series 4–0.

Emslie did not umpire the 1895 series—$25 per game was not enough to deal with Baltimore—but returned in 1896. Hurst and Tim Keefe had umpired in 1895, but champion Baltimore objected to the former and runner-up Cleveland to the latter, so Emslie and Sheridan agreed to call the 1896 series, which the Orioles won 4–0. Emslie had the plate for all games except the second, both umpires doing "excellent work" the entire series save for one "questionable decision" by Sheridan in the last game.[6]

Emslie was back with Hurst for the 1897 series between the champion Beaneaters and second-place Orioles, each umpire receiving $150, from which they had to pay their own expenses. Boston manager Frank Selee was delighted to have Emslie, who had also been recommended by Baltimore manager Ned Hanlon, call the games, agreeing with the *Boston Herald's* Jacob Morse that "no other member of the corps of umpires could begin to do justice to the occasion."

> It is very plain that he has no favorites, and knows neither club nor player while umpiring. He attends strictly to business, and shows rare good sense in handling a game. He makes due allowance for the feelings of players working under a great strain, but no player can over-ride him or make a spectacle of him before a crowd. He has great courage, and is afraid of no one. The players all know this, and they know his rare ability as an umpire. Umpires of his class are born, and not made. Undoubtedly he has got to be the best umpire who ever handled a game. Umpires there have been who have been as good in the mere minutiae of the game, but none to equal him when it comes to discipline, tact, personal habits, temperance, reliability and ability.[7]

Emslie umpired the plate in the first two games and the bases in the final game in Boston. En route to Maryland the teams played an exhibition game in Worcester on October 7 and in Springfield on October 8, Bob and Tim umpiring. In Baltimore Emslie called pitches on October 11 as the Orioles won 9–3 to take the Temple Cup 4-1. The umpires were to receive $100 each for the two games, but since the expected paltry attendance would mean a monetary loss for the players, they agreed to accept $50. It was an omen: the Temple Cup series was discontinued due to apathy of both players and fans.

Being selected to umpire the league's showcase games illustrated Emslie's rise to the top of the profession. Fans in western cities regarded him as "the best umpire in the league." The *Cleveland Leader* called him "by odds, the best umpire today." In 1896 the *New York Clipper*, terming his career "a brilliant one," published an extensive biographical article accompanied by a portrait, proclaiming him "generally perfectly cool and calm in the performance of his duties, and pretty nearly always correct in his decisions," and noting he was "seldom the butt of the merciless joke writer's wrath, or the spite of the disgruntled crank. He has a clear voice and is quick in making his decisions. His long service in the Major League is the best evidence that he has attended to his duties in an honest and fearless manner." That year *Sporting Life* named Bob "the best arbiter in the National League."[8]

FAMILY

As his professional career advanced, so did his private life. At age thirty-four in 1893, well past the age of matrimony for most men, he was prepared to settle down thanks to the financial security of being a Major League umpire. He had previously sought and welcomed the attention of young women but avoided serious romance, the fiscal uncertainty and itinerant lifestyle of a ballplayer and Minor League umpire making thoughts of domestic bliss unrealistic. Since becoming a professional umpire in 1887 he had lived with his parents in London, but after his father died in 1891 Bob moved to St. Thomas, boarding at the Grand Central Hotel.

In the city where he launched his professional career he met and became engaged to Helena Ward, one of the town's "most amiable young ladies."[9] Like Bob, she was second-generation Canadian. Born December 14, 1862, in Devonshire Frenans, England, she immigrated to Ontario in 1870 with her parents, Thomas and Elizabeth (Jackwell) Ward. When and how Bob met Helena are unknown, but it was a whirlwind courtship, as they married during the baseball season. Taking advantage of off days for Washington and Cleveland, Bob raced to St. Thomas after a game in Pittsburgh on September 4 for his wedding. He was raised Presbyterian, but Helena's faith was Church of England, so he acceded to his fiancée's preference and they were wed on September 5 in Trinity Anglican Church.

After a one-day honeymoon Bob left his bride and headed to Cleveland to umpire the Senators-Spiders game on September 7.

There is no inkling as to the reason for the unusually hasty and abrupt wedding, but questions do arise. Besides wondering what the Wards thought of their daughter's hurried wedding—to a baseball umpire, no less—the most obvious question is whether Helena was pregnant. Had she been employed as a chambermaid in the hotel where Bob resided in the off-season?[10] Since Bob left St. Thomas in early April, not to return home until after the season ended on October 15, did the matrimonial timing reflect the expected date of childbirth? Just as there was no announcement of the upcoming marriage in the St. Thomas newspapers, there is no record of a child born to the Emslies. Speculation, however called for, may be groundless and patently unfair to the newlyweds.

In any event, the decision to marry during the season would, in retrospect, be an omen for their marriage. Whether Bob fully explained the profession of umpiring to his prospective bride or she knew much about the demands of his career, Helena would come to know it as a central factor for the rest of her life; her husband would be away five months of the year. Bob celebrated their first anniversary in 1893 umpiring in Philadelphia; save for the 1912 season there would be no opportunity to celebrate their anniversary together for the next thirty years. With the arrival of a daughter, Helen Elizabeth, called Kitty, born October 27, 1895, and son, Robert John, called Jack, born December 17, 1900, Helena would be a single parent much of the year, as Bob was absent during part of the children's school year and all their free time during summers. Once married the couple resided at the Grand Central Hotel, but with Kitty's arrival they moved to a house at 380 ½ Talbot, then after Jack to larger home at 14 Queen.

However Helena dealt with an umpiring husband, for Bob marriage provided invaluable emotional grounding as his career advanced. Still, extended absences with reduced marital and parental relationships was difficult. He surely wrote home, and despite an oft-altered schedule received letters. Twice he was called home during the season for family emergencies. In 1895 he was summoned from Pittsburg on July 13 by the "serious illness" of Helena, then seven months pregnant with their first child; assured the danger had passed, he returned to duty on July 18. Exactly a month later, on August 13, he learned his sister-in-law, Kittie Ward, had died at age twenty-seven; after returning home for funeral services, he was back on the field on August 18. Two years later he hurried home from Philadelphia on July 6 to see his sick year-old daughter; after checking on Kitty and comforting Helena he left for a game in Pittsburgh on July 12.

TURMOIL AND TRAVAIL

From the time Bob called "Play" to start the contest and "Game" to end it he was the "master of the Field," given absolute authority, no player allowed to challenge his judgment save the team captain questioning rule interpretation. Or so the rule book asserted. In fact, the 1890s were sheer hell for umpires, who were besieged by excessive kicking, virulent profanity, and physical violence. Bram Stoker's 1897 novel *Dracula* was a metaphor for the the demonic curse of dispiriting kicking endured by arbiters. Historian Harold Seymour noted the "hoodlumism and dirty playing" was "worse than ever. There was scarcely an issue of the *Sporting News* that did not tell of kicking and wrangling with umpires, fights among players, indecent language, and incidents of rowdyism in general."[11] The reason, poetically put, was simple:

> How does the busy baseball player
> Improve each shining minute?
> He plagues the umpire all the day,
> Because—there's glory in it.[12]

The ethos of the game was partly to blame, baseball allowing managers and players to argue with umpires' decisions without penalty. Moreover, the demise of the Players' League and the American Association, reducing the number of clubs from twenty-four to twelve, not only increased the quality of play, but also made competition keener for available positions, which in turn led to more aggressive play. In 1891 the AA and NL rosters listed 409 players; 1892, with only 180 active players, was "the worst ever" for kicking, umpires "harassed almost to a point beyond endurance, and the efficiency of their work seriously interfered with." Kicking also increased with the arrival of former American Association teams, notably Baltimore, led by John McGraw, who played "dirty ball" and had "the vilest tongue of any ball player." The Orioles were "mean, vicious, ready at any time to maim a rival player" and "the things they would say to an umpire were unbelievably vile." The Orioles' success, thrice finishing first (1894–96) and twice second (1897–98), prompted other teams to adopt the same profane browbeating tactics. As Lynch noted, "Kicking was brought into the league by the American Association players and the other men took it up." With players "warring with every umpire" making "it hell on earth," Tim Murnane thought "the time will soon come when no person above the rank of garrotter can be secured to umpire a game."[13]

Predictably, rowdiness on the field spread to the stands and bleachers. For passionately partisan fans, seated much closer to the field than in modern stadiums—occasionally on the on the field itself—disparaging the umpire as a "thief, robber, thug and a bandylegged blackguard" was "one of the delightfully sweet privileges in a baseball crank's life." The *Brooklyn Daily Eagle*, noting the difference in the behavior of baseball and cricket fans, wondered if "professionalism" was "naturally and inalienably allied to vulgarity of speech and manner."[14]

Umpires also came under assault from newspapers and league owners for questionable decisions, tolerating kicking, and failing to curb rampant "dirty play," such as runners cutting in front of bases and fielders pushing, grabbing, and tripping runners to impede their progress. While challenging the competence and honesty of individual umpires and demonizing the profession was not wholly fair, it being impossible for a single umpire always to make accurate plate and field calls, there was an undeniable problem with the umpiring.

Responsibility for league umpiring fell to Nick Young, who in addition to a variety of administrative duties including setting seasonal schedules and compiling player statistics, was in charge of hiring, paying, and supervising umpires. On the one hand, he gave unqualified support to his beleaguered staff, vowing, "As long as I believe the umpire is acting conscientiously, I will indorse his work." So when St. Louis owner Chris Von der Ahe, a chronic complainer, a month into the 1892 season demanded Young remove Emslie for allegedly costing the Browns a game in Chicago, he received a pointed rebuff: "I have every confidence in Emslie, both as to his honor and ability." On the other hand, Nick understood that he worked for club owners, who regarded umpires less as dedicated professionals than temporary employees. Nothing was done about owners paying the fines umpires imposed on players and encouraging "scrappy" play to attract and incite fans.[15]

Young was not entirely to blame for the alleged poor performance of his umpires or the conspicuous staff turnover. Unable to observe prospective candidates at work, he had to rely on recommendations about their character, not evaluations of their actual performance. But he failed to supervise the umpires, rarely attending ball games other than those in or near Washington, as he had also been employed since 1874 as a clerk auditing war claims in the federal treasury department. Other than a brief preseason meeting to go over rules, Young's instructions to his staff were simply to wear a "neat blue flannel uniform," enforce rules "to the letter," keep their assignments "strictly confidential," practice "absolute sobriety," and immediately advise him as to their hotel upon arrival in each city so he could inform them of changes in assignment and be ready "to jump to some other city by first train." To Nick, Emslie was a model umpire: "So far as looking after the smallest details of his position is concerned, Emslie is the best man on the staff. He comes here before the season opens, give me a list of 12 hotels at which he will stop during the season, receives his instructions and is off, and from that time until the close of the season it is not necessary for me to see him again."[16]

Frequent turnover due to ineffective umpires being released and respected arbiters resigning because of incessant kicking and criticism was more than an administrative problem. Staff continuity signaled competence and resulted in better relations with players and managers, while inexperienced replacements predictably increased kicking.[17] But Young made poor hires, and bad umpires make for bad umpiring. With no means to evaluate the umpiring ability of applicants, Young had to hope his hires panned out. They usually didn't. In addition to an unprecedented number of inexperienced arbiters (among them Dan Campbell,

John Hunt, Fred Jevne, and Billy Long in 1895, and John "Bud" Lally and Horace McFarlan in 1896) he favored signing former Major League players, mistakenly assuming familiarity with the game would lead to "efficient and capable" umpiring.[18] But "nine times out of ten" they were found wanting.[19] Emslie and O'Day were the only Major League players to gain prominence as umpire; none of the other stalwarts Gaffney, Hurst, Lynch, McQuaid and Sheridan—had been ball players.

Bob experienced both rampant kicking and staff instability in his first season. In contrast to 1891, when eight regular umpires and seven players umpired games, in 1892 only twelve of the fifty who called games were regular staff. Of the initial hires, only three—Emslie, Gaffney, and Lynch—finished the season. Bob umpired 148 games, both the most of anyone on the staff and the most in a season in baseball history. Attrition worsened. In 1895 Young, desperate for umpires, lured George "Watch" Barnum out of retirement and pleaded for McQuaid, who left in disgust after 1894, to report for duty "if you are on earth," the unfortunately worded telegram arriving an hour before Jack died of appendicitis on April 16. In the greatest staff turnover to date, only fifteen of fifty-four umpires were regular staff in 1895. Emslie, "whom all hands agree is a first-class umpire," was the only one to work the full season, logging 130 games. The arrival on July 7 of Hank O'Day, Emslie's pitching rival in the American Association who also began umpiring by accident, strengthened the staff and started a lifelong friendship.[20]

TAKING TO THE FIELD

Scheduling assignments in a league that reached from Boston to St. Louis remained a headache for Young and his umpires even when the season was reduced to 132 games in 1893. Teams were given a season-long playing schedule, but umpires received monthly assignments. Geography was a consideration in Emslie's schedule. Perhaps because of convenient rail routes to St. Thomas, he opened the season from 1892 to 1896 in either Louisville or Cincinnati and ended four of five years in Cleveland or Chicago. To minimize travel he usually had regional assignments—three to four weeks in the western portion of the league followed by the same in eastern cities. As one of the league's best umpires, from 1892 to 1899 he worked more games in the east (616), where teams dominated the standings, than in the west (486). In the east he worked most often in New York (118 games) and least in Baltimore; in the west he worked by far the most games in Cincinnati (141) and the fewest in Louisville and Cleveland. Frequent rotation was the norm; Bob typically worked one series, occasionally two, in each city before moving on.

His schedule could change at a moment's notice. Some alterations were not a problem, as when in Brooklyn on July 16, 1894, he was dispatched to umpire the college baseball championship game between Princeton and Yale. He called the game at 12:45, then worked the league game. More troublesome were the sudden reassignments often caused by Young switching umpires from city to city as requested by managers and magnates. Arranging last-minute rail transportation was challenging, and the Pullman Strike, which disrupted rail traffic in the Midwest in June and July 1894, complicated Bob's travel to Cincinnati, Louisville, and Cleveland. He frequently arrived at the ballpark without having had a good night's sleep and more than once ended a game before nine innings to allow a team to catch a train. (The calculated average mileage per club—13,528 miles in 1892—was applicable to umpires as well.)[21]

Unlike his fellow arbiters, whose assignments were voided by partisan owners, Bob rarely missed umpiring in a given city. In 1894 Lynch was not assigned to three cities and assigned only three games in another, and in 1898 he skipped three cities and umpired only two games in a fourth. Meanwhile, from 1892 to 1899, in only four seasons did Bob fail to appear in every city, once missing two, twice only one, the absences due to scheduling needs rather than owners' opposition. New York's Andrew Freedman, especially emphatic about home umpires, did not want Lynch or Hurst but had no problem with Emslie. In 1896 Bob worked twenty-one games at the Polo Grounds while Hurst had six, Lynch three. Bob was missed. He was not assigned to Louisville in 1893, but on April 20, 1894, "by far the best umpire in the League" received "a hearty welcome from the crowd after his absence of a year." Even Browns owner Von der Ahe, known for his dislike of arbiters, complained to Young about "every umpire except Emslie" and was disappointed that Bob, who had given "entire satisfaction in St. Louis and not a single complaint was made," was "only permitted to remain here a few days and was then shipped away."[22]

Increasingly Emslie's schedule turned on being assigned to important games. During the tight 1897 race involving Baltimore, Boston, and New York, he umpired just 32 of 129 games west of the Allegheny mountains, and none after July 28. That, he admitted, "makes it hard upon me. You see, when a club has a hard series, it wants Emslie, and asks that I be assigned there. Now, I appreciate the compliment very much, but I also appreciate the fact that it gives me about all the games between the leading clubs in which the least adverse decision may turn the whole current of the game. Of course, I cannot blame President Young for putting me where he believes it will do the game most good, but it keeps me on the jump all the time."[23]

As pennant races heated up he was requested for crucial series between contenders. In 1893 Boston asked for either Emslie or Lynch, "the best of them all," to call the September 14–16 series in Pittsburgh between the first-place Beaneaters and second-place Pirates; Young assigned Emslie, who umpired in "the fair and even tenor of his way." In 1897 Baltimore requested Emslie and O'Day to work the series with Boston in Baltimore in September that might decide the pennant. Young sent Emslie and Hurst, whose umpiring was "admirable in every way" and received virtually no kicking by players or fans. Bob was then sent on September 29 to Brooklyn for the Bridegrooms' final two games with Boston, the pennant on the line. Surprised to see Emslie, Murnane thought Baltimore pressured Young to send him, hoping for favorable umpiring, but conceded Bob "umpired a good, clean game" as Boston clinched the pennant.[24]

He was also frequently assigned to mentor new umpires, though good intentions sometimes backfired, most egregiously in July 1895. It was reasonable of Young to send Emslie to the Polo Grounds when Baltimore came to New York for the first time since losing the tempestuous initial Temple Cup series to the Giants in 1894, but why he paired him with newcomer Ben Tuthill, an actor who had never before umpired, is a mystery. In his first game, on July 3, Tuthill's incompetence in calling pitches was so manifest Bob replaced him behind the plate after four innings. After the game Young ordered Emslie to Pittsburgh for an important Spiders-Pirates series on July 4 and 5, leaving Tuthill to the mercy of the rowdy Orioles and Giants. Bob's assessment that "it was a shame to leave two such clubs as New York and Baltimore at the mercy of a man so ignorant of the game and the rules and so lacking in perception as Tuthill" was accurate. Enduring "no end of trouble," Tuthill confessed, "I am doing the best I can. I don't know the game." He never umpired again.[25]

ILLNESS AND INJURY

The daily grind of umpiring was exhausting, but Emslie exhibited unusual stamina and dedication, missing remarkably few games. Twice, in 1894 and 1898, heat exhaustion kept him from umpiring the second game of a doubleheader. Surely wrong is the claim that Emslie in 1898 "took one look and fainted" after a wild pitch from Washington's Bill Donovan caught the fingernail on catcher "Deacon Jim" McGuire's middle finger, ripping the flesh from the bone.[26] In 1900 stress, the umpire's constant emotional companion, had physical repercussions. The first two games with the Giants in St. Louis went well, but in the final game of the series, on August 7, his umpiring was "frightfully weird," there being "constant kicking" on decisions both behind the plate and on the bases. It was "an exceedingly hot" day, but something else seemed to be wrong. The wrangling continued throughout the next series with Brooklyn, a Cardinals player saying "there is something the matter with Bob," others thinking "a short rest would do him good." Things were back to normal in the home stand finale, Bob's umpiring deemed "first class," but after moving to Cincinnati he again was "not well," unable to umpire the second game of a twin bill on August 15. The next day, he explained the problem: "I left my neuralgia medicine at the hotel." After taking the medication he returned to form.[27]

While press criticism and verbal assaults from players hurt his ego, Emslie also daily faced the prospect of bodily injury. Most injuries suffered by umpires were too common and inconsequential to warrant mention in newspapers, but as Bob could attest, umpiring behind the bat was injurious to health. His thin wired mask and light, cork-filled chest protector afforded scant protection from batted and pitched balls. Most dangerous were the foul balls, erroneously called "foul tips," that went straight back of the plate. On September 27, 1892, in Baltimore he was knocked out by a foul tip that caught him on the left side of the mask, driving it against his temple. The crowd, which had hissed a couple of his decisions, initially "cheered and applauded" before falling silent as Emslie was carried unconscious off the field. He was unable to umpire the next day, but showed up on September 29 in New York, no doubt with a terrific headache.

Emslie was injury free in 1893 and 1894, but thereafter battered annually. On July 19, 1895, in Cincinnati he was "pretty well shaken up," struck by foul ball on the left jaw so severely the reporter commented his "mask saved him from serious injury." The next year, on September 4, in the second game of a doubleheader in Chicago, he was "nearly knocked out" by a "hard blow" from a foul tip, but he was the lone umpire and shook it off after a few minutes and "pluckily resumed business." In May 1897 he escaped injury after tripping over the Pittsburgh batboy while hustling from home to make a first base call, but suffered two serious injuries later that year. In July a "sharp blow" from a foul tip over his left lung caused him to cough up "a large clot of blood." He was advised to rest for a week or two, but continued umpiring. Then, in Washington on September 7, 1897, a foul tip just below the kneecap "paralyzed" his left leg. Carried from the grounds, taken by carriage to his hotel, and placed under a doctor's care, he was unable to return until September 14. He was replaced during his absence by a local umpire, John Heydler, later president of the National League. In St. Louis on August 8, 1898, a foul struck his right ankle "with terrific force." Unable to walk, he was carried off the field by the Giants' Mike Grady and the Browns' Joe Quinn; he was out for three days and returned on August 12. The most serious injury occurred in Baltimore on September 12, 1899, when a foul tip dislocated his left shoulder. Unable to raise his left arm, certain movements causing the shoulder to "droop," he soldiered on to finish the game. The severity of the injury sidelined him for fourteen days, the longest recuperation of his career; he was unable to return until September 27, then had to work a lengthy, high-scoring doubleheader in Baltimore, the Orioles winning the first game 11–0 and the Phillies the second 15–0.

It was rare to be injured by a pitched ball, but it happened on September 9, 1895, in Baltimore. In the second inning Cy Young uncorked a wild pitch that hit "an obstacle" in front of the plate, bounced up, and hit Emslie in the temple. "Knocked senseless," he was taken to his hotel in a carriage, but was back behind the plate the next day. More unusually, he was even injured making base calls. In Brooklyn on August 4, 1897, while rushing to make a call at third base, he was "severely spiked" in the foot by Brooklyn's catcher, who was backing up the play. After the cut was dressed he "pluckily resumed" umpiring, but after the game his foot was so swollen he couldn't put on his shoe. Fortunately, the next day's game was rained out, and Bob was back to umpiring, a bit gimpy, on August 6. On May 1, 1900, in Brooklyn, a throw to catch a runner at third in the seventh inning hit Emslie "a terrific whack on the knee." Bob "winced and limped a little," but returned behind the plate as the crowd "cheered him." The only time he was hit with a batted ball had a humorous ending. Although "in great pain," the welt on his head "growing to the size of a goose egg" after being skulled by a line drive, he couldn't help laughing as the Giants' Kid Gleason, who caught the ball before it hit the ground, yelled, "What an assist, Bob, what an assist! Between you and me we certainly can play second base."[28]

PRESS BOX PERSPECTIVES

Emslie tolerated the inconvenience of frequent schedule changes and occasional injuries much better than criticism of his work. He understood that old axioms—an umpire is expected to be perfect from the first game and improve thereafter and had done a good job if fans did not remember who called the game afterward—were nonsense. Umpires are not inerrant, and calls on close plays that go against the home team are sure to evoke derisive comments about an arbiter's ability, eyesight, and parentage. He also knew criticism was part of the job and not to be taken personally. And he learned that crowds in various cities regarded umpires differently: fans in Boston and Brooklyn were "more partial" to umpires while rooters in Cincinnati "tested" the nerve of any umpire. He knew, too, that "people in the press box, forty feet from the ground, and on the bleachers" think "they can judge much better than the umpire."[29]

More difficult to stomach than players kicking and spectators hissing was newspaper criticism. Partisanship often trumped fairness in reportage. Bob was told his decisions in Chicago in one game were "gangrened and caused thrills of anguish to carom up and down one's spine," and in another he "could scarcely have made more mistakes if he had been blindfolded." In St. Louis his decisions were deemed "so rank that they were really laughable," and a Pittsburgh reporter, after admitting Emslie was "looked upon as the king of umpires," said his work "during the past few days has been awful." Others were more evenhanded, saying Bob was "rather rank in his decisions but he divided his favors fairly well." Reporters knew field and baserunning decisions were inherently difficult to make when working behind the plate, but Emslie was "roasted" for "an exhibition of incompetency" in calling a runner safe at second when "the runner was out by fully six feet" and for failing to see a runner impeded, and accused of being "manifestly unfair" in deciding a fly ball had been trapped instead of caught.[30]

Partisan reportage invariably followed crucial calls against the home team. The *St. Louis Globe-Democrat*, allowing Emslie was "one of the few umpires who is regarded as thoroughly competent," blasted him for "as sorry an exhibition of umpiring as has ever been seen at Sportsman's Park," saying he could "conscientiously have given the home club the benefit of a put-out at the plate in the close play of the ninth inning. It was a play in which a decision either way would have been justified." That reportage turned on the eye of the beholder was starkly illustrated 1896 in St. Louis when Emslie forfeited a game to Baltimore. The *Globe-Democrat* headline screamed, "Robbed by the Umpire. Emslie Gave the Game to the Baltimores," while the *St. Louis Post-Dispatch* said the forfeit was "properly decided."[31]

Critical press commentary, invariably on decisions against the home team, demoralized umpires and created negative views of umpires in the minds of spectators and the general public. Disturbed by partisan and unfair reporting, in 1896 Bob spoke out publicly for the only time in his career about reporters having "the power to make it pleasant or disagreeable for us by their stories." In a *Sporting Life* column titled "Ideas of R. Emslie," he blamed the scribe who, siding with players, "prints false excuses and holds the umpire up to ridicule for doing his duty," for being "largely responsible for the commotion in the stands and for unruliness on the field. If we could only have baseball reporters whose partisanship was mild enough to treat all alike the game would be greatly benefited in the end."[32]

If reporters were at times critical of Emslie's work, they were more often fulsome in praising it, even welcoming his appearance. "The presence of Professor Emslie was enjoyed by both players and public. There was no wrangling and the game went off with the best of feeling to the delight of every lover of the sport." "Bob is a top-notcher in the umpire line, and the local people should appreciate the fact that he is kept in the city, thereby insuring impartial and enjoyable contests." "One cause for congratulation is that the games will be umpired by Emslie." The *Post-Dispatch* tempered the comment that Bob was "human, and liable to err" by admitting "as a matter of fact, he errs less than most umpires," and the *New York Tribune*, while intimating Emslie may have made a mistake "as all umpires are prone to do at times," said his work "has always been of the best sort."[33]

Reporters sometimes even defended Bob's decisions. When Washington fans erupted on August 9, 1892, after he called out Tommy Dowd for over-sliding second base, the local paper deemed it "entirely uncalled for" as the decision was "perfectly proper," saying, "It's a very one-sided judgment that could find fault with umpire Emslie's work." When on June 19, 1897, he called the Senators' Charlie Reilly out at second while he was trying to stretch a single into a double and then threw him out of the game for arguing, the Washington press condemned both Reilly's "unreasonable and wholly unnecessary abuse" and the "hisses and groans" of the spectators, asserting that Emslie's decision was "correct" as he was "on the spot and had a clearer sight than the runner or the spectators."[34]

Most conspicuously and frequently, the press lauded his integrity. Impartiality and objectivity are goals of all umpires, but Emslie's work on September 11, 1893, so impressed Cleveland sportswriter Elmer E. Bates that he noted Bob had a "succession of hair breadth decisions to give, but every one was absolutely fair and impartial." To the *Sporting News* "there is no more conscientious umpire in the business than Emslie and if he makes a mistake it is of the head and not of the heart." Even Cincinnati sports editor Harry Welden, quick to blame umpires for Reds defeats, acknowledged “nobody has ever questioned Umpire Emslie’s integrity” as he “has always had the reputation of being honest and impartial.” Cleveland noted that “Emslie has the reputation of being one of the fairest umpire who ever lived, and the most chronic kickers in the League seldom find fault with him, even when he makes a glaring mistake, for they know he means to be fair.” The Washington press, too, calling Emslie a “star umpire,” thought “lovers of the game should not be too severe when his judgment does not meet their approval.”[35]

While many an umpire succumbed to the pressure exerted by crowds in home town games, to veteran baseball writer O. P. Caylor, “in correctness of decisions and impartiality to home and visiting teams Emslie is the best umpire in the League.” “No one,” agreed Jacob Morse of the *Boston Herald*, “will accuse him of being a home umpire”; he considered it the “highest compliment to Emslie’s fairness that he is taken to task by the partisans.” The backhanded compliment that Emslie was “a mighty good man on the road but too fair for home games” spoke to the no-win lot of the umpire. While the *Philadelphia Times* welcomed Emslie because he “cannot be accused of being a home umpire,” the *Cincinnati Enquirer* thought it “unfair” for the Reds to have him so often umpire home games given his “reputation of being the best umpire for visiting teams on the league staff. League teams would rather have Emslie away from home than any other umpire. They know that they will get an even break and possibly the best of it. Emslie, in his efforts to prove that he is not an ‘at home’ umpire, leans the other way and gives the home team the worst of it.”[36]

ENFORCING THE RULES

Emslie’s basic job was to enforce the rules of the game. Several rule changes made his job easier. With the infield fly rule he no longer had to decide whether fielders deliberately dropped a ball to make a double play, and balks were called if the pitcher made any motion after being set other than delivering the pitch. Requiring catchers to stand within ten feet of the plate made it easier to judge pitches, and redesigning home plate from a twelve-inch square with one corner pointing toward the pitcher to a seventeen-inch square with the straight side facing the pitcher, increasing the width of the strike zone by forty-two percent, made calling pitches—his most difficult task and the source of most arguments—much easier. Umpires were instructed "to give corners of the plate" to pitchers, but Bob drew on his experience in the box: "They [umpires] made me split the plate when I pitched, and I do to them as I was done." While invariably criticized from time to time, he was by 1896 regarded as "without a peer as the caller of balls and strikes"—an accurate assessment, as only three of twenty-six ejections from 1892 to 1900 came on disputed pitch calls.[37]

Two rules caused him difficulty. The first was in extending the pitching distance of sixty feet six inches in 1893, when a sixteen-by-four-inch white rubber pitcher's plate replaced the box. The white line of the box was clearly visible, but it was now impossible to see from behind the bat if pitchers were, as frequently charged, illegally delivering pitches several feet in front of the ground-level "rubber." Increasing the size of the slab in 1895 to twenty-four-by-six helped, but the problem was not resolved until the evolution of a raised mound, standardized at a maximum height of fifteen inches in 1903. Emslie's greatest trouble remained enforcing the rule against coaches giving directions to players other than base runners. Emslie admitted, "I cannot tell, for the life of me, what the coach is doing" because when "the cunning fellow held his hand to his mouth I do not hear a word."[38]

Emslie quickly became known for his command of the rule book, which made his umpiring "in striking and superior contrast" to the other umpires in terms of strictly enforcing the rules. On July 17, 1894, in Brooklyn, with Washington leading the Bridegrooms 3–2, the home team loaded the bases with one out. Tommy Corcoran then grounded to Nationals pitcher Win Mercer, who threw to catcher Deacon McGuire for a force out, who then threw to first base to retire Corcoran. But the ball hit Corcoran, who was running on the grass on the inside of the base path, on the right shoulder and then bounced into right field, letting two runners and Corcoran score to give Brooklyn the lead. When Bob called out Corcoran for interfering with the throw, ending the inning and negating the three runs, the fans howled, the Bridegrooms argued, and after the game Dave Foutz berated Emslie for "a clear case of robbery." Emslie replied, "Corcoran ran out of the line and I could do nothing else but call him out." The press, though charging that Emslie had "stretched a point" by strictly interpreting the rule, agreed that it was "a just decision." The next month, on August 12, Washington's Jim "Deacon" McGuire threw his bat to the ground in disgust at Emslie's strike call, whereupon Philadelphia's hurler threw a pitch over the plate before McGuire got back in the batter's box. Emslie called, "Striker is out!" as McGuire had failed to call time out. McGuire got no sympathy from his teammates or manager, Gus Schmelz, who said Bob's call was "perfectly right."

A stickler for rules, he steadfastly enforced them to the letter even when it meant countering accepted practice. On July 26, 1895, Cleveland's Cy Young grounded to short to start a double play, but runner George Tebeau blocked the throw to first. He had done nothing unusual, but Bob called Young out because of Tebeau's interference. Cleveland kicked, not to challenge interference, but to protest the application of a rule routinely ignored. Although the decision went against the Spiders, when Bob appeared on the field the next day, fans applauded in recognition of his fairness and adherence to the rules. He was no less assiduous in applying new rules, even at critical moments. On May 24, 1899, Louisville scored two runs to tie Brooklyn 5–5 and had a runner at third. Superbas manager Ned Hanlon ordered pitcher Joe Yeager to walk the Colonels' best hitter, Fred Clarke. When Brooklyn's catcher stepped out of the box to take the wide pitch, Emslie called a balk, thereby allowing the winning run to score from third. The Brooklyn paper noted "a rather closely drawn interpretation of the new balk rule," and the Louisville paper commented, "Very few umpires would have had the nerve to make that decision in the ninth inning."[39] Later that season he used common sense in applying the balk rule. On August 15 Giants pitcher Ed Doheny stopped in mid-delivery when his cap slipped over his eyes. Emslie did not call the obvious balk, and the Louisville team did not object.

With rules rapidly evolving in detail and application, Emslie sometimes had to rely on judgment. In Cincinnati on April 27, 1893, with the Reds' Henry "Farmer" Vaughn on third and George Henry on first, Charlie Duffee grounded to Chicago pitcher Gus McGinnis, who threw to third, trying to catch Vaughn off the bag. As Vaughn evaded three Colts in a rundown between third and home, Henry and Durfee circled the bases, passing Vaughn. Before they reached the plate Vaughn was tagged out. Assessing the unusual situation, Emslie decided both runners had scored, whereupon Anson and the Colts launched a "vigorous protest," arguing that Henry and Dufee should have been out for passing a base runner. In a rare postgame interview Emslie said he "never saw or heard of a play like that" and admitted he "cannot cite any rule in support of my decision, because the rules do not cover that point. It is one of those cases where an umpire has to use his own judgment. That is what I did today. I think I am right, but I may be wrong." He wrote to Young describing the play and urging the league to make a rule covering situation. Young decided Bob was "absolutely right" in thinking Vaughn, once put out, was not a base runner.[40] (If Vaughn had not been tagged out, instead returning safely to third, Henry and Durfee would have been declared out for passing a base runner.)

The judgment call that caused Emslie the most grief was terminating a game before nine innings had been played. Rules provided for calling games on account of rain after a thirty-minute delay but offered no guidelines for when it was too dark to continue effective play. With games typically beginning at three-thirty or four o'clock and generally ending in under two hours, both teams usually agreed when there was insufficient daylight to continue. But if a cancellation would affect the outcome of the game, disagreement ensued. (With no outdoor lights until the mid-1930s, terminating games on account of darkness was not an infrequent occurrence; in 1894 twenty-two games were so ended.)

Bob's worst encounter with a darkness call came in St. Louis on July 24, 1896. With dusk descending the Browns tied the score 8–8 in the bottom of the twelfth with none out. Baltimore, to prevent a possible winning tally, delayed play, hoping Emslie would call it on account of darkness—pitcher Bill Hoffer even threw the ball into the outfield, where it was "lost" for a time. The pace quickened when Emslie pulled out his watch, threatening to forfeit the game to St Louis. The Browns failed to score, and when Baltimore came to bat in the top of the thirteenth, St. Louis flagrantly stalled as darkness fell, deliberately misplaying balls and allowing the Orioles to plate seven runs to lead 15–8. When Browns outfielder Joe Sullivan made no effort to catch a fly ball that fell near him,

Emslie had enough of the nonsense, forfeiting the game to Baltimore 9–0. The *St. Louis Post-Dispatch* declared that in forfeiting the game, Emslie "upheld his dignity and that of the game when the Browns delayed matters." Less charitably, Browns owner Chris Von der Ahe protested the game and asked that another umpire be sent to replace Emslie. Young appropriately rejected both requests.

Not all rules are book rules. On September 29, 1900, at Pittsburgh's Exposition Park, Emslie encountered time-honored, if controversial, chicanery. With cross-state Philadelphia notorious for using binoculars and electronic signals to relay pitching signs to batters, Pittsburgh decided to engage in sign thievery.[41] In the eighth inning, with the score tied 1–1, Cincinnati shortstop Tommy Corcoran, who had earlier exposed Philadelphia's "signal bureau," asked Bob to investigate someone behind the center-field fence stealing the catcher's signs. Emslie refused, since sign stealing was not against the rules, but during the confab Reds right fielder Phil Geier scaled the fence and threw over an iron rod bent sharply at one end to Corcoran, who gave it to Emslie. Corcoran claimed someone behind the fence used binoculars to see the catcher's signals and then inserted the rod through a hole in the center of a large letter *O* in an advertisement, the bent end acting like the hour hand of a clock to identify the kind of pitch to be delivered—fast ball twelve o'clock, in-curve three, out-curve nine. After examining the rod Emslie smiled, then tossed it toward the Reds bench and bade the game go on. After the game Pirates owner Barney Dreyfuss "most emphatically denied" any knowledge of a sign-stealing scheme, but said the fence panel in question would be removed. "Those who should know" said that the device, operated by "an ex-ball player" paid $5 a game, was counterproductive, as the Pirates had batted poorly in losing three of four games to the Reds.

A MATTER OF STYLE

Making accurate calls and applying rules is the core of umpiring, but how an umpire executes his duties determines success. Emslie's personality and the manner in which he discharged on-field duties enabled him to control the game, thereby earning the respect of players and managers, praise from the press, and the admiration of league officials. Having been a Major League pitcher helped establish his credibility, and he sometimes played catch with players during lulls. On one such occasion in 1893 Emslie began throwing to Pirates third baseman Denny Lyons, who jumped out of the way as Bob's throws "came in too hot." As the ball rolled toward the bleachers Connie Mack winked at Emslie in recognition of his days pitching with Baltimore.[42]

His mechanics were first-rate. Players and spectators alike appreciated that he announced decisions quickly and decisively with the "clearest voice" of any umpire, hustled to be "always near to a base when a close play occurs," and anticipated plays. But as the lone umpire he couldn't see everything. In the eighth inning on September 26, 1896, while Cleveland players argued that Louisville's Charlie Dexter cut second base while running to third, the Spiders' Jesse Burkett pushed a smiling Dexter off the bag, Chippy McGarr touching him with the ball. Emslie did not see Burkett's trick so called Dexter out, which started an argument with Louisville.[43]

Most important was Bob's ability to run the game, to keep control of the players and himself. It was not easy to maintain composure and impartiality in the face of vile verbal assaults on his integrity and person, not to let anger influence the next decision or carry to the next inning, let alone the next game. Barnum, who quit in 1895, believed "no matter how much an umpire strives to be impartial, he will chafe under the eternal useless kicking of a team that makes life miserable for him from the time the call of 'play ball' is given until the finish." Sportswriter J. A. Williams agreed, thinking it "folly" for anyone to believe the "badgering" an umpire had to take "doesn't interfere with his judgment and injure his work." Since challenging an umpire's decision meant implicitly challenging his integrity or judgment, Henry Chadwick thought "every umpire is going to react negatively to charges of dishonesty or stupidity." Even Bob's cocksure colleague Bill Klem admitted, "Most baseball fans feel that these verbal and physical public humiliations go in one ear and out the other. Well, they don't. They go in one ear and go straight to the nervous system, eating away coordination, self-confidence and self-respect."[44]

Emslie did not have a porous epidermis or rabbit ears and understood, as Young admonished, "It is not necessary that you should hear every word that is spoken by players in the heat of a contest, unless it is vulgar, insulting or directed to or intended for your ear." However, he could not help but take the barbs personally at times, especially those questioning his integrity. During an argument in Washington on July 30, 1897, Baltimore's Jake Stenzel called the Senators' Jack Reilly a liar. Thinking the word was meant for him, Emslie ejected Stenzel, paying no heed to Stenzel's explanation.

Players' kicking was expected, but the gratuitous criticism from fans was harder to take. In a rare breach of decorum Bob once lost his cool with a spectator. When a fan in St. Louis, after roasting Emslie for a base call, added he was "unfair" and afraid to call strikes on Orioles pitcher Bill Hoffer, Bob lost his temper, turned around, shook his fist at the fan and yelled, "No, I am not and I'm not afraid to fight you after the game." What bothered him most was captains approaching him "with the most nonsensical claims on points they know to be absurd. They often do this with the hope that finally they will work a decision their way, but I question if it does any good. There would not be half the trouble in the games if the umpire wasn't bothered a great deal with things brought up without any cause."[45]

It is easy to see why Bob was annoyed, if not angry, by the constant bickering, much of it obscenely delivered, but he was able to control himself and the game because of his unshakable belief that an umpire's success depended on "perfect fearlessness in rendering a decision believed to be right, and, having rendered it, to let it be final and irrevocable." Cleveland's Patsy Tebeau, pilot of one of the rowdiest teams in the league, said Emslie, who "seldom makes a mistake," silenced kickers with, "That's the way I saw the play; I'm doing the best I can." Emslie was not prone to second-guessing, but sometimes wondered if he had missed the call, as in St. Louis on July 20, 1899. In a 2–2 tie with Jess Burkett on first, Boston third baseman Jimmy Collins gloved the Perfectos' Cupid Child's airborne bunt "about three inches above the grass" and fired to first to double off Burkett. But Emslie ruled the ball caught on the first bounce and so ruled out only Child. As so often happens after a crucial play, the next batter singled, scoring Burkett with the winning run. After the game Collins said he was willing to sign an affidavit that he had caught the ball cleanly while Bob, apparently troubled by the call, left without going to the dressing room.[46]

That Emslie had fewer reported confrontations than other umpires was due to his style of umpiring. With congruence of temperament and task, for Bob the rule forbidding players or coaches to "address him or question his decisions," allowing team captains alone to challenge rules interpretations, was not an absolute. The antithesis of egotistical, confrontational autocrats like Lynch and Hurst, Emslie earned the respect of players with his even-tempered, diplomatic style, a central component of which was discretion, distinguishing spontaneous protest and profanity from chronic carping. He had learned being red-assed was neither practical nor purposeful, the goal being to diminish antagonism, not provoke it. Understanding human nature, he sized up the personalities of players and managers, knowing the ones who needed to be put down promptly or ejected and those who warranted patience. Thus, knowing the "excitable temperament" of Lou Sockalexis, Emslie was commended for "excellent judgment" in not ejecting him when Cleveland's rookie outfielder became "obnoxiously aggressive."[47]

While Emslie was tolerant to a degree of profanity and allowed players to let off steam, "at no time did he permit the players to become openly offensive or ridicule him or his decisions." Cleveland sports writer Elmer Bates thought Emslie earned the respect of players and fans by umpiring "with just enough dignity not to appear arrogant and tyrannical," and *Sporting Life* said his career had been "comparatively smooth" because Bob "always had a listening ear to a complaint; he never turned away from a player as abruptly as he would turn from a whining dog. But though he listened he wouldn't argue the matter. Like a gentleman, he heard the objection and let the game proceed. And isn't there a deal of good sense in this line of conduct?" The *Washington Star* concurred Emslie was "highly esteemed" because he "understands the game in all the intricacies, maintains good order on the field, is quick in his decisions, decides plays as he sees them, and maintains his official dignity firmly, yet not offensively."[48]

Bob's diplomatic style of maintaining control included using a firm statement, stern look, authoritative gesture, or disarming quip to prevent confrontations. Baltimore's Wilbert Robinson's abuse ended when Bob walked over to the bench and said "something in a low tone." When Washington's Bill Joyce came up to argue, violating the rule that only team captains could approach an umpire, he abruptly wheeled about and headed to the bench after Emslie, in "mild and dulcet tones," asked, "Why, Billy, are you the captain of the club?" When Louisville rookie Fred Clarke turned around to glare at Emslie over a strike call, Bob taught the feisty rookie proper protocol. His query, "Don't you think you had better turn around and look straight ahead young man?" prompted a meek "Yes, sir." After Bob raised his hand with fingers outstretched, signaling a $5 fine, Chicago's Bill Everitt, who had protested a called strike "by jumping in the air, kicking out his heels, and wildly swinging his hat at the zenith," silently returned to the batter's box. And many were the times he ended arguments by pulling out his watch, threatening to forfeit the game. Sometimes a quip diffused a confrontation. When Cap Anson disputed a call, saying, "You don't say so," Emslie replied, "I do say so." To Anson's response, "But I don't," Bob's put-down, "How brainy and intellectual," sent Cap sheepishly away. Bob also used humor to counter criticism from the stands. When an obnoxious fan at the Polo Grounds yelled, "You're a robber and I know it!" Emslie turned around and said, "If you've got any money on this game and you lose it, come and see me and I'll make your loss good," the clever remark applauded by spectators as the fan slunk away.[49]

There were, of course, limits. Emslie refused to "stand any nonsense," at times becoming "nawsty when vexed." In Baltimore on June 18, 1894, Orioles pitcher John "Sadie" McMahon, preparing to pitch, discovered the ball had been cut, allegedly by Boston pitcher Charles "Kid" Nichols. Emslie threw him a new ball, which Sadie promptly rubbed in the dirt. Bob threw him the last new game ball, warning him not to dirty it again, since the rules specifically prohibited discoloring the ball with dirt and required pitchers to use a new ball. Petulant, McMahon threw a wild pitch—over the grandstand and out of the park. Sadie, too, left the field, $25 poorer.

Although "one of the most popular umpires in the League," Emslie inevitably had his share of rip-roaring encounters with players and managers. Most troublesome were the league's four notorious kickers: Cleveland player-manager Patsy Tebeau; John McGraw, Baltimore's fiery, foul-mouthed third baseman; New York's combustible "Dirty Jack" Doyle; and Chicago's cantankerous player-manager Adrian "Cap" Anson.

Of Anson's quibbling and quarrelling there was no end. On September 18, 1895, in Pittsburgh, the Pirates claimed Chicago left fielder George Decker had a glove larger than allowed. When Emslie called him in to show the glove, Anson told George to stay put. Even after Bob threatened to fine Decker, Anson ordered him not to come in. Emslie reluctantly went out to left field and found the glove legal, but Cap's petulance cost his player $25.

Anson's truculence was again on display in 1896. Kicking throughout the first game of a doubleheader on September 4, he was finally ejected after consigning Emslie "to a place where snow shoes are not the vogue." Anson defiantly took a seat on the Colts' bench, refusing to leave the field until Bob had a policeman escort him to a seat in the grandstand. Emslie smiled at the mulish behavior, but Cap did not return the grin and refused to speak to Bob during the second game. Later that month Anson pressed Emslie's patience to the limit in a bizarre display of managerial obstinance. Darkness approached on September 15 in Cleveland as the Spiders came to bat in the bottom of the ninth, trailing Chicago 6–3. When, after two outs, Cleveland scored twice and had the potentially tying run at third, Anson argued it was too dark to continue. Emslie demurred, whereupon Anson instructed the entire Chicago team to lie down on the diamond while he argued. Emslie ordered the Colts to return to their positions, but on Anson's command they did not do so "for fully five minutes." When Bob pulled out his watch and threatened to forfeit the game, Anson signaled his men to return to their positions. After play resumed the Spiders scored the tying run and had the winning run on third, whereupon Anson signaled the Colts to take another nap on the infield while he demanded Emslie call the game. Again to avoid forfeiture Anson sent his players back to their positions, but told Herbert "Buttons" Briggs not to pitch to the batter, threatening to fine him $1,000 if he threw the ball over the plate. After Briggs tossed two balls "ten feet wide," Emslie, exasperated by Anson's intention of leisurely walking batters until darkness descended, called the game a 6–6 tie. His patience had allowed the game to proceed to an equitable ending, but *Sporting Life* thought he should have received "a sharp scolding" for not forfeiting the game to Cleveland in light of Anson's delaying tactics.[50]

The next year Anson's antics endangered a win. On August 30, 1897, at the Polo Grounds, Chicago led 7–5 when in the top of the ninth Anson, hoping to preserve the victory, argued it was too dark to continue play. When Emslie ordered that the game go on, Cap shook his hand in Bob's face and called him "a name too vile to appear in print," for which he was fined $25 and ejected. Chicago then scored three runs to lead 10–5, but when New York came to bat in the bottom of the ninth the Colts had only eight players, Decker having replaced Anson at first base. Just as Bob was about to forfeit the game to the Giants, pitcher Danny Friend, who had already showered and dressed, rushed out of the clubhouse to left field wearing his Colts cap and light gray bathrobe buttoned down the front to conceal his civilian clothes. Spectators roared at the sight of him waddling out to left, one fan exclaiming, "It's a woman!" Not amused, Giants manager Bill Joyce protested Friend was ineligible to play as he was not in uniform. Emslie, nonplussed, replied, "How can I decide that Friend has no uniform on? Do you want me to search him?" When Joyce urged him to "go out there and look," Bob declined, no doubt recalling that the rules did not specify what constituted a uniform. Emslie ordered the game to continue, but after two outs Joyce threatened to lodge a formal a protest and ordered the next Giants batter not to hit. Faced with the prospect of a stalemate Emslie called the game on account of darkness, the score reverting back to the eighth inning and a 7–5 Chicago victory, whereupon Anson triumphantly exclaimed, "I carried my point! I wanted you to call the game and I made you do it." The next day Joyce said Bob was correct in ignoring Friend's attire since the rules did not "cover such a point." The next year the rules stipulated uniforms "shall conform in color and style."[51]

Worse than Anson's caviling were nasty encounters with Jack Doyle, whose proclivity for feuding earned him the nickname Dirty Jack. In 1894 when Doyle stepped out of the batter's box after the pitcher had begun his motion, Emslie appropriately calling a third strike when the pitch crossed the plate, Jack went ballistic, throwing his bat at Bob's feet and unleashing a "series of foul names unfit for publication." Bob responded to the "scorching effects of Doyle's diatribe" with a fine of $25 and ejection. In the Giants clubhouse after the game, used by umpires as a dressing room, Doyle spewed incendiary invective, but Emslie "wisely refrained from making any retort."[52] Worse still were Doyle's personal comments.

Bob Emslie took the field self-assured save for his acute sensitivity about wearing a toupee. Vanity aside, since it was commonplace for men in the late nineteenth century to regard hair loss as a sign of decreased manliness, by the mid-1890s Bob had donned a reddish-brown hairpiece, it being understandable for an authority figure like an umpire to hide baldness. Contrary to the belief that his hair loss was due to nerves or the constant stress of umpiring, the premature baldness was genetic—he had begun to lose hair while pitching for Baltimore in 1885.[53]

Even amid the execrable rowdiness of the 1890s there is no evidence Emslie was nicknamed "Wig," as is often claimed and inappropriately noted on his plaque in the Canadian Baseball Hall of Fame, and comments about his hairpiece were rare. An offhand reference in the *Cincinnati Enquirer* on May 10, 1896, to "bald-headed Bob" is the first known newspaper mention of his condition. In early March 1897 the *Boston Globe* felt it necessary to explain the racially disparaging comment that should Lou Sockalexis be overcome by "aboriginal instincts" it would be "disappointingly easy to scalp at least one umpire—Bob Emslie" by saying "for the benefit of those who may not know it" the Cleveland rookie "is an Indian and Emslie wears a wig." Later that year the *Baltimore Sun* used the only known mention of "Bob 'Wig' Emslie" in reporting a disparaging comment by Jack Doyle. Doyle had said "a good deal" without Bob taking offense until suggesting he get "a hair restorer," a comment that resulted in Jack being escorted from the grounds by a policeman. The most embarrassing incident occurred in 1898 when Doyle, angered by being called out, grabbed Emslie's hairpiece and ran off with it. Showing remarkable forbearance, Bob soaked him $20 without ejection; Jack said, "It was worth the laughs."[54]

More worrisome than words was the prospect of physical harm. Being the target of cushions, bottles, and other objects thrown by disgruntled spectators was disconcerting enough, as in Cleveland on May 26, 1894, when a leather seat cushion hit Emslie in the face. But requiring police protection when angry fans surged onto the field after the game was unnerving. Emslie's first encounter with postgame mobbing came in Cincinnati on May 9, 1896. With the score tied in the bottom of the tenth inning, the Reds pitcher tried to pick Brooklyn's Jennings off third, but Hughie ran into third baseman Charlie Irwin, knocking him to the ground, and scored the winning run as the ball rolled away. Fans, irate that Emslie had not called Jennings out for "dirty ball," poured onto the field intent on revenge. Harm was prevented by club-wielding policemen escorting the besieged umpire from the field.[55]

The most dangerous episode occurred in Brooklyn on September 7, 1899, at Brooklyn's Washington Park, already noxious from Gowanus Canal stench and nearby factory smoke.[56] With Brooklyn trailing Boston 2–1 in the bottom of the ninth, Bob called out the Superbas Tom Daly in a close play at home to end the game (the decision was termed "a bad call" by New York papers and "unquestionably correct" by Boston's.) As fans, incited by Brooklyn captain Joe Kelley's vehement protest, swarmed from the stands, Bob calmly walked to the Superbas bench to give the game ball to manager Ned Hanlon as the "bellowing throng" pelted him with vile words and "all sorts of missiles" including stones, handfuls of dirt, and pieces of wood. When one of the "ruffians" slapped him in the face, Bob grabbed the assailant by the collar and with "a swift uppercut" knocked him flat on his back. Further violence was averted when Daly and Bill Dahlen rushed to Bob's aid, swinging their bats "in a vigorous manner" to ward off the irate fans, and Brooklyn owner Charles Ebbets escorted the umpires off the field.

Emslie and his partner, Frank Dwyer, changed clothes in the safety of the dressing room, then defiantly refused the offer of a carriage to take them to their hotel and started walking up Third Avenue toward the elevated train station on Fifth Avenue. Escorted by police and Ebbets, the umpires fearlessly proceeded up the street as "fully a thousand" vengeful fans hurled "every kind of epithet" and debris, including stones. Upon reaching the station, Bob and Frank went up to the platform to await the next train as Ebbets and police blocked the howling mob at the foot of the stairs. When a train carried the umpires away, the crowd dispersed, "breathing vengeance against Emslie" when he next appeared on the field. The next day fifty bluecoats lined up in front of the grandstand and bleachers to ensure order, but their only function was to return foul balls. When Emslie and Dwyer nonchalantly walked onto the field, a few denizens of the bleaches "hissed" while the majority of the crowd of about seven thousand burst into "generous applause." Taken aback by the unexpected greeting, Emslie acknowledged the tribute by doffing his cap to the crowd.

Emslie's confidence had been bolstered by an unexpected visitor to the umpires' dressing room prior to the game. Ex-heavyweight boxing champion Jim Corbett, who had witnessed the brawl from a box behind the Brooklyn dugout, shook Bob's hand and congratulated him on the punch that flattened his assailant. "Finest job I ever saw done," said Gentleman Jim. The pugilist's compliment pleased Bob, but he admitted "what gave me the greatest satisfaction was the 'hand' I received the afternoon following the riot, when I went out to open the game. It was the first applause I had ever received and I appreciated it." It also started a lifelong friendship. Until his death in 1933 Corbett, who lived in Bayside, Queens, met up with Emslie whenever he was in New York or Brooklyn. (Did Bob umpiring against Corbett's younger brother ever come up?)[57]

The most "disgraceful scene" in Brooklyn baseball would have been much worse had not Daly and Dahlen protected Emslie and Ebbets escorted him off the field to the train station. The *Brooklyn Times* lauded Ebbets for defending the umpires and Emslie, "an old, experienced and excellent" umpire, for showing "no fear" in facing the angry crowd "with dauntless courage."[58] But after the game Ebbets, while saying he had "confidence in Emslie and believed him to be honest" and the "attack is to be deplored," there being "no use injuring the umpire for a mistake," said "I cannot blame the public for its action" because "it shows they are with the team and want the pennant to come here." Hanlon, though also condemning the assault, said "an umpire is sometimes to blame for what he gets," noting he had warned Emslie "several times against just such decisions [against the home team] at critical points, but he makes them."[59]

The comments of Brooklyn's owner and manager revealed they, and their counterparts in every other club, were largely responsible for the kicking and unruly fan behavior that had produced declining attendance and increasingly poor umpiring due to staff instability. Something had to be done.[60]

10

Standing the Gaff

It was a sunny day in spring;
The warbling birds were all a-wing;
An April sky of azure hue
Enchanted the fanatic's view,
And sultry was the atmosphere
Upon the first game of the year.
Upon the field His Umps appeared,
And, lo! the throng arose and cheered,
While all around the fife and drums
Played "Hail! The conquering
    Hero Comes."

—Grantland Rice, "The Ump's Midwinter Dream"

Attendance overall had risen since 1892 with the addition of four teams, but by 1895 fans increasingly stayed away. To Henry Chadwick, the "painfully conspicuous Hoodlumism—blackguard language; low cunning tricks, unworthy of manly players; brutal assaults on umpire and players; that nuisance of our ball field, 'kicking,' and the dishonorable methods comprised in the term 'dirty ball playing'"—was responsible for the "decided falling off in the attendance of the best class of patrons." The esteemed sportswriter blamed umpires for "moral cowardice" in not enforcing rules against kicking, but knew "the real cause" of indecisive umpiring was the failure of club owners "to do their duty." Faced with declining attendance, on-field turmoil, and poor umpiring marked by staff turnover, the owners finally overcame self-interest, personal antagonisms, and political squabbles to take steps to address the problems.[1]

FINES AND EJECTIONS

Imposing fines and removing players from the game have ever been the umpire's ultimate means of controlling behavior. In 1892 Emslie could impose fines of $5 to $25, but could not eject players except for continued repetition of the offense. Where other umpires were quick to fine, Bob fined the least, partly because it had no effect since all the clubs except Boston paid players' fines. He knew, too, that players inadvertently said harsh things in the heat of competition and when hot weather "turns the northeast into a blast furnace," players and spectators "turn ugly. They take the life out of the umpires and cause miscues. The more the players' quarrel, the worse it is for the umpire. He is cursed from the first inning to the last because everybody is out of sorts." Still, he did not hesitate to levy fines when warranted and was scrupulously impartial in doing so. Pittsburgh's venerable Connie Mack, after being soaked $5 for cussing Emslie from the coach's line, said Bob was "too good a friend of mine" to report the fine. He was mistaken; the fine was extracted.[2]

To curb kicking the owners increased the fine scale in 1894. Players other than captains who argued would be fined $10, those ejected $25, and anyone using "vulgar, indecent or other improper conduct or language" $25 to $100. The stipulation that umpires who failed to enforce the anti-kicking rules would be fined $10 for the first offense and $25 for the second was an empty gesture, since punitive action required supporting affidavits from a team captain and two reputable witnesses. Bob ignored Young's order to eliminate kicking or risk being dismissed, knowing strict enforcement of the rules would simply create more antagonism without support from club owners. By mid-season 1895, he alone had not fined a player; in 1897, a tumultuous year for kicking, Lynch and Sheridan fined the most, Bob the least.

With higher fines failing to curb kicking and the "disgraceful scenes" in 1895 "worse than ever before known in league history," the magnates for the first time consulted with umpires about the problem. At the December league meeting Emslie, Tim Hurst, and Tom Lynch testified that fining didn't work because umpires were loath to impose heavy fines and the money did not come from players' pockets. Struck by Bob's report about fine reimbursement by fans—Baltimore's Joe Kelley once told him "You may fine me much as you please, all my fines are paid, and not by me or the club"—the owners decided to abolish fining in favor of ejecting players after one warning.[3] Emslie had no illusions about the efficacy of expelling players from the game. He knew firsthand how the loss of a player could hurt a team and believed ejections caused far more animosity than fines. After his first ejection on July 21, 1892, expelling the Browns' Jack Crooks for "abusive language," Bob did not toss any the next year, but as the kicking and verbal abuse wore thin, his ejections increased; by the decade's end he had posted thirty-five ejections.[4]

COMPENSATION

Increased kicking raised the issue of umpire compensation. Chadwick argued in 1891, "It is plainly the best policy to make the amount so liberal as to insure the most intelligent and competent class of men for the position. The umpire's position is the most important and onerous known to the game and merits a high reward for effective service." To *Sporting Life*, the only way to improve umpiring was to increase salaries to "attract a better class of applicants." But in 1896 the league's top three umpires, Lynch, Emslie and Hurst, were still paid $250 per month plus train fare and were docked for every game missed. While $1,250, tax-free, for five months' work was well above the average workingman's income, Lynch pointed out the umpire was "the hardest-worked man in the game," having to stand during the entire game while making "about 250 decisions," mostly on balls and strikes. Emslie agreed. So did Hurst, saying in typically blunt fashion umpires should be paid like "those guys in the outfield, that get three or four balls a game and pick up $400 for a few minutes' work, while we slave the entire game, are abused and at times take our lives in our hands." So the trio decided to launch the first ever attempt by umpires to pressure the owners for more money.[5]

Prior to the December 1896 league meeting they presented a petition asking in the "best interest of the sport and justice to us to vote us an increase in salary." Their rationale was simple: "the duties and labor of an umpire are much more arduous than formerly; that the public demands more from, and in demanding more from, imposes graver responsibilities upon an umpire than in former years; that players, and even substitute players, are paid larger salaries than the most competent umpires." Columnist Ring Lardner disagreed with the "salary grabbers," saying there was no shortage of umpire applicants and "a majority" on the staff "know a good thing when they see it," but most sportswriters supported the petitioners, pointing out that umpires received less than regular players and about half that of top players, and since competent umpires were "rarer" than players, the best umpires should receive as much as "a first-class player"—three to four thousand dollars.[6]

Support for the umpires increased in January after the *Boston Globe*'s Tim Murnane, offended by Young saying all the clubs had lost money and the umpires were paid "all they are worth for their services," stressed that "the success of the game" depends on the umpires, whose job was "certainly hazard enough" to demand more salary. The *Baltimore Sun* was explicit: "Umpires, like poets, seem to be born, not made, and the crop is distressingly small. It requires a peculiar sort of talent to be a good umpire, as well as courage, coolness, patience and tact. It is besides a thankless job, sometimes an exceedingly disagreeable, and not unfrequently a dangerous one. First-class and experienced umpires should be paid in accordance with their real worth." In February the magnates passed the umpire compensation question to Young, who publicly said he could not pay more than $250 per month and denied any trouble with the staff, there being "not the slightest difference existing in relation to salary or anything else." However, hoping to undermine the threatened holdout of his best umpires, he increased Lynch's salary to $1,500, asking him not to tell Emslie or Hurst. Ever loyal, Tom promptly told Bob and Tim, who, after contacting Young, subsequently received the same amount. Young then gave the rest of the staff a $50 per month raise, boosting the annual base salary to $1,300.[7]

UMPIRE SUPERVISOR

Umpiring shortcomings stemmed not from "moral cowardice," as Chadwick claimed, but from owners refusing to discipline rowdy players and the league president failing to provide adequate supervision. Young attended games infrequently, relying on reports from club owners to assess umpire performance. Save for a preseason session to go over rule interpretations and periodic in-season instructions, each umpire was on his own. With gratuitous squabbling having a negative effect on fans' perception of both the game and umpires, the owners, believing Uncle Nick too old and too supportive of umpires to require them to enforce the rules, decided to appoint a supervisor to monitor the staff.

The appointment of an umpire supervisor was less a forthright effort to ensure quality than an honorific gesture. Baseball legend William Henry "Harry" Wright, fired as manager by Philadelphia after the 1893 season, was unanimously elected chief of umpires in February 1894 at a salary of $1,800. His duties were to assist Young in the selection of umpires, evaluate their performance, and make rule suggestions. *Sporting Life*, heralding the appointment as "a great advance," devoted its cover on March 9, 1895, to a picture of Wright surrounded by his six umpires.

Emslie was scarcely affected by the appointment. "Uncle Harry" had seen his share of umpires during his thirty-year career, but knew nothing of umpiring, having called only four games as a substitute. Besides, veterans like Bob did not need supervision and there was little chance Wright would be at games when new umpires encountered problems. With no substantive responsibilities or authority, Wright rewrote a couple of rules, attended some games, did nothing to curb kicking, and deferred all staff decisions to Young. Reappointed in 1895, Wright, ill most of the season and on the verge of blindness, chafed at Young's limited confidence in him, even giving some thought to resigning. When he died on October 3, 1895, the position went with him, the owners' memorial admitting the position was "created in recognition of his invaluable services to and lifelong connection with the national game, an office of which he was the only incumbent without predecessor or successor."[8]

With the position not filled and rowdiness increasing in 1896, *Sporting Life* urged the appointment of "an inspector of umpires" to observe game conduct and compel umpires to enforce the anti-kicking rules. The *Sporting News*, however, thought the money could be better spent on a double-umpire system or even designating one of the veteran umpires "chief of staff" who could serve as a replacement when needed.

In February 1897 the owners appointed one of their own, John B. Day, former president of the New York Giants, "Supervising Inspector of Umpires and Players." Day didn't want to be "a pensioner and nothing more," but that's what he was: an old colleague who had fallen on economic hard times given a nominal position devoid of authority. That was evident when the owners agreed to pay him $2,000, or $1,000 less than the committee recommended, while raising Young's salary $1,000 after he agreed to resign his government post (where he earned $1,800) in order to devote himself full-time to league business. Day's job was to report "on the habits and morals of the umpires and players" and make recommendations; Young would make all decisions and retain control of umpires.[9]

Emslie knew a supervisor would not solve umpiring issues and had nothing to do with dwindling attendance. The problem was increasingly rowdy behavior accompanied by a profusion of profane (culturally offensive), obscene (sexually abhorrent), vulgar (coarse or crude), foul (offensive), and indecent (offensive to standards) language. Owners knew it as well and in November 1897 finally decided to address both issues, no doubt eliciting, at least initially, a grin of satisfaction and relief from Bob Emslie.

BRUSH RESOLUTION

Language on the ballfields had devolved appreciably since 1845, when Ebenezer Dupignac Jr. was fined six cents for saying "s—t." In 1897 Cincinnati owner John T. Brush decided to do something after learning a Reds player responded to a spectator's pregame inquiry about the day's pitcher with "Oh, go fuck yourself" and proposed creating an independent board authorized to expel permanently from professional baseball anyone using "foul, indecent and obscene" language. The intent was not to eliminate cursing (damning) and swearing (blasphemy), both common currency on the diamond, but "vulgar and profane language which shocks the average man" and had "a tendency to keep women and respectable men away from the game." Consequently, the owners appointed an advisory committee of Brush, Boston's Arthur Soden, and Chicago's James Hart to define inappropriate language and determine the appropriate penalty.[10]

At the league's March 1898 meeting the committee, "to protect the patrons from the villainously filthy language" and to curb rowdy behavior, recommended blacklisting offenders for life. Some owners thought lifetime suspension too severe, but that something drastic needed to be done became evident when Brush read examples of the "malodorous English" and "salacious expressions" submitted by nineteen umpires, including Emslie, who provided "choice 'bon mots' of artistic profanity." The "shocking" verbiage elicited childish "roars of laughter" from the owners until the newspaper reporters present unanimously endorsed the proposal and said they would report any owner who did not support it as being "opposed to clean sport."[11]

The result was the unanimous adoption of the twenty-three-point Brush Resolution, hailed by Phillies owner John Rogers as "the greatest thing that has happened in the national game." Umpires, not only upon receiving disrespectful kicking or "obscene, indecent or vulgar language," but also if hearing or being told of "brutal use of vulgarity to a spectator or within the presence of spectators and within the hearing of ladies," were immediately to suspend the offender for up to three days and file a report to Young, who in turn would forward the case for final adjudication to a three-member Board of Discipline. The board, comprising experienced baseball men who had no current financial interest in the game, could suspend violators "for days, for months, for the unexpired season, for a year, or for life" depending on the offense. Named to the tribunal for three-year staggered terms were Louis C. Krauthoff of Kansas City, former president of the Western Association; Louis Kramer of Cincinnati, former president of the American Association; and Fred Stearns, ex-owner of the Detroit Wolverines. There would be no appeal of the board's decision save by unanimous vote of the owners based on new evidence. A copy of the "Purification Plan" with an explanatory letter was sent to the manager, players, and all employees of every club by express—not regular mail, because the examples of "villainously filthy" language "warm enough to burn holes in the envelope" (the mildest being "You cock-sucker!") would run afoul of postal obscenity regulations. Each player was asked, not required, to a sign the letter and return it as an indication they had read and agreed to the terms of the resolution.[12]

Prior to the season Young instructed the staff to eject anyone who questioned their decisions and report those whose objectional language violated the Brush rule. But Emslie knew he could not enforce the rules. With kicking routine and even the vilest language firmly embedded in diamond discourse, reporting offenders would come to no end other than increasing hostility from players and owners. He was prescient; the resolution soon engendered withering criticism. The *Washington Times* felt "an umpire like Bob Emslie was better protection to decency and good order than a 50-page volume of Brush laws." A board with authority so sweeping was sure to lead to a backlash. Enforcement became problematic when Francis Richter, publisher of *Sporting Life*, launched "with a vengeance" an attack on Brush and his resolution. Richter had spoken in favor of the resolution, but soured when Brush succeeded at the end of the meeting in abolishing *Sporting Life*'s self-designation as the league's official organ. Sore at being "thrown down," Richter pledged "to get back" at Brush. *Sporting Life* on March 12 devoted three columns to scorching condemnation of Brush and his resolution, arguing rowdyism, not profanity, was the bane of the league, and the resolution was "a sham reform not worth the paper it is written on" as it is "non-enforceable." Players refused to sign off, some thinking the penalty too severe, others thinking it an insulting "grand stand play" that made them look like "a foul-mouthed lot." Chicago's Tim Donahue thought the resolution would take "the ginger" out of some players and the special instructions, "making us out a lot of dogs," involved "mainly a little back talk between the players that doesn't do a great amount of harm," although "it's a little rough on the umpire sometimes." Louisville's Charley Dexter voiced the greater concern: "some of us will be sent up" since "in the heat of battle we are almost sure to lose our temper and say things that we are sorry for afterwards." Owners, too, began voicing opposition, fearing the lifetime suspension of key personnel. Dissent also stemmed from politics—passage of the resolution was considered an assault by western owners, especially Brush, Robison, and Hart, who had engineered the association merger in 1892, against the "Big Five" eastern magnates. (Two of the advisory committee members had been western owners, and all three members of the board were from western cities.)[13]

Despite laudable intent, the Brush Resolution was a dead letter. In the 1898 season 162 players were ejected from games, 60 for using noxious language, but "not more than half a dozen" were disciplined by club owners and none reported to the Board of Discipline. At the league meeting in December, Brush proposed increasing the board's jurisdiction to include any challenge to umpires' decisions and fights between players, with both players and umpires to be held accountable for failing to make charges or provide testimony. Instead, the owners at the spring meeting effectively nullified the Brush Resolution by stipulating charges against players had to be first heard by the league's board of directors (the owners) and a vote of fifty percent would be required to forward the case to the Board of Discipline. The board jurisdictionally emasculated, its members resigned.[14]

Sporting Life gleefully, in bold print, headlined reports of "Brush's Busted Board" and "The Brush Resolution Rendered Totally Innocuous." But *Sporting News* conceded, "Credit is due to Mr. Brush for instituting the reform in the interest of decency on the diamond and if it is necessary to renew the crusade, the better element of the followers of the game, will array itself under the banner the he raises."[15] But the problems of rowdiness and profanity remained. Actually, they worsened. The Brush Resolution was not the only casualty in 1899. With the jettisoning of four teams, the owners returned to a single umpire in 1900, the New York *Sun* presciently predicting "the old troubles are pretty certain to come back with only one behind the plate."[16] Maintaining decorum became much more difficult when Brush, he of the resolution against profanity, owner of the New York Giants from 1902 to 1912, employed as his manager foul-mouthed John McGraw, whose vitriol infected the league. The escalation of kicking and profanity resulted in a historic number of ejections during the first two decades of the following century.[17] So much for baseball's war on profanity.

TWO UMPIRES

With kicking, not blue language, as the major problem, the owners finally admitted the inherent shortcomings of a single umpire. The advantages of the double-umpire system, which had been used to good advantage in the Temple Cup series, was obvious to players like Fred Pfeffer, who thought the 1893 season demonstrated "clearly to every sane man that a single umpire cannot watch balls and strikes, and at the same time be in position to correctly judge a close base decision." Given penurious ownership the Louisville captain suggested six regular umpires always work the plate while an umpire hired by the home team made base calls; the latter was to be paid $5 per game and discharged if he gave the visitors "a raw deal." Pfeffer also prophetically advocated "a training school" from which the best umpires would be added to the regular staff.[18]

The league had experimented mid-season 1894 with two umpires for some games, usually pairing veterans with new hires. For Emslie it was disastrous. For nine games in August he found himself working with Will Hoagland, who was regarded soon after his debut on July 27 as the "rankest failure of the year, as he is not even familiar with the playing rules." In Boston the *Globe* thought Emslie "as usual did excellent work," but Hoagland did "not so well," the latter abruptly departing after the first game of a doubleheader on August 21, thereby ending his twenty-seven-game career. The next year Emslie teamed for ten games with newcomer John Hunt. Behind the plate Bob "inwardly convulsed" as Hunt kept changing bases decisions; he finally stepped forward to overrule his associate, who left after nineteen games.[19]

Given the kicking and staff instability in 1895 the Washington *Evening Star* thought it "probable that an entirely new system will have to be devised next season to settle the umpire problem." Chadwick thought the double-umpire plan was "the only method of securing anything like correct umpiring," and editorials in the two national baseball magazines used Emslie as an example in supporting two umpires. *Sporting News* argued it was "a necessity" when "even such an able official as Mr. Emslie has come in for repeated abuse," with *Sporting Life* agreeing, "If an experienced umpire like Bob Emslie cannot see all the movements during a game it is very evident that help is needed." During the 1896 season Young assigned two umpires to important games. With the value of the system demonstrated time and again the dual umpire system came up at the league meeting in November. Emslie, Hurst, and Lynch were again called in for advice. Young proposed staffing all games with two umpires, but the three veteran umpires, wearing battle scars and defensive of their ability to call games effectively, spoke against it, telling the owners umpiring would be easy if they made the players keep quiet. Bob said he would have "no trouble" as a single umpire if he had only to call routine plays, but having to watch for tricks, dirty plays, and illegal coaching "distracts his attention and makes it almost impossible to preside at a game alone satisfactorily." So instead of adopting the double umpire system, the owners decided to abolish monetary fines in favor of ejecting obstreperous players.[20]

Emslie did not think ejections would be effective once owners realized the impact of losing important players. He was right. Chadwick thought in 1897 the "outbursts of hot temper and questionable language and actions," reaching the "culminating point of low prize-ring tactics," had become a "positive danger to the good name of the professional baseball business." The *Chicago Chronicle*, citing "beer glasses for Lynch at Louisville, decayed eggs for Sheridan at St. Louis, mobs after Hurst in Pittsburgh," declared 1897 "superlatively the worst season that Uncle Nick Young's staff of diamond autocrats has ever experienced. Verily, this is the year of much woe for the umpire. If the present state of affairs continues much longer it will be hard to tempt a man upon a ball field to umpire a game at any price."[21]

Predictably, the abuse took a toll on the staff. Sandy McDermott quit at the end of June, Sheridan a month later. Lynch, who resigned in July, then returned eighteen days later out of loyalty to Young, said, "The players simply broke Jack's heart." On August 4 in Cincinnati Hurst lost his cool, picked up a beer glass thrown at him by a fan, and threw it back into the stands, hitting a spectator. Arrested and fined $100 for assault, Tim was not rehired for 1898.[22] By midseason Emslie had not experienced the difficulties encountered by other umpires and had even been cited as the only umpire to give "given general satisfaction" in St. Louis. Things changed during the dog days of August. Called out at the plate on August 21, New York's William "Kid" Gleason in a fury grabbed Emslie's coat while berating him in threatening fashion; a week later, on August 28, Chicago's Bill Dahlen, called out for oversliding third base, dragged Emslie around by the collar in "the most vicious attack on an umpire that year." Both were ejected and fined.[23] The *Boston Globe* asserted kicking had reached "a critical stage that threatens the stability of the national game. Something must be done to prevent the disgraceful scenes so frequently enacted upon the ball field." Even Giants owner Andrew Freedman, bane of umpires, felt "action must be taken or the game as a sport and as a financial enterprise must fail." Young, "to save the national game from riots and bloodshed," resigned his government post to devote all his time to the umpiring problems, including personal staff inspections.[24]

In November owners finally took three decisive actions to curb rowdiness. First they abolished the Temple Cup series. Attendance had plummeted, but Washington owner Earl Wagner alleged, with slight exaggeration, "Brawls and outbursts of hoodlumism on the ballfield were practically unheard of till the Temple Cup post-season games." Teams, primarily Baltimore, fought for a share of the money, "ever ready to engage in passage of sulphurous words with the umpire if they thought an inch of ground could be gained." Second, umpires were given absolute authority: players were expressly forbidden to question judgment calls, and those who did were to be immediately ejected and suspended for a period determined by the umpire and league president. Third, and most importantly, the double umpire system was adopted for the 1898 season.[25]

While praised by the press, umpires and players were skeptical of dual umpires. Players predicted there would be twice as many kicks with twice as many umpires. Veteran umpires like Emslie, O'Day, and Gaffney, who believed there was "too much work for one man, but there is not enough work for two," preferred working alone and thought having two umpires "will deaden the game." Gaffney felt the problem with a single umpire was the arbiter who too often worked behind the pitcher. Admitting he introduced the practice of switching positions, he did so "less than any man in the business," believing the only time the umpire should go on the field was when he suspected a first base runner intended to steal second.[26]

The double umpire system came about not only to facilitate more accurate decisions on the bases, but also to convince players and fans that the outcome of games turned on player performance, not umpire decisions. Cap Anson, who thought two umpires would not be any better than one, was spot-on: "The public and the players will perhaps think it is better, and that, after all, is all you want." Though the need for two umpires was obvious, it was adopted only "after stiff argument." Opponents argued against the increased cost (about $10,000 per year) and, given the rate of staff attrition, the inability to obtain six more qualified umpires. Gaffney agreed, saying, "I don't think twelve first-class umpires can be found in the whole country." To cover the cost of two umpires, the magnates increased the schedule from 132 to 154 games, adding eleven more home games per club, and abolished Day's position as umpire supervisor over Young's plea to continue it on the grounds that the double-umpire system required more than one man to look after the staff.[27]

Given decent pay and the prestige of being in the "big leagues," Young reportedly received some three hundred applications for the staff of twelve umpires. Instead of submitting a letter of inquiry accompanied by solicited recommendations as previously, applicants had to fill out a fourteen point questionnaire. Most of the questions were pro forma, but applicants were also asked about their experience as a ballplayer or umpire, their expected salary, and the names and addresses of references who could testify to their "honesty, sobriety and moral character, and as to your capability as an umpire." Pickings were slim. To fill the staff Young retained Emslie, Lynch, McDonald, and O'Day and hired two Minor League umpires, Ed Swartwood and Tom Connolly; two former players with no umpiring experience, Ed Andrews and George Wood; and personal friend and sportswriter John Heydler, who had called twelve games as a substitute. Young also lured from retirement Charlie Cushman, who last called forty-six games in 1885; Wes Curry, out since 1890; and Pop Snyder, who left in 1893. Emslie and Lynch, "in a class by themselves," received $2,000, while the other salaries ranged from $900 to $1,400. Tommy Connolly received $1,200.[28]

Optimism pervaded the start of the 1898 season. With the field umpire making base decisions something more than guesswork at long range and the Brush Resolution threatening ejection and suspension, there seemed "no reason why professional baseball should not be clean" with the elimination of "nine-tenths of the riotous demonstrations which have disgraced the diamond during past five years." It was wishful thinking; in fact, things got worse.[29]

The problem was twofold. Although having two umpires was nothing new, it took time for umpires to adjust to the new system. The designated "Umpire," a veteran like Emslie, was in charge of the game. He was to work permanently behind the bat and judge hits along the foul lines, watch for runners cutting bases, and make third base calls. The "Assistant Umpire," less experienced, would make the calls at first and second base. But umpires sometime overruled each other and differed in their interpretations of the rules, so Young sent out bulletins providing instructions on rules and responsibilities for each arbiter. The umpires were to assist each other in case of uncertainty or conflicting decisions, but often failed to help each other. It sometimes caused problems when they did, as when on July 7 Boston's captain, Duffy, argued that Bob had no right to help the assistant umpire on a base call. More importantly, not all new hires proved competent, and Young botched assignments. To start the season Emslie was paired with Andrews and Lynch with Connolly, but for some reason Nick teamed veterans O'Day and McDonald, leaving three unseasoned duos: Snyder and Curry, Cushman and Heydler, and Swartwood and Wood. Of the two teams that initially worked in Philadelphia, the press judged the umpiring of Snyder and Curry as "poor" and held that "the excellent work" of Emslie, "a very good umpire," was countered by Andrews' "awfully wretched decisions," concluding it was "far better to have one umpire who is a good one, than to have two, as an Andrews will spoil the splendid work of an Emslie every time." As the *Boston Globe* noted, two good umpires "have proved a grand thing for the game. One dummy, however, will make both umpires look like dunces." As it turned out, Curry, Cushman, Heydler, and Wood failed to last the season.[30]

Emslie was on hand for Heydler's denouement, which illustrated the problem umpires and Young faced. Heydler, inexperienced and temperamentally unsuited for the job, struggled with the incessant kicking. *Sporting Life* reported in June he had "lost in flesh and looks like a sick man. He is a gentleman and cannot stand the abuse which umpiring brings him." During a July 4 doubleheader in New York Emslie watched helplessly as Heydler, after calling out George Davis at second base, was berated and nearly punched in the face by Davis. After the game Giants owner Freedman told Heydler he was guilty of "barefaced robbery," dispatched his business manager to the umpires' dressing room to tell Heydler "it was the rawest deal he had ever seen," and sent an "inflammatory telegram" to the other clubs and a "wire Scorcher" to Young demanding Heydler be fired, asserting that Nick was guilty of favoritism in employing him. Shaken, Heydler resigned after the next day's game, explaining, "I can stand abuse from crowds and players, but when it comes from a president it is about time for me to retire." He later said the experience umpiring "added ten years to his life." That Freedman was not disciplined for his outrageous behavior spoke to the owners control of the president and his umpires.[31]

At the end of the 1898 season Young said the system had given "general satisfaction." Having received fewer complaints than ever before, he was confident the system would be continued, the public demanding it and the expense of additional umpires being "comparatively small." Emslie would agree. He had issued eight ejections in 1897, but only three in 1898. The owners, however, had other ideas. First, they took hiring umpires out of Young's hands. Instead of endorsing his proposed slate, the magnates in 1899 chose umpires from a list of Young's recommendations, the top selections ranked 1–6, the assistants 7–12, and possible substitutes prioritized. They dropped Lynch, Snyder, and Wood and hired Gaffney, John Hunt, and Billy Smith. Then, with the league returning to eight teams in 1900 by jettisoning the four former American Association clubs, they reduced the schedule from 154 to 140 games and returned to having one umpire per game. The change brought no significant staff changes: Emslie was the first chosen, followed in order by Swartwood, Connolly, O'Day, and Hurst. They were to follow a set schedule the entire season. Commensurate with taking control of umpires from Young, owners reappointed John Day as supervisor of players and umpires at $2,500. But without a need to monitor Emslie and the other experienced umpires or any authority over players, Day had little to do except "keep out of sight until pay day."[32]

No sooner had the 1900 season opened than it was obvious the owners had blown every decision. Bob soon learned his supposedly secret, season-long schedule, intended to prevent teams from objecting to certain umpires, would be frequently revised, often at a moment's notice. As the only umpire against whose arrival did not spark complaint, his staff-leading 129 games were assigned almost equally between eastern and western teams. And while both Emslie and O'Day worked in every city, Bob alone was not banned by owners. Hank early in the season called six games in Cincinnati and St. Louis, but following controversies never returned to either. Swartwood worked no games in Philadelphia and five in St. Louis. Hurst, not allowed to umpire Cincinnati or New York home games, worked no Giants and only five Reds away games. In the face of blatant favoritism in assignments, the owners decided in December 1900 that umpires would be henceforth be scheduled equally, working the same number of games in each city.

It was also soon apparent it was a mistake for owners to select umpires. Owners became more brazen with the umpires now directly obligated to them. After a game in Philadelphia the Phillies' John Rogers pointedly admonished Hurst, "We want the close decisions, Mr. Hurst. We do not care so much for the decisions at first base, but we must have those at the plate." Cincinnati's Brush admitted "it preferrable for one person to hire and control and be responsible for their performance."[33]

The worst mistake was returning to the single-umpire system. Umpires were once again permitted to work either behind the plate or on the field. Emslie, who like most umpires preferred to work alone, was outspoken about how the single umpire system should work. Conceding that umpiring behind the pitcher allowed for being close to plays on the bases, he argued, "No man can umpire properly from behind the pitcher. One must be behind the catcher to accurately judge balls and strikes as well as see the ball when hit along close to the foul lines, also to judge all close plays at the plate, where men often slide wide and avoid being touched out. The only way a man could umpire single handed, to even his own satisfaction, would be to remain behind the plate." Now facing greater responsibility and effort, he asked for a salary increase. Young's response is unknown, but umpire salaries increased. Connolly's was raised to $1,500 while Emslie, Hurst, and O'Day made "considerable more." Bob was probably the highest paid since with Lynch's departure he was the head of the staff.[34]

As the *New York Sun* predicted, "The old troubles are pretty certain to come back with only one behind the plate." Chicago's Clark Griffith agreed, not only because it was "almost impossible for one man to umpire even decently," but also because players, after becoming used to the double umpire system, will "kick on decisions they used to accept." Tommy Connolly, fed up with escalating kicking, quit after seventeen games; Adonis Terry left after thirty-nine. Games dragged on a half hour longer due to arguments and umpires moving back and forth from the plate to the field. A Boston a fan vowed not to attend games until the second umpire returned: "the single umpire business looks cheap after the double work one has seen at the league games for the last two years."[35]

Contrary to mounting press reports of rowdy play, Day said the single system was "working to the satisfaction of the club owners" and would be "permanently established." Why? Because the umpire, from behind the plate, "sees plays as a majority of the spectators see them, while the assistant umpire sees these plays from behind first base and from a different point of view from the majority of the spectators. While I admit the assistant's judgment may be correct, it differs from that of the majority of the spectators." Day's toady comments revealed the owners' preference for "conciliating a crowd rather than securing honest decisions." Notwithstanding extensive newspaper reports that umpires were "assaulted and abused in almost every game, and the players are starting riots over decisions that are not even close," the owners in July voted 6–2 not to return to two umpires, the objection being the additional expense.[36]

As the tumultuous season neared an end Young said the "the public demands" a return to two umpires next season. Chafing at criticism of the staff, he said, "Talk that there are not eight good umpires is all nonsense" and that owners "have abused me because of the unsatisfactory work of their own selection." But in December, owners showing no disposition to loosen purse strings, further reduced expenses by abolishing southern spring training trips and deferred consideration of the double umpire system, "unquestionably popular with the fans," to see if "eight good men" apply for the position.[37]

DIAMOND DUSTUP

During the disorder accompanying the return to a single umpire, Emslie had no problems, save for ejecting McGraw for disputing a base call on

June 2, until encountering the worst physical assault of his career in Cincinnati on July 4. Spectators who intermittently set off fireworks during the first game of the doubleheader witnessed a fiery explosion in the second. In the third inning the Giants' Jack Doyle tried to get to second base after being picked off first but was tagged out by Joe Quinn. It was a close play, Emslie rushing out from behind the plate to make the call, his view partially obscured by Quinn. Doyle, "livid with rage," grabbed Bob by the sleeve and spun him around, calling him "a name that is never seen in print." As Bob turned, heading toward the plate, Doyle punched him in the back of the neck. While falling to the ground he grabbed Doyle's arm, pulling Jack down with him, the two "fighting like two Kilkenny cats."[38] When several Reds players pulled the enraged player off the prostrate official, Doyle, whose "countenance" had sustained "considerable damage," tried to kick Emslie before heading to the Giants bench amid jeers, hisses, and cries of "Shame!" from spectators. Emslie, suffering only "a few scratches," ejected Doyle, then nonchalantly brushed the dirt from his uniform, dusted off home plate, and called for the game to resume.

Unlike other diamond dustups, this fight between a player and umpire wound up in court. Shortly after play resumed a police officer arrested Doyle as fans cheered, one shouting, "Beat his nut in with your club." Taken to the York Street station, he was charged with disorderly conduct but soon released on bail bond posted by the Reds' treasurer, N. Ashley Lloyd. After the game Emslie was also arrested on the same charge, taken to the station, and released on Lloyd's bail. The next day, instead of appearing in court, Doyle, who had left for Pittsburgh with the Giants, and Emslie, who remained in Cincinnati for the next series, sent in written guilty pleas. Judge William H. Leuders, believing there would be "no more such affairs" since the combatants were "now penitent," assessed them court costs and dismissed the case, as was common for a misdemeanor.[39]

The donnybrook became a cause célèbre and received extensive press coverage. *Sporting News*, believing if the case had been tried Doyle would have been "heavily fined" and Emslie's charge dismissed, thought some good might result from "one of the most outrageous affairs ever witnessed on a ball field" if Young invoked his power "to suspend for a definite period and to impose a fine not exceeding $200 upon any League manager or player guilty in public of gross misbehavior, including intoxication, fighting . . . or other scandalous conduct." But while newspapers throughout the league called for "Dirty Jack" to be "severely punished," everyone knew he would not be penalized. Immediately after the incident Brush said that while the assault was "a disgrace to baseball," it was "safe to predict that Doyle will not be disciplined" since league owners had dismantled the board of discipline that had been charged with handling untoward behavior. The *Washington Evening Star* agreed: "The idea of assaulting such a veteran and unbiased umpire as Bob Emslie is simply outrageous, to put it mildly, but the chances are that nothing will be done, as Magnate Freedman is back of Doyle." Doyle tried to gloss it over as an unfortunate accident. Declaring he and Emslie "are, and always have been, the best of friends," Jack said, "I lost my head for a moment." Terming the episode "comical" and "exaggerated," he claimed that when he ran up behind Emslie and "yanked his coattails" they both lost their balance and fell. Giants manager Buck Ewing repeated Doyle's untruthful account, asserting mendaciously that "Emslie was as much to blame as Jack." Upon learning of the Giants' account and no doubt realizing the eventual outcome, Emslie, too, tried to defuse the situation by untruthfully saying, "Doyle did not hit me," they were "both to blame," and since "the whole thing was a mistake," he would "make no charges against him."[40]

It must have been galling for Emslie to misrepresent the incident and not bring assault charges against Doyle. Did he simply want to avoid what might be a lengthy, perhaps technically unwinnable, court case? Was it a softhearted response by a former player who understood competitiveness getting out of hand? Did he think he may have missed the call as his view of second was partially obscured by Quinn? Was he worried that bringing charges might antagonize players and perhaps prompt club owners to terminate his job? Most likely he simply knew league officials would not penalize Doyle.

Whatever his thinking, it was another correct call. Predictably, Giants owner Andrew Freedman refused to discipline "Dirty Jack" despite his extensive record of rowdy behavior, including a fistfight with umpire Lynch in 1897. Nor, more tellingly, did Nick Young. After reading press accounts of the incident, Young said Doyle's "offense is of too serious a nature to overlook." While implored by the press to suspend Doyle immediately, the league constitution prohibited him from doing so until Jack received a hearing, so Young decided to obtain affidavits from Emslie and "disinterested parties," then go to Cincinnati to investigate himself instead of sending Day, the umpire supervisor, who offered no public statement about the assault and went on fishing trip.[41]

But Young decided to adjudicate the matter from his office in Washington after receiving a letter from Freedman pointing out that penalizing Doyle "will keep the New York Club down low in the race" and other players should have been penalized for "unbecoming conduct" during the season. Young got the message and simply sent Emslie's "full statement of the facts under oath" to Doyle for response and asked unnamed persons in Cincinnati to send him an account of the incident. Along with four other accounts, three by Giants teammates, Jack submitted a "sworn statement" falsely saying he "did not use any obscene language or strike or kick Mr. Emslie." The lone Cincinnati respondent said he was "so far removed from the scene of action that he could not say who was the aggressor." Given Doyle's statement and the lack of responses from Cincinnati, Young, ignoring the detailed newspaper accounts, to "avoid any complications" decided on August 21 he had "no alternative but to dismiss the case."[42]

The press, citing Doyle's record of combative behavior coupled with Emslie's well-known diplomatic style of dealing with confrontations, excoriated Young for dereliction of duty in failing to discipline Doyle. Terming the league president and umpire supervisor "baseball barnacles," *Sporting News* charged Young with "cowardly apathy" and a "gelatin backbone," contrasting his decision to allow Doyle to go unpunished with the prompt and decisive way Ban Johnson dealt with offenders in the American League, and calling for Day, who makes "a poor bluff at filling the position," to be "unloaded." Tim Murnane was disgusted: "Think of the league not being able to protect a man like Robert Emslie, who has given the greatest exhibition of all-around umpiring of any man who ever wore the mask." While the lack of support from Young must have been disillusioning to Emslie and the other umpires, it was not surprising. The league president was simply an employee, never permitted independent authority with the umpire staff, and "Old Nick" feared that offending Freedman would jeopardize his position.[43]

The Doyle incident was still fresh in Bob's mind during subsequent incidents in St. Louis. On August 11 he exercised great restraint when the Giants' William "Kid" Gleason, angered by being called out at second base, knocked the indicator out of his hand with "a sharp blow on the wrist." Bob calmly stepped back, rubbed his wrist, ejected Gleason, and ordered play to resume. He was uneasy when, after calling a game on October 7 in St. Louis after seven innings on account of darkness, which gave the visiting Pirates a 3–2 victory, angry Cardinals fans poured onto the field threating harm. Six policemen escorted him to the clubhouse, and after leaving the dressing room, Bob, surrounded by police, walked defiantly up the street for the streetcar to take him to his hotel through a crowd of "fully 1000" that hurled sticks and stones, two officers staying with him until he reached the hotel.[44]

Come season's end, Emslie had had enough. Postseason play resumed when the *Pittsburgh Chronicle Telegraph* sponsored a best-of-five series between the pennant-winning Brooklyn Superbas and the runner-up Pirates. Emslie and Hank O'Day, the league's best, were expected to umpire, but they refused to accept the embarrassingly low pay of $25 per game.[45]

STANDING THE GAFF

Given the turmoil and travails of the 1890s, how was Bob Emslie able, as Harry "Steamboat" Johnson aptly put it, to continue "standing the gaff?"[46] Dedication and determination are not enough to explain why Emslie endured the verbal abuse and physical confrontations of the 1890s. Love of the game was involved, as was the prideful satisfaction of ensuring orderly and fair play. And for the former player there was great pleasure in being close to the action of exceptional pitching, hitting, and fielding. For a home plate umpire, a no-hit game is a thrill despite mounting pressure to call pitches unerringly. Bob's first came on August 16, 1893, when the Orioles' Bill Hawke faced twenty-nine batters, walking two, in beating Washington 5–0 for the first no-hitter of the season and the first thrown since the pitching distance had been increased to sixty feet six inches. The second came on May 25, 1899, when Louisville rookie

Charles "Deacon" Phillipe blanked the Giants 7–0. And behind the dish he witnessed historic batting feats in three consecutive seasons. In 1896 "Big Ed" Delahanty became the first to hit four inside-the-park home runs in a game; in 1897 Bill Joyce tied George Strief's 1885 record with four triples; and in 1898 the Phillies' Bill Duggleby, in winning his first Major League start, became the first and only pitcher to hit a grand slam home run in his initial time at bat. Bob may not have been aware at the time of two other batting firsts. On August 7, 1893, left-handed Giants slugger Roger Connor, facing Brooklyn lefty George Sharrott, batted right-handed for the first time and hit two home runs. And in the final game of the 1898 season, Louisville's Jesse Burkett went 2–4 on September 26 to finish with a .410 batting average, the first player to hit .400 in back-to-back seasons.

Not all special games involved plays. On October 3, 1899, when Brooklyn's Charley "Duke" Farrell came to bat for his first time in Washington since being traded from the Senators, Emslie, who was umpiring the bases, interrupted the game to obtain from fans in the right field stands a beautiful fishing rod as a present to their favorite ex-Senators catcher. Reeling in the line, which extended into the right field seats, Charley landed an eight-pound catfish that flopped around on the plate, then responded to the gift by lining a base hit to right field. And unbeknownst to Bob, a personal celebratory event came in Philadelphia on July 21, 1900. Upon leaving the field neither he nor spectators or press reporters knew he had umpired 1,323 games, the most in Major League history. That the historic game passed without notice, baseball statisticians then keeping track of batting and pitching feats but not umpiring statistics, was perhaps fitting, as umpires are not in the game for personal glory or individual achievement.

There was also life beyond the ballpark. With games usually over by 5:30 p.m., Emslie found ways to decompress from the pressures of the diamond after tidying up and supping. The vibrant cities he visited during the season offered museums, theaters, musical performances, and learned lectures aplenty, but he probably took little advantage of these opportunities. Free time afforded by rainouts and some Sundays was rare, and recovering from the stress and strain of the game was the evening's priority. Bob was well aware of the decade's major attraction, the 1893 Columbian Exposition, but had little time to visit the fabled White City or the Canadian exhibit as he was in Chicago for only five days, May 20–24. Primarily a people person, he did not sit around hotel lobbies like Hank O'Day, preferring to visit friends old and new in various league cities, even regularly seeing old pals in Camden when umpiring in Philadelphia.

Emslie savored his off-season respite from the diamond wars north of the border. One of three umpires not born in the United States, he was the only resident of two countries, for seven months an itinerant worker in the United States, the other five a resident of Canada.[47] It would have been easier for him and his family to relocate, but as a proud Canadian to the core, he was unable to forsake his native land and preferred the familiarity and "small town" atmosphere of St. Thomas to the impersonal bustle of American cities. As with baseball, the world around him in both countries was rapidly changing. When he left St. Thomas in March 1898 construction had just begun on the city's first electrified railway line; upon his return in October it was operating to great acclaim. No doubt Bob paid the nickel fare and rode a streetcar around town. In 1900 he observed another new conveyance: the first car in St. Thomas, a "Winton" capable of speeds up to thirty-five miles per hour, but for Bob, who loved horses and kept a fine specimen to pull his carriage, owning an automobile was years away. Whether or not he took off-season employment—as was common among players and umpires—he unwound by visiting with friends from Toronto to Detroit, and, especially, pursuing seasonal sporting pleasures.

With Ontario rich in upland game birds, he traversed open fields with a twenty-gauge double-barreled shotgun and one of his cocker spaniels trained to scent, flush, and retrieve downed birds. (He bred spaniels and was eager to share with ballplayers who were hunters; Boston's Tommy McCarthy was not alone in receiving pups out of his prize stock.) After hunting season Bob became an avid and accomplished trapshooter, entering local and international tournaments in both live bird and clay target competitions.[48] A member of the St. Thomas Gun Club, Emslie, armed with a semiautomatic single-barreled open-bore twelve-gauge shotgun, competed in tournaments in Ontario (then, as now, the trapshooting capital of Canada) as well as New York. Whether shooting at the wild flight of live pigeons or the unpredictable angle of clay discs, each requiring different techniques, Emslie was a "crack shot."[49]

Always being identified as "the well-known baseball umpire" added pressure but also fueled his determination to succeed. In 1896 Bob made the highest individual record in a team match between the St. Thomas and Port Stanley clubs. In a heralded January 1898 duel with William Margette of Buffalo, after tying with twenty-one of twenty-five kills, Bob won the shoot-off 4–3, then proceeded to tie for second in the first sweep and win the second. In a March tournament he broke twenty-three of twenty-five targets in one event and all twenty in another. During the 1897 season he took advantage of an off day on May 7 to enter the Baltimore Shooting Association's club shoot with a borrowed gun; he was the only competitor to hit ten straight. After the season he copped $200 and a trophy for winning the St. Thomas International Handicap. On January 5, 1899, Bob Emslie reached the pinnacle of the sport, receiving the Gilman & Barnes International Championship medal for winning the Grand International Handicap. In November he bested sharpshooter Joe Coffey in a highly publicized match in St. Thomas. With extra-lively birds caught the night before and a strong side wind Bob missed his first shot, then nailed the next twenty-four to win the $50 purse. He did not fare as well in the Thanksgiving Day tournament in Buffalo on November 30, hitting seventeen of twenty, but rebounded on December 5 to tie for first in a high gun contest downing nine of ten live birds, and in another shoot posted a perfect 15–15 score. He ended the decade adjusting to the new Magutrap trapdoor release throttle. In January 1900, on the first day of the Grand Canadian Handicap, he finished eighth of thirty shooters. The next day, despite unfavorable weather, he hit eight of ten birds to place second. In the clay disc competition he scored 7–20 in the first event, improving to 13–20 in the second. By year's end he was back in the groove, carrying off prize money in multiple events.[50]

If trapshooting provided Emslie with recreational pleasure—and perhaps vicarious release of frustration with targets representing kickers—reports of Emslie's trapshooting marksmanship in league newspapers and *Sporting Life*, which had a section devoted to the sport, enhanced his reputation for visual acuity as an umpire. Given Bob's skill with the gun, the *London Advertiser* facetiously commented, "No more will he have to be escorted off the field by the police. Before entering the ball field Mr. Emslie will merely hang his fowling-piece across his shoulder, and make any decision he pleases with perfect sangfroid."[51]

With the onset of winter Bob turned to curling. Brought to Canada by Scottish immigrants, curling, like baseball, predates hockey as a popular participant and spectator Canadian sport. The St. Thomas curling club, established in 1877, played outdoors until the Granite Curling Club built an indoor rink in 1893. Among the seventy-five members, all male, was Bob Emslie. With his father a member of the Guelph curling club and three uncles being prominent Guelph curlers, he likely watched curling in Guelph and played it in London, but was not an experienced competitor when he joined the Granite Club. Nonetheless, he would quickly emerge as an accomplished curler, assuming the key position of skip (captain) of the club's best four-member rink (team).[52]

FIN-DE-SIECLE

As the decade, indeed the century, wound to a close, the National League was in crisis. Internecine ownership turmoil, unprecedented rowdiness on ballfields, and the ancillary problems of drunkenness and gambling called into question the integrity of the game and its place as popular commercial entertainment. Penurious club owners, after jettisoning four teams and expanding the schedule in hopes of increasing revenue, voided the Brush Resolution against profanity and rowdiness, appointed ineffective umpire supervisors, abandoned the double umpire system, and stripped the league president of control of the staff, all the while engaged in interleague warfare with Ban Johnson's upstart American League.

Suffering most were Bob Emslie and his fellow umpires. They were marginalized, disrespected really, in the annual *Spalding Guide*, which carried pictures of players as well as Major and Minor League and college teams, but nary a photo or even listing of umpires. They were constantly lambasted by reporters eager to cater to fans and defend home team players, the *Brooklyn Daily Eagle* and *New York Sun* acknowledging newspapers were responsible for "encouraging rowdyism by excessively criticizing umpires." Despite dwindling attendance in many cities, kicking and cussing increasingly off-putting to fans, ownership, unable "to see the handwriting on the wall" and "lacking backbone," failed to rein in players or provide adequate support for umpires. The *Sun* wondered by decade's end if "baseball was a contest between two clubs with ball and bat, or an assault upon the umpire by eighteen players armed with temper and bad tongues."[53]

Through baseball's most turbulent era Bob Emslie not only endured, but prospered. He alone of the illustrious coterie that began the decade umpired all ten seasons, four times working the most games (1892, 1894–95, 1900) and twice the second most (1893, 1897). By 1900 Emslie had risen to the top of the umpiring profession. Murnane regarded him as "the one great umpire left on the staff." Brooklyn skipper Ned Hanlon agreed he was the "best umpire now before the public" and Giants manager Buck Ewing thought that next to Lynch, Bob was "the best umpire he has ever seen."[54]

11

Deadball Veteran

I THINK THAT THERE SHALL NEVER BE
AN UMPIRE WHO CAN REALLY SEE
ABOUT WHOSE HEAD A HALO SHINES,
WHOSE MERITS RATES REPORTERS' LINES,
ONE WHO CALLS THEM AS THEY ARE,
AND NOT AS I WOULD WISH BY FAR.
A GENT WHO LEANS NOT EITHER WAY,
BUT LETS THE BOYS DECIDE THE PLAY,
A MAN WHO KNOWS THE RULES BY HEART,
AND USES JUDGMENT FROM THE START.
POEMS ARE MADE BY FOOLS LIKE ME,
AND ONLY GOD SHOULD AN UMPIRE BE.

—1959 PONY League pamphlet

The dawn of the twentieth century brought fundamental changes to Major League baseball and Bob Emslie's umpiring. The National Agreement of 1903, formalizing the merger of the National and American leagues as the Major League, ushered in a decade of unprecedented administrative stability and financial prosperity marked by a three-member National Commission to govern the game, the inauguration of the modern World Series, and new expansive concrete-and-steel stadiums. In 1904 the schedule increased from 140 to 154 games, the norm until another expansion in the 1960s. For Emslie the decade entailed adjusting to renewed staffing instability, dramatic changes in league administration, new on-field duties and mechanics, and coping with innovative styles of play as well as health issues and harsh criticism that threatened his career.

As the calendar turned to 1901 the league's best umpire, one of "the classiest handlers of the indicators the game has ever known," enjoyed "the confidence and respect of the public and players." Emslie was not only the most popular umpire but also a role model for Minor League arbiters. (Tom Cotter of the New England league was hailed as the "Emslie of league officials.")[1] Bob knew success as an umpire required the proper mental makeup as well as command of the rules and the ability to make accurate decisions. He was disappointed but not surprised that three Minor League umpires hired on his recommendation—Charlie Smith of St. Thomas, A. E. Knowlton of Boston, and E. Priest of Pittsburgh—failed to reach the Majors: "I've seen many a chap whom I thought was the making of a great umpire, and who really did great work, make an absolute failure of it, though his judgment could not be improved upon. Disposition, of course, is everything. It would never do for an umpire to lose his head, nor would it do for him to be too lenient or too strict. I have been umpiring a good many years now, and I am still not satisfied as to what the qualifications are for a good umpire."[2]

Actually, he knew his success was due to making accurate decisions and having an engaging personality, even temperament, and ability to control the game. To baseball writer E. B. Moss, Bob was "a most dignified arbitrator" who "has few peculiarities of action. He is very quiet and is always open to argument on a close decision. The players realize, however, that they cannot 'show him up' and it is seldom that he is compelled to banish a participant. Players and managers alike know that he is well-versed both as a player and arbitrator, and that he gives decisions just as he sees them without fear for favor. Furthermore, he means what he says."[3]

Emslie knew, too, that success depended "a great deal upon the impression an umpire makes upon the crowd in the stands as to whether he will make good or not. If the fans like a fellow's looks, think him honest and capable, he has little trouble, even though his work is not of the best. Another man may be much more capable and make fewer mistakes, yet the crowd is up in arms against him whenever he appears upon the lot." When asked how it felt to have thousands of people reviling him, he responded, "If he's a new man in the business he probably feels scared. If he has had experience, he feels inclined to smile, for he knows that they don't mean it, that they are wrought up with a desire for their home club to win, and therefore are pardonably prejudiced. But whether old or new in the business, the conscientious umpire steels himself against any loss of nerve by the feeling that he has done his best in rendering the decision that is criticized, and he is fortified further by the knowledge that he was closer to the play than any one save the players." He usually paid no attention to jibes from spectators but occasionally silenced taunts, as when, to the delight of other fans, he turned around and told a loud-mouthed critic he "should be on the stage." To help control his emotions he chomped on a wad of gum as if in "an endurance gum chewing contest."[4]

BY THE BOOK

The merger of two leagues with differing rules initially complicated life for the foremost rules expert. To discourage batters from deliberately fouling off pitches, the American ruled all foul balls strikes, while in the National only the first two were strikes. As a compromise, the joint rules committee in 1902 proposed drawing a line drawn across the diamond from third to first base and extending to the stands. A batted ball landing beyond the line would be a foul and one falling inside the line a strike unless the batter had two strikes already. Emslie presciently opposed requiring the plate umpire to make such precise spatial judgment calls and the unwieldy concept was rejected, each league retaining its own rule. But he endorsed the joint balk rule in 1904, which made enforcement easier: after the pitcher had come to a set position any movement, however slight, not resulting in a throw to first base or home plate would be a balk.

Bob enforced playing rules daily but only once had to attend to pregame instructions to ensure the field was properly laid out. On May 9, 1902, in Chicago, after the Orphans won two games, Giants manager Horace Fogel before the third game asked Emslie to measure the distance from the pitcher's rubber to home plate, which by rule was to be sixty feet six inches. Representatives of Chicago and New York, measuring with cloth tapes, disagreed by four inches, but Bob's steel measure found it to be thirteen inches short, so he ordered the groundskeeper to dig up the rubber and move it back to the proper distance, some 750 fans "shivering in the chilling breezes" during the half-hour delay.

Emslie remained a stickler for rules. Flat-sided bats were banned in 1893, but Brooklyn Superbas batters continued to use them. While some umpires, including Klem and O'Day, ignored complaints, Bob would not yield to custom. When Cincinnati catcher George "Admiral" Schlei protested Brooklynite Harry Lumley's bat in the first inning on August 29, 1905, Emslie declared it illegal. After Lumley switched to a regulation bat and slammed the first pitch against the right-field fence for a triple, Schlei figurately kicked himself, the Superbas players roared with laughter, and Emslie could not help but grin.[5] On the other hand, contrary to the rules, the one-time hurler allowed pitchers to warm up between innings until ordered to stop.[6]

Occasionally he had to use common sense in applying imprecise rules. Bob was the lone umpire in Chicago on May 13, 1906, when Brooklyn's Billy Maloney was thrown out at third after lining a shot into the right-field corner. Since the ball had rolled into a cluster of three policemen standing in foul territory, the Superbas argued Maloney was safe since the rules awarded three bases on a ball hit into a crowd of spectators, while the Cubs contended a trio of cops did not qualify as a crowd. Emslie pondered for a few minutes, then, admitting doubt as to what numerically consisted a crowd, called Maloney safe, deciding the policemen "corporeally" constituted a crowd.

Since the rules did not cover all possible situations, Emslie often relied on personal judgment. He had to decide whether to call a game on account of rain, but did so only once, when faced with a flood. The sun was shining brightly for the doubleheader in Pittsburgh on July 4, 1902, but soon after the morning game started water from the adjacent Allegheny River, swollen by the previous day's heavy rain, began to flooding into Exposition Park. Soon right and center fields became small lakes, fielders splashing through rising water, occasionally falling into the drink. With nearly eleven thousand fans on hand and no rules covering flooded grounds, Emslie bade the game go on, awarding one base on balls hit into the water and having a boy dry wet ones with a towel. It was thought the afternoon game would be canceled, the water knee-deep in center and right fields and within ten to twelve feet of second base, but with players eager to continue despite soaked uniforms and fans enjoying the aquatic play, Emslie called, "Play!" Despite the flooded outfield, each game appropriately ending when a player fell into the water after making a catch, the twin bill was remarkably well-played, the Pirates winning both, 3–0 and 4–0, each in ninety minutes. The next day the water had receded, leaving a muddy but playable field.

Bob found himself overruled only once, and then on a technicality. It happened the first time he encountered the "hidden-ball" trick—the deceptive practice of infielders concealing the ball in their glove or armpit, then tagging the unwary runner who strayed off the base. Incredibly, thirty-three such incidents occurred before Bob encountered one on July 22, 1910, in St. Louis. After Cy Seymour flew out the clever ruse was used on Fred Snodgrass, Emslie calling him out only to have home plate umpire Cy Rigler overturn the decision, saying after the flyout the Giants had called time to send up a pinch hitter. But St. Louis catcher-manager Roger Bresnahan argued Rigler had never called time and the new batter was awaiting the pitch when Snodgrass was caught napping. Bresnahan may have been right, but after the game Emslie, ever the loyal comrade, said Rigler was correct in calling play "dead" to announced the change in batters.

Emslie's reputation as a rules expert was legendary. When a reader posed a complicated hypothetical baseball question to New York newspaper columnist Bozeman Bulger, the scribe asked Giants players, who disagreed on the interpretation, and McGraw, who admitted he didn't know the rule. Bulger then asked Emslie, who in providing the correct answer cited the number of the applicable rule. Fans also queried him about rules. Once, when asked a question as he arrived at the ballpark in Philadelphia, Bob "pondered over the question long and deeply"—so long that he was late reaching the field for the scheduled start of the game.[7]

Stories circulated of Emslie's postgame encounters with fans on streetcars that demonstrated his rules expertise. Most often told were two incidents from Philadelphia related in detail by his contemporary in the American League, future Hall of Fame umpire Billy Evans. One involved Emslie sitting next to a fan who asked if he had been at that day's game. After an affirmative response, the fan queried, "What did you think of the umpire?" To Emslie's response—"He made a few mistakes, but on the whole I think he did fairly well"—the fan replied, "He gave the rottenest exhibition I've ever witnessed. I'd just like to meet him right now. They tell me Emslie is as bald as a billiard ball and wears a wig on the diamond. His bum decisions caused me to drop twenty, and I feel as if I'd like to scalp him of that false hair." Despite the ill-mannered reference to his toupee, Bob calmly replied, "Oh, I don't know. I've been coming to ball games for nearly twenty-five years, and I've seen worse and by the same fellow," and on departing at the terminal gave the fan his umpire's card. The next day at the ballpark he received a letter of apology that concluded, "No better supporter of Emslie now lives in Philadelphia."[8]

Another time, the day after being excoriated for a decision, he found himself riding to Baker Bowl with two fans who had been at the game and were arguing about the play. One asked Bob if he had been at the game. He replied affirmatively, and in response to the fan asking if he had seen the play, said he believed "no one could have been in a better place" to see it. The fan, having bet a five-dollar hat on the disputed point, asked Bob to settle it, whereupon the other fan asked if Bob "thoroughly understood the rules." Saying he "had made a careful study of them," Bob proceeded to explain the play "thoroughly so as to remove the slightest doubt in the mind of the man who had been stuck for the hat." When the trio arrived at the ballpark Emslie gave his umpire identification card to the loser and hurried away. The next day he received an order from a hat company for a new chapeau inscribed "It's on me."[9]

While the stories of Emslie's encounters with fans in which he answered questions authoritatively then surprised them with his identity are without firsthand documentation, it is unlikely that Evans made up out of whole cloth stories about a contemporary umpire whom he knew personally and had worked with in postseason games. True or not in detail, since Emslie was the original teller of the tales, they underscore his pride as master of the rule book.

DIAMOND UNPLEASANTRIES

Like a judge applying the law despite claimants' differing views of justice, Emslie inevitably faced disputes. The 1901 season opened fittingly on April 19, the anniversary of the first shots of the American Revolution being fired at Lexington, for in the first inning his out call of Chicago's Tully "Topsy" Hartsel's attempt to steal third base produced the initial volley of kicks that characterized the first decade of the century. Emslie's job of maintaining decorum during games became much more difficult in 1902 when Brush, he of the 1898 resolution against profanity, hired foul-mouthed John McGraw, poster boy for pugnacious treatment of umpires, as player-manager of the New York Giants. Small in stature and big of mouth, the crafty strategist routinely devolved into a vitriolic homunculus spewing vicious invective that infected his team, then spread throughout the league.

Nothing put Emslie and the other umpires in higher dudgeon than the second-most ejected manager in history.[10] On May 19, 1902, at the Polo Grounds, Bob had the distinction of giving McGraw his first managerial ejection for "raucously expressing disagreement" over whether Billy Lauder was hit by a pitch.[11] By 1910 he had tossed out "the boss kicker" eight more times for spouting "choice selections from his famous repertory of vilification" and also exiled twenty-seven Giants. New York was the most contentious team, in 1907 accumulating a fifth of all ejections.[12] The Cincinnati Reds were close behind: Bob tossed seven Reds, ejecting player-manager Joe Kelley nine times.

For Emslie, umpiring games between McGraw's Giants and Kelley's Reds was like going into a nest of vipers. During a series in Cincinnati in May 1904 he tossed three Giants and suspended Bill Dahlen and Kelley for three games. When the Giants returned to the Queen City during a twin bill on August 12, Bob tossed four New Yorkers as players on both teams "buzzed around his ears like Jersey mosquitoes in a cranberry bog." Emslie was so upset by the contentiousness that he uncharacteristically talked about the ejections to a reporter. "Umpires have been instructed not to let ballplayers kick over decisions and not to tolerate any abuse from them. I will not stand for any kicking from a player in the League, no matter who the man is. I will put him out of the game just as soon as I feel that he is talking back too much or uses language which he should not use." The next day he wasted no time benching the Giants' Frank Bowerman and the Reds' Jack Harper for "caustic comments."[13] After Emslie filed his report on the ejections, Pulliam indefinitely suspended

Kelley, previously suspended for three days after an altercation, and suspended McGarr and Harper for three days.[14]

True to his word, he showed no favoritism. He greatly admired Pittsburgh's Honus Wagner, but exiled the Pirates shortstop on July 13, 1901, for angrily throwing his glove across the diamond at Bob, and again on May 28, 1905, for demonstrating displeasure by "scornfully grasping his nose with this thumb and index finger." Bob's integrity and fairness were universal. On May 2, 1910, Christy Mathewson missed his third no-hitter when Brooklyn's official scorer ruled a slightly misplayed eighth inning grounder the only hit of the game; the scorer was roasted, but Emslie, despite greatly admiring Mathewson, told reporters he had seen the play clearly and backed up the ruling. And when John "Jack" Taylor, who admitted taking $500 to throw three games in the 1903 Chicago intercity series, was accused the next year of throwing a game against Pittsburgh on July 30—the first formal allegation since 1877 of players conspiring with gamblers to fix a game—Emslie, the plate umpire for the game in question, who as former pitcher would be alert to suspicious performance, submitted an affidavit stating that Taylor "had done his best." Consequently, Taylor, in the process of setting a Major League record of thirty-nine consecutive complete games, was exonerated of crookedness, but fined $300 for drinking heavily the night before the game.[15]

Emslie struggled with kicking. As Giants manager Bill Joyce observed, the former "scrappy" ballplayer "sympathized with the boys and overlooked a good many things." Threatening "Ten and out of the game," Bob's usual means of cutting off arguments, didn't suppress rowdy behavior, and his reluctance to eject players led to leniency. On July 13, 1901, he did not toss Pittsburgh's Fred Clarke after a raucous outburst, saying after the game that he had not been called any "vile names," the worst being "coward," and it was the first time in years Clarke had argued. The press praised Bob's "good judgment" in ignoring the "loud talk of the excited player," concluding, "Emslie is a wise man. He simply ignores the kickers." When angry Giants piled dirt on the plate, he just swept the dirt off the plate and called, "Batter up!" He even showed remarkable forbearance to his nemesis McGraw. In 1904, after being grabbed by the arm during an argument, he ejected but did not suspend Muggsy when he apologized profusely, saying he had not meant to touch Bob. And when McGraw, after being ejected, returned two or three times to "slap his hands" in Emslie's face and even "shook his fingers under his nose," Bob "stood there stoically without retaliation."[16]

Emslie tolerated disagreements over decisions, but would not abide being "shown up" or ridiculed before the crowd. In New York on May 21, 1902, he ejected Luther "Dummy" Taylor, the Giants' deaf and dumb pitcher, after he threw his glove toward Bob, did "a pantomime that showed his displeasure," and "doubtless said more swear words mentally than this paper would care to print."[17] The worst derogatory incident occurred in Chicago in May 25, 1908, when McGraw ended an argument by suggesting Emslie get a box of hairpins to fasten his toupee. Only a few players heard the mean-spirited comment, so the next inning he repeated it loudly enough to be heard by fans. As the cruel remark meant to embarrass "swept from stand to bleachers," later passing around town, Bob, "crimson from white collar to the edge of the maligned wig," ejected his antagonist and hit him with a sizable fine. McGraw "smiled a wicked smile" as he left the field "amid the jeers of the spectators," Emslie regarding the wanton humiliation as "one of the most tragic, brutal cases of 'show up' he had ever experienced."[18]

Bob had fewer confrontations than other umpires, but kicking bothered him to the point of expressing his views in a rare interview:

> I think the thing that gets an umpire most is to have old friends among the players jump on him. Of course, he expects his best friend to protest if a decision on a close play is against him, but when it comes to profanity and that sort of thing, an umpire, being a human being, feels just as you would. It's a hard job at best, but I guess no harder than any other, and when a man does his best he finds satisfaction in that which outweighs all the jeers, hisses and groans. You may get a notion how effective is that philosophy when you consider how few baseball umpires ever answer back or give any sign that the protests of the players or the shouts of the crowd have been noticed by them.[19]

Sometimes the kicking was justified. On August 15, 1904, in New York Bob rushed from behind the plate to make a call on an attempted steal at second base. Seeing the fielder tag the runner, he turned and headed back to home, thereby not seeing the fielder drop the ball. After the game he admitted he blew the call: "I realized the instant I heard the spectators yell that the ball had been muffed, but I had not seen it. I really felt badly about the mistake."[20]

Verbal abuse was commonplace, physical assaults by players and fans rare. At the Polo Grounds on August 6, 1902, the Giants' Jim Jones argued a strike call, then flew out, grabbed Emslie's arm, and took a swing that knocked off his mask and cap. With the Doyle incident embedded in his consciousness, Emslie "kept cool," showing "admirable self-control by not retaliating," simply ejecting and fining his assailant. The Giants suspended Jones for the season, the banishment made easier since he was "not so valuable to the club that his services will be missed." (He never returned to the Majors.) Emslie's only other physical encounter came in Philadelphia on June 18, 1908, when "a smart shove" in the back by the Phillies' Sherwood Magee resulted in banishment.

Fan violence was the greater and omnipresent danger. Occasional objects thrown from the stands were disconcerting but not dangerous, as they invariably fell short of the target, as on July 31, 1907, when a Chicago fan signaled displeasure by throwing a pop bottle at Bob; the missile missed and the fan was promptly ejected from the grounds. More frequent and dangerous were postgame mobbings, invariably prompted by game-ending decisions against the home team. Emslie demonstrated his mettle with aplomb by twice disdaining police protection in Pittsburgh in 1901. When fans stormed the field on July 13 after Bob called a Pirates player out at home to end the game, Pittsburgh officials dispatched a squad of police to protect him, but he "fearlessly waved them off" and calmly walked through the angry crowd to the clubhouse. Less than a week later, on July 19, after another out call ended the game, several hundred bleacherites invaded the field, some yelling Bob should be jailed, others suggesting "a lynching bee." Brooklyn players provided initial protection and when police arrived Emslie "stood his ground manfully," again waving them off and heading unescorted for the clubhouse. Recalling he had forgotten his mask he returned to home plate, nonchalantly looked for the mask, then proceeded through the hooting and hissing crowd to the dressing room, the press reporting the "cool and gentlemanly conduct of the umpire was admired by the majority of the club's patrons."[21]

Home team fans were not the only ones given to rowdy behavior. At the Polo Grounds on July 4, 1906, Emslie called Brooklyn's Tim Jordan's hit a foul ball, negating a three-run homer that might have won the game. After Jordan struck out to end the game, angry Superbas rooters made a rush for Bob. This time, several policemen surrounded Emslie, warded off his assailants with clubs, and escorted him off the grounds.

Prior to the 1907 season, the *New York Sun* on February 25 published a poem, "Gentle Spring Thoughts":

> The violet will shortly blow,
> The crocus lift its cup;
> And in the fields the hemp will grow
> To string the umpire up.

It was prophetic: on May 21 came Emslie's closest call yet with fan violence. He and O'Day were sent to the Polo Grounds for an important series, Chicago one game behind league-leading New York. In the last inning of the first game a "vehement protest" by the Giants' Bresnahan when Emslie called out him out for running out the baseline so inflamed the crowd that after the final out, the Cubs winning 3–2 to tie for first, "fully 10,000" fans surged onto the field bent on assaulting Bob. Several Giants came to his aid, in particular pitcher Joe McGinnity, who protectively put his arm around Emslie's shoulder, yelled for the crowd to desist, and deflected several blows intended for Bob's head. Security officers provided a protective cordon as Emslie and O'Day walked toward their dressing room under the center-field grandstand surrounded by fans "wildly howling for their blood"—"Punch the robber! Knock his block off!"—and hurling cushions, bottles, and other debris. Emslie was hit on the head with a broom, and when punched in the ribs, he smacked the violent offender on the nose. Fans blocked access to the dressing room until a policeman fired his pistol into the air and several mounted officers rode into the throng. A squad of officers followed the umpires all the way to the 155th Street elevated train station. Displaying courage and the dignity of their profession, Bob and Hank "smoked cigars unconcernedly" despite being pelted with "hoots and catcalls," rocks, and rolled-up newspapers, one knocking off Emslie's hat. The next day the regular police squad stationed outside the stadium as a precaution was not needed. Fans gave the umpires an ovation when they appeared on the field; Bob was behind the plate when McGinnity, who received a letter from Pulliam commending him for his "manly action" in protecting Emslie, pitched the Giants to a 7–1 victory.[22]

ILLNESS AND INJURY

Displaying remarkable stamina, Emslie missed remarkably few games, routinely calling about 90 percent of the games each season. He led the staff in games umpired in 1901, 1902, and 1908, the latter season's 156 the most in his career. Umpiring almost daily from April to October was physically taxing. Games were usually completed in well under two hours, but he constantly ran back and forth from behind the plate to make base and foul line calls. Absent a time limit or maximum number of innings, a baseball game theoretically can go on forever, and some threatened to do so. During the decade Bob called 123 extra-inning games. Most went for ten to thirteen innings, but in 1909 one went to seventeen; twice he had two sixteen- and seventeen-inning games in a season. He found doubleheaders, more frequent as the season drew to an end, exhausting; he said the "strain is terrific and the effects are bad." From 1901 to 1910 he worked 178 twin bills, 20 to 22 of them in four seasons, and 24 in 1904; six times he umpired 3 of them in a row and thrice umpired 4 straight.[23]

Since beginning umpiring in 1887 Emslie generally enjoyed good health during the season, but in 1901 he began suffering a series of ailments. Games starting at 3:30 or 4 p.m., the hottest time of the day, could be enervating. With "sizzling heat" in Boston on June 28 producing sixteen deaths and "scores of prostrations," Emslie struggled under the "broiling sun" until collapsing in the fifth inning. After treating the fallen umpire, Boston's club physician accompanied Bob, "completely prostrated," to his hotel. Since he did not umpire again until July 11,

Emslie probably suffered not from heat exhaustion or dehydration, the normal recovery time being twenty-four to forty-eight hours, but heat stroke (hyperthermia), whose effects can last two months or more.[24] On August 20, under a "scorching sun" in Brooklyn, he was again almost overcome in the first game of a doubleheader. He completed the game but felt so sick he refused to umpire the second game "at any price." Bob umpired the next three days, then, feeling ill again, went on the sick list for two days. After umpiring in Cincinnati on September 7, ptomaine poisoning put him out of action for four days; he returned on September 12 even though he had not entirely recovered. He suffered no physical maladies in 1902, but in New York on May 30, 1903, in the second inning of the morning game of a doubleheader, Bob suddenly was unable to stand upright from an attack of sciatica. With a look of agony on his face as the intense lower back pain from a herniated spinal disk radiated along the sciatic nerve through his hip and down his leg, he was carried to the Giants bench, where he lay curled up for a time before hobbling to the dressing room. But he refused to have players umpire, so he took a painkiller and umpired the afternoon game.

Injuries were far more common and serious than illnesses. At the onset of the 1901 season it was noted that "the hairless one" had had "many hard knocks since he donned the umpire's mask," but they were nothing like the physical injuries Emslie would suffer during the upcoming decade. Most injuries umpires received from batted and thrown balls were minor, but several of Bob's were serious enough to warrant mention in the press.[25]

Standing behind the plate wearing a mask and a padded leather chest protector did not prevent blows to Bob's body, and his bones hurt more and bruises lasted longer with age. He got through 1901 and 1902 unscathed; then the battering came in bunches. On June 27, 1903, "smote with terrific force" by a foul on the left forearm at the elbow in St. Louis, Emslie fell to his knees, groaning in pain. A doctor who happened to be in the stands determined no bones were broken, so Emslie resumed umpiring. He stoically continued to umpire in great pain for several days as the arm "turned black" from elbow to wrist. (The discoloration likely came not from "blood poisoning"—bacteremia or septicemia resulting from infection—as reported at the time, but from deoxygenated blood pooling from the blow.) In 1904 doubleheaders in Pittsburgh proved particularly hurtful. In the first inning of the second game on July 29 Bob had to leave after being hit "several times" on the left wrist by foul tips, with players substituting after his departure. The next day he umpired another twin bill with his left arm in a splint; in the second game fouls raised "two severe bumps" on the side of his head. On August 29, in another twin bill in Pittsburgh, a foul tip in the second game so badly bruised his right knee he was unable to umpire on August 30, two players again substituting. By season's end the frequency and severity of the peppering caused *Sporting Life* to comment on October 15 he had been "hit on the shins so often by foul tips that he can hardly navigate."

Emslie was not the only backstop for backwardly batted baseballs. O'Day was seriously injured on July 23 by a foul that struck him on the ear and caused him to miss almost two months. But Pulliam called on Hank to join Bob on September 15, both "suffering from injuries that practically incapacitated them." Until season's end three weeks later, O'Day, unable to don a mask, worked only the bases, while Emslie, hobbled by a bad leg, had the plate.[26]

The pounding worsened in 1905, the press proclaiming Emslie had "more hard luck" with foul tips than other umpires. "A wicked foul tip" to a kneecap on June 26 in Philadelphia, the "ugly blow heard all over the grounds," was serious enough to suspend play for twenty minutes while a physician dressed the injury. Bob, the lone umpire, finished the game and was back at it the next day, a bit gimpy. A week later, in Philadelphia on July 5, he got rapped on the shins so severely that, while he completed the game, he was unable to umpire again until July 11. His bad luck was good fortune for a Minor League player. While home recovering from the leg injury, Bob spotted Jack Graney pitching for the St. Thomas Saints of the Canadian League and recommended him to the Chicago Cubs. Graney reached the Majors in 1908, and after fourteen years with Cleveland, in 1932 became the first former Major Leaguer to broadcast games on the radio, all with the Indians.

Bob's most serious foul encounter came on September 24 in Chicago, when in the second inning he was "staggered" by a foul tip just over the heart. Bob thought the "intense pain" would wear off, but after the next pitch, he dropped "as if shot." Players rushed to his side and fans poured from the stands to see what had happened to the fallen umpire, fearing him dead as he "never moved a muscle." A doctor worked over Emslie for more than twenty minutes before he regained consciousness and struggled to his feet, "dazed and with a face white as chalk." After resting a few minutes on the Cubs bench, to everyone's surprise, Bob "in great pain, concealed his suffering," donned his mask and ordered play to resume. At the remarkable display of courage and resilience of the lone umpire, fans "stood for several minutes and cheered him wildly." But for the next three-game series in Pittsburgh, O'Day was summoned to call pitches while Emslie worked the bases. Bob returned solo to the plate on September 28.

He was free of serious injury in 1906 but not in 1907. Three times he was "badly jarred" when hit: by a foul tip flush in the center of the mask, by a passed ball on the neck that required medical attention, and by a backswing of the bat that "dented his kneecap" and produced a "prominent welt." None of the blows were disabling, but on September 15 in Chicago Bob was struck so hard on the shin by a bat flung by Frank Chance after getting a hit that he went home to St. Thomas to recuperate for three days before returning to duty.[27]

Exchanging the external leather chest protector for an "air cushion" worn under his jacket, wearing "leather cups" over his elbows, and donning "formidable shin guards" did not protect him from injury in 1908. By the end of May Emslie was "still leading all of the umpires in getting hit by foul tips."[28] There was nothing new about him getting "nearly knocked down" by a foul tip in Cincinnati and getting "a hearty hand" when he resumed umpiring on July 1, but on July 23 he had a career day for misfortune in Pittsburgh. In the second inning his London pal George "Mooney" Gibson, after hitting the ball, "viciously flung his bat away," striking Emslie on the knee and knocking him to the ground. In the fourth inning, after a foul tip hit him on the shoulder, he had hardly finished rubbing the ache when another foul hit him on the same spot. Later that inning Bob was nailed in the ribs, and to top it off he suffered "a hard fall" after tripping on a catcher's mask while racing to cover a base play. Emslie stoically carried on while "the heartless fans only giggled at Mr. Emslie's ill luck." The blow to his knee was so severe he was unable to bend; Bob umpired only the bases for the next three series (thirteen games), finally returning behind the plate on August 7. Truly, as the *New York Sun* observed on September 4, 1909, "Emslie has had more hard bumps behind the bat than all the rest of the umpires put together."

Umpiring the bases was much safer. But the day after he returned from heat exhaustion in August 1901 he was hit "with terrific force" by Bill Dahlen's line drive in Brooklyn. Bob "winced," called Dahlen out at first, then gamely carried on, but was out for five days afterward, not returning until September 2. The next year Bob was felled by a thrown ball for the first time in his career. On July 1 in Brooklyn Phillies catcher Fred Jacklitsch's throw to second to thwart a steal attempt hit Bob with a whack below the right ear so hard it was heard in the grandstand by Nick Young, who immediately ran for a physician. Bob, unconscious for several minutes, finally struggled to his feet and "in a dazed sort of way" dusted off the plate as the fans "generously applauded his pluck in resuming duties." His penchant for injury was such that when umpiring the bases in Boston May 21,1903, he was almost knocked out by a ball not in play. While watching the play on the Reds' George Magoon at first, Bob was felled by "a wicked blow" on the head from an earlier foul ball thrown back onto the field. Magoon was out, but since Emslie did not see it, he ordered the play done over. Magoon then struck out, making two outs in one at bat.

Bob twice missed games due to family emergencies. Before a game in Chicago on October 3, 1905, he received a telegram saying that his sister lay paralyzed from a stroke (hemiplegia). He left with the score tied after the ninth inning to catch a train to St. Thomas, leaving two players to call the final four innings of the 5–5 game. Assured of her survival, he returned to finish the season in New York on October 5. When she died, five years later to the day, he left St. Louis after the game on October 4, 1910, to attend burial services, then returned to Cincinnati on October 8 to work the last two games of the season.

Along with bodily injuries, Emslie suffered emotional blows. For all his self-assurance he remained acutely sensitive about his baldness, even trying to make light of his alopecia with quips such as "The law of gravitation explains why a thing falls down, but it doesn't explain why hair falls out" and "In trying to take time by the forelock you occasionally find that it wears a wig." Players and managers knew he wore a toupee, but as late as 1907 it was not generally known he wore a hairpiece. "It used to be quite the fad in the League to josh Bob about his wig," Christy Mathewson recalled in 1912, "but that pastime has sort of died out now because he has proven himself to be such a good fellow." There are no references to Bob ever being called "Wig" to his face or even within hearing by a player or manager as an immediate fine and expulsion would result. The amiable and even-tempered arbiter would stand for a lot of abuse, but woe to anyone who made wisecracks about his toupee.[29]

Occasionally the hairpiece came to attention on the field. The Cardinals' Jimmy Burke claimed that Emslie refused to speak to him for a week in 1905 when, angry for being called out on strikes, he accidentally knocked off Bob's cap and "red wig," exposing his bald head.[30] In 1906 McGraw had Cy Seymour take the field in Cincinnati on August 25 wearing a red beard as a disguise, fearful that fans would not take kindly to the former Reds player after being sold to the Giants. When umpire Hank O'Day objected to the ploy, McGraw countered, "If Emslie can wear a false wig when umpiring, there is nothing in the world to stop Seymour from wearing false whiskers in the outfield." O'Day conceded the point, but Seymour, after grounding out to end the first inning, removed the "chin-chillas."[31]

On September 3, 1909, at the Polo Grounds, a foul tip produced a foul reaction from Bob. Hit by "a staggering wallop on the head that seemed hard enough to kill an ox," he fell senseless to the ground. Christy Mathewson arrived with a bucket of water to revive the stricken arbiter, and as Roger Bresnahan applied a wet sponge to Emslie's head the wig slipped off. Upon regaining consciousness, Bob, realizing his "nude pate was exposed to view," furiously pushed Bresnahan away, struggled to his feet, "like a tiger" shooed away his attendants, refitted his disheveled wig "to cover his naked head and hide his humiliation," and ordered play to resume. The blow to the frontal bone likely would have fractured his skull had the toupee not cushioned the impact; as it was, Bob was out for two days, and then, with a terrific headache, worked only the bases for the next two games. The incident played on his mind. Several weeks later, when he next encountered the Giants, Emslie asked Mathewson if Bresnahan removed his wig. To Christy's reply, "No, Bob, he was only trying to help you," Emslie said, "I thought maybe he took it off while I was down and out and showed me up before the crowd." To Mathewson's assurance, "Listen, Bob, I don't believe there is a player in either league who would do that," the relieved umpire said, "I'm glad to hear you say that, Matty" as he prepared to go to work.[32]

UMPIRING CONUNDRUMS

The belief that the American League in 1902 had "a majority of the star players" while the National had "by long odds the best staff of umpires ever got together" was wrong. With Lynch, Gaffney, Connolly, Hurst, and Sheridan gone, the National suffered from poor hirings and turnover. Emslie, O'Day, and Jim Johnstone, hired in 1902, umpired the decade; not until the arrival of Bill Klem in 1905 and Cy Rigler in 1906 was the staff equal in stability and ability to that of the American. There was far less bickering and berating in the American owing to Ban Johnson supporting umpires and suspending players guilty of flagrant misconduct while insisting his arbiters be tactful, not combative, in dealing with rowdiness. But in the National an umpire had "practically no backing except his own fists." The contentiousness was such that veteran John Gaffney quit after 1901, preferring a job as streetcar conductor at $13 per week over umpiring for $300 per month. To the *Boston Globe*, "The umpires of the American league are making the most pronounced success, while those of the National league, Emslie excepted, look like playthings for players, magnates and spectators." *Sporting News* bluntly editorialized, "It is time for the National League to clean its skirts."[33]

Instead, the owners made life much more difficult for Bob and his cohort. First, in April 1902 they replaced the office of league president with an executive board comprising three owners and instructed Young, now reduced to being the board's secretary, to move the league offices from Washington DC to New York City, home of the Giants' Andrew Freedman, a notorious umpire critic. Then, hoping to stop rowdy play, umpires were ordered to eject, not fine, players who used offensive language or disputed their decisions.

Emslie thought the belief ejections instead of fines would curb kicking was a pipe dream. After he tossed Frank Chance on April 19, 1902, he complained, "Some of these players would rather lose an arm than give up a five-dollar bill, but with all power to keep them in check taken away from him the umpire is subjected to more abuse than ever. Look at the way the Chicagoes acted today. What can I do? Eject nine or ten men from the bench?"[34] As a former player he disliked ejecting players, as it hurt the team, but with increased kicking his ejections spiked from two in 1901 to eight in 1902, sixteen in 1903, twenty-one in 1904, and nineteen in 1905, before decreasing as he increasingly umpired the bases: he issued seven in 1906 and 1907 and only three in 1910. Notwithstanding increased kicking, he remained hesitant to pull the trigger, each season tossing the fewest players of any umpire on the staff: Augie Moran tossed twenty-eight in 1903, Johnstone thirty in 1904, Klem twenty-six in 1905 and twenty-eight in 1907, Rigler twenty-seven in 1907 and twenty-eight in 1909.

Emslie got caught up in, or rather took advantage of, the discord among National League owners following the American League's assertion of Major League status in 1901. In December 1901, after four magnates left the league's annual meeting, the rump session elected Albert Spalding to replace the aged Nick Young as president. His appointment was immediately challenged, but Spalding attempted to consolidate his position by offering contracts to the league's two top umpires, asking them to "name their terms." Hank O'Day asked for $300 per month, amounting to $1,800, and Bob requested $2,000. Then, whether inspired by Spalding's preemptive overture or the interleague competition to sign the best umpires, the three best umpires in each circuit—Emslie, O'Day, and Tom Brown from the National and Tom Connolly, Jack Sheridan, and "Pongo Joe" Cantillon from the American—refused to sign contracts for 1902. O'Day and Cantillon, fingered as the organizers of the holdout, said they had not combined to pressure the owners, but simply decided not to sign until given "fair salaries," adding, "None of us are in a hurry to do business, but if the magnates are willing to talk business, we stand ready to meet them half way." The denial was too emphatic by half; it was unreasonable to believe the best umpires in each league would simultaneously, independently decide not to sign contracts. It was the first organized umpire holdout in history.[35]

Emslie knew from previous experience that asking for a salary increase was a tough sell, but the involvement of three American umpires and the uncertain times seemed to bode well. But despite support from the press, which argued, "Considering the scarcity of good men, and the onerous duties they are called upon to perform, the umpires are a poorly paid lot," the quest for higher salaries was a fool's errand. National League owners were famously indifferent, if not downright hostile, to umpires, regarding them as replaceable employees. The American League's Johnson, while supportive of umpires, was cheap, and like the owners, regarded umpires as easily replaceable ancillary employees instead of skilled professionals central to the game. When Johnson began hiring Minor League umpires, the sextet lost their bargaining position, and signed contracts in April, just before opening day.[36]

Notwithstanding the abortive salary quest, the lot of National League umpires improved. Ownership disputes and the executive board's inability to deal effectively with issues led in December 1902 to deep-sixing the ruling troika and reestablishing the position of president with "Old Nick," now sixty-one, replaced by the youthful Harry Clay Pulliam, the thirty-three-year-old secretary of the Pittsburgh Pirates. The move initially concerned Bob as he and Young were great friends, often socializing after ball games, but he quickly found the former newspaper reporter cum baseball executive an effective advocate for umpires. While Young had been the nominal head of the league with only routine secretarial duties, Pulliam immediately assumed an active role, convincing the owners to give the president unprecedented power to handle rowdy behavior. Finally recognizing that without strong leadership the league "will be a bundle of straws" and influenced by Johnson's authority in the American, NL owners adopted a resolution giving the president "full and absolute power to maintain order and discipline on the ball field" and stipulating that "in all cases where the penalty fixed is either a fine or suspension his decision shall be final." A subsequent amendment proposed by Cincinnati's Max Fleischmann prevented clubs from paying a player's fine or salary while suspended. (Chicago's James Hart proposed the primary resolution making the president "the absolute dictator and supreme ruler of the field," but it was subsequently called the Fleischmann rule.) It was a gutsy move by Pulliam, but also indicative of the depths to which the game had fallen in the National League.[37]

Prior to the 1903 season Pulliam established both fines and ejections as penalties for untoward behavior, but Emslie remained hesitant to impose severe penalties. He was the first to apply the Fleischmann rule, ejecting Cincinnati's Joe Kelley for verbal abuse. When Pulliam ruled Kelley's action "justified immediate suspension," Bob argued the penalty should instead be "a severe reprimand." In deference to the league's senior umpire, Pulliam honored Bob's "gracious" request, adding it was "the first in which lenience is shown and it will be the last." Pulliam did not appreciate Emslie's "easy going ways," ordering him "in the most positive terms that he must be less lenient with the kickers."[38]

Emslie's initial restraint proved prophetic. In December 1904 the owners increased the fine for violating playing rules from $5 to $10 and added $10 for each day of suspension, but recognizing the potential for losing players given Pulliam's sweeping authority, surreptitiously failed to renew the Hart-Fleischmann resolution, thereby reverting presidential authority to the earlier Brush resolution, which required a hearing before the imposition of a suspension. Consequently, in 1905 when Pulliam, mistakenly thinking the resolution still effective, hit McGraw with a $150 fine and a fifteen-day suspension for taunting Pittsburgh owner Barney Dreyfuss on May 19 in New York, saying he should umpire instead of Emslie as it "would be all the same thing." After the owners absolved McGraw of "abusing" Dreyfuss—a slap at Pulliam—the wily manager, undoubtedly advised by Giants owner Brush, filed a bill of equity in the Massachusetts Superior Court against Pulliam's penalties on the grounds that he had not been given a hearing. When the judge issued an injunction against enforcement since the lapse of the Hart-Fleischmann resolution required a hearing before suspensions, Pulliam rescinded both penalties.[39]

McGraw and Brush won the battle, but Pulliam won the war. After the season Brush and his ally, Cincinnati's Garry Hermann, tried to oust Pulliam, but he was unanimously reelected (the two conspirators did not vote.) He immediately exercised his influence by implementing a slightly revised Hart-Fleishmann resolution that made the president's decisions on fines and suspensions final. Support for umpires increased in 1906 when the league created the separate office of secretary-treasurer, giving Pulliam more time to pay attention to the staff. Emslie was vastly pleased with the appointment of John Heydler, whom he knew well as a former Orioles teammate and 1890s umpire.

Other improvements followed in 1907. Requiring ballparks to provide a "proper and suitable" dressing room for umpires was greatly appreciated, as was Pulliam's unsuccessful attempt to ban the sale of intoxicants and liquids in bottles. For the first time umpires, Emslie and Connolly, were added to the joint rules committee, Ban Johnson thinking the men charged with implementing the rules would have valuable suggestions. And the Hart-Fleischmann resolution, formerly a rule, was added to the league constitution. Moreover, umpires finally achieved official public recognition, appearing for the first time in an edition of *Spalding's Official Base Ball Guide*. Among the photos of players from each team were pictures of four National League umpires—Carpenter, Johnstone, Klem, and O'Day—and four American League umpires—Connolly, Evans, O'Loughlin, and Sheridan—in addition to the two 1906 World Series umpires, Johnstone and O'Loughlin, each shown in game-action shots for all six games.[40]

UMPIRING ADAPTATIONS

During the Deadball Era (1901–20) Emslie found himself umpiring a faster-paced style of play. A combination of balls made "dead" by design and overuse and pitches scuffed and "doctored" with saliva and other substances improved defensive play. An array of outstanding pitchers (think Grover Cleveland Alexander, Mordecai "Three-finger" Brown, and Christy Mathewson in the National and Walter Johnson, Rube Waddell, and Cy Young in the American) produced low-scoring games in which teams relied on an offensive strategy—bunting for hits and to advance runners and stolen bases—that made it more difficult for a lone umpire stationed behind the plate to make base calls.[41]

Bob also adjusted to new umpiring techniques and equipment. Since 1887 he had stood erect behind the catcher when calling balls and strikes, but following the lead of Jack Sheridan, now in the American, he began crouching and shifting position to track the ball's flight. To protect his legs from fouls and pitches he pioneered the use of shin guards. He appeared in 1900 wearing cricket pads, dark brown reinforced canvas pads stuffed with cotton. (Since 1907 catchers had been wearing thick shin guards strapped to their legs, and by 1911 umpires commonly wore a thinner version inside their pant legs.)[42] Instead of switching to a chest protector worn inside the jacket, as advocated by Bill Klem, Emslie continued using an outside protector, but he donned a full-torso pad unlike O'Day's shield-shaped breast cover. To improve traction while running to make calls he attached spiked plates to his shoes, and after a player in 1904 sprained an ankle tripping over the broom used to dust off home plate he carried a whisk broom in his pocket. With the construction of larger stadiums making it difficult for spectators seated farther from the field to follow the action, he was given a greater role in providing information. Announcing with a megaphone the batteries and changes in team personnel was not a problem for Bob, whose "sonorous voice" once prompted the observation he could make a fortune as a railroad conductor—a view seconded by Sheridan, who said he would "give a good deal to have a clear, resonant voice like Bob Emslie."[43]

More difficult was adopting arm movements to signal pitch and base decisions. Umpires for years used various ways of indicating calls, but most were vocal. With the record crowds on hand for a series in Chicago unable to hear the calls of "bullfrog" Jack Sheridan, on September 9, 1901, he wore a red sleeve on his right arm to signal strikes and a white one on the left to indicate balls, but the experiment was not repeated. Cy Rigler, who used hand and arm gestures in the Minor Leagues in 1905 to inform outfielders of his calls, found when he got to the Majors in 1906 that Klem had started using them. In February 1907 the joint rules committee, impressed by the use of hand signals in the 1906 World Series, proposed uniformity in calling pitches: umpires would raise the right arm for strikes while making no motion for balls.[44] The proposal failed on opposition from Emslie and Connolly, each league's head umpire pointing out that umpires often used both hands to hold up chest protectors, needed to sprint onto the field to make base calls, and had individual preferences for signaling decisions. Absent a specific official requirement, the presidents in both leagues decided to require the use of arm signals in 1907 without specifying what they should be. Standardization was slow in coming. For pitches, O'Day raised his left hand for ball, none for strike, while Johnson and Carpenter raised the right arm for strike; for base decisions, most like Emslie raised his right arm, index finger extended, for "out" and a downward palm for "safe." It took time for Emslie to adjust; a month into the 1908 season Bob "more than half the time forgot to raise his right arm for a strike."[45]

DOUBLE UMPIRES

Emslie eventually also had to adjust to working with another umpire. He had done so more often after both leagues began using five umpires in 1901. When the National adopted six regular umpires in 1906 Emslie was usually paired with new hires, most of whom, like George Bausewine in 1905, John Conway in 1906, and Frank Rudderham in 1908, lasted only one season. If a second arbiter facilitated base calls, Emslie found problems occasionally arose when the arbiters disagreed on a decision or, more often, when neither made a call, thinking the other would do so. Some disputes were quickly resolved, as on July 12, 1905, in Chicago: controversy arose over whether Emslie and O'Day had made different judgments on a play at third base, but it ended when the umpires agreed both had made an out call. But a month later, on August 5, when Bob teamed with Bausewine for an important series between the first-place Giants and second-place Pirates in Pittsburgh, confusion about a call produced a riot. With the score tied 5–5 in the bottom of the ninth, Bausewine, the plate umpire, called the Pirates' Claude Ritchey safe on a close play at third base. As the Giants swarmed angrily about George in protest, McGraw appealed to Emslie, who said he hadn't seen the play as he was watching a runner at second and, besides, it was Bausewine's responsibility to make calls at third. When the Giants refused to stop arguing, McGraw pushing both umpires in the chest, Bausewine pulled his watch and forfeited the game to Pittsburgh. During the ensuing melee Muggsy shook his fist in George's face, Christy Mathewson tried to knock the watch from his hand, and Emslie lost his temper. Provoked by "a particularly uncomplimentary remark," Bob, after either delivering "a hard punch" to "Turkey Mike" Donlin's face or bloodying Art Devlin's with a "good right fist," walked "quietly and unconcernedly" to the umpires' dressing room as Pirates fans hurled rocks and all manner of debris at the Giants as they left the field and fled in carriages over the Allegheny River and out of town. Bausewine did not umpire with Emslie again and was terminated after the season.

Indecision resulted in one of the most embarrassing moments of Bob's career. On May 2, 1908, in New York, Rigler called the Giants "Cy" Seymour out trying to steal second base—a seemingly obvious call as he was out "by ten feet"—but Seymour protested, claiming he slowed down because he heard Emslie, the plate umpire, call, "Foul." After conferring with Bob, who said it was a foul ball, the play by rule being dead, Rigler reversed his decision, sending Seymour back to first. Now the Phillies protested. The umpires again huddled and Emslie changed his mind, so Rigler again called Seymour out. Pandemonium erupted as the Giants argued the second reversal. Reports in both New York and Philadelphia newspapers thought there was "little doubt" Emslie called a foul, Seymour rightly being allowed to return to first. Why did Bob change his call? Had he made a mistake? The Philadelphia's catcher's quick throw to second was possible on a foul tip—a live ball caught—but not a foul, the ball dead on falling to the ground. Was Seymour so easily out, as he admitted, despite slowing up a factor? With no postgame press interviews at the time, there is no explanation of the confusing decision. Whether or not the *Philadelphia Inquirer* correctly concluded that "there is no rule covering this point, and it is probable the umpires knew their proper course when they declared Seymour out," fans understandably "hissed Emslie vigorously" for the rest of the game.

It was obvious a lone arbiter was unable to follow the action of "small ball" or "inside baseball," so both leagues in 1909 regularly used two umpires, one behind the plate, the other on the bases. Ever stubborn and self-reliant, O'Day opposed the move, arguing he found it "more trouble than working alone as he often not only had to make his own decisions, but his mate's as well." But Emslie, who like Hank had previously opposed two umpires, now recalling he had "stood a great deal from the players when we had the single umpire system," was a zealous convert, proclaiming the dual system, which "should have been in vogue long ago" was the answer to easing the umpire's duty and reducing arguments. "I am for it first, last and all the time," he announced. "Anything that minimizes the labors of the umpire is a blessing. Two umpires are a deal better than one for the simple reason that two men can see more than one. There are very few players that can get away from two umpires. There is more confidence in the umpires when there are two men working."[46] Still, as Bob learned to his embarrassment, a second umpire did not preclude mistakes. On September 4 in Cincinnati, the pitcher picked off the runner at second after fielding the ball, but Bob, anticipating a throw to first, missed it. When the runner, knowing he was out, left the base and was tagged, Emslie then made the correct out call.

The American League routinely used two umpires for every game, switching their positions from the plate to the field every other day, but Pulliam assigned double crews for three games with a single umpire working the fourth game solo "to ginger him up." To take advantage of each umpire's particular skills, he assigned those "with the keenest eyesight," Klem and O'Day, to the plate in almost every game with the others primarily working the bases, expecting each "will do better work than when he is shifted around every day." Pulliam also regularly paired Emslie and O'Day to important games and series. They were the only veterans working as a team; the other regulars worked with "second string men."[47]

In loosening the purse strings to hire a second umpire, league owners and administrators finally recognized that a stable corps of competent umpires was essential for the welfare of the game. By facilitating better umpiring on the bases, the double umpire system significantly reduced the frequency of stressful confrontations that had contributed to annual turnover and shortened careers. In contrast to the instability that had long characterized umpire staffs, continuity would henceforth be the norm.

OFF SEASON

Come season's end Emslie headed to St. Thomas to unwind from umpiring stresses and strains as well as to reunite with his family. Whether or not Bob took an off-season job, as was common for umpires and players, he headed out for more competitive action in the popular Ontario sports of hunting, trapshooting, and curling. Traipsing across fields in search of game birds brought pleasure and relaxation, while curling and trapshooting fueled his competitive instincts.

After the 1901 season, plagued by injuries and kicking, ended on October 5, he raced home, eager to release frustrations by trapshooting, a sport popular among baseball players.[48] He promptly entered the October 9–11 tournament in St. Thomas. The first day, still unnerved by the turbulent season, he finished sixth in the clay target shoot, breaking seventy-two of ninety discs, then picked up, finishing third in three live bird events and fourth in another target contest, blasting forty-seven of fifty-five clay pigeons. He soon became a top gun. In 1904, in addition to having administrative duties when elected secretary of the St. Thomas Gun Club, he tied for second in an unusual jack rabbit shoot, finished second in the first sweep of a live bird that he co-sponsored, then won another by missing only one of thirty-six shots. In 1905 he again won the Gilman and Barnes Trophy in the live pigeon Grand International Handicap, besting over eighty crack shots from the United States. In 1906 he was elected vice president of the gun club and captain of the team that in succeeding years won multiple local, regional, and international competitions.[49]

When snows came and temperatures fell he headed to the rink. When the touring Scottish Royal Caledonian Curling Club team visited St. Thomas in January 1903, Emslie was on one of five rinks taking on the Scots at the Granite Club, described as the most "majestic" and "palatial" they had seen on their North American tour. Unaccustomed to playing indoors and at night, the visitors did not do well.[50] Bob, rapidly increasing his proficiency on the ice, by 1908 became skip (captain) of the foremost St. Thomas team competing in bonspiels (tournaments) from Ontario to Saskatchewan, and apropos his prominence was elected president of the Granite Club in 1910. The sport almost cost him his life. In February 1908 he was "laid out for a minute" when hit by a six-foot iron crowbar accidentally dropped by a worker prying ice from the eaves of the rink. The point of the crowbar pierced his hat, "inflicting a nasty cut" on his scalp. He was lucky; "a half inch either way probably would have fractured his skull." Of the painful but not serious, injury, Bob quipped, "Having often received foul tips on the head, I don't mind a crowbar or two now and then."[51]

If the off-season brought respite from the diamond wars, trekking through fields, moving across trap stations, and sliding down rinks could not shake from his mind the growing criticisms of his umpiring. Kicking over decisions was frustrating, but impugning his ability was disconcerting. And the adoption of double umpiring brought significantly fewer home plate assignments. Why? From the beginning of his umpiring career, the press occasionally criticized him for alleged missed calls, which was routine for a single umpire, but in recent years reporters increasingly charged him with poor eyesight.

Questions of visual acuity have been the bane of umpires since the game was invented. Ridiculing arbiters' ocular ability was a cultural meme long before Gladys Gooding, on May 17, 1942, (in)famously played "Three Blind Mice" on the Ebbets Field organ when umpires took the field. The children's ditty was taken up by the Brooklyn Sym-Phony band when calls went against the Dodgers until the league banned the disparagements. Umpires took charges of blindness in stride, but there was some truth to the partisan ribbing.[52] Because of poor eyesight Gaffney had to retire in 1900 and Sheridan in 1910. Bob Emslie could empathize with his former colleagues as an ocular issue fundamentally altered his career.

Once regarded as the best in the league at calling balls and strikes, Emslie was now increasingly criticized for his work behind the plate. At the beginning of the 1903 season a St. Louis reporter said Emslie "umpired a good game, being especially good in his ball and strike rulings," but players and scribes increasingly believed Bob's eyesight was failing. McGraw even wagered that he could not stand at second base and distinguish an apple from an orange set on home plate, a proposition *Sporting News* deemed "ridiculous" given his marksmanship "ranks with the best trap shots in the Dominion."[53] If the belief that Emslie's umpiring suffered from vision loss seemed not to make sense given his performance in trap shoots each fall, the sports entailed markedly different visual acuity. Calling pitches required precise linear judgment of erratically moving speeding spheroids, while trapshooting involved gauging the horizontal distance over which to spray a field of pellets.

Beginning in 1904 the criticism became frequent and nasty. It was hard to turn away when told, "You're a joke as an umpire," harder still to read ridicule in newspapers. The *Cincinnati Enquirer*, noting "a drop of witch hazel in each eye will clear out all foreign matter and make the vision clear and perfect," thought Emslie's "poor eyesight" would need "at least two gallons in each of his optics." In arguing a pitch call, the Giants' Bill Dahlen handed Bob a cup and sign inscribed "I am blind." Fans laughed at the "picturesque exception," but Bob, not amused, handed Dahlen a $50 fine and a three-day suspension. A New York reporter suggested fans chip in to buy "the veteran umpire a pair of gold rimmed spectacles." The *Pittsburgh Press* agreed, "Uncle Bob should wear glasses" because of his "notoriously bad eyesight," and the *Cincinnati Post* bluntly asserted, "He belongs in an asylum for the blind." A Brooklyn scribe thought, "It would appear quite natural if a man suffering with poor eyesight should quit umpiring," but "nobody would have the temerity to suggest this to Emslie." Pirates owner Barney Dreyfuss did: "Emslie has been in the business too long. He needs a rest. I would gladly contribute toward any fund that would serve as a pension for the veteran. It is ridiculous to keep him on the staff longer. He has outlived his usefulness and his present work has driven away many patrons from the grounds."[54]

One can imagine Bob's reaction to reading press criticism and ridicule, as he surely did, but he was not without defenders. Tim Murnane noted there was no criticism of Emslie's eyesight in the 1907 Boston intercity series; people rejected the notion he was unable "to see as well as of yore" because "he could see well enough to handle the rifle with the best of 'em." Pulliam, admitting "a great many persons" thought Emslie had poor eyesight, claimed the veteran umpire "can see as well, if not better than any of his other arbiters." At the banquet concluding the annual league meeting in December, Bob told the club owners he was "not blind" and promised "as soon as it was impossible for him to perform his duties he would be the first one to let them know," whereupon Pulliam pledged Emslie "will be on my staff of umpires so long as he desires. I know that when Mr. Emslie believes that his eyesight is failing, he will be man enough to come to me and say so. Until he does, I will pay not the slightest attention to any reports about him."[55]

The avowal of ability and vote of confidence and notwithstanding, criticism escalated in 1908. It was bad enough a Brooklyn paper headlined an account of alleged miscalls "Umpire Emslie Should Consult an Oculist" and Cincinnati's Joe Kelley impertinently told Bob, "You old, wall-eyed son of a tinker, you ought to be in a grave alongside [Henry] Chadwick." To make matters worse, Bob became forever and most famously (or infamously) known for his role in the so-called Merkle Boner game.[56]

At the Polo Grounds on September 23, with two outs in the bottom of the ninth, the score tied 1–1, rookie Fred Merkle, at nineteen the youngest player in the league in his first start, singled, putting Giants on first and third. After Al Bridwell lined what appeared to be the game-winning hit, Merkle, thinking the game over, headed for the Giants' clubhouse before advancing to second base. As elated fans poured onto the field, Cubs second baseman Johnny Evers obtained a ball—which ball and from whom are unclear—and, touching second base, claimed to Emslie that Merkle had been forced for the third out. Bob, who fell down to avoid being hit by Bridwell's line drive, had not watched Merkle, so asked O'Day if he had reached second base. Hank, as home plate umpire responsible for seeing if Merkle reached second, said he hadn't, so Emslie called Merkle out, thereby ending the inning and negating the winning run. O'Day was prepared for the play. Less than three weeks earlier, on September 4, Evers and the Cubs tried the same ploy, causing Hank to say that in the future he would be on alert for such a play. He "came within an ace" of telling Emslie about the incident when Bob joined him to work the Giants-Cubs series, but decided it was simply his duty to watch the runners. As the Giants raged in protest, the most experienced arbiters retreated to the umpires' room—a wire cage under the stands—to discuss the situation, ultimately ruling the force out was valid and called the game because it had become too dark to continue. Pulliam subsequently endorsed their decision, ordering the game replayed if the two teams ended tied at season's end. They did, for the first time in Major League history; on October 8 the Cubs won the makeup game 4–2 and went on to defeat Detroit in the World Series.[57]

Ruling the game a tie and providing for a makeup was appropriate, but the subsequent criticism of "Bonehead" Merkle and Emslie was unfair. Fred forgetting the rule was unfortunate, but leaving the field on a walk-off hit was common practice. And watching to see if he touched second was not Bob's call. As O'Day reported to Pulliam, Emslie had been properly watching to see if the batter-runner completed the primary play; had Bridwell veered into the infield in celebration without touching first base, he would have been called out.[58] In the end, as *Sporting News* observed, "Baseball came out of the experience all the richer, Emslie and O'Day went into the history of the game as intrepid fighters for the right." If nothing else, the incident underscored the truth of the admonition on a sign in Pulliam's office: "Take nothing for granted in baseball."[59]

After the game McGraw reportedly dubbed Emslie "Blind Bob." If true—no contemporary verification can be found in newspapers or statements of contemporaries—the denigrating epithet was short-lived. The lone such reference is Clark Griffith in 1909 saying Emslie was "blind as a bat." Historian James Kahn says McGraw once bellowed to Bob, "You're as blind as a mole," but provides no substantiation.[60] Also unverifiable are oft-repeated stories of Emslie showing up at a Giants practice session hefting a rifle, not to shoot McGraw but to demonstrate his visual acuity. According to one account, the morning after McGraw compared Emslie "to a bat and advised him to see an oculist," Bob from behind the plate blasted a dime off a matchbox on second base and, having proved his point, walked off the field without saying a word. Another version says he placed a dime on the pitcher's rubber, retreated behind home plate, took aim, and sent the coin "spinning into the outfield." On another occasion, after McGraw challenged Emslie, saying, "I'll bet you that I can put an apple and baseball down on second base and you cannot tell the difference from home plate," Bob responded, "I'll tell you what we'll do. Let's come out here tomorrow morning and put an apple on second base and shoot at it. I'll bet you five hundred dollars I hit more apples than you do." McGraw declined, quipping, "Maybe you can see apples, but you can't see baseballs!"[61] Although lacking original documentation, the stories of Emslie's marksmanship countering allegations of vision loss, whatever the exact details, were told by contemporary reporters, players, and McGraw himself.

Perhaps owing to mounting criticism capped by the Merkle game, Emslie, an intensely private man not given to publicity, agreed to discuss his umpiring experiences for the November issue of *Baseball Magazine, which had been* founded by Boston sportswriter Jacob Morse in May 1908. In the aptly titled "Ramblings of an Umpire," the first comprehensive public commentary about umpiring by an umpire, Emslie did not relate the confrontations with players and managers or amusing tales both tall and true so many of his colleagues were eager to tell.[62] Instead, adhering to the umpire's axiom that what is said on the field stays on the field, he penned a candid, if a bit defensive, commentary intended to educate readers about the trials and tribulations of umpiring. Mincing no words, his opening sentences went to the heart of the matter: "Umpiring is more difficult today than ever before. Under any circumstance it is a most trying task, and few can fill the bill satisfactorily."

Emslie addressed first and in greatest detail kicking, the aspect of umpiring most discussed by the press and fans. He acknowledged, "It is inevitable that players will protest when a decision is given that seems to them erroneous. Umpires make mistakes the same as other people and it is only natural that there should be a protest if the player gets the small end of a decision" and a player "will say much in the heat of a moment that he will be sorry for afterward." However, he wrote, "What incenses an umpire most is when is protest is registered at some trivial point where none deserves. There is absolutely no reason for a player to turn on an umpire when the latter happens to miss a ball and call it a strike." He also stressed that there was little an umpire could do to curtail arguments, it being "well-nigh impossible" to keep a player from leaving his position to protest a decision, and that ejecting players, "even when they deserve such treatment," was difficult as it would "spoil a contest." Because "the hit and run game" and the prevalence of bunting kept the lone umpire busy "watching the man at the bat and the man on the bases,"

Bob thought the way "to lighten the labors of the umpire, to cause less friction, [and] to please players and the public" was the double umpire system "for the simple reason that two men can see more than one." By reducing kicking and erroneous calls that could affect a game, the dual umpire system "should have been in vogue long ago, the expense would be as nothing compared with the benefits that would accrue."

Hoping to increase appreciation for umpires, he said, "Few people realize the dangers that confront an umpire in the discharge of his duties. Thoughtless people seem to find it extremely amusing when he is solidly struck by the horsehide and fairly leaps from the pain. I have received so many blows on my anatomy that it would take a mathematician to count them up. Suffice it to say that I have walked or hobbled on the field to umpire a game when my body was covered with bruises. It is a case of work, however, as long as one can stand on his feet." Underscoring that Emslie's purpose was education, not personal promotion, the essay ended with a brief summation of his playing career and entry into umpiring.[63]

EMOTIONAL TRIBULATIONS

If releasing his thoughts about umpiring boosted Bob's spirits, the effect was short-lived, as 1909 was by far the most trying year of his career. Criticism of his eyesight worsened. It was reported in May that "critics are unanimous in the opinion that Uncle Bob Emslie's eyes are on the 'blink' and that he ought to be kept away from the rubber." In July Bob's "poor eyesight" was blamed for calling the Phillies' John Titus's hit fair when it was "foul by a foot," Titus even stopped running until urged on by the first base coach. If Bob erred, as the lone umpire standing behind the pitcher he did not have a good angle on the ball. Two days before he followed "the course of the leather perfectly" from behind the bat, correctly judging the ball fair as it "barely cut the corner of the first base bag, a field umpire likely calling it wide."[64]

Harder to take than press criticism was the drastic alteration of assignments. After the league in 1904 began using two umpires for some games, the percentage of Emslie's annual base assignments (27 or 28) was comparable to that of other members of the staff, but after the adoption of the double-umpire system in 1909 his work at home plate declined dramatically, as Pulliam conceded Emslie had a problem calling pitches. In working a record 156 games in 1908, he umpired 112 games behind the bat, but in 1909 he called only 70 of 146 games at the plate, 12 of them as the lone umpire.

Adding injury to insult, he suffered a distressing personal loss at the Polo Grounds on July 21. Before the game he took off his gold ring with a diamond insert, tucked it into his purse with his money, and put the purse in his pants pocket. At the end of reportedly the longest 8.5-inning game in modern history—two hours and thirty-two minutes—the purse was gone, having fallen from his pocket during the game. A fan probably picked it up, as a search of the grounds and inquiries of players failed to produce it. Disconsolate, less because of the money than what likely was his wedding ring, Emslie reported the loss to concessionaire Harry Stevens (purported inventor of the ballpark hot dog) who offered in vain a reward for its return. (Beginning in 1908 all clubs were supposed to provide "suitable and separate dressing rooms" for umpires, but not all clubs had complied, and those that did provided no security.)

Finally, there was a succession of emotional blows. Death, not kicking or criticism, weighed most heavily on him. In May he learned his nephew, William Alexander Emslie, had had committed suicide. After Bob's brother James died in Waterville, his widow and young son moved to Atchison, Kansas. Will became a competitive bicycle racer and rose to prominence in the community, in 1907 purchasing a fire insurance agency and in May 1908 marrying Grace King, daughter of mayor Samuel S. King. But increasing difficulties with his vision were worrisome, especially since as a young boy he had lost sight in his right eye after a playmate shot him with a slingshot. He went several times to Kansas City to see a specialist, the latest examination ominous: "Eyesight destroyed in one eye; corneal nebulae on the other eye; vision eighteen-seventy-fifth. The sight of the eye he could see out of was less than one-fourth normal." During the afternoon of May 7, 1909, less than a year after his wedding, Will went to his insurance office, took a seat behind the desk, stuck a Colt 38-caliber revolver in his mouth, and pulled the trigger. He had been contemplating the fatal act for some time, unable to accept the inevitable onset of blindness.[65] For Bob the tragedy was particularly unsettling. Given complaints about his eyesight and knowing eye disease was often hereditary, a close relative having congenital degenerative vision leading to blindness must have given him pause, making him wonder if he, too, might eventually suffer loss of sight.

Two weeks later, on May 23, in Brooklyn, he received word that his aunt and mother-in-law had both died. He headed to St. Thomas after the game on May 26 to attend to funerals and family affairs, returning to the diamond on June 1 in New York. The next month, in rapid succession, two National League club owners died unexpectedly: Boston's George Dovey on June 19 and Philadelphia's Israel Durham on June 28. Games canceled out of respect, funeral services, and flags flying half-mast at ballparks cast a pall over the game and Bob Emslie.

A month later he received another emotional blow when Pulliam died on July 29 of a self-inflicted gunshot wound—a final response to lingering illness, the efforts of some owners to replace him, and possibly anxiety about his homosexuality. Wrenchingly reminiscent of his nephew's suicide less than three months earlier, Pulliam's death affected Bob deeply. Harry, a dear friend, was responsible for Bob's initial hiring as a Major League umpire in 1890; as league president since 1902 he had provided unstinting support amid mounting criticism. Bob dutifully went to Pittsburg for two games before mournfully going to Louisville with the entire staff for Pulliam's funeral on August 2 in group recognition of his unwavering support for umpires. After the services Bob went to St. Louis, working two series alone and sorting through emotions about the recent events that so underscored the tenuous nature of life itself.

CAREER CROSSROAD

The emotionally charged season ended with a change in league administration that would fundamentally alter Emslie's career. After a bitter week-long fight over the presidency, the owners on December 18 elected a compromise candidate, Tom Lynch. Lynch prevailed primarily because the president's principal duty was to supervise the staff, a task for which he was well suited, having umpired league games for thirteen years from 1888 to 1902. Surprised but pleased at the appointment of Lynch, whom he knew and respected from their umpiring days in the 1890s, Bob hoped he would be "as good a president as he was an umpire."[66]

Lynch, realizing his job depended on stabilizing the staff and curtailing rowdy play, immediately tried to reduce the noxious confrontations between players and umpires. Less than a week after taking office he wrote to the six staff veterans asking, "Where did most of your trouble with the ballplayers last season come from, the teams playing the game, the coaches, the managers or the players siting on the bench?" Learning from Emslie and his comrades it was mainly "nagging from the bench, which heats the umpire into a state of resentment," he pushed through in January 1910 a rule adopted by both leagues allowing umpires to fine and eject "loudmouth" substitutes, and announced his intention to "watch the umpires closely" to ensure the rule against protesting an umpire's decision would be "enforced to the letter."[67]

In early April Emslie headed to New York for a staff meeting. After six hours reviewing the rules and last season's protested games, Lynch laid down the law, pointedly telling his umpires to remember they, as "the monarchs of the field," were to be "less lenient with the kickers than they have been in the past," to avoid "flippancy, facetiousness or undue familiarity" with players, and always to carry a rule book on the field to clear up disputed points. Upset by the staff enduring "terrible language" and "barroom names," he notified club owners any player benched for "profane or indecent language on the field" would be suspended indefinitely. And to minimize distractions and possible interference with umpires, photographers would no longer be allowed near the diamond after the game started.[68]

During the 1910 season Bob learned that Lynch meant what he said about curtailing rowdiness and controlling the staff. After McGraw "kicked too vehemently" against Emslie and Rigler at the Polo Grounds on August 15, his behavior inciting fans to toss bottles and other missiles at the umpires and requiring police protection for them from an angry mob after the game, Lynch attended the next two games, observing McGraw "continually nagging the umpires." At series end on August 17 he came down "like a ton of bricks on the Little Napoleon," suspending him indefinitely, declaring, "I will tolerate no longer this umpire-baiting and these tactics of putting the crowd on the umpire." Lynch brooked no nonsense from umpires either, fining Bill Klem and Steve Kane each $25 for mistakenly going from St. Louis to Pittsburgh on August 25 instead of to Chicago as scheduled, thus requiring two players to umpire a Cubs-Giants game. Reflecting Lynch's strong support of umpires, by season's end, twenty-two players had been suspended and fourteen fined, $330 added to the league treasury. Emslie had few notable encounters with players; his three ejections since 1902 were by far the fewest.

If Bob was pleased by Lynch's unstinting support, he was disappointed with his umpiring duties. Given pervasive comments about his vision and reduced plate assignments in 1909, he expected to work more on the field than behind the plate, but in 1910 he was restricted to the bases, calling pitches in just 2 of 145 games, both second games of doubleheaders, on May 30 and June 13. What had happened? Neither Bob, his fellow umpires, newspaper reporters, nor league administrators publicly explained why he no longer umpired behind the bat. Was it solely Lynch's decision? Did Emslie, affected by criticism, request only field assignments?[69]

In addition to Bob's difficulty calling pitches, the decision reflected the league's practice of assigning umpires to positions according to their special abilities. And the veteran umpire was an invaluable mentor. For example, Lynch paired Emslie with hotheaded Cy Rigler, hoping Bob's diplomatic demeanor would mitigate Cy's quick trigger. In three seasons after joining the staff in 1907, Rigler tossed sixty players, twenty-eight in 1909 alone. From the season opener on April 14 Bob worked every game with Cy until the last game on October 9, which he worked with Bill Brennan in Cincinnati. It was the only time in Emslie's career he had the same partner all year, and likely the only time in history umpires were paired the entire season. It worked. Of Rigler's twenty ejections in 1910, nine came in June; he removed only seven players in 1911, and thereafter exercised restraint (save for in 1914, when he threw out a career-high thirty-one players).

Before heading home, the October 9 game the season finale for Emslie as well Cincinnati and Pittsburgh, the avid sportsman may well have stayed to watch the Reds and Pirates compete in eight postgame "field day" events—Beating out Bunts, Fungo Hitting, Circling Bases, Catchers' Accurate Throw, Pitchers' Control, Outfielders' Accurate Throwing,

100-Yard Dash, and Long Distance Throwing. He certainly needed a diversion. By the end of the disquieting season rumors circulated at full throttle: Emslie would either be retired owing to diminished eyesight or appointed supervisor of umpires, the position that had been abandoned in 1900. It was not the first such talk. In 1903 it reportedly was "almost certain that Bob Emslie is playing his farewell engagement on the National league circuit, and that next season will see him relegated to the minors or to oblivion. He has lost control of the players on the field and of his eyesight and the combination is enough to put any man out of the business." In 1905 Bob repeatedly denied reports he was going to retire after the season, and in 1908 talk of appointing him "a sort of supervising umpire" came to naught; the American had no umpire supervisor and Pulliam, disinclined to let anyone interfere with his staff, declared he did not need a supervisor.[70]

Whether Bob knew it—and he likely had an inkling, being aware of rumors and the opposition of some magnates—his termination moved closer to reality at the league's meeting in December. After the owners reelected Lynch to another one-year term as president, refusing to give him a three-year contract (Ban Johnson had a ten-year deal), and rejected the suggestion of interleague games, they tried to jettison the oldest umpire on the staff. Cincinnati's Max Fleischmann, co-owner of the Fleischmann Yeast Company, proposed league umpires undergo eye examinations, adding if it should "prove a hardship to any faithful men" the "unfortunates would be taken care of." Lynch was instructed to order eye tests; anyone with visual problems was not to be retained. It was, in fact, a craven way of retiring "the old warhorse," as was evident in the Cubs' Charles Murphy's thinly veiled sarcasm: "If we have some umpires who cannot tell a lemon from a baseball at a distance of sixty feet the sooner we find it out the better." Brooklyn's Ebbets, assuming Bob could not pass an eye test, successfully moved he be given a pension in recognition of his long service. Murphy, on returning from the meeting, announced Emslie "has outlived his usefulness on the playing field" and will be voluntarily "retired on a pension owing to failing eye-sight," gratuitously adding that aged umpires like Emslie should not be retained "out of loyalty," but should "step aside" in favor of "younger and more capable men."[71]

Bob was not the only visually challenged umpire. The American League's Jack Sheridan also found his home plate assignments drastically reduced in 1909 to 45 of 146 games. The next June he complained of "violent headaches" from eyestrain, saying "looking through a mask for twenty-five years does not have a tendency to strengthen one's eye." Ban Johnson, eschewing mandatory eye exams in favor of selective tests, ordered him to see a Chicago oculist, who found Jack "suffering severely from astigmatism." While off the field for two months after June 25, scouting for umpires in the Minors and providing instruction for new league arbiters, he wore glasses; when he returned to umpiring on August 30 he worked only the bases and rejected Johnson's suggestion that he wear glasses "for fear of being ridiculed by fans." No doubt to provide the league's senior arbiter with a $500 bonus and an honorific career capstone, Johnson assigned Sheridan—despite his deficient eyesight—to umpire only bases in the 1910 World Series, the only time a member of a four-man crew did not work the plate. Jack said he would "never go behind the bat again"; except for one game in 1911 he exclusively umpired the bases until retiring in 1914.[72]

Unlike Sheridan, Emslie never complained of eyestrain and his diminished vision came not from astigmatism (a curvature of the cornea or lens that blurs vision) but from hyperopia (farsightedness), a difficulty focusing on close objects easily corrected by eyeglasses. While it was uncommon for Major League players to wear glasses until the 1920s, it was an unspoken rule that umpires should not don spectacles as it would be taken as an indication of visual deficiency. The eyeglass ceiling for umpires that unnecessarily compromised Emslie's career was not broken until 1956.[73]

News of the first retirement of an umpire with a pension came as a surprise and with puzzlement to some. Since Emslie was "expert with the gun" in trapshooting, a Pittsburgh club official thought that Bob suffering from vision loss "doesn't sound reasonable" given his winning trap shoots each fall. Bill Brennan, who umpired with Bob in 1909 and 1910, flatly declared it untrue that his eyesight "wasn't keen." Tim Murnane thought, despite "a consensus of opinion that he is not the umpire that he once was," Emslie was "better than some of the new men recently tried out." O'Day was willing to wager that any replacement "will not be as good a man by far as Bob is."[74] There were also farewell encomiums. *Sporting News* editorialized, "Probably no one else could have held his position as long as Bob had and do no better work than he sometimes did, but he had the good will of players and press and, in fact, of all who knew him. Everyone will miss Bob's pleasant smile and will be glad to remember, when missing it, that the league to which he gave the best years of his life is giving him at least a slight reward for his services and it may be greater than 'slight.'" The retirement of "a great official" saddened American League umpire Billy Evans: "No finer fellow ever lived than Bob Emslie. No umpire has done more for the game than the former dean of the National league staff."[75]

Murphy's announcement and retirement accolades were premature. Lynch, regarding an eye exam as acceptable but removing Emslie as a test of his authority, refused to give Bob a pension. Flouting the long-standing unwritten rule that the opposition of five owners meant the dismissal of an umpire, he declared that the president, not the magnates, would determine the makeup of the staff.

At home in St. Thomas Emslie, having received no word from Lynch or other league officials—a callous display of disregard for the veteran umpire's feelings—was shocked to learn from newspaper reports of his apparent retirement, which was anything but voluntary, and that umpires were to undergo eye examinations. Considering Murphy's charge of diminished eyesight "without foundation and uncalled for," Bob defiantly said he "does not want and will not need to accept any pension from the league." Still, persistent criticism of his eyesight, being relegated to base duty, the owners' desire to get rid of him, and the impending eye examination prompted bitter philosophizing: "Distance lends enchantment to the view. It is only in the Winter that a small boy is ambitious to be a baseball umpire."[76]

There is no way of knowing what was going through Bob's mind, but it is easy to imagine that, while feeling disappointment, even anger, he may have thought about retiring. At fifty he was the oldest member of the staff. He had passed the age of average male life expectancy at the time and had worked the most years and games in history. When umpiring at the South End grounds on June 13, 1910, the *Boston Globe* mused that no member of the Reds or Doves had been born when Bob started umpiring in the league. (Cy Young was the only player still active when Emslie began his Major League career in 1890: Bob began on April 17, Cy on August 6.)[77]

No doubt his absence from home and family for up to six months each year weighed heavily on the eldest surviving male Emslie sibling. In truth, 51 Elgin Street was largely an off-season retreat, marital and parental time and responsibilities lost from March to October. He had yet to celebrate a wedding anniversary with Helena; if present for Christmas and his children's birthdays, he missed much of the formative childhood years of Kitty, now fifteen, and Jack, ten. Even while at home he had been frequently off to fields, traps, and rinks. Continuing to umpire would mean further diminishing his relationship with Helena and being absent during the children's crucial teenage years.

Certainly, he harked back to the trials and tribulations of a quarter century of umpiring. Tim Hurst's witty response to Silk O'Loughlin's complaints about umpiring—"Yis, but kin ye beat thim hours?"—missed the point.[78] It was not backbreaking labor or ten- to twelve-hour shifts, as was common in the workforce, but the concentration required amid frequent vociferous and often virulent criticism was mentally exhausting, and the peripatetic lifestyle, toting umpiring gear and personal effects from city to city, was physically taxing. There was also more waiting than working. When asked what he did when he wasn't umpiring, he replied, "I mind my own business. It is literally true. I go away from the field and try to forget all about my business. The baseball umpire goes to his dressing room when the game is over, changes his clothes, and leaves the field to mingle with his fellow-men, just like the ball player does." His social life consisted mostly of a network of on-the-road acquaintances; rainouts or rare days off, usually Sundays, were spent visiting friends old and new. He had visited exciting cities, but with little time to enjoy their amenities. In 1904 he was in St. Louis only on July 9 and 10 for doubleheaders, giving him no time to visit either the Louisiana Purchase Exposition known as the St. Louis World's Fair or attend the Summer Olympic Games simultaneously held in St. Louis.[79]

Still, he could look back with pride at officiating special nonleague games. He umpired two collegiate championships, the Yale-Princeton finale in 1903 and the two final games of the 1904 Harvard-Yale series. The additional compensation was welcome, but he begged off future collegiate assignments because while there was little kicking "the language the young men used to each other was more than he could stand."[80] He subsequently earned extra money umpiring the popular intracity and interstate games played in October concurrent with the World Series. Complaints about his eyesight notwithstanding, Bob was chosen to umpire the 1905 Boston City Championship series, the 1907 Boston series, and the 1909 intercity series between the Giants and Red Sox. Managers of the Phillies and Athletics in 1907 chose him to go south with Connolly to work the preseason series between the two Philadelphia teams, which began in Marlin, Texas, then meandered northward to Philadelphia. Spring training was canceled in 1908, but Emslie and Connolly again were chosen to umpire preseason games between the Phillies and A's in Philadelphia. And in August 1910 he and Billy Evans were hired to umpire a postseason barnstorming tour of American and National league all-stars, but had to return their certified checks after the National Commission squelched the tour. Bob also had the pleasure of umpiring the bases on June 29 in the last game in Pittsburgh's Exposition Park and umpiring the plate the next day for the inaugural game at Forbes Field.

Pleasant memories may have been tempered by not being assigned to any of the seven World Series games from 1903 to 1910. The league presidents chose umpires for the Fall Classic, initially one from each league, then in 1908 two-man crews alternating games. In 1909 the crews combined in Game Three to form the first four-man crew, two umpires manning the foul lines owing to the difficulty of judging balls hit into overflow crowds on the field. Hank O'Day understandably was called five times, but the league's senior umpire was passed over in 1906 for Jim Johnstone, then in his fourth year, and Bill Klem, after his third season in 1908. It was reported that Emslie would officiate the 1907 series, as he and Hurst were considered "the only logical selections," but Bob had already signed to umpire the Boston city series.[81]

He understandably was not chosen after 1909 when relegated to the bases, but why not before, as he was selected by managers to umpire intercity and interstate postseason games and spring training exhibitions? Concerns about Bob calling pitches likely precluded his selection, but Johnson picked Sheridan for 1910 despite his poor vision, restricting him to the bases. Did Bob, recalling the tempestuous Temple Cup series, decline to serve? At that time umpiring the World Series was more about extra pay ($400, increased to $500 in 1910) than professional recognition. Connolly declined to umpire the 1907 World Series, preferring to "take a train for a little place down in Massachusetts, where I'll hear no hisses and no groans, and where I'm not a robber and a thief."[82] Whatever the reason, not umpiring in the World Series, the lone omission in his résumé, would detract from Emslie's recognition in umpiring history.

Being increasingly subjected to harsh and sometimes personal criticism, battered by foul balls, relegated to base umpiring, and believed no longer capable of effectively doing his job by owners not only threatened his career but also assaulted his pride in a reputation forged over more than two decades. A lesser man, wounded of ego but proud of unequaled career credentials, would have headed posthaste to retirement. But Bob decided to stay the course.

Why stay with it? He didn't need the money. By 1910 the highest salary in the National League was $3,000; only four umpires earned more than $2,000, but Emslie, Klem, O'Day, and Rigler were surely paid top dollar. (With mandatory double umpires in 1912 arbiters earned about $2,500.) He was financially comfortable enough to purchase for $12,000 the Franklin House, the finest hotel in Port Stanley, a popular vacation spot called the Coney Island of the Great Lakes, nine miles south of St. Thomas. First and foremost he wanted to stay in the game that had been the focus of his life since boyhood, and to continue as an umpire, experiencing the pleasure of witnessing firsthand the skilled performances of some of the greatest players in the game's history and the satisfaction of making decisions that affected the progress, even the outcome, of a game. Besides, an umpire is a dramatist, the ballfield a stage on which he performs, not simply where he works. Billy Evans admitted there was a "thrill that comes with occupying the limelight, of having supreme command, of having a big crowd of people hang in expectancy on every word one says, the feeling of responsibility that goes with absolute authority."[83]

Ultimately, for Bob Emslie retirement was an idea whose time had not yet come. He simply was not ready to put away the indicator. Evans was right in saying, "A good umpire must start out with an ambition to be an umpire and stick to it," the job becoming "an obsession with him."[84] Bob Emslie just did not want to give it up. He couldn't quit. Umpiring was not what he did; it was his way of life, his identity. As hard as it was, he was able to accept a reduced level of responsibility given his dedication to the game and to umpiring and because he believed he still had something to offer the league as a base umpire and premier rules authority. He would be back if he passed the eye test and Lynch would have him.

12

Dean of Umpires

Let me be umpire.

—Shakespeare, *Henry IV*, Act 4

Come 1911, Emslie's celebration of his fifty-first birthday on January 29 was tempered by the owners' attempt to jettison him and the impending eye test. By mid-January he still had no word from Lynch about his reported superannuation, but defiantly declared, "I don't propose to accept a pension, but to umpire regularly in the National League next season." Agreeing with Hank O'Day "the trouble is with the optics of the players," Bob was confident about the eye exam: "I know that I can see as well as I ever could. I can pass the eye test. No honest oculist will find anything the matter with my optics." Still, the consensus seemed to be that while "a man of more sterling integrity than Emslie never officiated in any baseball league," Bob "will not serve actively on the diamond this year" since players have "openly doubted the accuracy of his vision."[1]

In the meantime, curling and trapshooting provided fun and self-assurance. At a February trap meet in Dutton, snow blanketing the ground and swirling in the air, he nailed ten straight white pigeons at the maximum thirty-one yards. Of the only perfect shooter a competitor commented, "They tell me your lamps are gone. Well, you may not be able to see a baseball, but I can say that you can still see the birds, all right!" His achievement in Dutton also brought vindication from sportswriters. Bill Murphy asserted anyone thinking Emslie suffered "from senile decay, blind staggers and kindred things" would be laughed at given his clean score; *Sporting News* agreed, "He must have something left in the eyesight line." Joe Vilas, dismissing charges of faulty eyesight inasmuch as Emslie "pierced numerous live birds and bullseyes in Canada this winter," predicted Bob would be back as a regular umpire.[2]

In late January and early February 1911 league umpires called on doctors in their hometowns for the required eye examination. On February 10 Emslie went to the office of Dr. John Harper Cormack. Cormack was not a certified ophthalmologist, there being no ophthalmological training in Canada until the 1940s, but the eye, ear, and nose physician was knowledgeable about optic issues.[3] He was also familiar with his patient—he lived at 47 Queen, across the street from the Emslies. In the most detailed report Lynch received, Cormack found Bob's vision "better than normal," adding the exam "tends to convince me that the out-of-door life, wide vistas and instant vision required of the baseball devotee must increase the efficiency of the visual function. At least, this theory offers another argument in favor of the great American game." As Bill Brennan recalled, Lynch stipulated that it was to be "a real examination" and the umpires were not to go to "some friendly oculist," but there is no reason to think Emslie passed the exam because of neighborly benevolence, as it likely consisted of a basic eye chart reading. *Sporting News* opined that the tests would "not be so severe but that a person with normal eyes can pass it."[4]

To ward off any question of favoritism from hometown doctors, Lynch submitted the examinations for review to Dr. Royal S. Copeland, preeminent New York City ophthalmologist, who concluded every test had been conducted according to "universally employed" standards and "indicate normal vision in every case, and, in several instances, vision far above the average." O'Day had "perfect vision," Klem "above normal," Rigler "unusually acute." Lynch hoped all umpires' passing scores would convince owners, players, and fans that if an arbiter made a mistake "as they are bound to do" it was not because of faulty eyesight.[5]

REPLACEMENT UMPIRE

Although Emslie passed the examination, for the first time in twenty-one years he was not appointed a regular member of the staff. Instead, Lynch designated him the replacement umpire, stationed either in New York or Chicago depending on the regional playing schedule to facilitate quick transportation to league cities. Cormack's report notwithstanding, since it was obvious Emslie's vision was deficient for calling pitches, he would no longer umpire behind the bat.

Why did the league retain an aging umpire to work only bases? Bill Klem, whose talent for self-promotion was as considerable as his umpiring ability, boasted for years that he was responsible for Bob not being released. He told J. G. Taylor Spink, publisher of the *Sporting News*, that when Emslie "got into trouble with Lynch and appealed to the league board of directors to hold his job, I volunteered to team with Bob and work at the plate every day. I did that without a break for nine years." (He later erroneously said he umpired exclusively behind the bat for sixteen consecutive seasons.) To John Kieran he said he told Lynch he'd work the plate so Bob would have "the easier job on the bases." To Harold Parrott he said, "McGraw was out to get Emslie fired. And to save Emslie's job, I volunteered to work every day behind the plate if they would let Emslie stay to umpire on the bases." He subsequently told the story with slight variations to Harold Burr and Tommy Holmes who, like Parrott, hadn't covered baseball during the Deadball Era and thus knew nothing of Emslie's career.[6]

Klem's claims that Bob appealed to owners to keep his job, that McGraw wanted Emslie fired, that he was responsible for saving Emslie's job by working the plate so Bob could work only bases, and that he umpired exclusively behind the plate for sixteen years are palpably untrue.[7] He did not make those claims in his 1951 autobiography. Unexcelled in calling pitches, Klem began working primarily behind the plate in 1910 and called pitches in every game in 1915 and 1919 and all but one in 1916–17. However, he had virtually no association with Emslie during the four years when Bob's future was uncertain and he was restricted to base duty. Klem did not umpire with him in 1910, 1912, or 1913; they partnered for Bob's first fifteen games in 1911, June 2–17, but not thereafter that season. They did, however, mostly work together from 1915 to 1920.

Two interrelated considerations explain Emslie's retention as a replacement umpire restricted to base duty. League policy was to maximize staff abilities by assigning some umpires—notably Klem, O'Day, and Rigler—primarily behind home plate and the others on the field; newcomers were always assigned mostly to base duty. Farsightedness compromised Bob's ability to call pitches, but not his ability to umpire bases. Moreover, he was valuable as an expert in the rules and for his experience in handling players and managers. Emslie's reaction to what amounted to a demotion is unknown, but it surely hurt his ego and professional pride. That he accepted the appointment reflects his loyalty and belief that, given the opportunity, he would prove himself worthy of a regular appointment.

The season opened on April 12, Bob agonizingly whiling away the days waiting for dispatch to the diamond. It was also difficult to accept Jack Doyle being added to the staff. Doyle's hiring was shocking given his reputation as an umpire-baiter in his playing days and that he had gotten into a fistfight with Lynch in 1897. Christy Mathewson said that to learn the umpiring craft Doyle was paired with Emslie and that they "got along like Damon and Pythias."[8] The "Big Six" was wildly off in this delivery. Bob never umpired with Doyle, who always teamed with Klem. Unsurprisingly, the hothead failed as an umpire and was released on June 1, after forty-two games, for excessive ejections, poor judgment, an unacceptable demeanor, and not knowing the rules. His replacement on June 2? Bob Emslie.

It was fifty-one days into the season before Emslie took the field. Until August 9 he worked with various members of the staff, then from August 16 until season's end with Klem. Bob's umpiring confirmed Sheridan's belief "he is a good man to run a ball game." O'Day telling a reporter that Bob "never umpired better ball in his life than he is doing now" was not the backing of an old friend; sportswriter Billy Murphy declared, "Klem and Emslie are really good."[9]

Bob was glad to be back but disappointed that Lynch, in the face of growing pressure from owners, retreated from Pulliam's policy of ejecting players for "even the slightest protest," instead instructing umpires "not to pay any attention to kicks made by players unless they were accompanied by abusive language." Emslie, knowing restraint would increase rowdiness, witnessed riotous behavior in Brooklyn on July 8, 1911, with fans throwing bottles at newcomer Ralph Frary and threatening to mob him after the game for chasing Robins manager Bill Dahlen and sending four bench players and the team mascot to the clubhouse. Shaken by the upheaval, Bob publicly challenged his boss for the first time in his career: "The players are taking advantage of Mr. Lynch's kindness and the umpires are the sufferers. There is only one way to break up such scenes as we have just witnessed, and it is to have every player distinctly understand that the minute he turns around to question a decision he will be put out of the game." Allowing that Lynch was "actuated by kindly motives," Bob thought he would now "realize that drastic measures will have to be taken without delay, else people who do not like to witness wrangling on the diamond will withdraw their patronage and we will soon be back just where we were before Harry Pulliam drew the lines so closely."[10] It didn't happen.

At season's end Emslie thought umpiring 103 games without a single reported complaint demonstrated his ability to serve as a regular member of the staff.[11] O'Day agreed: "I honestly think his work on the bases was the best of the league. While we were together there was less kicking made on his decisions than on any other man who worked with me. In fact, there was hardly any. Of course the players yelled, but they never objected strenuously. His eyes surely cannot be bad when he wins a shooting match every fall."[12] But given his pointed public criticism of the league president and Lynch hiring Garnet Bush and Clarence "Brick" Owens for 1912, it seemed Emslie might be among the luminaries (including Cy Young) passing the torch in 1911. That feeling increased when Hank O'Day, his close friend and frequent umpiring partner, left to manage the Cincinnati Reds.

When the 1912 season opened on April 11, Emslie was again a bases-only reserve ensconced in league headquarters in New York. Upon reading the *Titanic* had sunk on April 15, Emslie may well have wondered if his career was also going down. But just four days later he was sent to Chicago when Owens, who had a "voice like a sea lion," developed a sore throat from exclusively calling pitches. Brick's ill fortune was Bob's good luck, giving him the opportunity on April 20 to umpire O'Day's first game as Reds manager in his hometown. Before the game Hank, dressed in a blue suit, gray coat and hat, and patent leather boots, was given a solid gold watch and chain, a pair of diamond cuff links set in platinum, and a gold-handled knife, all etched with his initials. He then retired to the Reds bench, decorated with an eight- to ten-foot floral display inscribed in white flowers with "Hank O'Day" over a pair of stockings made of red posies. Bob watched with pleasure as his friend was lavishly honored, no doubt regretting they were not umpiring together.

After the game, won by the Cubs 5–4 in ten innings, Emslie returned to New York. He did not umpire again until June 8, when Rigler had to retire in the top of the fifth inning at the Polo Grounds after being hit by a foul on his left ear. Bill Finneran umpired alone until Bob arrived in the bottom of the sixth inning to cover the bases. He then worked a forty-game stretch through July 16, but umpired only seven times after that, August 21–26 and October 5–6.

At season's end Bob again had mixed feelings about umpiring. He was pleased about umpires' increased salaries—most now earned about $2,500—and unprecedented recognition; the names of the staffs in both leagues were now listed in the annual *Spalding Guide*, which also in 1913 for the first time had pictures of the arbiters in each league. But he was insulted by the owners' mandate that umpires lose a day's pay if they failed "for any reason"—including injuries suffered during games—to work an assigned game and their order that Lynch "fine, remove, suspend or expel" an umpire who failed to enforce rules or was guilty of "any improper or ungentlemanly language or conduct."[13]

In December for the first time Emslie thought seriously about leaving. It was one thing to be restricted to bases, but quite another to be called on for a career low of forty-eight games. (Eleven of the games involved Cincinnati, and while umpires are neutral, it must have been difficult not to fraternize with O'Day and to watch the Reds lose seven times, including in a humiliating, season-ending 16–6 whipping.) Already disheartened by limited assignments, he was utterly disillusioned in December when Lynch, deciding he had no use for a part-time umpire only able to work the field, sent him notice of discharge and a check for $500. He got a reprieve when the owners, determined to reassert control by undermining the president's authority, ordered Lynch to rehire Bob at his old salary.

His umpiring future insecure, Emslie explored other opportunities. He initially considered offers to purchase the St. Thomas club in the Canadian League, backing off when warned it would preclude being reappointed an umpire. But when in January 1913 the team's new owners made Bob an attractive offer to manage the Saints, his reputation a draw for the hometown club and a boost for the league, he was not averse to the idea of a new challenge and being at home with the family; besides, O'Day had managed without abandoning the possibility of a return to umpiring. Negotiations and rumors persisted throughout February as Saints owners were confident Bob would accept the job. But he finally declined, the decision perhaps influenced when O'Day, released by the Reds, signed a contract to umpire.

For the 1913 season Lynch hired newcomers Bill "Lord" Byron and Bill Guthrie with the two veterans as substitutes. The season began on April 9 with Bob and Hank cooling their heels in New York and Chicago, respectively, until May 6, when they again became regulars owing to the misfortune of Owens and Guthrie. Partners in a floral business in Chicago, they worked as a team until released "for the good of the game" on May 5 after frequenting some "white lights" (gambling houses) in Pittsburgh. Lynch, sensitive to persistent charges of gambling in the game and a stickler for proper deportment for umpires as "representatives of the league," had hired detectives to trail several umpires suspected of patronizing gambling parlors, taken ipso facto as evidence of betting on games. No specific charges were ever made against either umpire; they may have been playing games of chance instead of betting, but Owens having been charged (albeit later vindicated) with giving a gambler $100 to bet on a game when umpiring in the Minors in 1906 likely played a role in the dismissal. *Sporting News* reported, "the general impression is that there is something behind the discharge for Owens that has not been told."[14] (After doing penance by umpiring in the Minors, both returned to the Majors with the American League: Owens from 1916 to 1937 and Guthrie in 1922 and 1928–32.)

Returning to duty on May 6 in Brooklyn, Emslie and O'Day were paired the rest of the year, save for seventeen games from June 30 to July 16 when Bob worked with newcomer Ernie Quigley during Hank's absence owing to serious health issues. Teaming the league's two senior umpires was a success. The *New York Times* reported the July 21 game at the Polo Grounds was "a sort of reunion of old-timers, Uncle Hank O'Day and Uncle Bob Emslie being the umpires. They worked right through the game like young fellows." Given the opportunity, Emslie demonstrated his ability and increased his prospects for continuing as a regular member of the staff by umpiring nearly a full season of 131 games.

After punctuating the successful season by calling balls and strikes in the finale in Chicago on October 5, the third time he had been behind the plate, he was chosen to umpire the postseason intercity series between Cleveland and Pittsburgh with Billy Evans. In game six, in Pittsburgh on October 13 Bob experienced the pain and pleasure of being a plate umpire. He was hit four times: once on the ankle by a slipped bat and three times on the head by fouls, two smashing him in the mask and one cutting the side of his head just above the temple, the blow requiring treatment by the Pirates club physician. As he carefully placed his mask over the bandage and went on with the game, the crowd applauded. The painful injuries did not diminish the pleasure of calling Vean Gregg's thirteen-inning 1–0 masterpiece in which he struck out nineteen, allowed only five hits, and walked just two. Emslie may well have reflected on his pitching career as Gregg relied almost exclusively on a sharp-breaking curve. After the game Bob said, "I have seen all the great ones: Rusie, Radbourne and Mathewson, but I am confident that I never saw any pitcher show the stuff that Gregg had." Evans agreed, saying he had umpired great left-handers like Rube Waddell and Eddie Plank, but "none boasted a curve ball that compared with Gregg's."[15]

Emslie's hopes of continuing as a regular in 1914 received a jolt when the ownership cabal that had been trying for two years to unseat Lynch finally succeeded, replacing him with John K. Tener, then the governor of Pennsylvania. Emslie could scarcely have predicted his teammate for one game with Baltimore in 1885 would one day be his boss as league president. On June 8 Emslie watched from the bench as the rookie right fielder recorded no hits, put-outs, or assists but three errors to cost the Orioles the game as "he could stop nothing, and several fly balls which could have been caught by half the amateurs in Baltimore he let go by."[16]

Emslie was understandably uneasy about what Tener's appointment meant for his future. Previous league presidents had had long service in Major League baseball, but Tener, who had briefly pitched in the Majors and had umpired one game in 1889 and one in 1890, had fashioned a career in business and politics, serving one term in Congress before being elected governor in 1910. Still, he was a baseball enthusiast. A Republican member of the 61st Congress, he initiated (with support from Texas Democrat Sam Garner, future vice president of the United States) the first interparty Congressional baseball game on July 16, 1909, in which the Democrats drubbed the Republicans 26–16. But he had no administrative experience in baseball. Would he be as umpire-friendly as Lynch? And, more to the point, would he retain Emslie? There were indications Tener would relieve the veteran "knight of the indicator" of field duties, appointing him a "traveling supervisor of umpires" charged with assessing umpires' skills and players' behavior.[17]

Should Bob not be retained, a possible alternative was joining the Federal League, operating as a third Major League in 1914 and 1915. Offering increased salaries and freedom from the reserve clause, the upstart circuit lured stars from the two established leagues, but as with the Players' League, it was easier to entice players than umpires; only Bill Brennan defected. The Federal may not have been interested in an umpire restricted to the bases, but Emslie likely would have spurned an offer anyway given his league loyalty and apprehension the new organization might not succeed.

REGULAR STAFF

In any event, Bob's concerns were allayed when he was rehired as a regular member of the 1914 National staff. He may well have had an assist in the appointment. Tener did not want baseball business to interfere with gubernatorial duties until his term ended in April 1915, so he turned over league administration to John Heydler, who as de facto president was given an unprecedented three-year contract. Emslie was delighted. Heydler was not only well-versed in league affairs, having served as secretary-treasurer since 1903, but also had firsthand knowledge of umpires and umpiring, having called eighty-three Major League games in the 1890s. Moreover, he knew Emslie as an umpire—Heydler had worked eight games with him 1898 and observed his work for a decade as league secretary.

The relationship with Heydler was a plus, but Bob earned reappointment because he was a good umpire, his base work recognized and praised, his hustle invariably putting him in position to make calls. *Sporting Life* noted Emslie "is along in years, but he has a clear eye and the pep to get around and sees the plays." The *Brooklyn Times* agreed: "There are few umpires who use the judgment Emslie does in rendering decisions and there are none who can be found in the correct position to judge on any base play as Emslie invariably occupies. He is rarely caught napping on any play." The *Cincinnati Post* thought he was "a good base umpire" because experience "taught him the best way in which to get into proper position to judge plays, and he is usually correct in any decision he renders." When McGraw argued a call at third, the *New York Tribune* said Emslie was "right on top of the play," the *Sun* concurring, "It was close, but Emslie was right there." Photographs in *Baseball Magazine* show Bob "going at full speed" in "a spirited thirty-yard sprint" to get in "exactly the right position" to the make the correct call at third; the runner was safe by "not more than two inches." It was no exaggeration: Pittsburgh shortstop Honus Wagner regarded Emslie as "the greatest of all the umpires on base decisions. Some kind of instinct seemed to guide him on all close plays. If a man was stealing second and I missed touching him by a quarter of an inch Emslie would see it."[18]

His retention was also due to being the league's foremost authority on the rules. At the end of the 1911 season both leagues abandoned the practice of owners formulating rules in favor of appointing a special rules committee consisting of a club owner, a team manager, and an umpire. Lynch appointed John Ward, co-owner and president of the Boston Rustlers; Roger Bresnahan, pilot of the St. Louis Cardinals; and Bob Emslie. (Connolly served for the American.) By the end of 1912 Ward left Boston and Bresnahan was fired, but Emslie continued as the cornerstone of the committee for the rest of the decade and was praised in the press not only as "one of the most competent umpires in the majors," but also as the "best versed man on rules in the National League; whenever President Tener or Secretary Heydler is in a quandary over any technicality in the rules they call on Emslie to straighten them out, for he is said to be one of the brightest and best informed men on the rules in the business." Emslie was respected not only for his knowledge of written rules. Wagner praised Bob's "fine judgment on plays not covered by the rule book. He saved many a bad situation by making a quick decision on some point not covered by the rules. Nine times out of 10 the players would feel satisfied that he had done right." Fellow umpires, too, acknowledged his expertise, Cy Rigler forthrightly declaring, "Bob Emslie knows more about the baseball rules than all the other National umpires together."[19]

Good base umpiring and rules expertise aside, Emslie proved valuable in mentoring fellow arbiters—usually new hires, but also regular members of the staff, the chief examples being quick-triggered Ernie Quigley and Bill Byron. They knew how to umpire, but Emslie taught them to be an umpire.

Ernest Cosmos Quigley, on coming to the league in the middle of the 1913 season, cautiously ejected six players, but the next year tossed twenty and obstinately refused a reasonable request to move out of a batter's line of sight. Unused to challenges or backtalk while refereeing football and basketball, he officiously signaled a foul as a roundball official by yelling "You Can't d-o-o-o that!" instead of blowing his whistle.[20] In 1915, after Quigley's physical encounter on July 22 with Johnny Evers, for which both combatants were fined $100, Tener decided to pair Emslie with his fellow Canadian for the rest of the season in hopes of calming Ernie down. It worked. He issued twenty-three ejections before teaming with Bob but only three thereafter, and became the league's supervisor of umpires upon retiring in 1936.

Two years later Bob was called on to mentor William Jeremiah Byron, whose penchant for lighthearted but annoying "sing-song" commentary earned him the nickname Lord Byron after the famous English peer and Romantic poet who would have been appalled by his namesake's silly verse. Like Quigley, Byron came into the league in 1913 and immediately displayed a fast thumb. In his first four seasons he led the staff in ejections, averaging twenty-eight each year. Bill opened the 1917 season with Quigley and frequently ejected players—six on June 5 alone. After a game in St. Louis on June 21when a squadron of police was required to protect him from a mobbing, Tener, responding to complaints from the Cardinals' new president, Branch Rickey, about Byron's unpopularity and behavior, immediately dispatched Emslie to St. Louis to work with the volatile umpire. Cardinals fans were treated to a novel three-man crew on

June 24, Emslie stationed at third base. He remained there through July 4, working eight of the next nine games at third base while monitoring Byron's behavior and counseling the fiery arbiter. Again, he had a calming effect. In forty-eight games prior to Emslie's arrival, Byron had ejected twenty-one players, one more than all American League umpires; after working with Bob, he tossed seven the rest of the season and thereafter toned down his work, removing only nine in 1918 and fourteen in 1919, his last season in the league.

Simply put, Emslie became a regular member of the staff because he was a better and more accomplished umpire than any of the new additions and most of the veterans. Umpires came and went, but Bob remained. As a regular for the rest of the decade, he umpired home plate just six times: thrice in 1913 and 1918, all in second games of double-headers except for spelling O'Day behind the plate in the season finale on October 5, 1913, a meaningless game in which both teams fielded mostly prospects and reserves.[21]

ON THE FIELD

After attending a preseason get-acquainted staff meeting with Tener in April, it was back to normal for Emslie in 1914, working a full schedule of 149 games. With O'Day, his usual partner, again bolting, this time to manage the Chicago Cubs, Bob teamed with Cy Rigler from April 14 to May 31, then with Ernie Quigley until June 9, and from June 10 to season's end with Klem. Along the way he called thirty-four games involving O'Day's team, no doubt silently pleased the Cubs won twenty of them. Umpires routinely pay no attention to spectators save for their outbursts of protest, but on June 5, when the principal of Brooklyn's Girls' High School brought one hundred "pretty students" to the Robins-Cub game on June 5, the *Brooklyn Times* reported both teams and the umpires were "affected by the feast of beauty." It claimed that Quigley called pitches with "one eye peeled on the grandstand" and Emslie, in trying "to watch the bases and the school girls at the same time, gave some terribly raw decisions," though both assertions were wildly apocryphal. More accurate was the *Brooklyn Daily Eagle* thinking the sloppy play gave the girls "a pretty low opinion of the Higher Baseball which they have been studying."

Before the 1915 season Emslie and the staff went in March to Warm Springs, Virginia, for a "physical and mental" training course. O'Day, fired by the Cubs, returned, but not until August 8, so Emslie continued pairing with Klem. Despite Tener's order for one umpire to always work behind the bat and the other on the bases, crews regularly switched positions, except for Klem and Emslie—Bill "about the best" calling balls and strikes, Bob "winning general praise for his efficiency" on the bases. The league's premier crew would continue as a pair to the end of the decade.[22]

In returning to regular status Emslie participated in several historic games. In 1913 Charles Ebbets chose him as chief umpire working the plate for the inaugural game at Ebbets Field on April 5, an exhibition game with the New York Yankees. The highlight of the 1915 season came on August 18 in Boston, when for the third time he umpired the inaugural game of a new stadium: Braves Field, touted as "the greatest baseball plant in the world," with a capacity of 43,500 people. Among the dignitaries on hand was Helen Hathaway Britton of the St. Louis Cardinals, the first woman owner of a Major League club.

The next year Bob was involved in a critical game of the Giants' purported twenty-six-game winning streak, the longest in history. Having set the record at seventeen earlier in May, the Giants reached twelve when the second game of a doubleheader on September 18 at the Polo Grounds was suspended in the ninth inning because of rain, then called on account of darkness. Since suspended games were not resumed at a later date until 2007, the game was replayed the next day as part of a twin bill. The Giants won both contests, but the winning streak had technically been broken, the historic mark actually being consecutive games without a loss, not consecutive games won. But for Bob, September 19 was historic: the doubleheader was played in record time, the first game finishing in one hour and thirty-five minutes and the second in one hour and twenty-three minutes.

In 1917 Emslie umpired in another record-setting contest: the longest game by time and number of innings played in the National League. On August 22 at Ebbets Field, in the first game of a scheduled doubleheader, the Robins and Pirates battled for twenty-two innings before Pittsburgh won 6–5 in four hours and fifteen minutes. (Pirates second baseman

Jake Pitler also set a record with fifteen put-outs.) Thinking the day done after the marathon, the players headed to the showers and fans for the exits, but Emslie, relieving an exhausted Klem behind the plate, called the second game at six o'clock. Two scoreless innings and twenty minutes later he ended the game on account of darkness, the teams having playing twenty-four innings in four hours and thirty-five minutes. The forty-five innings in consecutive extra-inning games (ten, thirteen, and twenty-two) set the record for innings in a three-game series.

With umpiring the bases less mentally and physically demanding than working the plate and kicking decreasing in frequency, the second decade of twentieth century was by far the least stressful of Emslie's career. He could quickly answer Grantland Rice's rhetorical question, "Are the first or the last twenty-five years the hardest?"[23] He was well aware of the difference in kicking from his early days.

> I stood a great deal from the players some years back when we had the single umpire system and very little backing up from the executive office because I did not care to deprive any of them of any part of their salary, but patience ceased to be a virtue at times for some of them would take advantage of my leniency and become so very abusive that I have been obliged to protect myself, as well as the best interests of the game. Kicking in the days I speak of was "rowdy intelligence." Today to kick and get away with it is called an art. There are some players yet who think that an umpire is only on the field to be held up to the ridicule of the crowed, and they lose no opportunity of showing this. They will kick over everything with no conceivable idea of what they were kicking about, only they have a notion that they must do something to cover up other shortcomings.[24]

That Emslie thought umpiring "a cinch compared to years ago" was due to the double-umpire system, which produced better umpiring not only by allowing better views of base decisions but also providing an extra pair of eyes.[25] Bob benefited from it on July 14, 1912, in St. Louis, when he was stationed near first base and missed seeing the Cardinals pulled a hidden-ball trick on Fred Snodgrass at third base; plate umpire Mal Eason saw it and waved Fred out. But two umpires can't see everything, as Emslie learned on two plays in Boston in 1914. On May 9, when plate umpire Cy Rigler ruled that Snodgrass made a fair catch of an outfield fly, Boston manager George Stallings protested, arguing that Bob as the field umpire should have made the decision. Heydler disallowed the protest, pointing out since there were two men on base at the time, Emslie had all he could do to watch them without trying to follow the ball, so Rigler properly made the call. Later that year, on August 8, as Rabbit Maranville threw to first to attempt a double play, Fred Clarke, running to second base, threw up an arm. The ball hit him and bounced into right field; instead of ending the inning with a double play, two runners scored. It looked like a deliberate interference, but Emslie, running to first base to call the play on the batter-runner, did not see it, and Klem, when appealed to, said he did not see it either.

The system required umpires to respect each other. Bob refused to be drawn into controversy when Klem appealed to him when McGraw launched a "Bolshevick movement" against Bill in 1919 over a call at third base. But the next year, when unsure of a call at first base while watching another base runner, Bob appealed to Klem, who made the call since he was in a better position to see the play. He even once saved his partner from a fight. After the game in Boston on April 27, 1916, McGraw, angry that Klem had ejected him for the second straight day and also cleared the Giants bench, waited for Bill at the entrance to the umpires' dressing room and assailed him with "scurrilous remarks" of "unprintable language." Klem initially ignored the attack, but after "a slurring reference" to one of his close relatives, leaped at Muggsy "in a wild rage." Bob jumped between them and dragged his partner away, averting what would have been a nasty, highly publicized brawl.[26]

During the decade Emslie had no major controversies and his ejections declined dramatically. Skewed slightly by the abbreviated 1912 season, in which for the first time since 1894 he did not eject anyone, from 1911 to 1920 he tossed only thirty players, five in each of three seasons (1911, 1914, and 1919), and only one in 1917. All the ejections were for disputes over safe or out calls besides tossing Fred Clarke in 1915 for fighting,

Fritz Mollwitz in 1918 for arguing a catch/trap call, and Bill "Pickles" Dillhoefer in 1919 for arguing a strike call by Klem. He had the most trouble with Heinie Zimmerman and John McGraw, ejecting each three times. He tossed McGraw for the last time on July 18, 1916, at the Polo Grounds for throwing his glove and pouring out "the vials of his wrath."

Emslie made errors, most inconsequential, some egregious, but always based on what he saw or thought he saw. He knew mistakes were inevitable, but remained greatly troubled by what might have been a wrong call. "Particularly blue" after roasted for a decision in Pittsburg, he uncharacteristically confessed to a reporter, "I may have been wrong, but God knows I thought I was right. I decided the play just as I saw it, but everyone else on the field and in the crowd seem to see it from an entirely different angle." When told a veteran of nearly a quarter century of umpiring shouldn't let criticism bother him, he replied, "I hate to make mistakes during a game. I'll never be any other way. I simply cannot help it."[27]

That Emslie experienced few arguments and criticism was less, as one scribe said, for being "pretty nearly always correct in his decisions, and therefore seldom the butt of the merciless joke writer's wrath, or the spite of the disgruntled crank," than for being "generally perfectly calm in the performance of his duties." While often praised for the accuracy of his calls, it was Bob's style of umpiring that kept confrontations to a minimum. Not autocratic like Klem or O'Day, Emslie had a relational attitude to players. Bob, thought Tim Murnane, "seems to have a knack of keeping out of trouble" by always "running away from the player rather than mix in an argument." It was an exaggeration to say "arguing with old Bob is just like arguing with a wooden Indian," but he was "the best listener in baseball." Christy Mathewson said Emslie, understanding the competitive spirit and that players saw close plays differently, "will listen to a reasonable argument. He is one of the finest umpires that ever broke into the League, I think. He is a good fellow. Emslie is the sort of umpire who rules by the bond of good fellowship rather than by the voice of authority."[28]

Emslie often disarmed potential kicks with a smile that signaled his dismissal of a complaint. Brennan, who had umpired with Bob for four years, recalled, "Many a fellow has looked at Emsie's smile just once and started no more arguments. The result is that Bob has never said a thing that was held against him by a ball player and you can bet there is more dissatisfaction with his work in the grandstand than there is on the player's bench." Even McGraw conceded Emslie was "fair and would listen to a protest." And when Klem berated league umpires by name in his syndicated column, only Emslie and Al Orth escaped criticism. The *Boston Globe* believed, "Most fair-minded fans will readily admit that Bob holds high rank among the fairest and squarest of the men who have played the difficult role in the memory of fandom."[29]

He also exercised restraint in handling volatile situations. On September 7, 1914, at Fenway Park, Fred Snodgrass "loudly taunted" Boston pitcher George Tyler after being hit by a pitch. Tyler responded by pretending to drop a fly ball, imitating Snodgrass's error that helped the Red Sox win the 1912 World Series. Upon taking his place in center field, Fred "thumbing his nose" to catcalls from Boston fans prompted a barrage of bottles, whereupon Boston mayor James Curley jumped out of the grandstand and demanded Emslie remove Snodgrass for inciting the crowd. Bob refused, saying Snodgrass had done nothing that warranted ejection, and "half-pushed" Curley back to his seat. The next day Curley demanded Tener punish Snodgrass for his "flagrant and unwarranted insult" to fans and censure Emslie for not removing him from the game. Nothing came of the request, as Emslie had shown proper restraint in not ejecting Snodgrass.

At times Emslie's tolerance seemed excessive. The partisan New York press thought it "a wonder" he didn't toss Lew McCarty out for persistent kicking. Neither did he eject Johnny Evers, who attempted to step on his feet, snapped fingers under his nose and insultingly asked if the Federal Census tally of blind persons included Bob. Even more remarkable, given his sensitivity about his eyesight, was his failure to eject McGraw, who argued throughout the game and asked Emslie between innings if he had ever been to Camden, South Carolina. When Bob replied in the negative, McGraw said, "You ought to go there, just the place." "How's that?" Emslie asked. "Lightning struck a woman down there and restored her eyesight," replied McGraw, handing Bob a newspaper clipping. Apparently dumbstruck by the clever if biting ruse, Bob said nothing as Muggsy walked, smiling, to the coaching line.[30]

Emslie would take a lot, but there were limits. He ignored McGraw protesting a call by throwing his glove, but when he peevishly said Bob was "losing his eyesight," Emslie tossed him with the comment, "I can still see the clubhouse." And he cut short beefs with curt responses. When Miller Huggins complained that McGraw, whom Emslie had ejected, was not leaving the field fast enough, Emslie tossed the Cardinals manager as well: "Suppose you set the pace for him." When Zimmerman, after Emslie thrust his right arm upward signifying him "out" at second base, yelled, "You're crazy Bob, I ain't out!" and threw his cap to the ground, Emslie threw up his hand again, saying, "Now you're out twice, Heinie. Take your hat and drag yourself to the clubhouse." Players knew when to cease kicking. When the Cubs' Bill Killifer realized Emslie was about to eject him, he abruptly returned to his position as the fans laughed.[31]

Bob treated players with respect, and they in turn respected him. Brennan thought Emslie was "the most popular with the players. I do not believe that I ever heard Emslie speak a harsh word to a ball player and I am just as positive that I never saw one put over anything on him." While he got to know players fairly well after seeing them repeatedly over the years, he steadfastly avoided undue fraternization. His advice to aspiring umpires was emphatic: "Don 't mingle with the players either before or after the game, in fact, treat them as utter strangers at all times. If a chance acquaintanceship is cultivated it only leads to trouble with a big T. Keep away from them at all times." However, umpiring the bases afforded opportunities for amiable banter with runners, fielders, and coaches. Emslie particularly enjoyed an encounter with John McGraw in 1911 when Philadelphia's sensational rookie Grover Cleveland Alexander was flummoxing the Giants. Late in the game McGraw, perhaps to bring luck, switched from coaching third base to the first base coaching line. After two outs, the second on Emslie's close call at first, Bob remarked, "Boys are not hitting much today." "Nope," answered McGraw. "That Alexander is quite a pitcher," Bob added. "Yep," replied McGraw. "Certainly worked a swell game," Bob continued. "With the assistance of a couple of blind umpires, he is doing immense," scowled Muggsy. After the third out McGraw headed to the bench before Bob could reply, but he "enjoyed a smile without letting McGraw observe it."[32]

Emslie also benefited from the respect and recognition of his long and faithful service. Umpires came and went, but Bob stayed on, the press often deferentially referring to him as "the veteran," the "venerable Bob Emslie," "old Bob," and "Uncle Bob." Players, "no matter how turbulent," also showed respect by restraint.

> Good old Bob Emslie never has a harsh word shot at him. No matter how badly the ancient arbiter may miscall a play, no athlete kicks, and it is a pleasing thing, when some novice starts a roar, to see how rapidly three or four old men rush on the boy and shut his face. It is the unwritten law of the game that Emslie, old now and really missing lots of the close ones, shall never be insulted or even troubled; the boys all conspire to make his road an easy one, and good old Bob goes on his way as if he were the great Nawab of baseball, the high judge whose decisions never err.[33]

When McGraw raged at Emslie, St. Louis columnist L. C. Davis mused poetically:

> At old Sir Robert Emslie McGraw has been kicking;
> He flies at old Bob in a towering rage;
> It looks as if Muggsy were fond of soft picking—
> Why doesn't he pick on some guy of his age?[34]

Deferential spirits notwithstanding, kicking and arguments there were. Occasionally questionable close base decisions raised hoary comments about his deficient "ocular nerve" or suggestions that he "sorely needed some optic assistance," a headline once querying, "Is Bob Emslie Blind?" Understandably sensitive about his vision, he continued to use marksmanship in defense of his eyesight. When he challenged McGraw to a shooting match for a side bet, the Giants' skipper replied, "No, Bob, you're all right. I give it to you." And to McGraw's quip that from behind home plate Bob couldn't tell the difference between an apple and baseball on second base, he retorted, "Some of your players act as if they did not know the difference either." Honus Wagner recalled when some Giants players offered to bet that from home plate Emslie couldn't tell an apple from an orange on second base, Bob ignored them, then ended the jest that fall by winning a prestigious trapshooting contest. Similarly, Bob recounted with pride the time in 1911 when players challenged him to get a pair of glasses; that fall he hit ninety-nine of one hundred shots to win a trap shoot.[35]

Umpires, like players and managers, become the central character in oft-told tales, some true, some tall. As Emslie became something of a national celebrity, stories circulated about amusing ejections. In 1914 it was reported Bob, tired of Boston bench jockeying, shouted, "Willis, off the field! Get out of there." When Vic failed to leave Bob rushed to the dugout, only to find him "sound asleep and snoring with his head resting against the side of the bench." As the Beaneaters convulsed with laughter, Bob woke up Willis and ordered him off the field, the "only instance on record when an umpire put a man out of a game who was asleep." But Emslie never once ejected Vic. The basis for the story is Augie Moran ejecting Willis in Boston on June 13, 1904, for coaching from the bench. On reaching the dugout Moran discovered Vic presumably napping, his elbows on his knees and face between his hands, but tossed him anyway. Willis left "with a smile"; it was the only ejection in his thirteen-year career.[36]

On April 11, 1916, the *St. Louis Star* published McGraw's story about Emslie tossing Luther "Dummy" Taylor at the Polo Grounds. The game began in the rain, and when it intensified, the Giants skipper tried in vain to get Emslie to call the game. To prove his point, McGraw sent Taylor to coach at first base wearing a pair of rubber boots borrowed from the groundskeeper. Taylor, a deaf mute given to antics to make his point, waved his cap above his head to represent an umbrella as he sloshed around, pretending to sink. Unamused, Emslie ejected him and, by opening and closing his fist twice, signaled a $10 fine. But the story isn't true. Emslie ejected Taylor only once, in 1902, for protesting a pitch call by throwing his glove.

HAIL TO THE CHIEF

On January 27, 1916, Bob Emslie turned fifty-six and prepared to begin his thirtieth season umpiring, twenty-seven in the Majors. Over the years he had rendered at least 125,000 decisions. Baseball fans of all ages knew about the lengthy careers of ballplayers like Cap Anson (twenty-seven years), Cy Young (twenty-two), and Nap Lajoie (twenty-one), but it took Bob Emslie's entry into his fourth decade of umpiring for public attention to be given to "a work unequaled in length of service and efficiency." On the eve of World War I newspapers as far away as Hawaii began recounting Bob's umpiring career, "which has never been surpassed in length or devotion to duty." The publicity prompted the visiting Washington team's batboy from the 1890s to recall an incident with Bob. The lad, when told one day Cincinnati didn't want a batboy but lacking money for admission, asked Emslie as he approached the gate, "Mr. Emslie, take me in, please." Bob did, his kindness receiving a backhanded compliment: "Umpires are not so bad, after all, at least I did not think Emslie was that afternoon."[37]

In 1916 the baseball world took note of his quarter century in the National League. A flood of biographical articles summarizing the playing and officiating career of the "Dean of Umpires" appeared in papers across the United States and Canada, Emslie becoming "known to every baseball fan in the country." *Sporting Life* praised Bob for setting "a world's record for continuous service as an autocrat of the diamond." The *Boston Globe* noted his "record of a quarter of a century in the big show has never been equaled by any other umpire in the history of the sport." The Trenton *Times* was impressed that for thirty years he "survived the slings and pop bottles of outrageous fortune as an umpire," the *Philadelphia Inquirer* declaring he had "done as much in his way to boom baseball as any of the great pioneers of the game." It was even suggested that for his heroic service as an umpire Bob be awarded a Carnegie Hero Fund, created in 1904 to honor acts of civilian heroism in the United States and Canada.[38]

National League owners, too, recognized Emslie's unparalleled career. In February they honored baseball's senior umpire at the league's fortieth anniversary dinner at the Waldorf Astoria in New York and on August 9 voted to commemorate his twenty-five years of service with a "fitting tribute" between games of a doubleheader in Brooklyn on August 12, the occasion dubbed "Emslie Day" by Charles Ebbets. (The owners moved up the historic milestone by a week; Bob was scheduled to umpire in Cincinnati on August 19, the place and date of his first National League game.) He was supposed to work the Braves-Robins series with Klem but was given the day off, replaced by Byron. Between games Klem escorted Bob, "all togged out in a shining new seersucker suit," to home plate from the grandstand, where he had watched the first game with his wife, who had hurried down with friends from St. Thomas for the occasion. He was surrounded by players from both teams and several umpires from days past, all removing their caps as President Tener complemented "Modest Bob" on a quarter century of continuous service to the league:

> You have been a credit to baseball, both as a player and as an umpire. You have not only had the respect but the affectionate regard of your associates. You have so long been connected with the game in the official capacity as umpire that it may be said you have the greatest knowledge of the rules of the game, not only in familiarity with the letter of the rules today, but a complete understanding of why each rule was adopted.
>
> In twenty-five years of continual service you have never been suspended, fined or censured for any breach of conduct. You have ever held the confidence, the respect and the warm personal regard of the presidents of the league under whom you have served and have also won the friendship of the players who have come and gone during your long term of service to the great American game.

Tener then presented Bob with a leather bag containing twenty-five gold double eagle coins worth $20 each, one for each year of service. Emslie "smiled happily" at receiving $500, then "broke into a broader grim" when Klem gave him a diamond stickpin on behalf of his fellow umpires.[39]

With a mixture of pride, humility, and perhaps a bit of embarrassment, the man who shunned publicity left the field accompanied by the "warm, enthusiastic applause" of the capacity crowd of 35,000. An ardent New York fan, regretting he could not attend the ceremony, wrote Bob a letter expressing the "pleasure of witnessing ball games at which you umpired" and sending "my most heartiest congratulations and best wishes to Bob Emslie the gentleman umpire."[40] Bob also appreciated a brief vacation: he was off duty until August 18, when he rejoined Klem in Cincinnati.

The next day, as twenty-five years earlier, the Reds lost, this time to the Phillies. The *Cincinnati Enquirer*, which had noted Emslie's debut in 1891, made no mention of the occasion.

Among the encomiums accorded Emslie, Grantland Rice, America's most famous sportswriter, in his nationally syndicated column "Sportlight" on August 14 reached hyperbolic heights in a "Ballad of Heroes" about World War I, saying "hats of the universe should be doffed to Mr. Emslie":

When Hindenburg held the Russ at bay
 His name was entered upon Fame's hall;
When General Joff checked the Teuton army,
 The Red Game bowed to his mighty thrall;
The Lily of France crept out of the pall
 And medals were pinned on his gleaming coat;
Who is the greatest hero of them all?
 Emslie's the entry that gets my vote!

The Trooper faces the shrapnel's spray,
 And he is a hero beyond recall;
To face grim death in the deadly fray,
 To give your life at the country's call—
Where has glory a greater haul?
 Show me the chance for a greater gloat!
On the Field of Honor the heroes fall;
 But Emslie's the fellow that gets the vote!

Haunted and taunted, day by day,
 For a thousand weeks by the sore fan's squall,
Branded a thief upon each called play,
 Hissed and hooted on each pitched ball;
Held to scorn in the biting scrawl,
 The One and Only Eternal Goat—
Come, ye heroes and crowd the stall—
Emslie's the entry that gets my vote![41]

Press coverage of the first day honoring an umpire failed to mention that Emslie had umpired the most games in Major League and National League history (3,374 and 3,237, respectively), but noted the absence of World Series assignments. The *Boston Globe* lamented he had been "overlooked" and other papers thought it a "peculiar fact" he had not worked the fall classic, arguing that "since he umpires the bases all season" he "should be given a place among the four umpires in the fall classic, even if he does not work behind the catcher. He is a great credit to the game and especially the National League, and has done as much in his way to boom baseball as any of the great pioneers of the game." Assigning an umpire exclusively to the bases would have interrupted the normal rotation, but that was hardly a significant problem. Just as Ban Johnson had honorarily assigned Sheridan to umpire bases exclusively in 1910 despite his inability to pass an eye exam, giving Emslie the limelight in 1916 would have been appropriate for an umpire who had contributed so much to the game. Of no matter at the time other than losing out on $650, the lack of recognition attendant on umpiring in the World Series would ultimately detract from Emslie's place in umpiring history.[42]

BOMBS AND BUGS

While being recognized for his career, Emslie was affected by two developments beyond the ballpark. World War I, which broke out in June 1914, became personal when Great Britain declared war on Germany on August 4 and Canada quicky dispatched troops to European theaters. Bob's son, Jack, was too young to be mobilized for active duty, but the family endured wartime exigencies.[43] When the United States declared war on Germany on April 7, 1917, military preparations affected professional baseball. Tener wanted his umpires to be in shape, so in March 1918 sent them south for spring training, like military recruits reporting for basic training. Veterans O'Day and Emslie took "a light training course," but the others drilled "as strenuously as the players." Bob and Klem then went to Hot Springs, Arkansas, to call Red Sox and Robins exhibitions. After the teams broke camp the umpires accompanied them for games in Texas, Louisiana, and Tennessee en route home to open the season.

During spring training Bob learned of the second external threat, the highly contagious deadly H1N1 virus of avian origin commonly (if inaccurately) called the Spanish flu that would ravage North America after breaking out in early 1918 at Camp Funston in Fort Riley, Kansas. Baseball spring training camps had avoided contagion, and while communities across the country implemented regulations to combat the disease, neither the National Commission nor league presidents discussed contingency measures to protect umpires, players, or spectators against influenza during the upcoming season. Major League baseball, like the national government, was more concerned about the war than public health; *Sporting News* had not a word to say about the threat of the deadly virus to the game and its personnel. (Owing to the war *Sporting Life* ceased publication in 1917, resuming in 1922.) Fortunately the flu abated during the summer and Emslie, his umpiring colleagues, players, and managers escaped the disease. Whether Bob or others individually took precautionary measures is unknown.[44]

Emslie opened the 1918 season with Klem on April 16 in Philadelphia, the game beginning with the band evoking patriotism by playing "The Star-Spangled Banner." Thereafter Bob was affected daily by the war. He faced travel restrictions as troops and matériel transport, given priority, jammed rail lines. At ballparks baseball supported the war by selling Liberty Bonds, collecting war tax, and having players (armed with bats instead of rifles) engage in pregame "drill" on the field. Attendance declined sharply as war dominated fans' attention, and the quality of play declined as an increasing number of players—eventually some 38 percent—donned military uniforms following Secretary of War Newton D. Baker's "work or fight" order in July. Although the Minor Leagues were hit hardest—out of ten circuits only the International League finished the season—American League president Ban Johnson proposed ending the Major League season on August 20. National League owners, however, insisted on carrying on until Labor Day, so teams played 124 to 131 of 154 scheduled games. During the rush to end the season Emslie worked five consecutive doubleheaders from August 24 to September 2.

Among the season's uncertainties, none was more immediately concerning for Emslie than when Tener, fed up with intra- and interleague ownership infighting, abruptly resigned on August 6. Bob's apprehension about his fate under a new president evaporated in December when the owners, opting for continuity amid uncertainty, elected John Heydler, friend to umpires, president. To ensure stability they returned to tradition by having the president also serve as secretary-treasurer and gave him a three-year contract, the first time a National League president had been hired for more than one year. The descriptions of Heydler—"not flashy, but faithful and capable," with a "firm but quiet and modest manner of conducting the business of the league," "well versed in every department of the game," "a sportsman of the highest ideas of equity and fairness," "plays no favorites, and nothing ruffles his temper"—applied equally to Bob Emslie.[45]

Despite the disruptions and distractions Emslie logged another successful season, working 129 games, the second most on the staff. On September 2 he finished the abbreviated season where he began, in Philadelphia, calling a doubleheader between the Robins and Phillies with O'Day. In the ninth inning of the first game a squadron of six Navy planes circling the city flew over the baseball field. As they appeared O'Day called time while the band played "the National anthem"—"My Country, 'Tis of Thee"—as the crowd stood, hats off, singing the words until the planes disappeared. When directly over the playing field each plane jettisoned leaflets reminding people to support the war effort, though none fell inside the park.[46]

After the game Bob may have headed home, arriving on September 5 in time to celebrate his wedding anniversary with Helena for the first time in twenty-six years. Or he may have gone with O'Day to Chicago, where Hank umpired the World Series between the Cubs and Red Sox, the earliest start and only time the fall classic was played in September instead of October. With a nod to warnings from health officials about the spread of the virus, the "spitball" was disallowed and each player and the four umpires, all of whom for the first time worked in the infield and rotated positions after each game, wore surgical masks. As a patriotic gesture the club owners agreed to contribute ten percent of gate receipts to war charities, the players doing likewise from their revenue share and the umpires from their salary, which had been reduced from $1,000 to $500. Then in the first game, on September 5, during the seventh-inning stretch of Game One, a military band impromptu played "The Star-Spangled Banner" as a salute to the servicemen in attendance; the crowd rose, sang, and at the end "exploded into thunderous applause" in a burst of patriotic fervor. It was a historic event: played during each succeeding game of the series, the song, not designated as the national anthem until 1931, was thereafter played at the opening games of the season and in every World Series. (The custom of playing the anthem before every regular season game began during World War II.)[47]

The early season ending was fortunate, likely sparing Emslie, fellow umpires, and players from the massive mid-September outbreak of the flu in Boston and Philadelphia that set off a wave of illness and death across the country during the late fall and winter of 1918–19; of some 22 million infected Americans, 675,000 would die. The virus claimed several people related to baseball, but the only active participant was Francis "Silk" O'Loughlin, an American League umpire who died from the disease at age forty-six at his home in Boston on December 20, 1918. (John McNulty, a Federal League umpire in 1913, the year before its designation as a Major League, also died from the disease.)[48]

Back in St. Thomas, Emslie watched the progress of both the war and the pandemic. While his concerns about the impact of the Great War abated with Germany's unconditional surrender on November 11, he probably remembered, upon reading about Eddie Grant, the first Major Leaguer killed in combat on October 5, that he had given the likeable Phillie his first ejection for arguing a call at third base on May 21, 1908. Undoubtedly Bob and the family took precautions to protect themselves from the virus that ravaged the Dominion and the province of Ontario, where at least nine thousand and perhaps as many as twenty thousand died of influenza.[49] With the pandemic still raging in the winter of 1918–19, he wondered if the 1919 season would be shortened or even canceled. Absent vaccines and pulmonary equipment, national preventive initiatives and adequate public health services, health officials in many communities canceled sporting events and large gatherings or required people to wear masks in public. University of Missouri basketball fans had to mask, and to comply with a Pasadena ordinance two Southern

California Winter League teams, umpires, and spectators wore masks covering their noses and mouths for eleven innings in a game on January 26, 1919, reportedly "the first and only time" this was done in an American city. (The rule was rescinded four days later.)[50]

Faced with a pandemic and the likelihood that returning troops would cause extensive railway disruptions, Major League owners, anticipating a poor season at the gate, in December 1918 agreed on a reduced season of 140 games for 1919. The decision was prudent but unnecessary as the epidemic attenuated by March. Spring training proceeded as normal, the unusually high attendance at games portending enthusiasm for baseball as a release from the anxieties and impacts of war and disease. Indeed, attendance increased dramatically, every club showing a profit at season's end; the Minor Leagues also rebounded with fifteen circuits, initial attendance numbers promising new records for crowds during the season.

RETURN TO NORMALCY

Emslie opened 1919 with Klem in Boston on April 19, four days before the official start of the season. The Braves had been given special permission to host a doubleheader with Brooklyn as part of the Patriots' Day celebration commemorating the opening shots of the American Revolution at Lexington and Concord. Emslie and Klem hung around for the Braves' season opener on April 23, then teamed through season's end on September 28. In logging 139 games, missing only 4, August 9–12, Bob had again performed well; "his eye still is keen and he gets about the diamond as sprightly as some of his younger contemporaries." As a result he had received respect from players, and even fans were "usually contented that when he calls a decision it is right." Sportswriter Fred Lieb was among those thinking the league had "done well" in putting him back on the regular staff, writing, "Old Bob continues to hold his own with the best."[51]

Every game, however routine, contained special elements of play, and 1919 was a banner year for unusual games. When Emslie and Klem walked onto the Polo Grounds on May 4, 1919, they confronted 37,000 fans, the largest crowd ever to watch a regular-season game in New York. What made umpiring the otherwise lackluster 4–3 Phillies victory special? It was the first Major League game played on Sunday in New York City, the crowd validating the wisdom of the state legislature in lifting the ban on Sunday baseball. (A record crowd of 25,000 was also in attendance in Brooklyn.)

If at times the former pitcher thrilled at outstanding mound performances, he also felt sorry for hurlers who endured difficult outings. Both emotions obtained on May 15 at Ebbets Field when Brooklyn's Al Mamaux and Cincinnati's Hod Eller pitched twelve shut-out innings, the Robins right-hander collapsing in the thirteenth as the Reds scored ten unearned runs to win 10–0. There were times when the old-time hurler ached when a pitcher simply didn't have it. He watched with amazement on July 20 at the Polo Grounds when Christy Matheson, bereft of his fastball and legendary control, was driven from the mound after 1.1 innings, perhaps the worst outing of his career, certainly of the season in which he led the league with 1.99 ERA.

History was made two weeks later with Emslie and Klem in Cincinnati for a series between the first-place Reds and second-place Giants. The teams split the first two games, attendance increasing each day, so Heydler, anticipating an overflow crowd at Redland Field on Sunday, August 3, summoned William "Barry" McCormick and Peter Harrison from St. Louis to form the first four-umpire crew assigned to a regular-season game in Major League history. Heydler's decision was wise. The record crowd, a third more than seating capacity, filled the stands and spilled over both foul lines and along the outfield fences, save for an open space in deep center. Klem worked the plate and Emslie the bases while the other two umpires manned the foul lines, McCormick in left field, Harrison in right, to rule on balls hit close to the foul lines and into the crowd. The quartet "admirably handled" the game and there was "no strenuous kicking" by either team.

The final week in September brought a remarkable ending to an unusually eventful season for Bob and Bill. In Cincinnati on September 21 they umpired a game that set two Major League records. It took only fifty-five minutes for Brooklyn to beat the Reds 3–1, and Cincinnati's Harry "Slim" Sallee, while failing to win his twenty-first game, threw only sixty-five pitches to best Christy Mathewson's previous mark of sixty-nine.

Three days later, in Philadelphia, Bob was on hand for Fred Luderus Day, celebrating the Phillies' first baseman setting the Major League record for consecutive games after reaching 479 on August 3. To wind up the eventful month Bob umpired another historic game on September 28, the Giants beating the Phillies 6–1 in the first game of a doubleheader at the Polo Grounds. Although the New Yorkers recorded thirteen hits, every batter getting at least one, owing to "groove pitching and first ball hitting" as well as players from the sixth inning on running to and from their positions when it became apparent that they "could do something unusual," the game took only fifty-one minutes, to date still the shortest game in Major League history.[52]

In 1920 Robert Emslie, age sixty-one, reached the end of his third decade and thirty-first year of Major League umpiring. Only Klem, O'Day, and Rigler remained from the 1911 staff, Hank alone having umpired before the twentieth century began. Admired in baseball circles in America, Bob was a revered, iconic sports figure in Canada. It was reported that the governor general of Canada, the viceregal representative of the monarch, "always nods to him" and the premier, the head of the national government, was known "to slow up his car to permit Emslie to have the right of way."[53] When the erstwhile Dean of Umpires opened the season in St. Louis on April 14 the *St. Louis Star* concluded a biographical sketch by saying, "The oldest umpire in the game in point of service, and without question one of the most competent who has ever handled an indicator," who by a "conservative estimate" had made "something like 150,000 decisions," was "ready for another long season."

Indeed he was. With the return to a 154-game schedule Bob worked 156 games, matching his career high in 1908, all with Klem except the final seven with Bob Hart. Emslie's season ended on October 3 as it had begun on April 14 with a ten-inning game, bracketing a career high of twenty-seven extra-inning games. There was a bonus: his salary, which had been reduced in the 1918–19 war years like that of the rest of the staff, was restored to its 1917 level. There were also downsides. As a former pitcher who had plunked his share of batters, he was shaken by news that Cleveland shortstop Ray Chapman, hit in the head by a pitch on August 16, died the next day, the first and only player ever to die from an injury sustained during a game. And though well aware that gambling had increased in recent decades, including rumors of World Series fixes in 1917 and 1918, he was troubled by mounting talk that eight Chicago White Sox players had conspired with gamblers to throw the 1919 World Series to the Cincinnati Reds, as two of his colleagues, Cy Rigler and Ernie Quigley, had umpired the games. Quigley, behind the plate in games three and seven, said, "I never saw a team try harder to win and they were beaten on the square by the superior strength of the Reds," but all eight Chicago players were permanently banned from organized baseball.[54]

Exclusively umpiring the bases was far less stressful and physically taxing than working the plate. Doubleheaders (he worked 169 during the decade) were less strenuous, and he was able to rest between the morning and afternoon games. But there were occasional demanding stretches, especially late in the season. In 1916, from August 28 to September 5, he had six twin bills in seven days, four in a row, winding up with eleven in September. The next year from August 31 to September 26 he umpired twelve doubleheaders in sixteen games, including seven straight from September 5 to September 18. In 1918 he had five in a row to end the season; in August 1919 he had six in seven days. Extra-inning games were also increasingly tiring. From 1913 to 1920 he worked 135 extended games, usually 12 to 14 per year, but had 18 in 1917, 19 in 1919, and a phenomenal 27 in 1920. Eight times he worked back-to-back extra-innings games.

On the bases Bob was no longer incessantly battered by foul balls. But there were different dangers. Twice he was injured by first basemen making plays. On August 25, 1916, in St. Louis, the Phillies' Fred Luderus, chasing after a wild throw, bowled over Emslie, who was kneeling just outside the foul line preparing for a close decision. Bob, badly shaken, had to continue for three more batters before the game ended. On June 10, 1918, in Brooklyn, the Pirates' Fred Mollwitz, after diving for a hot grounder, raced to the bag for the put-out and crashed into Emslie, striking him a "severe blow" in the head. Emslie fell to the ground, "knocked out for several minutes." When he arose, "slightly dazed" and boasting "quite a bump" on his forehead, the crowd cheered his pluck. Thrown balls could also be hurtful. In the first game of a doubleheader in Cincinnati on June 24, 1919, left fielder Fred Merkle's throw to third base hit Emslie on the left wrist. Although several players urged him to leave the game, he worked both games despite the badly bruised wrist "giving him constant pain." After the game it was determined he had suffered a broken bone, so he umpired for several days with a bandaged left arm.

HOME, SWEET HOME

Winding up the 1920 season, he returned to St. Thomas on October 7 looking "quite fit" at age sixty-one and feeling proud of the being the oldest umpire in history. But while continuing to perform well on the field, it was obvious that age was catching up with him. As a sign of time passing, he tapered off some in his off-season activities. He spent more time strolling down Talbot, the main street, chatting with friends in St. Thomas, and driving with his wife to Toronto, Port Huron, Michigan, and Toledo, Ohio, visiting "a host of friends among the sporting class." And to prepare financially for the inevitable end of his career, he became an original stockholder and member of the board of directors of the St. Thomas Metal Signs company.[55]

To be sure, he continued to feed his competitive urges by trapshooting; no local, regional, or international meet considered complete without his participation. Advancing age did not diminish his accuracy. In February 1911, with snow on the ground, he downed ten straight mostly white birds to win the championship, and in December, despite strong winds, he won an International Tournament in St. Thomas. In 1912 he tied for first twice in January and won another title in February. When O'Day visited Emslie in February 1912 he found Bob wearing "a classy diamond medal" for winning a trap shoot. To see for himself, Hank went with Bob to the range and watched him kill forty out of forty-five birds, a testament to his visual acuity. In 1915 he tied for third in a twenty-bird shoot and second in two ten-bird shoots with nine kills. Heralded as "the King of Trapshooters" by baseball writers, he lived up to the billing by winning a ten-live-pigeon team event in December 1916 despite unfavorable weather.[56]

But he gravitated increasingly to administrative duties with the St. Thomas Gun Club, the finest grounds in Canada with five sets of traps for clay targets and Fulford traps for live birds. Bob was elected vice president in 1911 and 1912 and president in 1913, serving for at least two years.[57] Bob made his mark as administrator as well as shooter. In 1914 he spearheaded splitting the St. Thomas Grand International Tournament, which had grown to be the largest tournament in North America save for the Grand American, into two sections: a four-day target shoot in September and a three-day live bird meet in December. In organizing the Grand International meets he convinced customs officials to allow shooters from the United States to bring their guns into Canada, although they still had to pay duties on their ammunition. As Bob's competitive shooting declined, he increasingly attended meets as a spectator; he also served as the referee in trap tournaments—"a cinch" compared to "calling balls and strikes on things which whizz, curve, drop, jump and do a whole lot of other things rendering quick, almost snap decisions on close plays at the bases; listening all the while to rough stuff that is not always sotto voce and that is dosed out alike by fans, players and sometimes managers!"[58]

Come winter he continued competing in curling bonspiels with great success, invariably described as "the umpire-curler." His rink again won the Ross Trophy as the top curling squad in Ontario in 1911, lost in the final round of the Toronto championship in 1912, and in 1913 took the Tecumseh trophy in London and the McDonald-Emslie trophy in St. Thomas. As skip, at the advanced age of fifty-eight, he tossed the final two stones that won the Glenn Cup in 1917; the following year he won both the Winnipeg bonspiel and the Western Ontario classic in London; and in 1920 he handily won the largest bonspiel ever held in Owen Sound. His success was such that when his team faltered in a London match on January 6, 1919, the press noted, "By some mysterious stroke of luck Bob Emslie, the veteran baseball umpire and knight of the stone, did not even reach the finals." He also contributed to the advancement of curling off the rink when elected to the executive board of the Granite Curling Club in 1917 and 1918 and vice president by 1920. His pride was unbounded when Jack also took to the rink, rising to the position of skip.

Trapshooting and curling were not his only sporting enthusiasms. Umpiring summers left little time for golf, but he took up the sport after the St. Thomas Golf Club opened a new course in Pinafore Park in 1909. An admirer of good horseflesh and owner of a stable of "fast harness horses," he regularly hitched up one of his "fast steppers" to ride around St. Thomas, "ever ready" to challenge another driver to a road race.[59] There is no record of him attending prizefights—not the sort of thing mentioned in the press—but given his interest in the "Sweet Science" and his visits with Corbett when in New York, it takes no stretch of the imagination to envision him occasionally ringside. Indicative of his avid interest in prizefighting, Bob got into an animated discussion with Hans Wagner in 1910 over a highly publicized upcoming fight in Reno on July 4. Billed as the "Battle of the Century," former champion James Jeffries, dubbed the "Great White Hope" by the press, had been enticed out of retirement in hopes of reclaiming the heavyweight title from African American Jack Johnson. When Wagner mentioned that he thought Jeffries would win, Emslie, "quite a fight fan," thinking Johnson would win, started "fussing." Hans recalled they walked off the field amiably but excitedly "shaking our fists at each other and making quite a lot of noise." (Johnson's victory brought both celebrations and race riots across the nation.)[60]

DECADE'S END

The personal repository of the league's institutional memory since 1891, Emslie at the end of 1920 could look back on profound changes without and within the ballpark over the past three decades. In addition to umpiring during World War I and the Spanish flu pandemic, he also lived through the 1918–20 Red Scare that swept across Canada and America in response to the Russian Revolution in 1917 and the Red Summers of 1917–19, the race riots ignited across the United States by the exodus of southern Blacks to northern cities and conflict between Black and white soldiers returning from the war. Emslie did not work in the cities where major violence occurred—St. Louis in 1917, Philadelphia in 1918, Chicago in 1919—but he surely heard and read about them.[61] Whether or not his wife was involved in the suffrage movement, Helena was surely pleased with the granting of national voting rights for women, partially in Canada in 1918 and in the United States in 1919. In the United States American

Indians, men and women, were granted suffrage by act of Congress in 1924. Canadian national suffrage extended to black and white women except in Quebec, which did not grant voting rights to women until 1940. “Minority” men and women were excluded, Asians receiving the right to vote in 1948, Inuits in 1950, and First Nations people in 1960.[62] But Bob, who enjoyed alcoholic libations, was displeased by the enactment of Prohibition laws on both sides of the border, first in his home province of Ontario in 1916 and then in the United States in 1920.[63]

Of more direct consequence were changes in the game itself. Some were obvious. He had served under five league presidents and saw the three-man National Commission that had fractionally governed the majors since 1902 replaced after the Black Sox scandal in 1920 by the game’s first commissioner, the autocratic former federal judge Kenesaw Mountain Landis, in a move strongly supported by Heydler. He had also witnessed the rise and demise of a third Major League, the Federal, as well as profound changes in where and how games were played. He saw wooden bandboxes replaced by expansive brick, steel, and concrete stadiums, even umpiring inaugural games in three of them—Forbes Field in 1909, Ebbets Field in 1913, and Braves Field in 1915—and the Deadball Era’s “scientific baseball” replaced by the free-swinging slugging launched by Babe Ruth.

Changes in umpiring were more subtle. Two 1920 rules, banning “doctored pitches” and requiring umpires to remove the gloss on balls before games by rubbing them with mud, did not affect Emslie as the field umpire. While umpires continued to be vexed by arguments with players, insults from fans, and occasional flying objects, the physical and verbal abuse abated and threats of postgame mobbings were things of the past. With greater front office support, the two-man system, more favorable press coverage, greater staff stability, and higher salaries, umpiring had become a vocation instead of a short-term job; an umpire who passed muster in the first two or three years could look forward to a long career. The enhanced stature of umpiring was due largely to the personalities and performances of the men who served in the first two decades of the twentieth century. It was the Golden Age of Umpires, the finest, most colorful and popular collection of umpires ever to grace the diamond;

four of the ten arbiters in the Hall of Fame hail from the Deadball Era.[64] Grantland Rice, lamenting "the color" the game had lost in the last few years, thought the best place to look for "unique or distinctive types" was among the umpires: "Hank O'Day, Bob Emslie and Lord Byron will live long in the annals of the game."[65] Truly, 1920 marked the end of an era for baseball—and Bob Emslie.

13

Umpire Supervisor

> Umpires might come and umpires might go,
> but Bob Emslie appeared to go on forever.
>
> —*Sporting News*, January 4, 1923

Having survived the First World War and the concurrent viral pandemic, Bob Emslie in 1921 began his fifth decade of professional umpiring, the fourth in the National League. It had been rumored the league would open without its two senior umpires, Emslie being pensioned and O'Day opting for better weather and less travel in the Pacific Coast League, but both were on the staff come opening day and would work the full season.

For the opener in Boston on April 13, Bob teamed with Bill Brennan, returning after seven years. The pairing proved difficult due to frequent arguments over Brennan's decisions and, in one embarrassing instance, his inattention to duty. When in the eighth inning on May 28 in Pittsburgh Brennan called a Pirates player safe at home to tie the score, Cincinnati pitcher Dolph Luque threw the ball to the ground in disgust. On seeing the ball roll into the Reds dugout, Clyde Barnhart, who was on second, headed for third, thinking he was entitled to the extra base. But someone in the dugout threw the ball to Reds catcher Ivey Wingo, who tagged Barnhart out, Emslie making the call. Pittsburgh manager George "Mooney" Gibson immediately protested, saying the ball should have ruled dead for going out of play and Barnhart allowed to advance. But neither umpire saw the ball go into the dugout; Emslie was running toward third to make the call on the advancing runner, and Brennan neglected to watch the ball. Heydler upheld the protest and the game was replayed from the contested place in the eighth inning in Pittsburgh on June 30, the Pirates winning in ten innings on Charlie Grimm's walk-off homer.

Emslie continued with Brennan until being seriously injured on June 23. In the ninth inning of the first game of a doubleheader in St. Louis, an errant throw to first base struck Bob, crouching behind the bag to make the call, in the knee. His leg muscles paralyzed from the blow, he fell to the ground in great pain and was carried off the field and taken to a hospital, where an examination by Cardinals physician Dr. Robert Hyland found no broken bones, but "a shattered nerve" behind the badly bruised knee that would keep Emslie off the field for "at least three or four days."[1] In fact he was out for fourteen days. Bob returned to duty on July 3 and worked with Klem through August 9, then joined Bob Hart until August 13. Whether owing to continuing knee discomfort or simply needing to rest, he umpired only eleven games thereafter—a single game on August 19, six games from August 28 to September 2, and four from September 27 to the finale on October 1. He wound up calling 107 games, the fewest in nine years, all but one at first base.[2] On September he umpired at third base for the second time in his career and previously recorded a first as part of a four-man crew in Brooklyn on May 8.[3]

It was difficult season, perhaps the most frustrating of his career. Like every umpire, he was firm in not changing his decision unless proven wrong, but in 1921 he uncharacteristically twice reversed himself on the spot. On June 11 in St. Louis, on a "very close" play, Bob initially motioned Rogers Hornsby safe with his right palm down, then snapped his arm up to signal an out. "The Rajah" rarely criticized umpires, but this time "objected vigorously," not to the decision but to Emslie reversing it. Emslie stood firm. On July 24 in New York, "the ancient arbiter" again changed a decision on a close play at first, initially calling Ross Youngs out, then ruling him safe.

He had few confrontations during the early part of the season, his only two ejections on the bases occurring by June 22, but the dog days of August brought some of the harshest criticism he had ever experienced. On August 1 in Pittsburgh, after charging Emslie with "three doubtful calls," the Braves "fretted and fumed" when he called Rabbit Maranville safe in stealing second; Emslie stoically withstood the abuse, but Klem ejected Hank Gowdy for throwing a cup of water at Bob. After the game Emslie and Klem followed the Braves to Chicago where all hell broke loose during the second game of a doubleheader on August 3. In the seventh inning, after consecutive decisions termed "awful" and "ridiculous,"

Bob was "hooted and jeered" and showered with pop bottles and "other missiles." After the game, fans still enraged despite the Cubs' 7–5 victory, threw bottles and debris as Bob, beleaguered, headed to the dressing room. Heydler, who happened to be in the stands, after witnessing "the poor work and the wild demonstration of protest," decided to give Emslie a breather, replacing him with Brennan for the series finale on August 5.

Criticism kept coming. On August 28 in Brooklyn "frequent barkings" increased after he reportedly "erred egregiously" as the only one in Ebbets Field to think Pittsburgh's Davey Robertson was safe at third. Bob seethed but turned a deaf ear to the "jibes and jeering" cascading from the stands and ignored the solitary pop bottle thrown at him. The *Daily Eagle*'s Abe Yager quipped that Emslie, having "labored long and fulsomely in the baseball vineyard" was "entitled to all consideration, consisting of much veneration for his age and a lot of doubt as to his judgment," but if Bob had erred so "egregiously" at the Polo Grounds he "doubtless would have met with a sudden and painless demise."

If uncharacteristically faltering on calls, Emslie was sharp as ever on rules, as befit his appointment to the new interleague rules committee. Called "the rule book wizard" by fellow arbiter Cy Rigler, his expertise was often called upon when working with Brennan and even when working with Klem, now the head of the staff, who despite his exalted reputation behind the plate was known to be lackadaisical about enforcing rules and may have been involved in more overturned and controversial contests than any other umpire in history.[4] On July 4, in the first game of the holiday twin bill in Chicago, Klem failed to notice the Reds batting twice in the wrong order. When the Cubs complained in the third inning, Klem did not know what to do, so Emslie came in to explain what should be done. The next inning the Cubs again protested and Emslie again explained the situation. Klem finally got it right, Cincinnati thereafter batting in the correct order. Bob was unable to correct Klem's failure to call an infield fly on July 27. With Pirates on first and second base, George "Possum" Whitted "lifted a high fly above the plate" that on the way down hit Giants catcher Frank Snyder's glove and fell on the infield grass. Snyder quickly picked up the ball launched a double play, ending the inning. The infield fly rule was explicit, but Klem, not being in proper position, failed to call it. Since Emslie from beyond first base could not see if the ball had landed in fair territory, he was unable to override the decision.

The 1921 season ended as it began, Emslie teaming with Brennan for the last game on October 1 in Brooklyn. But it marked a career change for both. Brennan's contract was not renewed, so he returned to Southern Association. Emslie would take a different course. After the season it was rumored the league's senior umpires, Emslie and O'Day, would be pensioned, or if Hank decided to leave for the warm climes of Pacific Coast League, Bob also would depart. But talk that the game would lose two of its "oldest notable characters" were unfounded. O'Day decided to stay for his twenty-fifth season, Emslie for his thirty-second. As Heydler noted, "nothing proves the difficulty of getting good umpires more than the fact that Connolly, Emslie, O'Day, Klem and Evans have all been umpiring 20 years or more [sic] and are still at it."[5]

With both leagues starting the 1922 season experimenting with a trio of umpires on two crews, Emslie opened on April 12 in St Louis with Charlie Moran and Ernie Quigley. He worked at third base in the first game, moved to first base for the second game, then umpired the plate for the finale on April 15, no doubt impressed with Jesse Haines's three-hitter. Bob left the field unaware it was the last time he would call pitches.

After the game he headed to Chicago to attend the April 16 funeral services of Adrian Constantine Anson, one of most influential figures in the league's formative years. Among the numerous baseball dignitaries Emslie was the lone umpire. That Bob went to pay respects to the nemesis who caused him such aggravation in the 1890s spoke to his character. He returned on April 20 and worked until May 15, umpiring all but three of eighteen games at third base, in the process tossing the Cardinals' Milt Stock in Cincinnati on April 23 for disputing a call by throwing the ball in disgust. It would be his last ejection. On May 16 the final game of the series in St. Louis was rained out, the gloomy day and downpour apropos a dramatic change in his career: after twenty-one games, all but four spent at third base, he was abruptly removed from regular duty. There had been no criticism of his work, but the league decided, doubtless to save money, to abandon three-man crews. (The last American League trio worked on June 28.)[6]

For the rest of the season Bob worked an occasional game or single series as a replacement umpire. The seventeen games passed without incident save two. On June 4 in Brooklyn, with the Robins nursing a 4–3 lead in the top of the ninth, the Giants began a rally given life by a crucial call from Emslie. With two outs, he initially signaled Heinie Groh out on a force play at second, then reversed the call and signaled him safe. Instead of the inning ending with a Robins victory, the Giants plated two runs to take the lead and a fusillade of pop bottles flew in Emslie's direction; fortunately none struck the intended victim. After the game he was besieged by angry fans as he made his way to the clubhouse. There would be no more bottle showers, but on July 14 in Pittsburgh he was skulled by a baseball. A "sizzling grounder" took a bad hop, striking him in the head. He fell down dazed, but after a few minutes resumed work with a headache.

Emslie's season's highlight was the invitation to umpire the Old Timers' game in Boston on September 11. The more than fifty luminaries of yesteryear, now unfamiliar to many fans, were divided into American and National league teams and wore numbered jerseys corresponding to names printed in the score card. Bob, who umpired the plate while Jack Stafford, former American arbiter, called the bases, thoroughly enjoyed watching players he had seen in their prime—"some gray haired, some baldheaded and some fat and shortwinded"—pound out fifty hits while committing only two errors. He might have grimaced as the Americans won 28–7, but smiled at the humorous antics of Nick Altrock, Washington's coach, who in addition to pulling familiar stunts added a new one, twice climbing up the screen in front of the stands to the press box "like a squirrel."[7]

Umpiring a game played by retired ballplayers was an omen. Bob's eyes were still sharp. At sixty-three, an age when most men wore glasses, Emslie, like O'Day, donned spectacles only for reading. Umpire Billy Evans marveled at the two senior umpires' "extraordinary power of sight," their ability to see things "clearly at a distance." But Bob had slowed down. His legs were not as strong, his stamina not as great, his reflexes not as quick. His face was now deeply etched by age and the stress of umpiring for thirty-six years, strikingly visible in the rare portrait taken in 1922 by renowned photographer Charles M. Conlon.[8] Friends begged him to quit, to take it easy, but he carried on, "perhaps because necessity compelled him to do so."[9] But it was time to stow the indicator, as demonstrated by the increasing criticism of his work.

By end of the 1922 season, in which he umpired only thirty-eight games, Bob's career seemed to have come to an end, a *New York Herald* headline blaring on December 14, "EMSLIE'S DAYS AS UMPIRE ARE OVER." Not quite. At the league's annual meeting on December 13, Heydler announced Emslie's retirement, praising him for thirty-one consecutive years of service in the "most trying of professional callings" and noting he had been "rated as the past-master of patience and diplomacy among baseball officials, and his honesty has never been questioned." He said Bob would not be leaving, but "in appreciation of his long and faithful service," would assume a new position, supervisor of league umpires, to be called on to work games only in "extreme emergency."[10]

Bob Emslie, at age sixty-three, had achieved another historic milestone: he was the first former umpire to hold the official position as supervisor of league umpires, a post vacant for twenty-one years. It was a fitting tribute to his long and distinguished service as well as recognition of his importance to the league and the respect he enjoyed from fellow arbiters. The appointment surprised no one. In 1908, amid concerns about his visual acuity, there was talk of assigning him as "a sort of supervising umpire" to travel around the league evaluating the performance of umpires, and in 1917 rumors had Bob pensioned and appointed to the new position of "chief of umpires and general assistant" to supervise the staff and resolve disputes over their decisions.[11]

It was with mixed feelings that Emslie accepted the appointment. He knew he couldn't call 'em forever, but was reluctant to leave the field. Still, he was pleased with the honor—an unprecedented one, at that—and gratified not to be summarily released. If no longer able to undertake the daily rigors of umpiring, he was proud the league regarded him as a font of umpiring and rules knowledge and believed that he still had something to contribute to the good of the game. Retirement from field duty was not the end of his umpiring career but the beginning of a new, challenging phase that avoided the wearisome travel of calling games.

News of Emslie's appointment as umpire supervisor was met with an outpouring of accolades for both Emslie and Heydler. The *Cincinnati Enquirer* called it a fitting honor for "one of the best umpires the game has ever known and also one of the best known and loved men of sportdom, a high-class man, gentle, kindly, diplomatic with a positive genius for his work." The *St. Louis Star* congratulated Heydler for reestablishing the lapsed position and appointing "not only one of the most capable men in the arbitrating business, but one of the best posted men generally in baseball."[12] *Sporting News* said it was "a noble thing" for Emslie "to be placed on the sunny side of Easy Street" with "a good salary" by those he had "served faithfully and well," adding, "May God bless them for that."[13]

The appointment was, in fact, a demanding one. In addition to being available for rules consultation, Bob was to travel to league ballparks to observe umpires and the conduct of players and fans, provide counsel to new members of the staff, and scour the Minor Leagues evaluating prospective new umpires. And he kept his mask, protector, and indicator handy for a possible return to the diamond in emergency situations. He did not have to wait long.

It came as the result of a tragedy. On April 17 Leopold Theodore "Paul" Sentell opened his second season in Chicago. Suffering from increasing abdominal pain attributed to indigestion, he struggled to finish the series, and after heading to Cincinnati on April 21 was rushed to a hospital to undergo an emergency operation for a ruptured appendix. Bob, fortuitously stationed in Chicago for possible assignment, replaced Sentell for four games in Cincinnati from April 21 to April 24 and one in St. Louis on April 25. At Sportsman's Park he witnessed another first: the left sleeve of Cardinals players displayed a black numeral corresponding to the number next to their names on the scorecard. In reporting the innovation, the *Cincinnati Enquirer* thought numbered jerseys would not catch on because the numerals were so small and fans were not interested. (They didn't, until 1929.)[14]

On April 27 Paul Sentell died. He was forty-four. Flags at National League ballparks flew at half-mast on April 29, and on April 30 games were halted for a moment of silence in memory of the first umpire to die in season.[15] Emslie's first official duty as umpire supervisor was to attend Sentell's funeral in New Orleans as the league's representative. During the funeral service held at Sentell's home, Bob no doubt thought again of Peter Harrison, his colleague from 1916 to 1920, who succumbed to tuberculosis on March 10, 1921. Bob would experience a second such tragedy in 1928 when Frank Wilson, forced to leave the field after being stricken with appendicitis in Brooklyn on June 3, died from surgical complications on June 12.

After returning from New Orleans, Bob sat idle until June 22, when he was behind the plate for the Harvard-Yale college playoff game in Boston. He did not umpire a league game until September 26, when for one game in St. Louis he replaced new hire Jack Powell, whose debut he had evaluated on September 14. It was Bob's final field assignment of the year.

Called on to umpire only six times in 1923, the head of the corps worked even less in 1924. He was the plate umpire for two amateur games: the Memorial Day game between the military and naval academies on May 31 in Annapolis and an Ontario Baseball Amateur Association exhibition game on June 12 in St. Thomas, giving both the hometown Saints and the Chatham Briscoes "satisfaction" and letting the fans see "how a big league umpire works." In the National League he took the field just four times, all with newcomer Monroe Sweeney: on April 26 in Boston, September 27 in Cincinnati, and September 28 in St. Louis for a season-ending doubleheader between the Reds and Cardinals. The games at Sportsman's Park were historic in two respects. Rogers Hornsby would win his fifth straight league batting title, this time with a record .424 average. For Bob Emslie, it would be the last time he donned the blue suit as a Major League umpire.

His assignment to meaningless games between the fourth- and sixth-place teams was likely an honorific gesture by Heydler, graciously allowing Bob to end his storied career on the field. In 1923 Everett Scott, for his "iron man" record of one thousand consecutive games, was acclaimed as "the greatest ballplayer in point of service and achievement that ever trod the diamonds of America," and Connie Mack was heralded on his birthday as "one of the few men in baseball who have reached the age of 60 years." But Emslie's historic last game went unnoticed by players, press, and fans. Bob simply walked off the field and into baseball history as the oldest man, at sixty-five years and eight months, to umpire a Major League game, and as the one who had worked the most years (thirty-five) and called the most games (4,231).[16]

From 1925 on much of Emslie's work as umpire supervisor was routine. He attended league and rules committee meetings, consulted with Heydler about the staff and application of new rules, traveled to ballparks to evaluate the staff, scouted the Minors for new umpires, and represented the league on special occasions. Highlights were the various activities in 1925 marking the league's golden jubilee. He attended the kickoff dinner in New York on February 2 at the Broadway Central hotel, where the league had been founded on February 2, 1876. Ceremonial games were held in each league city; Bob was in Boston on May 8 for the initial game between the Braves and Cubs, the two remaining charter teams; on hand were three members of the 1876 Boston Red Stockings and ninety-three-year-old Billy McLean, a fellow Scot, who umpired the league's first game on April 22. Bob then headed to New York, where at the commemorative banquet on May 14 he paid tribute to the Giants fireballer Amos Rusie, confessing he "always had an uncomfortable feeling" when calling the "the Hoosier Thunderbolt's" swift, unpredictable pitches. Bob was also present for the anniversary games in Cincinnati on June 12 and in Pittsburgh on June 19, receiving "a big hand" when introduced.[17]

He may well have been present at a more somber event. His favorite pitcher, Christy Mathewson, died on October 7, the funeral held three days later in Lewisburg, Pennsylvania. In accordance with Mathewson's wish there was no funereal "fuss," only private services held at his mother-in-law's home, but numerous baseball celebrities came to file past his bier, including President Heydler. Given Emslie's admiration for "Big Six," he may have been there as well. In 1921 Bob had joined the other National League umpires in sending best wishes and a $300 contribution to the "Matty Day" testimonial game between American and National "old-timers" in Boston on September 21 to help defray the expenses of his treatment for tuberculosis at a sanatorium in Saranac Lake, New York. The next year, when Mathewson's former teammates and opponents gathered for a three-inning game on July 7 at the Polo Grounds to raise money for the Matty Memorial Benefit Fund, Emslie umpired the plate.

Scouting for umpiring prospects was a rewarding and important aspect of the job. He agreed with Heydler that "collecting champion umpires" was "no less a task than collecting championship players," and knew well the difficulty of finding umpires with the "ability, the courage, judgment, determination, tact, the executive capacity to run a ball game and bear the brunt from the contending players and the criticism of the public."[18] On Bob's recommendation, the league hired George "Jack" Powell in 1923, Monroe Sweeney in 1924, and Peter McLaughlin in 1925. Each of them umpired only three years.

Two of Bob's finds went on to great careers. It was déjà vu of sorts in 1927 when he saw a college arbiter fill in at an Eastern League game for the assigned umpire, who had broken his arm. Bob was so impressed with the substitute's performance that he recommended him to Heydler, who promptly hired Albert "Dolly" Stark, the league's youngest umpire at twenty-seven, as Hank O'Day's replacement. During his career (1928–40) players named him best umpire in 1934, and in 1935 New York fans gave him a "Dolly Stark Day." Then, on September 21, 1933, Bob, taken by the courage of the New York-Penn League umpire to make tough calls and withstand getting beaten after the game, enthusiastically recommended him to Heydler; two days later Bill Stewart broke into the Majors and stayed for twenty-two years, umpiring five World Series and four All-Star games. (Like Emslie, Stewart was at home on the ice, serving as a National Hockey League referee from 1928 to 1936 and from 1940 to 1941 as well as the Chicago Black Hawks coach from 1937 to 1939.)

Keeping a hand in the profession and game as umpire supervisor eased Emslie's transition from the field, but administrative work was not completely satisfying after umpiring for thirty-eight years. Visiting ballparks major and minor brought back memories of calling games, the emotional embers of umpiring banked, not extinguished. If he couldn't suit up and take to the field for regular-season games, spring training would do. So in early March, as the curling season wound to a close, he packed his rule book and gear, leaving snowy and overcast Ontario for the sun and warmth of the southland.

It began in February 1924, when Brooklyn's Charles Ebbets announced Emslie would head to Clearwater, Florida, to officiate all Brooklyn spring training games. Paired with Clarence "Pants" Rowland, beginning his second year in the league, Bob almost always umpired the plate with nary a beef. In addition to games throughout Florida, they umpired the annual Yankees-Superbas series as the teams worked their way north through Alabama, Tennessee, Georgia, the Carolinas, and Virginia before heading home to open the season. Bob's acute historical memory came into play while umpiring a game between the Superbas and Milwaukee of the Class AA American Association. Impressed by Brewers shortstop Jimmy Cooney, Bob asked if he was the son of Jimmy Cooney, whom Emslie umpired against in the Western in 1889 and the National in 1891 and 1892. The response affirmative, he exclaimed, "Please introduce him to me—I want to shake hands with old Jim Cooney's son. You know, the boy is as great a player as was his daddy."[19] As it turned out, Jimmy advanced to St. Louis that year, playing third base for the Cardinals in Emslie's last game on September 28. There had been a previous family connection. Jimmy's brother, Johnny, pitched for the Boston Braves, and Emslie had umpired two of his games, on April 19, 1921, and September 2, 1922.

It was back to spring training in 1925. Heydler did not send his regular arbiters, saying they did not need to "tune up" and "intimacies are likely between the umpire and the players that will work out to the detriment of both."[20] Since Emslie was not a regular official, he was exempt. That year another promising player caught his eye, a touted Canadian pitcher, diminutive southpaw Danny McPhee from St. Thomas, in camp with Brooklyn. McPhee, who had a good fastball and nothing else, never did make the Majors, but a rookie American League umpire assigned to Emslie for mentoring did. Throughout the spring Emslie umpired the plate while Bill McGowan, future Hall of Fame arbiter, called the bases.

For 1926, Heydler decided again to use regular umpires because there had been so much criticism of the umpiring last spring. Emslie also was sent, again exclusively working the plate, and encountering no criticism save for a brief "scowling match" over a strike call with Babe Ruth in Atlanta. In 1927 Emslie, now sixty-eight, made his fourth and final trip to spring training. The five-week excursion ended, as usual, at Ebbets

Field for the Yankees-Robins finale, the April 10 game typical, Ruth hitting a home run and Emslie umpiring the plate.[21]

In March 1928 Emslie got sick enough from an unidentified illness to mention it in his memoir. It was emotionally a double blow. First, he said, "Up to that time, I never knew what it was to be sick, but since that time, I have not been so good." Second, he said being unable to continue working spring training "was the end of my umpiring career." The importance of umpiring to Emslie was so great that his memoir identifies the years he worked spring training, but does not mention being appointed umpire supervisor or his duties in that role.[22]

It had been a pleasurable, even thrilling experience for Emslie to don the mask and work the plate, demonstrating that despite being assigned to base duty for the final years of his career, he was still able to call pitches. Emslie's plate assignments, after not being behind the plate for many years, drew enough notice that newspapers printed a picture of him donning his gear. (He used the new lighter and more protective mask designed in 1921 by former colleague Jim Johnstone.)[23] The only downside of the spring training years was a brief resurgence of embarrassment about his wig, as related years later by Brooklyn's James "Zack" Taylor:

> I was catching for the Dodgers when we played the Yankees in Nashville on our way North one year. Bob Meusel tore in from third and I blocked him off the plate. Bob Emslie, the umpire was not only on top of the play but also on top of me. When Meusel hit, all three of us went pinwheeling. The collision shook Emslie loose from his toupee. We never had suspected that he wore a rug on his head. Emslie was so embarrassed that he forgot to put on his mask when he shouted, "Play ball." All he put on was his wig. The pitcher was already winding up when Dazzy Vance shouted a warning from the bench. "Forget about the wig, Baldy," he yelled. "If you really want to stay pretty, you'd better put on your mask."[24]

Finally having to stow his gear, administrative duties now filled Emslie's agenda for the next seven years. Nationally known as the "professor of umpiring" who "teaches the young umpires to call 'em as they see 'em," he received an assist and companionship when O'Day left active duty after the 1927 season. Their career parallels are striking. Like Bob, Hank's retirement was predictable. He worked a full schedule of 147 games, but only 12 were behind the plate, and save for 3 games he umpired only first base after May 25, at his request. Like Emslie, O'Day's last game was in St. Louis, and when he walked off after working third base, also without fanfare, he may or may not have been the oldest umpire to call a game in Major League history, his sixty-eight years and eighty-six days perhaps eclipsing Emslie by five months and eleven days.[25] And like Bob, he stayed in the game, retained by Heydler to scout the Minor Leagues for umpires and mentor new members of the staff.

As a member of the league's advisory board, Emslie continued to serve on the American-National joint rules committee, albeit now in an advisory role. In 1926 he supported permitting pitchers to apply resin to the ball over the objections of Connie Mack and Tommy Connolly, and in 1930 he endorsed ruling a batted ball that bounced from fair territory into the stands or over the fence an automatic two-base hit instead of a home run and a sacrifice fly simply an out and time at bat.

Two proposals particularly caught the former pitcher's attention. In 1928 Heydler suggested permitting a tenth player to bat in place of the pitcher. Emslie's thoughts are unknown, but surely, given his own experience at bat, he could not have argued with "the inability of pitchers to hit." While the *Chicago Tribune* agreed "the batting efforts of many pitchers provide a needed laugh" and some National League owners favored the idea, with American League opposition the proposal came to naught until, ironically, it was adopted by the American in 1973.[26] Another discussion of special interest involved the main object of attention for a pitcher: the baseball. It was inevitable the onset of power hitting exemplified by Babe Ruth's home runs would lead to allegations of a "lively ball." Despite the insistence that balls were manufactured with identical methods and materials, it was thought American League hitters were far outpacing National batters in power hitting with a ball said to be twenty percent livelier than the National's "slightly heavier" ball. The issue was finally resolved in December 1933 when the National agreed to adopt the American's ball as the standard for use in both leagues. Emslie and

O'Day were on hand to inspect the new ball to be used in 1934, the only season the sphere was stitched with blue and red thread.

To Bob's unbounded pleasure, a variety of special guest appearances complemented supervisory duties. He especially enjoyed participating in celebratory ball games. In 1932 he was in Cincinnati on August 21 for Old-Timers' Day, a reunion of greats of yore including Chief Bender, Hans Wagner, Cy Young, and Mordecai "Three-Finger" Brown. When Emslie and O'Day walked onto Redland Field to join some hundred players in vintage uniforms, the legendary umpires were greeted with "hearty" applause. He attended another Old-Timers' game the next year on May 1 in Philadelphia that marked the Phillies' fiftieth anniversary. This time Emslie, described as "one of the greatest of his time," had an active role. After announcing the batteries for the game, he umpired the bases as the current Phillies battled National League stars of seasons past. His enjoyment of the afternoon surely increased as he watched Dolly Stark umpire home plate in the day's regulation game. (For the first All-Star Game, held in Chicago on July 6, 1933, Heydler sent Secretary Harvey Traband to represent the league, so Emslie probably did not attend.)

Although involved daily for many years in Major League baseball, Bob's enthusiastic interest in baseball in his hometown and native province never waned, as illustrated by his rush to Guelph after the 1922 season to watch the Ontario Baseball Amateur Association (OBAA) senior championship on October 25. A longtime member of the executive board of the St. Thomas senior team in the OBAA, he was often seen at games throughout the province. If the competition was not the caliber he was used to watching, baseball being baseball sometimes produced never-before-seen experiences, as in London on August 10, 1926, when with two outs St. Thomas pulled off a double steal he had never seen before: with runners on second and third, the Saints batter laid down a bunt, both runners scoring as he beat out the throw to first.

The venerable umpire was also called on as keynote speaker at baseball banquets ranging from honoring the London Braves, champions of the semipro Western Ontario Intercounty League, to advising the young players in the Niagara Falls, Ontario, Amateur Baseball Association, perhaps reflecting on his youthful days, "to pay strict attention to their studies."

Bob also returned to the field. In June 1930 he went to Harriston for the first time since 1881 to umpire ball games during Old Home Week and in August 1933 was invited to umpire OBAA playoff games in Kitchener. Pleased with his performance behind the plate, Bob said there were only two pitches the entire game that might have been questioned.[27]

His supervisory duties did not afford any more time with the family, but it was too late anyway. He was present when Kitty married Harold Victor Montgomery, a tool maker in the automobile industry in Detroit, on October 24, 1921, and when Jack married Velma Agnes David on June 19, 1927, but marriage perforce altered Bob's parental relationships with his daughter and son. He would continue to see Jack, who settled in St. Thomas, but saw less of Kitty, who moved to Detroit. It was too late to make up for lost time with his wife. Bill Klem's wife, Marie, childless, often traveled with him during the season, but Helena, with two children to raise, never did. Now, the woman of "charming disposition" who had many friends and was an active member of the Woman's Auxiliary of Trinity Anglican Church, two blocks east of home, had been an invalid for several years, cared for by her unmarried sister Mary Ward, a tailor, who had long lived with the Emslies.

Bob's steady income as supervisor provided comfortable family financial support during the depths of the Great Depression and allowed him to pursue his avocational pastimes without interruption.[28] His involvement in trapshooting passed from competitions to administrative activities, but he remained a central figure in curling on and off the ice. As captain of the Granite Curling Club's most successful rink in February 1921 he won the first round of the Vendrom Cup Series in Sarnia, but lost in the final 16–12. Ever the competitor, his overcoming a six-point deficit to win a final medal game in March was the "feature of the competition." In 1922 his victories—more than a few against Major Leaguer player and manager Mooney Gibson, pilot of the London Thistles—included the district title and advancement to Toronto to compete, unsuccessfully, for the Ontario Cup. Despite advancing age Bob was able to slide the rock with the best of them. His rink admonition, "Go on! Go on! It'll go all the way!" proved prophetic as he led his teams in 1924 to bonspiel titles in St. Thomas, throughout Ontario, and in Detroit, at age sixty-five winning both the

Glenn Trophy and the President's Cup, emblematic of the Ontario provincial championship. Not restricted to competition, he continued as a member of the Granite Club's executive board and, unsurprisingly, was elected umpire for numerous club and championship meets, not only applying rules and settling disputes but also running the events.

In recognition of his prominence in the sport, on April 6, 1923, ninety members of the GCC staged a banquet at the Grand Central Hotel to honor the "chief," W. K. Cameron, the club's founder and current secretary-treasurer, and Bob Emslie, called the "boss" for his success on the rink and role in "bossing" club curlers like he did ballplayers. After the sumptuous repast featuring salmon and prime rib concluded with green apple pie and vanilla ice cream, the honorees were treated to a musical program, given an engraved sterling-silver loving cup, and received congratulatory toasts, Bob's being,

> Twas his constant care
> His heart's supreme ambition,
> To be fair.

The purpose of the banquet a surprise, and Bob was "almost overcome with emotion." "Too surprised for words," he said simply, "It is entirely out of my line to give a speech. This token of appreciation touches me and I really don't know what to say or how to thank you and express my gratitude. It is certainly fine." It was a big deal. The newspaper report of the event, covering almost five full first-page columns, indicated both the importance of curling as a community enterprise and the esteem accorded the two honorees, as did the souvenir program containing toasts to each guest of honor from all twenty-five skips of club teams.

Emslie held baseball "foremost in is heart," but wished more youngsters took up curling, "a great sport." He was proud and gratified that his son, Jack, played youth baseball and as a curler "distinguished himself by his good play," becoming proficient enough to become a member of Bob's crack rink, the father-son pair posting multiple victories in a tournament in January 1927. A few weeks later, in the opening round of a bonspiel in Toronto, Bob, described as "one of the grand old young men of sportdom," led the team to two victories in four matches played "with brief respites" over the course of nineteen hours from 9 p.m. to 4 a.m.[29]

In the rink Emslie was an ageless wonder. The *Toronto Telegram* wondered if his ability as a curveball pitcher accounted "for his skill now in curling a stone about a well-guarded 'house.'" In 1929, at age seventy, he took home the Meiser Cup, winning the championship of an international bonspiel in Detroit by defeating the hometown's top club 21–11. In 1930 in Toronto he reached the fourth round of the Ryrie-Birks championship, and the next year advanced to the second round of the Royal York trophy series. In 1934, at age seventy-five, he took his rink to Detroit for another international bonspiel, finishing second of twenty entries.

The insatiable competitor embraced two other winter sports: five- and tenpin bowling. A regular at fivepin alleys, Bob headed a crack St. Thomas team that challenged squads around Ontario. He was also the mainstay of the Talbot Club's tenpin bowling team, showing up "almost every day in the winter months" at the Strand bowling alleys. Since newspapers regarded bowling primarily as recreational activity, there is no record of Emslie's competitive achievements as a kegler.

In 1925 Bob decided to master, late in life, golf. To gain proficiency he played eighteen holes "almost every day when he can spare the time," often in challenge matches, to sate his competitive instincts. That included taking advantage of unusually warm weather on January 18, 1928, to schedule a game on the difficult Union course at the St. Thomas golf club. After three years of playing, at age sixty-nine he shot forty-four for the first nine holes. The other members of the foursome, all younger men who played regularly, shot thirty-eight. He would later enjoy golfing's supreme achievement with a hole-in-one on number 14, "quite a difficult hole," 260 yards to the green.[30]

But his mind was always on baseball, and he never passed up an opportunity to talk about the game. Although loath to give interviews while umpiring, he graciously, and no doubt enjoyably, at his home in St. Thomas entertained for a couple of days a Cincinnati reporter, who found it "a treat to talk over old times with this alert and active veteran who was more highly respected by the athletes than almost any other member of his precarious profession." Emslie responded to questions without elaboration except when asked how he was able to get along so well with players, even those "of the most critical temper." Bob replied forthrightly, "I got along with the boys pretty well mainly because I never allowed myself to bear malice, no matter how great the provocation might be. I never had it 'in' for any player, even if he had been madly abusive the day before. The next day a new slate was opened with the old one wiped clean." It was not a self-serving spin on old days; the response squared precisely with his umpiring style during his career.[31]

It was a special treat when umpiring comrades Bill Byron, Ernie Quigley, and Hank O'Day came to St. Thomas. Bill and Ernie shared umpiring stories while Ernie, the only year-round sports official in history, also told tales of working college football and basketball games. O'Day was the most frequent visitor. The closest of friends, Bob and Hank were in some respects an odd couple, markedly different in personality, lifestyle, and style of umpiring. Emslie had a family, a wide circle of friends, and enjoyed sports other than baseball, while O'Day, called by Heydler "an umpire and nothing else," was a lifelong bachelor and stone-faced social loner—Klem called him a "misanthropic Irishman"—whose sporting interest other than attending Cubs and White Sox games was going to the track to watch horse races. But they bonded, first as competing pitchers in the 1880s, then as fellow umpires devoted not only to no-nonsense enforcement of the rules and game decorum, but also to the umpiring profession. The two kindred spirits occasionally traveled together about Ontario, but mostly whiled away the hours sitting on Bob's front porch, their thoughts and memories passing in silence.[32]

Bob increasingly became a legend in his own time, sportswriters frequently relating stories about his career. Sid Keener, commenting on the recent umpires who "blunder so frequently," said he'd like to see Emslie and O'Day returned to active duty. Jack Ryder related how a batted ball hit Emslie in the head and bounced to Kid Gleason for the out. Ed Hughes recalled Emslie tossing McGraw for suggesting he get a hairpin for his toupee, and C. P. Winstead remembered Bob as a "top-notch" pitcher in the 1880s. Bob even became a trivia question. In 1927 a *Boston Globe* reader asked, "For how many years was Bob Emslie an umpire in the National League?" The answer given, 1891–1926, was incorrect; he retired in1924.[33]

Emslie was especially pleased his work received recognition from players. Honus Wagner, who retired in 1917 after twenty-one years, in 1923 identified the most outstanding players at every position he had seen during his career and named Emslie second among the umpires, ahead of O'Day and Klem, future Hall of Famers. When Hans in 1930 formulated his "All-Time All-America" baseball nine comprising both American and National league players, he said "the ideal umpires would be Bob Emslie and Bill Klem." Ty Cobb, the peerless competitor, mentioned Emslie among the five umpires he most admired for handling games "without friction," thereby earning the "respect and confidence of the players." And upon receiving in 1933 from Heydler an inscribed copy of the first edition of *Who's Who in Major League Baseball*, Bob was delighted to see his biographical sketch begin, "Whenever old-time fans get together and start chattering about diamond immortals you'll hear them paying tribute to Bob Emslie who was one of the greatest of them all in the days of Hurst, O'Loughlin, Sheridan, O'Day and Tommy Connolly."[34] But he was distressed to learn that his boss and dear friend, John Arnold Heydler, had resigned as league president on November 2, 1934, owing to ill health. What might the loss of his loyal supporter mean for Bob's future as umpire supervisor?

14

Late Innings

He that shall live this day, and see old age,
Will yearly feast his neighbours,
And say 'To-morrow is [game day]:
Then will he strip his sleeve and show his scars.
And say 'These wounds I had [in games].
Old men forget: yet all shall be forgot,
But he'll remember with advantages
What feats he did that day: then shall our names.
Familiar in his mouth as household words
[O'Day, Klem, Johnstone, Rigler]
Be in their flowing cups freshly remember'd.
This story shall the good man teach his son;
And [baseball seasons] shall ne'er go by,
From this day to the ending of the world,
But we in it shall be remember'd;
We few, we happy few, we band of brothers.

—William Shakespeare, *Henry V*

On January 27, 1935, Robert Emslie celebrated his seventy-sixth birthday and began his forty-ninth year of umpiring service. These days his agenda comprised more staff and league meetings than ballpark visits, so he typically remained at home in St. Thomas before being summoned to New York. Ever on the lookout for prospects, in late June he accompanied a Detroit Tigers scout to London to check out Joe Krakauskas, a young Lithuanian-Canadian southpaw Bob had also recommended to the Giants and Senators. (Krakauskas, who pitched in the Majors from 1937 to 1946, is best known for yielding the last of Joe DiMaggio's fifty-six consecutive hits in 1941.) An emotional jolt accompanied the outing:

Hank O'Day, who had been ill for several years, died in Chicago on July 2 of bronchial pneumonia.

Bob promptly boarded a train to Chicago to pay last respects to his dear friend and longtime colleague. Upon arriving in the Windy City he saw the Cardinals and Cubs were playing a July 4 doubleheader, so he headed for Wrigley Field, sharing stories "with old cronies" about Hank. The next day, as the official representative of the National League, he attended the funeral mass for O'Day at St. Jariath's Catholic Church. Among the many baseball notables present were Commissioner Landis; Heydler, who had retired as league president in 1934; Hank's former colleagues Byron, Quigley, and Klem; and American League chief of umpires Tommy Connolly. Six umpires, three from each league, served as pallbearers. For Bob the funeral was deeply personal. Profoundly saddened by the loss of a beloved friend with whom he had experienced baseball wars since 1883 and concerned about the consequences of Heydler's retirement, he likely knew his career, too, would soon come to an end; indeed, it would be his last assignment as supervisor.

At the league meeting in Chicago on December 11, 1935, Robert D. Emslie was unceremoniously retired. Earlier that year the St. Thomas newspaper noted Bob's birthday would be celebrated "in characteristic Emslie fashion, without fuss, totally devoid of frills." The same was true of his retirement. Although the league had recognized his silver season with a day in his honor and gifts, there was no announcement of his leaving after forty-five consecutive years, then the longest service to a single employer in baseball history. Reporters covering the meeting didn't mention it; the *Philadelphia Inquirer* alone simply noted, "Bob Emslie, oldest of all umpires, was retired." Instead of Bob's departure, newspapers reported Cy Rigler was not only retired from active service after twenty-eight years and appointed supervisor of umpires, but was also the first recipient of the new umpire pension plan providing $1,500 per year after fifteen years of service, increased by $100 for each season thereafter up to a maximum of $2,400. The two league presidents, the National's Ford Frick and the American's William Harridge, gave Bob a solid silver lifetime pass to Major League games inscribed "in appreciation of long and meritorious service." It was the least they could have done. Placing him retroactively on the new umpire pension plan would have been appropriate.[1]

Thumbed out of the game that had been his life since childhood, Bob headed home. He took with him memories of games and players, cities and ballparks, praise enjoyed and criticism endured. And he was pleased that his role as supervisor proved so valuable that the league continued the position with Rigler and that the American had appointed Tommy Connolly the circuit's first chief of staff umpires upon his retirement in June 1931. But if he were glad to be freed of the increasingly tedious desk work and wearisome travel to ballparks, it was emotionally difficult to retire mere months after losing two longtime friends and to not be involved in professional baseball for the first time in fifty-six years.[2]

For starters, he would be home year-round. Players, managers, league administrators, and fellow umpires had been his primary family since 1887. Even after his marriage in 1893, during off-seasons he was frequently out of town hunting, trapshooting, and curling. He was absent much of the time when Kitty and Jack were growing up; now they had lives of their own. Neither had children, so he missed the pleasures of grandparenting. Relations with his daughter, living in Detroit, were distant, but he was in frequent contact with Jack, who resided in St. Thomas at 25 Pearl Street, five blocks from his parents. Bob transferred his stock in the Thomas Metal Signs company to Jack in 1931, but his son struggled with alcohol and gambling. Relatives wondered if an oft-absent father contributed to the addictions, the drinking so serious it ultimately may have cost him his share in the business.[3]

Retirement would not bring marital bliss. He finally had ample time to spend with his wife, but Helena was now seriously ill. Just over a year after Bob retired, she died at home on March 15, 1937, from myocarditis (inflammation of the heart muscle) complicated by senile gangrene (deterioration of tissue in extremities caused by inadequate blood supply) and arteriosclerosis (hardening of arteries). On March 18 an intimate funeral service was held at the Emslie home, awash in floral tributes sent by relatives and friends including John Heydler, National League president Ford Frick, and the Intercounty Baseball League. To pay personal respects, Bill Byron came up from Ypsilanti, Michigan, and Billy Reid,

Bob's teammate on the 1882 Atlantics, came down from London, as did Helena's sister Gladys Ward. The Venerable Archdeacon J. W. J. Andrew of Trinity Anglican Church conducted the services. Interment followed in the Elmdale Memorial Park mausoleum.

For some people retirement means opening a new chapter of your life, perhaps taking on a new interest, traveling, or relocating to a new residence. But not for Bob Emslie. For him, making the psychological adjustment to retirement and determining what do with his time was easy: he just kept doing what he had been doing, albeit less frequently and at a somewhat slower pace. Living by some margin beyond the normal man's life expectancy of fifty-five years, he had enough energy to do what he wanted in playing out his last innings.

There is no evidence of interest in books, music, or the arts; Bob Emslie was a doer, not a thinker. Competition in traps and rinks were distant memories, but he remained physically active. For recreation he occasionally shot traps in fall and curled in winter, played golf in summer, and bowled year-round. Bob could be found most nights at the Strand, even celebrating his eighty-first birthday at the lanes. He enjoyed the tenpin game, maintaining a 180 average, but especially liked the fivepin variety so popular in Canada.[4] He also did a bit of lawn bowling. For a senior citizen his stamina was remarkable; it was not uncommon for him to play thirty-six holes of golf in the afternoon and bowl three or four games in the evening.

Aside from sports, he took pleasure puttering around in the garden behind his house, breeding Boston bull terriers, and heading two blocks north to Talbot, the main street, to kibitz with merchants and townsfolk. He regularly dropped in at Jackson and Cruickshank's barber shop, even when he didn't need a haircut, all the while tugging at his ever-present cigar. There were also fellowship activities aplenty for the member of the Elgin Golf and Country Club, Trinity Anglican Church, St. David's Lodge No. 302, and Talbot Lodge No. 44 A. F. & A. M. While it was sometimes "very hard to get through the outer 'shell' of this quiet, unassuming man of few words and undisputed honesty" with a "gruff" manner of speaking "acquired because for many years he had to deal harshly with players while in the majors as an arbiter," retirement and the enviable slowing down enabled him to cultivate many "genuine and lasting" friendships and enjoy activities previously curtailed by his umpiring life.[5] But it was baseball, always baseball, first and foremost on his mind and schedule. It had been the center of his life since childhood and still was. Purely and simply a baseball guy, his life continued to revolve around the game.

The big leagues never far from mind, Bob attended numerous regular-season and World Series games, his attendance frequently noted in the press. He took special pleasure in watching former colleagues umpire games and meeting up with old baseball buddies. Heydler was a frequent visitor to St. Thomas, talking ball and joining Bob for many a round of golf. After O'Day died Emslie spent more time with Byron, who, single like Hank, often came up to visit. They, too, were an unusual pairing, Emslie diplomatic and reserved, Byron a quick thumb whose sophomoric, mocking commentaries antagonized players, but a common love of the game and Bob's mentoring of Bill in 1917 cemented their friendship. At games, they occupied choice front-row box seats and always headed first to press headquarters in search of former ballplayers, Casey Stengel a favorite. On June 12, 1939, Bob and Bill went to Cooperstown to attend the dedication and first induction ceremony of the Hall of Fame Museum; in 1941 Emslie was the only former umpire among the five baseball executives on a committee appointed by Commissioner Landis to complete the selection of nineteenth-century players.[6]

But it was local baseball that commanded most of his time and attention. He had not been around to watch his son's games or to give him advice, but now delighted in encouraging youngsters to play ball, giving pitching and hitting instruction, telling stories about old-time players, even explaining the duties and techniques of umpiring. He was a member of the board of the St. Thomas Tomcats, a semipro team comprising college and former professional players in the Ontario Baseball Association's Intercounty League. The ballpark ever a magnet, Bob was frequently seen at Pinafore Park taking in the games played by amateur city teams or the Tomcats. Occasionally he ventured out of town; he was on hand for a benefit game in Stratford on July 8, 1939, watching the professional Stratford Nationals whip an Intercounty League all-star contingent 14–0.[7]

Although long since retired, Bob was still an umpire at the core. He conducted clinics for umpires, traveling in 1937 to Woodstock to address the umpires and give them their instructions before the Intercounty League All-Star game on June 3. Each spring he confessed to wanting to don his gear and call a game. Sometimes he did, taking advantage of his local celebrity status to call 'em for a few innings of amateur games at Pinafore Park. Commemorative gatherings also offered opportunities to return to the diamond. On June 27, 1936, Emslie, Fred Goldsmith, Mooney Gibson, and other old-time local baseball notables were in London for the "Booster Day" game to raise funds to repair the historic Tecumseh ballpark recently ravaged by flooding. Bob umpired the plate, calling pitches "with marked accuracy" while Gibson worked the bases. A week later, on July 4, he umpired the Intercounty League All-Star game in Kitchener. Two years later, at age seventy-nine, he groused, "I don't see why I couldn't go out and umpire a ball game tomorrow if I felt like it." Bob and Bill Byron were scheduled to umpire an old-timer's game in Windsor in August 1938, but Byron had to call the game solo as Emslie took sick, the unidentified illness also causing him to miss the World Series for the first time in many years.[8]

The venerated former umpire was frequently called on for guest appearances at special occasions. When in 1937 Toronto civic and sports leaders arranged a banquet on December 1 in honor of the inaugural season of Brooklyn outfielder Goodwin "Goody" Rosen, the lone Toronto native in the Majors, Emslie and Dodger skipper Burleigh Grimes were the featured special guests. The next year he was invited to speak at Detroit's Old-Time Baseball Players' Association banquet on October 30, where Bob was delighted to see again his youthful pitching idol, Fred Goldsmith.

Guest appearances fueled nostalgia, a conspicuous feature of retirement. He took with pride and pleasure many a stroll down memory lane, flipping through his mental album of images—some badly faded, others starkly clear—of his fifty-six years in baseball as a player, umpire, and supervisor of umpires. In 1935 legendary Southern League umpire Harry "Steamboat" Johnson chronicled his thirty-seven-year career in the first book-length umpire autobiography, but while Bob was much too private a person to divulge his experiences in a book, he was now eager to talk baseball with anyone, anytime, anyplace, telling stories about yesteryear and offering opinions about the present state of the game. For most of his career he eschewed press interviews after being misquoted by a New York reporter, but now he was willing to talk with local reporters, admonishing them "to secrecy."[9]

Finally, on his seventy-eighth birthday he opened up, speaking candidly and at length for the record, less about his umpiring career than the great players he had seen and changes in the game. As for his umpiring days, he briefly recalled the umpire and catcher standing well behind the plate, moving closer after the batter had two strikes, and how the game sped up after the first two foul balls were called strikes and batters were no longer able to deliberately off pitches hoping for "wonderful records for getting bases on balls." He offered no comment about the kicking and criticisms that peppered his career, simply saying, "I always got along very well with the players and I don't think I ever had an enemy in the game."[10]

Like many old-timers, he cherished yesteryear. Of the players and style of play that now dominated the game, he groused, "There's more hitting, it's true, maybe more base-running and high batting averages, but there's less inside baseball which I like." Not surprisingly, he regarded Deadball Era players as superior to the current crop. Admitting players were "generally faster" and play "better, faster ball today than they ever did," he maintained there were "no better pitchers than Mathewson, Cy Young or Rube Waddell, no better hitters than Ed Delahanty or Willie Keller, no better first baseman than Hal Chase and no better all-around players than Honus Wagner or Larry Lajoie." Defensive glove work? "There was never a smoother working piece of baseball machinery" than the Cubs' Tinker-to-Evers-to-Chance, who made the infield "as tight as man ever made it." As for the home run hitters who now dominated the offense, he said "Big Ed" Delahanty would have "hung up a record the present-day Kings of Swat would have had trouble touching" inasmuch as he "got his home runs with great regularity against the less lively ball, and the fences were farther back then than they are now."[11]

While umpiring Emslie didn't play favorites, but he had a favorite. He had worked behind some of the greatest catchers who ever crouched behind the plate—Roger Bresnahan, Duke Farrell, Johnny Kling, Deacon

McGuire, and Jack Clements, the greatest and last regular left-handed catcher—but the former hurler was most impressed with moundsmen, regarding Christy Mathewson as the greatest pitcher he and the game had ever seen. Granting there were now some "remarkably able" pitchers, just as there were "clever" ones in the past, he declared Mathewson remained "the chief of them all. He had everything a pitcher ever had and he knew how to use it. Besides, he was a gentleman—always. And he normally pitched every other day, invariably a complete game, while today's pitchers consider themselves overworked if they have to pitch every third instead of fourth day." As for umpires, Bob rated Bill Klem "the greatest of umpires," without equal calling balls and strikes.[12]

As many do in their advancing years, he reflected on those who had gone before. Losing O'Day and Rigler in 1935 and two years later Bob Hart and Cy Pfirman reminded him of the numerous umpiring colleagues who had died. It was sobering to realize he had outlived every American Association umpire he broke in with in 1890 as well all his regular cohorts from the first decade of the Deadball Era save Bill Klem, all passing on younger than he now was.[13] His sense of mortality surely increased upon learning that Charlie White, the International Association president who gave him his first umpiring job; Bill Watkins, his Atlantics manager; and many of his Atlantics and Orioles teammates had also left the earthly field.[14]

He was affected, too, by the passing of baseball friends. He was saddened by the death in 1930 of Arthur J. Donnelly, the St. Louis mortician who had sent a chauffeur to drive Bob and every other umpire to and from hotel and ballpark every game. Perhaps, when in St. Louis as supervisor, he went to the Calvary Cemetery, as did every umpire during the season, to lay a bouquet of flowers at Donnelly's headstone and to stand with head bowed for a moment in silent respect for the "friend of umpires." When John McCloskey, the second-least-successful manager in Major League history, died penniless in 1940, *Sporting News* launched a campaign to raise money for his wife and two daughters. Bob, who knew "Honest John" when he led the Louisville Colonels in 1895–96 and the St. Louis Cardinals in 1906–8, contributed $5 ($109 in 2023 dollars.)[15]

Bob was not alone in recalling times past. He was lauded more as a hometown celebrity in retirement than he had been as an umpire. Nary a birthday approached without the local paper relating his baseball career and retirement activities. Newspapers in the United States and other parts of Canada also periodically ran articles about his career and retirement; *Sporting News* was impressed that Emslie, still active at eighty-two years old, "in summer plays golf, travels to see big league games and never misses a world's series." Bob was so well-known across the Dominion and America he sometimes received mail addressed only to "Bob. Elgin Street. St. Thomas."[16]

As he approached his eightieth year, the physical frailties and infirmities of old age became apparent. He was slighter in build and now wore glasses. The strength and coordination in arms and legs ebbed, but he still regularly patrolled the streets and continued bowling and golfing until unable to walk nine holes. Ever up for a challenge, he took on a new, more sedentary activity: refinishing furniture. With antique maple and oak chairs, tables, dressers, and highboys filling both floors of his home, he set about scraping off old paint or varnish, then sanding the wood to original condition. Proudly showing off to a newspaper reporter the satiny finish on a tall walnut dresser that had been thick with old varnish, he said, "I'll bet I scraped off fourteen coats." It was a time-consuming task requiring patience, determination, and attention to detail, reflecting the temperament that served him well umpiring. Of the many hours of tedious toil, he said, "Once you get at it, it's kind of hard to stop"—just like umpiring.[17]

Come 1943, Bob's health precipitously declined. Illness kept him mostly confined to bed for several months during an unusually cold and snowy winter, able to take only very short walks and car rides about town with Jack. Friends were sure that come warm spring weather he would again be seen traipsing down the streets, making his usual rounds. It was not to be. On April 26, 1943, newspaper headlines announced the inevitable: "EMSLIE, GREAT BASEBALL UMPIRE, DEAD" and "DEAN OF UMPIRE DIES." After enduring two years of increasingly debilitating illness, he took a turn for the worse on Saturday, April 24, and at 2 a.m. on April

26, almost exactly two months into his eighty-fourth season, Bob Emslie closed his eyes and left the game of life, thumbed out by "chronic myocardial dysfunction (cardiac arrest) due to hypertension."[18] Just as when he began umpiring, Bob worked his last inning alone; befitting his long career, he exceeded the normal life expectancy by almost three decades, escaping tuberculosis, the fatal disease that prematurely claimed his four older brothers at young ages: James at twenty-two, J.A. at twenty-six, John at thirty, and William at thirty-six.

Numerous friends and guests crowded the Emslie home amid floral tributes aplenty for funeral services on Wednesday afternoon, April 28, with the Reverend M. B. Johnson, rector of Trinity Anglican Church, officiating. His eulogy undoubtedly echoed the epitaph from the *St. Thomas Times-Journal*: "Of him as an umpire and as a citizen, it can be said: He was a man of few words, quick and accurate decisions and undisputed honesty." Illness prevented John Heydler from attending, but he sent condolences for the loss of "a fine gentleman and a great umpire and sportsman." Among the baseball notables on hand to pay respects were National League vice president Harvey Traband; umpire colleagues Bill Byron and Bill Klem; Ontario baseball legends George "Mooney" Gibson, J. S. "Dad" Lyons, Robert Reid, and the late Billy Reid's son Stan, vice president of the Intercounty League; and Frank Adams, veteran *London Advertiser* reporter. Byron, Klem, Gibson, and Lyons were honorary pallbearers. After services concluded Robert Daniel Emslie was interred next to his wife in section ninety-two of the mausoleum in the St. Thomas cemetery.[19]

Bob Emslie's death was more than a local event. American newspapers in Major League cities and from Camden to Salt Lake City and Sacramento carried news of his passing. The *New York Times* and *Sporting News* carried lengthy obituary commentaries about the playing and umpiring career of the "grand umpire, a gentleman of the Old School" who survived a time when "umpiring baiting was common" by the "even temperament that ruled his conduct on the field." The *Buffalo Courier-Express* declared, "There never was a better umpire than Bob, and few as good," and the *Detroit Free Press* proclaimed the "Lion of the League" was "a giant of the game," his "iron nerve and courage" making him "one of the greatest of all baseball umpires."[20]

Canadian newspapers from Nova Scotia to British Columbia offered even more fulsome remembrances. The *St. Thomas Times-Journal* correctly predicted that while Bob would be remembered locally "for his many fine personal qualities and his record as a citizen of substance, it was for his achievements in baseball that he would be most honored," declaring he had "brought more distinction to St. Thomas in the realm of sports than any other of its citizens. His was a unique, and in some respects unrivalled record." Bill Gaynon, sports editor from Niagara Falls, Ontario, with due respect to such fine Canadian ballplayers as Jimmy Archer, Mooney Gibson, Jack Graney, and George Selkirk, declared Emslie "the greatest individual ever to leave the Dominion for big-time ball," indeed "the greatest landmark which Canada ever had in organized baseball." The *Montreal Gazette*'s Austin "Dink" Carroll thought Emslie "among the all-time greats in the umpiring profession."[21]

J. P. Fitzgerald, sports editor of the Toronto *Telegram*, pointedly asserted Emslie, "easily the greatest of all umpires," deserved a plaque in baseball's Hall of Fame in Cooperstown as "the importance of a man of the honesty of purpose, the keenness, and the ability of a Bob Emslie can't be overlooked in any galaxy of stars." The suggestion found favor not only with St. Thomas residents but also with John Heydler, who as league administrator had observed Bob as umpire and supervisor from 1907 to 1934. As a member of the Major League's advisory council charged with proposing nominations to the Hall of Fame, he said, "I shall be only too proud to present the name of Robert D. Emslie" as the first umpire to be nominated for enshrinement.[22]

That Bob Emslie or any umpire should be included in Cooperstown was an idea before its time. By the spring of 1939 the list of luminaries elected to the Hall of Fame had swelled to nineteen, all former players, but when *Sporting News* on May 25 advocated honoring "men who, during 100 years of baseball, have stood for honesty and integrity on the field of play," Emslie was mentioned among the "boys in blue" deserving the honor. Since the Baseball Writers Association of America could elect only former players, the Hall of Fame's Permanent Committee, which later became the Veterans Committee, on April 23, 1946, and announced the creation of "the honor rolls of baseball, created to honor those who made outstanding contributions other than as active players." Five managers, eleven executives, twelve sportswriters, and eleven umpires were chosen; Robert Emslie was one of the arbiters selected.[23]

It was a fitting gesture, but being named to the honor roll was "a phony type of baseball beatification," as *Sporting News* on May 2 aptly put it. "Either a man is worthy of the Hall of Fame, or he isn't. If a man was a great umpire or an outstanding writer, he should be elected to the diamond Pantheon, and not placed in an annex of that edifice." Still eligible for formal induction, Emslie and the other honor roll umpires were annually nominated for enshrinement, but none were chosen until 1953, when Bill Klem and Tom Connolly became the first umpires to enter baseball's pantheon of heroes. Emslie was on the list of nominees in 1954 and 1955, but no umpire was chosen, and his chances disappeared when the Veterans Committee decided in 1955 to elect only players. That would hold until 1973, when Billy Evans, who after putting away his indicator served as the general manager for the Cleveland Indians and Detroit Tigers, became the third of ten umpires to be enshrined in the Hall of Fame.[24]

While denied immortalization in Cooperstown, Bob lived on in the annals of baseball as sportswriters looking for human interest stories told Emslie tales, often exaggerated and erroneous, from personal memory, morgue files, or interviews with former umpires and players. He even appeared once again as a trivia question posed in 1955 by the inestimable historian and statistician Harry Simmons: "What Canadian was in the Major Leagues the longest?" And his longevity was not forgotten, as *Maclean's*, Canada's popular current affairs news magazine, reminded readers that as a player, umpire, and supervisor Emslie had served longer in professional baseball than anyone other than Connie Mack.[25]

St. Thomas decided to create a pantheon of its own for Bob. In April 1953, the St. Thomas Baseball Association proposed perpetuating "the memory of one of the great figures in baseball history" by naming the baseball grounds in Pinafore Park in his honor. The suggestion widely supported, the city council on May 5 unanimously endorsed the naming of Emslie Field. Dedication of the facility, the first ballpark ever named in honor of an umpire, was appropriately postponed to June, just before an

Intercounty League game between the Elgins of St. Thomas, his place of residence since 1880, and the Royals of Guelph, the city of his birth. To this day it remains a fitting, living memorial to the distinguished career of Canada's pioneering man in blue. Would that the players who take the field, umpires who supervise the action, and spectators who watch the games ever recall the achievements and contributions to baseball of Robert Dean Emslie.

Epilogue

Lion of the League

How does an umpire last so long—
Calling 'em right—calling 'em wrong?
Egging and bottles are tough on the hide,
Cuss words and catcalls cut deep
down inside.
Foul tips are murder to ankle and shin,
Foul language worse on the sered
soul within:
Stormed at by players and stoned by
the press,
Ridden by fans when he makes the
wrong guess;
Friendless, forsaken—a social outcast,
How long can a martyr like this hope
to last?
Yet [Emslie] had done it for 30-odd years,
Riding the tempest—sans anger, sans tears:
Keeping his courage, retaining his laugh,
Asking no quarter and "standing the gaff."
How does an umpire last so long?
"By calling 'em right, son—never one wrong."

—"Umpire's Epitaph," *Memphis Press-Scimitar*, February 20, 1951

With his last breath, a century after the first recorded game, Robert Dean Emslie's lifelong love affair with baseball that began when he was a youthful batboy and was ever foremost in his brain and heart came to an end, and with it one of the most extraordinary careers in baseball history. He had spent fifty-six of his eighty-four years, from 1880 to 1935, in the professional game, eight as a player and forty-nine as an umpire; in forty-six years in the Major Leagues he called 'em in thirty-five seasons (1890–1924), and served thirteen years (1922–35) as the umpire supervisor.[1] It is not an exaggeration to say that his forty-six years in the Major Leagues constituted a "unique, and in some respects unrivalled record."[2] Of the sporting arenas through which Emslie passed, none were more loved than baseball, none more comfortable and compatible with his abilities than the ballpark, but the avid sportsman and gifted athlete also won international championships in trapshooting and curling—sports requiring very different skills—and late in life became an accomplished bowler and golfer.

Emslie's baseball career was exceptional in another sense. It transpired during a time of profound technological, industrial, commercial, transportive, and demographic change as well as two world wars, a devastating viral pandemic, and the Great Depression. Growing up in a house with a wood stove, icebox, gas lighting and without running water and using horsepower transportation, he came to enjoy indoor plumbing, a gas stove, refrigerator, electric lights, a telephone, radio, and an automobile. If national and international developments affected him personally and professionally in undeterminable ways, he was dramatically impacted by experiences during five decades in the confines of ballparks.

Bob Emslie began his entry into the annals of baseball history as a professional pitcher in 1880, reaching the Major Leagues for three seasons (1883–85), playing all but four games with the Baltimore Orioles of the American Association. His only full season, 1884, portended a brilliant career; with a devastating curve he posted a 2.75 ERA in leading sixth-place Baltimore in innings (455) and wins (32), striking out 264 while walking only 88. Although a shoulder injury ended his career in 1885, Bob's first and true baseball love was pitching—his brief memoir details the highs and lows of his pitching career but glosses over his years umpiring.

With no room for Bob Emslie as a player in the firmament of great baseball players, he claimed his place as an umpire, the most exclusive club in the Majors, there being far more opportunities for players than umpires; by career's end he had done it longer than anyone else in history. Exhibiting remarkable endurance and dedication, in thirty-five seasons he failed to complete only eight games: four times when injured, thrice because of illness, and once when he left after the eighth inning order to catch a train home to attend to a family illness. The acknowledged master of the rule book, as evidenced by long service on the interleague rules committee, Emslie, fellow arbiter Cy Rigler declared, knew "more about the baseball rules than all the other National umpires together."[3]

Twenty years of service were a hallmark of supernumerary service and three years the average length of an umpire's career, but Bob obliterated both marks by umpiring for thirty-eight years, from 1887 to 1924. His longevity is the more remarkable, indeed unthinkable, because he toiled during the three most contentious and difficult decades umpires ever faced, 1890–1920. Only seven who broke into the Major Leagues before 1900 worked double-digit years and more than 1,000 games, Emslie's thirty-five seasons and 4,231 games and Tommy Connolly's thirty-four seasons and 4,769 games preeminent among them.[4] Excelling in a profession that looks easy but that few can master, Emslie demonstrated that umpires are born, not made. First donning the mask without instruction or experience, he learned the craft "so thoroughly that for all time he will be regarded as one of the best umpires."[5]

Emslie's place in umpiring history is due to working a record number of years and games and being the first umpire to hold the position of staff supervisor, but his reputation during his career came from performing the common aspects of umpiring in an uncommon way. Respected by players and managers for his temperament, handling disputes, and ability to run games in an efficient and orderly manner, he posted each season the fewest fines and ejections on the staff. Of the eighty-nine Major League umpires who worked more than three thousand games through 2021, ten of the twelve with the highest ejection rates per game are from the Deadball Era, all but two in the National League. Emslie tossed one player every twenty-six games compared with Bill Byron (six), Jim Johnstone (eight), Bill Klem and Cy Rigler (fifteen), Hank O'Day (seventeen) and Ernie Quigley (nineteen).[6] His conciliatory approach foreshadowed the way umpires typically handled confrontations after World War I.

When Emslie died in 1943, he had personally witnessed and experienced more professional baseball history than anyone ever had.[7] As a pitcher he transitioned from throwing underhand to overhand from a surface-level "box" fifty feet from home plate to batters who called for high or low pitches, used flat-sided bats, and experienced the racial integration of the Major Leagues. As an umpire he adapted to ever-changing rules, adjusted from the single to the double-umpire system, switched from standing erect behind the catcher to crouching behind home plate, learned to called pitches from the "slot" between catcher and batter, adopted hand signals, and acquired new protective equipment (perhaps pioneering the use of shin guards when he showed up in 1900 wearing cricket pads). Most importantly, he saw umpiring evolve from a much-maligned short-term job to a respected career; formal training provided with the advent of umpire instructional schools in 1935.[8]

He experienced baseball's evolution from amateur to professional sport and from regional business to commercial entertainment industry. He was on hand during baseball's transformations from two leagues in the 1880s to three in 1890, one in 1892, two in 1901, and three in 1914, then finally reverting to the familiar two circuits in 1916; he saw wooden ballparks with small seating capacities replaced by expansive steel and concrete stadiums, umpiring the inaugural games in three: Pittsburgh in 1909, Brooklyn in 1913, and Boston in 1915. While serving under eight league presidents he experienced governance pass from separate league presidents to a tripartite interleague commission and finally to a single independent commissioner. As his career wound to a close he saw fundamental changes in the game—the "big bang" home run–slugging of the 1920s replacing the "inside game" of the Deadball Era, the founding of the Negro Leagues in 1920, radio broadcasts of games in 1921, the All-Star game in 1933, night baseball in 1935, and the use of three umpires for regular-season games by the 1930s.

Were he able to look into the future he would have been delighted that ten umpires, especially his contemporary and pal Hank O'Day, are enshrined in the Baseball Hall of Fame, if confounded that John Heydler is not, and pleased the organization of an umpires' union in 1963 has produced increased salaries and benefits.[9] He would, given his dedication to the profession, have welcomed Black, Latino, and female umpires.[10] The old-time umpire who hustled to be in position to make base calls might have looked a bit askance at the adoption of four-man crews in 1952 and have mixed feelings about television replays that, while usually demonstrating the accuracy of decisions, sometimes reverse base calls due to inches unseen in real time.[11] But surely the die-hard National Leaguer would have rued the creation in 2000 of a single Major League staff that eliminated distinctive league umpiring.

Emslie worked with some of the finest, most colorful, and most popular umpires ever to grace the diamond: John Gaffney, Tim Hurst, Tom Lynch, Jack Sheridan, Bill Klem, Hank O'Day, Cy Rigler, Ernie Quigley, and Lord Byron. Four of the ten umpires in the National Baseball Hall of Fame were his contemporaries: fellow National Leaguers Klem and O'Day and Tommy Connolly and Billy Evans of the American League. Today the least known of the lot, Emslie reached the pinnacle of the profession and achieved more historic firsts than any of them.

When he called his last game in 1924, the "Dean of Umpires" left with numerous Major League umpiring records. He had umpired the most seasons (35) and the most games (4,231); he was the oldest to umpire a game, the first to work four decades, to call 2,000 (and 3,000, and 4,000) games, to be given a day in his honor, and the first umpire to be appointed staff supervisor. He retired in 1935 with two service milestones: the most consecutive years in a league (45) and the most years in the Major Leagues (49).[12] He witnessed numerous records set by players and notched a few of his own. His National League record for most no-hit games, four behind the plate and four on the bases, was broken by Frank Secory in 1969, but Bob still holds with Klem the record for umpiring the fastest game in baseball history—fifty-one minutes on September 28, 1919. He also achieved two personal distinctions: he was the first Canadian full-time Major League umpire and the only umpire to wear a toupee on the field.[13]

The duration and notable achievements of Emslie's career raise the issue of his place in baseball and umpiring history. It is problematic to compare umpires or players from different eras, but two things are clear: Umpiring was most difficult by far prior to World War I, and Bob ranks with the best of his day. He and O'Day are the only umpires included as "stars" of the Deadball Era.[14] Statistically, he is firmly entrenched in the Major League record book. He is tied for sixth in years of service with three who umpired on four-man crews and sixteenth with Al Barlick in the number of games umpired. Bob has the most in both categories by an umpire working in a single or two-man crew. Ranking fourth in games worked at home plate (2,356) is the more remarkable since for fifteen years he umpired only the bases. All of his umpiring career marks are the highest by a former Major League player.

More indicative of Emslie's prominence than career records, the product of longevity, are the views of contemporaries who had firsthand knowledge of his umpiring. Honus Wagner, the great Pittsburgh shortstop, ranked Emslie the best National League umpire he had seen during his twenty-year Hall of Fame career (1897–1917), and for his "All-Time" baseball team made up of personnel from both leagues said "the ideal umpires would be Bob Emslie and Bill Klem."[15] Hans regarded Emslie as "the greatest of all the umpires on base decisions" and part of "the best umpiring team the game ever knew—Klem at the plate, Emslie on the bases."[16] Hall of Fame umpire Billy Evans called Emslie "one of the greatest umpires the game ever produced." Sportswriters agreed. To Tim Murnane, Emslie gave "the greatest exhibition of all-around umpiring of any man who ever wore the mask," and John Kiernan regarded Emslie, O'Day, and Klem as "the greatest umpires of all time." The *New York Time*'s Isaac Falk labeled as the "greatest umpires, Klem, Emslie and Barlick."[17]

Records and personal acclaim notwithstanding, for Bob Emslie umpiring was a noble calling, ensuring that the game would be played in a fair, orderly, and efficient manner. What made him so dedicated to umpiring? Maybe no reason other than the pleasure of doing something he enjoyed and did well. But surely there is more to it than that. Success and staying in the game he loved do not explain Emslie enduring for so many years the rigors of travel and pressures of umpiring, lengthy absences from family, numerous injuries, and harsh verbal abuse from players, fans, and press. Everyone searches for meaning in life; Emslie found it in umpiring. Just as his youthful determination to switch from the outfield to the pitcher's box involved being the most important player on the field and the focus of spectators' attention, for him trapshooting and curling were less recreational activities than competitive contests; so, too, serving as "master of the diamond" in front of thousands of people brought personal pleasure, psychological gratification, and self-esteem.

Whether Bob Emslie belongs in the National Baseball Hall of Fame is for others to determine, but his reputation and career statics equal or surpass most of the ten umpires enshrined in Cooperstown. Emslie's thirty-five seasons as a regular member of the staff is second only to Bill Klem's thirty-seven and at least a decade longer than four other honorees. Immediately after Emslie's death, former National League president John Heydler called for his enshrinement in Cooperstown. Although only players were then eligible for election Emslie was among the eleven umpires named to the Hall of Fame's honor roll in 1946.

Despite Emslie's achievements, several factors have worked against his selection. First and foremost, umpires are given short shrift. After Klem and Connolly, the best-known umpires of the day, were elected in 1953, twenty years passed before Billy Evans, who after umpiring had been a prominent executive with three teams, followed in 1973. Second, as with players, the Veterans Committee privileges contemporary candidates; five umpires—Connolly, Jocko Conlan, Cal Hubbard, Al Barlick, and Doug Harvey—were elected while still alive. Third, voters are unfamiliar with the careers of umpires from the nineteenth century and the Deadball Era; four are in the Hall of Fame, and of those only Hank O'Day and Tommy Connolly began their Major League careers before 1900, in 1897 and 1898, respectively. After Evans, four decades and the elections of six more umpires would pass before O'Day was elected in 2013.[18] And self-promotion brings more recognition than self-effacement. Emslie shunned publicity and rarely gave interviews, as evidenced by his slim file in the Hall of Fame library. Garrulous Jocko Conlan, who two years after retiring from the National League in 1965 published an autobiography, in 1974 became the fourth umpire enshrined. Of Conlan's election, perhaps not coincidentally the year after the American League's Evans was inducted, sportswriter Bob Broeg mentioned Emslie among seven umpires who arguably "deserved the honor before Jocko."[19]

But the primary reason Emslie has faded into obscurity is the lone omission in his long and distinguished career: he never umpired in a World Series. Great players, including fellow Canadians Ferguson Jenkins and Larry Walker, who never played in the World Series are in Cooperstown because of their regular-season performances, but for umpires, who lack meaningful seasonal statistics, the Fall Classic provides public recognition. If the inability to effectively call pitches is assuredly the reason Emslie never was assigned to a World Series, the exclusion was unnecessary, as glasses would have corrected his hyperopia (farsightedness), but the eyeglass ceiling for umpires was not broken until 1956. In any event, not umpiring in the World Series unquestionably has precluded proper recognition by historians and sportswriters.

Bob Emslie eventually, if posthumously, found a place in baseball pantheons. In 1986 he was inducted into the Canadian Baseball Hall of Fame, and in 2004 he was enshrined in the Guelph Sports Hall of Fame as a player and umpire. Befittingly, he was the first of three umpires for whom a baseball facility was named, Emslie Field in St. Thomas the lone survivor.[20]

Bill Klem's pronouncement, "Baseball is more than a game to me; it's a religion," is hyperbolic, but it is no exaggeration to say that baseball was Bob Emslie's life. The line between his professional and private life was porous; while participating in trapshooting and curling tournaments he was regularly identified as a former player and a famous umpire. A man of few words even in death, the plaque on his tomb contains only his name and the years of his birth and death. An appropriate additional inscription would be *Umpire*.

Notes

PREFACE

1. For works on umpires, see Reid Duffy, "By the Book: Writings By and About Umpires," in Larry R. Gerlach and Bill Nowlin, eds., *The SABR Book of Umpires and Umpiring* (Phoenix AZ: Society for American Baseball Research, 2017), 444–51.
2. Bob Luke, *Dean of Umpires: A Biography of Bill McGowan* (Jefferson NC: McFarland, 2005), and James M. Kahn, *The Umpire Story* (New York: Putnam, 1953). There are three other slim biographies: John Bacchia, *Augie: Stalag Luft VI to the Major Leagues* (Bloomington IN: Indiana University Press, 2011) primarily deals with Augie Donatelli as a prisoner of war; Mary Bell Hubbard, *Strike 3! And You're Out: The Cal Hubbard Story* (self-published, 1976) is a family-oriented portrait by Hubbard's sister; Adrienne Cherie Ashford, *Strrr-ike! Emmett Ashford, Major League Umpire* (Bloomington IN: Author House, 2004) is a brief account by Ashford's daughter.
3. David Cicotello, "Bob Emslie," Society for American Baseball Research, https://sabr.org/bioproj/person/bob-emslie; and "Robert Daniel Emslie" in David Nemec, *Major League Baseball Profiles, 1871–1900*, vol. 1 (Lincoln: University of Nebraska Press, 2011), 60–61. But see Larry Gerlach, "Bob Emslie," in Andrew North, ed., *Our Game, Too: The Development of Canadian Baseball* (Phoenix AZ: Society for American Baseball Research, 2002), 108-114.
4. David L. Porter, ed., *Biographical Dictionary of American Sports: Baseball, Revised and Expanded Edition*, 3 vols. (Westport CT: Greenwood Press, 2000) and Matthew Silverman, Michael Gershman, and David Pietrusza, eds., *Baseball: The Biographical Encyclopedia* (Kingston NY: Total Sports Publishing, 2000), xi. Nor is he in Donald Dewey and Nicholas Acocella, *The New Biographical History of Baseball: The Classic*, rev. ed. (Chicago: Triumph Books, 2002); Robert L. Tiemann and Mark Rucker, eds., *Nineteenth Century Stars* (Phoenix AZ: Society for American Baseball Research, 2012), or Frederick Ivor-Campbell, Robert L. Tiemann, and Mark Rucker, eds., *Baseball's First Stars* (Cleveland OH: Society for American Baseball Research, 1996), which includes umpires. The only encyclopedia mention is in Mike Shatzkin, *The Ballplayers: Baseball's Ultimate Biographical Reference* (New York: Arbor House, 1990), 311.

5. *Toronto Globe*, July 9, 1974; *Toronto Mail*, July 9, 1974.
6. *St. Thomas Times-Journal*, April 26, 1943; *Sporting Life*, September 6, 1913 and February 26, 1916; *St. Louis Star*, April 14, 1914.
7. Larry R. Gerlach, *The Men in Blue: Conversations with Umpires* (New York: Viking Press, 1980; repr., Lincoln: University of Nebraska Press,1994).
8. Harriet Eleanor Smith, ed., *Autobiography of Mark Twain*, vol. 1 (Berkeley: University of California Press, 2010), 220–21.
9. Henry James, *Partial Portraits* (London: Macmillan, 1888).

PROLOGUE

1. *The Tempest*, Act II, Scene 1; William Patten and J. Walker McSpadden, *The Book of Baseball: The National Game from the Earliest Days to the Present Season* (New York: Collier, 1911).
2. The most comprehensive histories of nineteenth-century baseball remain Harold Seymour, *Baseball: The Early Years* (New York: Oxford University Press, 1960), and David Q. Voigt, *American Baseball: From the Gentleman's Sport to the Commissioner System* (Norman: University of Oklahoma Press, 1966). For early years see John Thorn, *Baseball in the Garden of Eden: The Secret History of the Early Game* (New York: Simon and Schuster, 2011); William J. Ryczek, *Baseball's First Inning: A History of the National Pastime through the Civil War* (Jefferson NC: McFarland 2009); Peter Morris, *But Didn't We Have Fun?: An Informal History of Baseball's Pioneer Era, 1843–1870* (Chicago: Ivan R. Dee, 2008); Warren Goldstein, *Playing for Keeps: A History of Early Baseball* (Ithaca NY: Cornell University Press, 1998); Tom Shieber, "The Evolution of the Baseball Diamond," *Baseball Research Journal*, (Cleveland OH: Society for American Baseball Research, 1994), 3–13.
3. "The Constitution of the Olympic Ball Club of Philadelphia," Dean A. Sullivan, ed., *Early Innings: A Documentary History of Baseball, 1825–1908* (Lincoln: University of Nebraska Press, 1995), 6.
4. Sullivan, *Early Innings*, 6; Ryczek, *Baseball's First Inning*, 224–25; Thorn, *Baseball in the Garden*, 71–77; Robert Peterson, *The Man Who Invented Baseball* (New York: Scribner's, 1973), 68, 77.
5. Henry Chadwick, ed., *Beadle's Dime Base-Ball Player* (New York: Beadle, 1862), 15–16, 28–30.
6. William J. Ryczek, *When Johnny Came Sliding Home: The Post–Civil War Baseball Boom, 1865–1870* (Jefferson NC: McFarland, 2006); William J. Ryczek, *Blackguards and Red Stockings. A History of Baseball's National Association, 1871–1875*, rev. ed. (Jefferson NC: McFarland, 2016).
7. *New York Clipper*, November 15, 1871; *Beadle's* (1875), 82.

8. A. G. Spalding, comp., *Spalding's Official Base Ball Guide for 1878* (Chicago: Spalding, 1878), 36–37, 40, 51.
9. *Philadelphia Times*, July 3 and July 6, 1882; *Cincinnati Enquirer*, July 3, 1882; *Cincinnati Enquirer*, July 9, 1882; Elizabeth K. Martin, "The Development of Baseball Umpires' Uniforms, 1846–1996," (MA thesis, University of Rhode Island, 1997): ii, 2–4; "Hey Blue!" *National Pastime: A Review of Baseball History*, vol. 7 (Cleveland OH: Society for American Baseball Research, 1988): 36–46.
10. *Cincinnati Enquirer*, December 3 and December 8, 1882; *Chicago Tribune*, November 19, 1882; *Philadelphia Times* and *Boston Daily Globe*, December 8, 1882; *Spalding Guide* (1883), 87–88, 91; *Chicago Tribune*, July 7, 1883.
11. The UA, which lasted one year, paid substitutes $10 per game. *Chicago Tribune*, December 19, 1883; *Wright & Ditson's Base Ball Guide* (Boston: Wright & Ditson, 1884), 38–39.
12. Daniel E. Ginsburg, *The Fix Is In: A History of Baseball Gambling and Game Fixing Scandals* (Jefferson NC: McFarland, 1995), 37–51. Umpires had to pay all their expenses except railroad fares until 1940, when they received a $750 travel allowance, a sum that covered only about half of their expenses. In 1970 the leagues provided umpiring equipment.
13. *Spalding Guide* (1883), 87–93, 103; Larry R. Gerlach and Harold V. Higham, "Dick Higham: Umpire at the Bar of History," *The National Pastime: A Review of Baseball History* (Cleveland OH: Society for American Baseball Research, 2000), 20–32; "Dick Higham, Star of Baseball's Early Years," *National Pastime* 21 (2001): 72–80; Harry V. Higham, "The Disqualification of Umpire Dick Higham," in Larry R. Gerlach and Bill Nowlin, eds, *The SABR Book of Umpires and Umpiring* (Phoenix AZ: Society for American Baseball Research, 2019), 402–7.
14. *Sporting Life*, July 30, 1884.
15. *Sporting Life*, July 30, 1884; *Chicago Tribune*, October 13, 1886; Richard Hershberger, *Strike Four: The Evolution of Baseball* (Lanham MD: Rowman & Littlefield, 2019), 105–12, 223–32.
16. *Spalding Guide* (1883), 30–31, 74.
17. For duties and equipment see Bob Webster, "The Evolution of Umpires' Equipment and Uniforms," in. Gerlach and Nowlin, SABR *Book of Umpires and Umpiring*, 259–62; and Peter Morris, *A Game of Inches: The Game on the Field: The Stories Behind the Innovations That Shaped Baseball* (Chicago: Ivan R. Dee, 2006), 31–36, 368–95.
18. *Spalding Guide* (1876), 39; *Spalding Guide* (1884), 95; *Spalding Guide* (1889), 120. For arguing an opponent's steal of third base on May 25, 1889, Dave Orr of the American Association Columbus Colts became the first player ejected

in MLB history and Fred Goldsmith the first umpire to toss a player. *Brooklyn Daily Eagle*, May 26, 1889.

19. *Spalding Guide* (1876), 21.
20. David Q. Voigt, "America's Manufactured Villain—the Baseball Umpire," *Journal of Popular Culture*, 3 (Summer 1970): 1–21; reprinted in Voigt, *America Through Baseball* (Chicago: Nelson-Hall, 1976), 162–80.
21. *Spalding Guide* (1885), 86.
22. *Sporting Life*, July 16, 1884.
23. *Spalding Guide* (1876), 39; 1878 *Spalding Guide*, (1878) 38; Peter Morris, "'A Motion as Near Flying as Any Human Being Could Attain': The 19th Century Umpire as Sprinter," *Base Ball: A Journal of the Early Game* 2, no. 2 (Fall 2008): 18–25.
24. *Detroit Free Press*, April 5, 1888.
25. Jerry Lansche, *Glory Fades Away: The Nineteenth Century World Series Rediscovered* (Dallas: Taylor, 1991); *Chicago Tribune*, October 17, October 18, and October 19, 1886; *Inter Ocean*, October 19, 1886; *St. Louis Post-Dispatch*, October 18, 1886; *St. Louis Globe-Democrat*, October 20, 1886; *Sporting Life*, October 20 and October 27, 1886. During the regular season the alternating umpires were players from each team.
26. *St. Louis Post-Dispatch*, October 10 and October 11, 1887; *Detroit Free Press*, October 10, October 20, and October 25, 1887.
27. *Sporting Life*, November 30, 1887.
28. *Rochester Democrat and Chronicle*, April 11, 15, 1886.

1. GROUNDING IN GUELPH

Epigraph from Robert Emslie's unpublished memoir, Elgin County Museum, St. Thomas, Ontario.

1. His marriage certificate includes the third given name "Kean." Ontario, Canada, Marriages, 1826, microfilm, Church of Jesus Christ of Latter-Day Saints Family History Library, Salt Lake City, Utah. Perhaps for convenience, he subsequently dropped Kean, possibly a maternal clan name, just as his mother used Gray as her surname instead of Graye, the traditional spelling.
2. Christopher Daniell, *From Norman Conquest to Magna Carta: England, 1066–1215* (London: Routledge, 2003), 13–14; George F. Black, *The Surnames of Scotland* (Edinburgh: Birlinn, 1998); Charles Wareing Bardsley, *Dictionary of English and Welsh Surnames* (London: Frowde, 1901).
3. The family history is recorded in the family bible, *Evangelical Expositor Commentary Holy Bible* (Glasgow, 1825), Elgin County Museum, St. Thomas, Ontario. Strathdon christening records identify Anna as the couple's eleventh child while the family bible lists ten children, so one, almost certainly a twin, Jean,

must have died in infancy. Christening records include a Jean on October 23, 1821, who is not mentioned in the family bible, the family likely bestowing the same name in memory of the first Jean.

4. Lucille H. Campey, *An Unstoppable Force: The Scottish Exodus to Canada* (Toronto: Natural Heritage Books, 2002), 18; Lucille H. Campey, *The Scottish pioneers of Upper Canada, 1784–1855: Glengarry and Beyond* (Toronto: Natural Heritage Books, 2005).
5. Neil Oliver, *A History of Scotland* (London: Weidenfeld & Nicolson, 2009); Magnus Magnusson, *Scotland: The Story of a Nation* (London: HarperCollins, 2000); John H. S Burleigh, *A Church History of Scotland* (Edinburgh: Hope Trust, 1988).
6. The two provinces formed by the Constitutional Act of 1791, Lower Canada (Quebecois French Catholics) and Upper Canada (English-speaking Protestants), were merged by the Act of Union in 1841 and renamed Canada West and Canada East to form the United Province of Canada. The Dominion of Canada, created on July 1, 1867, divided the Province of Canada into Quebec and Ontario. Martin Brook Taylor and Doug Owram, *Canadian History: Beginnings to Confederation* (Toronto: University of Toronto Press, 1994); Randall White, *Ontario, 1610–1985* (Toronto: Dundurn, 1985); Robert Bothwell, *A Short History of Ontario* (Edmonton: Hurtig, 1986).
7. Bob's grandfather John's obituary in the *Guelph Daily Mercury and Advertiser*, May 18, 1891, said he arrived in 1838, but his uncle John said he came to Canada with the family at age thirteen, making it 1836.
8. Leo A. Johnson, *History of Guelph, 1827–1927* (Guelph: Guelph Historical Society, 1977); David Allan, *About Guelph: Its Early Days and Later* (Guelph: Guelph Historical Society, 2012); Robert C. Lee, *The Canada Company and the Huron Tract, 1826–1853* (Hamilton ON: Dundurn, 2011).
9. 1861 Canadian census; Peter Wilson, *Building with Scottish Stone* (Edinburgh: Arcamedia, 2005), 9–13; Leanne Piper, "Quarries and Quarrymen: The Limestone Industry in Guelph," *Historic Guelph*, 46 (2007).
10. Robert W. Stuart Mackay, *The Canada Directory: Containing the Names of the Professional and Business Men of Every Description in the Cities, Towns, and Principal Villages of Canada* (Montreal: John Lovell, 1851), 92.
11. Johnson, *Guelph*, 33; *Guelph Herald*, February 26, 1850; Robert W. Stuart Mackay, *The Canada Directory* (Montreal: Lovell, 1851), 92; Linda Morton, "The Training of a Tailor," *Dress: The Journal of the Costume Society of America* 8, no. 1 (1982): 22–26; Judith Flanders, *Consuming Passions: Leisure and Pleasure in Victorian Britain* (New York: Harper, 2007).
12. *Guelph Herald*, May 13, 1851.

13. Population figures are inexact but close enough. William H. Smith, *Smith's Canadian Gazetteer* (Toronto: Rowsell, 1846), 72–73, says the population in 1845 was 3,400 and in his *Canada: Past, Present and Future*, vol. 2 (Toronto: MacLearn, 1851), 103, gives the population in 1829 as 778 and in 1850 as 4,399. Johnson, *History of Guelph*, 83 and 108, says 1,480 in 1847 and 4,730 in 1852–53.
14. *The Canada Directory for 1857–58* (Montreal: Lovell, 1857),160; *Guelph Herald*, January 7, 1851.
15. *Guelph Evening Mercury*, November 28, 1868; Johnson, *Guelph*, 109–10.
16. As of 2020 249 Canadian-born players reached major leagues, half (124) from Ontario. The first was Bob "the Magnet" Addy of Port Hope, believed to have originated sliding into a base. The next four players all came from Guelph: Tom Smith, Dan O'Connor, Jim Cockman, and William "Bunk" Congalton. The next Guelph native was Scott Diamond in 2016. Technically, there were three earlier Canadian-born Major Leaguers, but William "Silver Bill" Phillips, Arthur "Doc" Irwin, and Charles "Pop" Smith moved at young ages to the United States, where they learned to play baseball.
17. For the Beachville game see Nancy B. Bouchier and Robert K. Barney, "A Critical Examination of a Source on Early Ontario Baseball: The Reminiscences of Adam E. Ford," *Journal of Sport History* 15, no. 1 (Spring 1998): 75–90, and Brian Martin, *Baseball's Creation Myth: Adam Ford, Abner Graves and the Cooperstown Story* (Jefferson NC: McFarland, 2013). For overall history see William Humber, *Cheering for the Home Team: The Story of Baseball in Canada* (Erin ON: Boston Mills Press, 1983), and *Diamonds of the North* (New York: Oxford University Press, 1995); Samuel L. Hill, "Baseball in Canada," *Indiana Journal of Global Legal Studies* 8, no. 1 (Fall 2000): 37–46.
18. David L. Bernard, "The Guelph Maple Leafs: A Cultural Indicator of Southern Ontario," *Ontario History* 58, no. 3 (September 1992): 1–23; Tim Bonney-James, "More Than A Game: The Interaction of Sport and Community in Guelph" (MA thesis, University of Guelph, July 1997).
19. *Toronto Mail*, May 1, 1886; Emslie, Memoir; *Detroit Free Press*, October 3, 1899.
20. J. L. Mitchell and A. O. Loomis, comp., *Grand Trunk Railway Gazetteer* (Toronto: Chewett, 1862), 28; J. L. Mitchell, comp., *Mitchell's Canada Gazetteer* (Toronto: Chewett, 1864), 29; W. H. Irwin and George R. Burnham, *Gazetteer and Directory of the County of Wellington* (Toronto: Rowsell, 1867), 125; Johnson, *Guelph*, 85, 201.
21. Leavenworth's population increased from 7,429 in 1860 to 17,873 in 1870, growing 141 percent. William R. Petroski, *The Kansas Pacific: A Study in Railroad Promotion* (New York: Arno Press, 1981); Keith L. Bryant, *History of the Atchison, Topeka, and Sante Fe Railway* (Lincoln: University of Nebraska Press,

1974); Sheffield Ingalls, *History of Atchison County, Kansas* (Atchison KS: Standard Publishing Company, 1916); William G. Cutler, *History of the State of Kansas* (Chicago: A. T. Andreas, 1883; repr., Topeka: Kansas State Historical Society, 1976).

22. *Strong City Derrick*, January 18, November 20, 1896, and May 7, 1897; *Chase County Courant*, January 23, 1880; *Chase County Republican*, April 2, 1891.
23. *Atchison Daily Champion*, November 27, 1870, April 5, 1882, and May 18, 1903; *Waterville Telegraph*, January 29, 1870 and January 24, 1873; *Blue Rapids Times*, January 15, 1874; *Marshall County News* (Marysville KS), January 24, January 31, 1874, and May 17, 1879.
24. Bob said they moved when he was nine, which would be 1868. Emslie, Memoir. Alexander's last mention of being in Guelph is 1867. *Gazetteer and Directory of the County of Wellington* (Toronto: Irwin & Burnham, 1867), 125.
25. For the Maple Leafs see Hilary Stead, *Guelph: A People's Heritage, 1827–2002* (Guelph ON: City of Guelph, 2002), 49; for the 1874 Watertown tournament see Bonney-James, "More Than A Game," 88.
26. *The Canadian Illustrated News* quoted in Humber, *Cheering for the Home Team*, 27, 31.

2. COMING OF AGE IN LONDON

1. 1871 Census of Canada, District 10, London Ward No. 1, 20–21; *London City Directory 1872–73* (Montreal: Cherrier & Kirwin, 1872), 75, 130. London sorely needs a scholarly history. Frederick H. Armstrong, *The Forest City: An Illustrated History of London, Canada* (Northridge CA: Windsor, 1986); Nancy Z. Tausky, *Historical Sketches of London: From Site to City* (Peterborough ON: Broadview ,1993); Michael Baker, ed, *Downtown London: Layers of Time* (London ON: City of London, 1998); Orlo Miller, *This Was London: The First Two Centuries* (Westport ON: Butternut, 1988).
2. *St. Thomas Times-Journal*, January 26, 1939; Paul Axelrod, *The Promise of Schooling: Education in Canada, 1800–1914* (Toronto: University of Toronto Press, 1997); Susan E. Houston and Alison Prentice, *Schooling and Scholars in Nineteenth-century Ontario* (Toronto: University of Toronto Press, 1988).
3. Brian Martin, *The Tecumsehs of the International Association: Canada's First Major League Baseball Champions* (Jefferson NC: McFarland, 2015); R. David Edmunds, *The Shawnee Prophet* (Lincoln: University of Nebraska Press, 1985); John Sugden, *Tecumseh: A Life* (New York: Henry Holt, 1997).
4. Humber, *Cheering for the Home Team*, 27, 31.
5. Spencer Norris Lang, "Experimenting with Professional Baseball: An Examination of the Guelph Maple Leafs and the London Tecumsehs in Canadian

Baseball's First Professional Era, 1872–1878," (MA thesis, University of Western Ontario, 2003).

6. *London Free Press*, August 14, 1873.
7. Emslie, Memoir; *St. Thomas Times-Journal*, January 26, 1939.
8. *Gazetteer and Directory of the Great Western Railway and Branches* (Toronto: Polk, 1874), 228–38; *London City Directory, 1874–5* (Detroit: Polk, 1974), 246, 261, 268; *McAlpine's London City and County of Middlesex Directory* (London: McAlpine, Everett, 1875), 80; *London City Directory, 1874–5* (Detroit: Polk, 1974), 91.
9. St. Andrew's, with a congregation of about five hundred, opened on October 31, 1869. John M. Gunn, *Almost a Century: St. Andrew's United Church, London, Ontario, 1833–1933* (London ON: St. Andrew's, 1933), 21–22. For Emslie contributions, mainly by Mary after 1877, see "Report of the Deacons' Court and Managing Committee of St. Andrew's Church, 1869–1875," and "Annual Report of the Managing & Other Committees of St. Andrew's Church, 1875–1891."
10. In 1872 the otolaryngologist Dr. Brewster M. Higley VI wrote a poem, "My Western Home," whose words became the lyrics to "Home on the Range," the state song of Kansas. Kirke Mechem, "The Story of Home on the Range," *Kansas Historical Quarterly* 17, no. 4 (November 1949): 11–40.
11. *Waterville Telegraph*, October 9, October 16, and December 18, 1874; *Atchison Daily Patriot*, December 10, 1874.
12. Harold C. Evans "Baseball in Kansas, 1867–1940," *Kansas Historical Quarterly* 9, no, 2 (May 1940): 175–92; *Waterville Telegraph*, June 14, July 12, July 19, September 6, and October 6, 1872.
13. *Topeka Daily Capital*, March 24, 1940; Emslie, Memoir.
14. *St. Joseph Gazette*, June 26 and August 3, 1875.
15. *St. Joseph Gazette*, August 19 and August 31, 1875; *Atchison Daily Champion*, September 1, 1875.
16. *Atchison Daily Champion*, September 4, 1875. The *Atchison Daily Globe* on August 13, 1912, and May 3, 1913, incorrectly said Bob Emslie, "current National League umpire," had pitched against St. Joseph and St. Louis in August 1875, and the *Topeka Daily Capital*, March 24, 1940, erroneously identified him as "a Kansan" from Waterville who became a major league umpire.
17. *Atchison Daily Champion*, July 29, 1875, March 29, March 30, and April 8, 1876; *Blue Rapid Times*, April 13, 1876; *Atchison Daily Champion*, April 5, 1882; *Waterville Telegraph*, April 9, 1882.
18. *St. Joseph Gazette*, November 4, 1875; *Chase County Courant*, March 30, 1877; *Chase County Leader*, May 10, 1877.

19. Emslie, Memoir.
20. Les Bronson, "Old Time Baseball and the London Tecumsehs of the late 1870s," 1972 transcription, London Public Library; Frank Adams, "Some Baseball History, Both Amateur and Professional, in the City of London, Synopsis of Tecumsehs, the Renowned Champions of Early Days," *Canadian Science Digest* 4, no. 3 (March 1938): 214–15; Havi Echenberg, "Sport as a Social Responses to Urbanization; A Case Study-London, Ontario, 1850–1900" (MA thesis, University of Western Ontario, 1988); Spencer Norris Lang, "Experimenting with Professional Baseball: An Examination of the Guelph Maple Leafs and the London Tecumsehs in Canadian Baseball's First Professional Era, 1872–1878" (MA thesis, University of Western Ontario, 2003), x.
21. Goldsmith to Frank Adams, March 24, 1938, quoted in Adams, "Baseball History," 216, and *London Advertiser*, August 20, 1927. Years later Goldsmith said he was offered $300 per month, a preposterous sum. *Sporting News*, March 30, 1939. While Goldsmith, who claimed to have invented the curveball, was one of its earliest practitioners, the pioneer was likely William A. "Candy" Cummings. Martin Quigley, *The Crooked Pitch: The Curveball in American Baseball History* (Chapel Hill NC: Algonquin Books, 1984).
22. *London Advertiser*, July 4, 1876.
23. Forrest Capie and Geoffrey Wood, "Great Depression of 1873–1896," in David Glasner and Thomas F. Cooley, eds., *Business Cycles and Depressions; An Encyclopedia* (New York: Garland, 1997).
24. *McAlpine's London City Directory*, 159, 280; Emslie, Memoir.
25. Robert K. Barney and Riley Nowokowski, "A Canadian Distinction of Note: London, Ontario's Labatt Memorial Park, Baseball History's Oldest, Continuously Operating Baseball Precinct," *Ontario History* 113, no. 2 (Autumn 2021): 128–50.
26. Humber, *Cheering for the Home Team*, 41.
27. Undated newspaper clipping about Old Boy's game, *London Advertiser*, June 1936. The adulation was not universal. When Rowena Lavinia Rooks, age nineteen, an aspiring concert pianist, married Goldsmith on July 24, 1877, against the wishes of her family, she was disowned for marrying a professional ballplayer. "Rooks of London, Ontario, Canada—Message Board," www.ancestry.com.
28. *London Advertiser*, April 15, 1878; *London Free Press*, April 15, April 20, and April 21, 1878. Emslie recalled his first game in detail, identifying eight Tecumseh players, but mistakenly said the game was on "a Good Friday," which was April 19, and that the score was 3–2. Emslie, Memoir.

3. PITCHING FOR PAY

Epigraph from Henry Chadwick, Chadwick's Base Ball Manual (London: Routledge, 1874), 17.

1. Emslie, Memoir.
2. Judy Tuck, *A History of Harriston* (Mildmay ON: Mildmay Town Crier, 1978), 17, 20; Clifford M. Harrison, *A History of Minto Township* (Minto ON: Township of Minto, 1978), 120–36; *Guelph Daily Mercury*, October 13, 1880; "Harriston Browns: A Baseball Story," Wellington County Museum and Archives, https://www.wellington.ca/en/discover/mus-harriston-browns.aspx.
3. Tuck, *History of Harriston*; *New York Clipper*, June 19, 1880; *Listowel Banner*, March 26 and April 23, 1880; *New York Sun*, July 28, 1918; *New York Times*, April 29, 1943.
4. Records of the *Harriston Tribune* are not extant for 1879–80. The paper in Listowel, fifteen miles south, offers scarce mention of the Browns. Records of Guelph games appear in the *Guelph Mercury*.
5. *New York Clipper*, October 30, 1880.
6. *Guelph Mercury*, July 2 and July 20, 1881; *Toronto Globe*, July 8 and 23, 1881; Jesse Edgar Middleton, *The Municipality of Toronto: A History*, vol. 2 (Toronto: Dominion, 1923), 749; Alan Metcalfe, *Canada Learns to Play: The Emergence of Organized Sport, 1807–1914* (Toronto: McClelland and Stewart, 1978), 90.
7. Emslie, Memoir.
8. Emslie, Memoir.
9. Ron Brown, *The Lake Erie Shore: Ontario's Forgotten South Coast* (Toronto: Dundurn, 2009); Wayne Paddon, George Thorman, Don Cosens, and Brian Sim, *St. Thomas: 100 Years a City, 1881–1981* (St. Thomas ON: St. Thomas Centennial Committee, 1981). St. Thomas today remains a railroad city, hosting the North American Railway Hall of Fame in the restored Canada Southern Railway Station as well as the Elgin County Railway Museum.
10. *St. Thomas Times*, June 27 and July 6, 1882.
11. Robert D. Emslie, "Ramblings of an Umpire," *Baseball Magazine*, November 1908, 18.
12. Emslie, "Ramblings of an Umpire," 18. For details of the excursion see Larry R. Gerlach, "The St. Thomas Atlantics 1882 U. S. Tour," in Andrew North, ed., *Our Game, Too: The Development of Canadian Baseball* (Phoenix AZ: Society of American Baseball Research, 2022), 125–31.
13. They defeated Auburn 15–3 and 14–5; Oswego 17–0 and 14–3; Syracuse 3–2 and 11–7; and Binghamton 2–0 and 10–2.
14. *New York Times*, August 10, 1882; *New York Sun*, August 10, 1882; *Brooklyn Daily Eagle*, August 10, 1882.

15. *Reading* (PA) *Times*, August 15 and 16, 1882.
16. *Philadelphia Times*, August 16, 1882.
17. *St. Thomas Times-Journal*, April 26, 1943.
18. *St. Thomas Times-Journal*, April 26, 1943; Emslie, Memoir. He erroneously said the trip began on May 24 and ended June 30, the team lost eight games, and New York and Philadelphia were National League teams. He also claimed to have been the only pitcher, but as the trip progressed, he played at least three games in right field. His also incorrectly recalled game sites, probably confusing games with those he played with Camden in 1883.
19. Organized in 1882, the team was named after the merchant Albert Merritt, who had underwritten the club in hope of currying favor with voters in the state senatorial election. For a history of the Merritt see Larry R. Gerlach, "The Camden Merritt, New Jersey's Premier Nineteenth-Century Baseball Team," *New Jersey Studies* 9, no. 2 (Summer 2003): 35–57.
20. Horace L. Traubel, comp., *With Walt Whitman in Camden*, vol. 2 (New York: Mitchell Kennerley, 1915), 330, and vol. 4 (Philadelphia: University of Pennsylvania Press, 1953), 508.
21. His recollection fifty-some years later, of arriving on July 7, is slightly off. He correctly recalled playing the outfield the first game, but it was center, not left, and he did not pitch against Baltimore the next day but on September 15. The score was 3–2, not 3–0. Emslie, Memoir.
22. *Post*, December 20, 1883; *Courier*, December 20, 1883; *Post*, October 21, 1883.
23. *Courier*, October 27, 1883.
24. *Courier*, December 14, 1883; *Post*, December 16, 1883.
25. *Courier*, December 14, 1883; *Post*, December 16, 1883.
26. *Post*, June 2, 1883, and *Courier*, June 4, 1883.
27. On June 5, 1894, Duke Esper of Washington achieved the first officially recorded three-pitch inning.
28. Comparing teams from different times and places is a highly subjective, but the Merritt surely ranks with the other most heralded teams of the nineteenth century, the Tecumsehs of London, Ontario (which won the 1877 IA championship) and the 1878 IA champion Buffalo Bisons. Brian Martin, *The Tecumsehs of the International Association: Canada's First Major League Baseball Champions* (Jefferson NC: McFarland, 2015); "Joseph M. Overfield, 'The First Great Minor League Club,'" *Baseball Research Journal* 6 (1977): 1–6. New Jersey's 1937 Newark Bears, winners of the International League pennant with a 109-43 record, is generally regarded as the best team in Minor League history; the 1932 Bears (109-52) are also worthy of consideration. Ronald A. Mayer, *The 1937 Newark Bears: A Baseball*

Legend (New Brunswick NJ: Rutgers University Press, 1994); Randolph Linthurst, "The Newark Bears," *Baseball Research Journal* 6 (1977): 10–13.

29. *Sporting Life*, on July 30, 1883, incorrectly reported each of the three signees received $400.

4. CURVEBALL ARTIST

Epigraph by Honus Wagner, quoted in Jonathan Fraser Light, The Cultural Encyclopedia of Baseball (Jefferson NC: McFarland, 1997), 774.

1. In addition to Baltimore, the league comprised the Cincinnati Red Stockings, Louisville Eclipse, Philadelphia Athletics, Pittsburgh Alleghenys, and the St. Louis Browns. David Nemec, *The Beer and Whisky League: The Illustrated History of the American Association—Baseball's Renegade Major League*, rev. ed, (Guilford CT: Lyons, 2004); Richard Hershberger, "The First Baseball War: The American Association and the National League," *Research Journal* 49, no. 2 (Fall 2020): 115–25.
2. Mathew A. Crenson, *Baltimore: A Political History* (Baltimore: Johns Hopkins University Press, 2017); Sherry H. Olson, *Baltimore: The Building of an American City*, rev. ed. (Baltimore: Johns Hopkins University Press, 1997); Robert J. Brugger, *Maryland, A Middle Temperament: 1634–1980* (Baltimore: Johns Hopkins University Press, 1988).
3. James H. Bready, *Baseball in Baltimore: The First Hundred Years* (Baltimore: Johns Hopkins University Press, 1998.) Ireland's Patrick Loughlin appeared in one game on May 9, and Bill Reid from London, Ontario, played in twenty-four games until dismissed by Barnie on June 6.
4. Thom Karmik, "A Cricketer on Baseball," *New York Sun*, July 28, 1918; *Philadelphia Times*, September 29, 1883.
5. *Baltimore Sun*, September 1, September 3, and September 6, 1883; *Baltimore American*, September 5, 1883; *Sporting Life*, September 10, 1883.
6. *Louisville Courier-Journal*, September 16, 1883; *Baltimore Sun*, September 17, 1883.
7. It took seven pitches for a walk. The number was lowered to five in 1885 and finally to four in 1889.
8. *Baltimore American*, October 8, 1883; *Sporting Life*, February 20, 1884.
9. *Baltimore Sun*, October 6, 1883.
10. In 1829 the 178-foot, 8-inch obelisk designed by Robert Mills, who later designed the 1885 Washington Monument in the nation's capital, was placed on the cornerstone that had been laid on July 4, 1815. The first Washington monument to be completed, a forty-foot tower, was erected in Washington Monument State Park in nearby Boonsboro in 1827.

11. *Baltimore Sun*, October 9 and October 15, 1883; *Sporting Life*, February 27, 1884; *Baltimore Sun*, April 28, 1884.
12. *Baltimore Sun*, February 24, March 22, and March 29, 1884; *Sporting Life*, March 5 and April 9, 1884; *Baltimore American*, March 19, 1884. For Kimball, *Baltimore Sun*, June 13, June 17, and June 27, 1884.
13. *Toronto World*, February 7, 1884; *St. Thomas Times*, April 4, 1884; *Baltimore Sun*, April 7, April 8, April 19, and April 22, 1884; *Sporting Life*, April 16, 1884.
14. *St. Louis Post-Dispatch*, May 1, 1884.
15. *Sporting Life*, February 6 and April 23, 1884; *St. Louis Post-Dispatch*, May 6, 1884. Roscoe Conkling (1828–88), senator and congressman from New York, was known for making sarcastic speeches.
16. *Baltimore American*, June 16, 1884; *Baltimore Sun*, June 17, 1884; *Sporting Life*, June 18, 1884. Marty Payne, "The Undesirable Position," *Base Ball: A Journal of the Early Game* 1, no. 2 (Fall 2007): 104–14.
17. The account of the brothel row and aftermath is drawn from the *St. Louis Post-Dispatch*, July 2, 1884; *St. Louis Republican* and *Baltimore Sun*, July 3, 1884. The *St. Louis Globe-Democrat*, a morning paper, did not report the incident.
18. *St. Louis Globe-Democrat* and *St. Louis Post-Dispatch*, July 3, 1884; *Baltimore Sun*, July 3 and July 5, 1884; *Baltimore American*, July 4, 1884.
19. Barnie knew from the outset that Gardner was troublesome. As a Merritt in 1883 he evinced a drinking problem, and before signing him Barnie had to fork over $800 to get him "out of scrape" in Philadelphia—an assault on Mrs. Bertha Van Tullen. *Philadelphia Times* July 16, 1884; *Baltimore Sun*, June 19, 1884; *St. Louis Post-Dispatch*, July 2, 1884; *St. Louis Globe-Democrat*, July 3 and July 10, 1884; *Baltimore American*, July 5; 1884; *Sporting Life*, July 16, 1884. See also Dennis Thiessen, *Tip O'Neill, and the St. Louis Browns of 1887* (Jefferson NC: McFarland, 2019), 29.
20. *Baltimore American*, July 4 and 5, 1884; *St. Louis Globe-Democrat*, August 9, 1884; *Baltimore Sun*, July 23, 1884; *Philadelphia Times*, July 23, 1884.
21. Hecker, 52-20, led the American Association in games started and completed (73, 72), innings pitched (670.2), wins (52), strikeouts (385), and ERA (1.80).
22. Emslie, Memoir.
23. Technically, the first may have been William Edward White, a member of the Brown University team, who on June 21, 1879, played a game as a substitute first baseman for the Providence Grays of the National League. John R. Husman, "June 21, 1879: The Cameo of William Edward White," Society for American Baseball Research, https://sabr.org/gamesproj/game/june-21-1879-the-cameo-of-william-edward-white. For the Walkers see David Zang, *Fleet Walker's Divided Heart: The Life of Baseball's First Black Major Leaguer* (Lincoln: University of Nebraska Press, 1995).

24. *Baltimore Sun*, June 3 to June 5, 1884.

25. *Baltimore Sun*, October 23 and 24, 1884; *Sporting Life*, October 29, 1884. Smiley, who had played for St. Louis and Baltimore in 1882, started 1883 with the Richmond Virginians of the Union Association. Retrosheet, Baseball Reference, and Baseball Almanac do not list Smiley as a member of the 1883 Virginians, although box scores in the *Baltimore Sun* on May 9 and May 10, 1884, list him as Richmond's second baseman.

26. *Baltimore Sun*, October 22, 1884.

27. *New Orleans Daily Picayune*, October 9, October 23, and November 2, 1884; S. Derby Gisclair, *Early Baseball in New Orleans: A History of 19th Century Play* (Jefferson NC: McFarland, 1911), 99–100, 113–14, 138; Samuel C. Shepherd, Jr. "A Glimmer of Hope: The World's Industrial and Cotton Centennial Exposition, New Orleans, 1884–1885," *Louisiana History* 26, no. 3 (Summer 1885): 271–90.

28. Lawrence N. Powell, *The Accidental City: Improvising New Orleans* (Cambridge MA: Harvard University Press, 2012); Errol Laborde and Peggy Laborde, eds., *New Orleans: The First 300 Years* (Pelican, 2017); Arnold R. Hirsch and Joseph Logsdon, eds., *Creole New Orleans: Race and Americanization* (Baton Rouge: Louisiana State University Press, 1992).

29. *New Orleans Daily Picayune*, December 1 and December 8, 1884.

30. *New Orleans Daily Picayune*, November 14, December 7, and December 12, 1884.

31. *New Orleans Daily Picayune*, December 12, 1884; Emslie, Memoir.

32. *Baltimore American*, April 21, 1885; *Sporting Life*, April 22, 1885.

33. *Baltimore American*, May 29, 1885.

34. *Baltimore American*, June 7, 1885; *Baltimore Sun*, June 23, June 25, and June 26, 1885; *Philadelphia Inquirer*, June 25, 1885; *Philadelphia Times*, June 25, 1885; Emslie, Memoir.

35. *Philadelphia Times*, July 5, 1885; John Shiffert, *Baseball in Philadelphia: A History of the Early Game, 1831–1900* (Jefferson NC: McFarland 2006), 105–12.

36. *Sporting News*, February 1, 1896.

37. Tear of the superior labrum anterior and posterior cartilage where the humerus bone joins the scapula (shoulder blade) to stabilize the shoulder joint.

38. For pitching rules changes see William F. McNeil, *The Evolution of Pitching in Major League Baseball* (Jefferson NC: McFarland, 2006), 119–22.

5. COMEBACK TRAIL

Epigraph is excerpted from Andrew Peters, "I'm A Pitcher," Baseball Almanac, 2004, https://www.baseball-almanac.com/poetry/po_im_a_pitcher.shtml.

1. *Newark Evening News*, August 4 and August 7, 1885; *Baltimore Sun*, August 4, 1885; *Sporting Life*, August 12, 1885.
2. *Rochester Democrat and Chronicle*, September 1, 1885.
3. *Buffalo Commercial Advertiser*, February 19, February 20, February 21, and March 5, 1886; *Sporting Life*, February 3, February 10, February 17, and March 31, 1886. See also Bill O'Neal, *The International League: A Baseball History, 1884–1991* (Austin TX: Eakin, 1992), 6–8.
4. The Toronto Baseball Grounds, nicknamed Sunlight Park after the nearby Sunlight Soap Factory, was a four-story wooden structure with seating for 2,200 fans. Louis Cauz, *Baseball's Back in Town* (Toronto: Controlled Media Corporation, n.d.), 13–17.
5. *Toronto Mail*, September 8, September 9, and September 11, 1886; *Toronto World*, September 16, 1886.
6. *Sporting Life*, September 23, 1886; *Rochester Democrat and Chronicle*, May 9 and 10, 1886; *Toronto Mail*, May 10, 1886; *Toronto Globe*, May 17 and May 31, 1886; *Buffalo Times*, June 1, 1886. The term *mascot* derived from Parisian composer Edmond Audran's 1880 comic opera "La Mascotte" in which a young woman magically brings good fortune to her benefactor. *Mascotte* is French slang for "bewitch," "charm," or "spell."
7. *Syracuse Standard*, July 24, July 27, and July 28, 1886; *Buffalo Times*, July 28, 1886.
8. "De nigger on de fence" was a racist song circa 1863–65. Like "nigger in the woodpile," it referred to something undisclosed that was suspicious or wrong. The derogatory N-word, which was used frequently during the integration of the IA, is retained in this quotation and in the song titles to illustrate the racism of the 1880s and to retain accuracy of the historical material. See Gregory Bond, "Jim Crow at Play: Race, Manliness, and the Color Line in American Sports, 1876–1916," PhD diss., University of Wisconsin, 2008, 74–84; Gail Bederman, *Manliness and Civilization* (Chicago: University of Chicago Press, 1995); Michael Kimmel, *Manhood in America: A Cultural History* (New York: Free Press, 1996). See also James E. Brunson III, *The Early Image of Black Baseball: Race and Representation in the Popular Press, 1871–1890* (Jefferson NC: McFarland, 2009); and "Empire and Pastime: The Objectification of Black Baseball" and "The Politics of Performance: Music, Minstrelsy and Black Baseball" in *Black Baseball, 1858–1900: A Comprehensive Record of the Teams, Players, Managers, Owners and Umpires*, 3 vols. (Jefferson NC: McFarland, 2019), 437–51, 1331–35.
9. *Buffalo Times*, July 15, 1886. Alan W. C. Green, "'Jim Crow,' 'Zip Coon': The Northern Origins of Negro Minstrelsy," *The Massachusetts Review* 11, no. 2 (Spring 1970): 385–97; James Dormon, "Shaping the Popular Image of Post-

Reconstruction American Blacks: The 'Coon Song' Phenomenon of the Gilded Age," *American Quarterly* 59 no. 4 (December 1988): 451–71; Leah Kathleen Cothern, "The Coon Song: A Study of American Music, Entertainment, and Racism" (MA thesis, University of Oregon, 1990).

10. *Toronto Globe*, August 9 to 13, September 7, and September 9, 1886; *Toronto Mail*, August 6 and August 9, 1886; Cauz, *Baseball's Back*, 18.
11. *Toronto Globe* and *Toronto World*, August 16, 1886.
12. *Sporting Life*, October 6, 1886.
13. *Toronto Globe*, August 16, 1886; *Toronto World*, August 16, 1886; *Sporting Life*, October 6, 1886; Marshall D. Wright, *The International League: Year-by-Year Statistics, 1884–1953* (Jefferson NC: McFarland, 1998), 15.
14. *Rochester Democrat and Chronicle*, September 28, October 14, and November 6, 1886; *Toronto World*, November 24, 1886; *Toronto Mail*, February 14 and February 27, 1887; *Sporting Life*, February 23, March 2, and March 16, 1887.
15. Emslie, Memoir.
16. *Rochester Democrat and Chronicle*, September 28, October 14, and November 6, 1886; *Toronto World*, November 24, 1886; *Toronto Mail*, February 14 and February 27, 1886; *Sporting Life*, February 23, March 2, and March 16, 1887; Emslie, Memoir.
17. Emslie, Memoir.
18. *Savannah Morning News*, April 16, April 18, and April 21, 1887; *Nashville Banner*, April 27, 1887.
19. *Savannah Morning News*, April 15, April 16, April 17, and April, 19, 1887. Virtually nothing is known about the team. See Brian Harold Lee, *Baseball in Savannah* (Mount Pleasant SC: Arcadia Publishing, 2012).
20. *Savannah Morning News*, April 15, 1887.
21. *Savannah Morning News* and *Nashville Daily American*, April 25, 1887. On Sabbatarianism see Charlie Bevis, *Sunday Baseball: The Major Leagues' Struggle to Play Baseball on the Lord's Day, 1876–1934* (Jefferson NC: McFarland, 2003).
22. *Nashville Daily American*, April 24 to April 28 and May 15, 1887; *Nashville Banner*, April 25 to April 30 and May 12 to 14, 1887. Bill Traughber, *Nashville Baseball History: From Sulphur Dell to the Sounds* (South Orange NJ: Summer Game Books, 2017), 19–20, mentions the game without detail.
23. *Nashville Daily American*, May 3, 1887; *Savannah Morning News*, May 6, 1887, The only player indicted was Blues catcher Jack Hayes, perhaps because of his reputation as a troublemaker; in April he had been fined $50 and suspended temporarily for being "very unruly." *Nashville Daily American*, April 19, May 18, and May 22, 1887; *Nashville Banner*, May 19 and May 27, 1887.
24. Emslie, Memoir.

25. Marshall D. Wright, *The Southern Association in Baseball, 1885–1961* (Jefferson NC: McFarland 202), 19, 22–23.
26. *Savannah Morning News*, May 28, 1887.
27. *Savannah Morning News*, May 29, 1887.
28. Bill O'Neal, *The Southern League: Baseball in Dixie, 1885–1994* (Austin TX: Eakin Press, 1994),1–7; Lloyd Johnson and Miles Wolff, eds., *Encyclopedia of Minor League Baseball* (Durham NC: Baseball America), 111–12.
29. *New York Sun*, July 28, 1918; *New York Times*, April 27, 1843; *Sporting News*, May 6, 1943.

6. LEARNING TO CALL 'EM

Epigraph from address given by Harry "Steamboat" Johnson at the National Association of Professional Baseball Leagues meeting 1922. Baseball Commissioner Kenesaw Mountain Landis called it "the best exposition ever put together on the profession of umpiring" and requested copy for his files. "Steamboat" Johnson, Standing the Gaff: The Life and Hard Times of a Minor League Umpire (Nashville TN: Parthenon Press, 1935, repr. Lincoln: University of Nebraska Press, 1994), 119–20, and Phoenix Gazette, March 25, 1933.

1. Emslie, Memoir.
2. Emslie, Memoir.
3. Emslie, Memoir; *Stratford (Ontario) Beacon-Herald*, April 26,1943.
4. Emslie, Memoir.
5. Emslie, "Ramblings," 18.
6. In 1888 American Association umpire John Gaffney made "an ingenious breast and stomach protector" of pasteboard sections to wear under his jacket, saying "he was hit so often in the chest and over the heart that he had to take some means to save his life." By 1891 most umpires donned cork chest protectors. New York *Sun*, April 22, 1888.
7. "Look Out He's Loaded," *Wilkes-Barre (PA) Evening Leader*, August 17 and August 21, 1887.
8. *Toronto World*, July 13, 1887.
9. *Wilkes-Barre Morning Leader*, August 21, 1887.
10. *Scranton Republican*, July 22, 1887; *Wilkes-Barre Morning Leader*, August 14, 1887; *Camden Daily Telegram*, August 20, 1887.
11. *Rochester Globe and Democrat*, August 24, 1887.
12. Peter Mancuso, "July 14,1887: Color Line is Drawn—Chicago at Newark," in Bill Felber, ed., *Inventing Baseball: The 100 Greatest Games of the 19th Century* (Tempe AZ: Society for American Baseball Research, 2013), 189–92.

13. *Rochester Democrat and Chronicle*, June 28 and July 15, 1887; *Buffalo Morning Express*, June 15, 1887; *Toronto Globe*, July 16, 1887; Jerry Malloy, "Out At Home: Baseball Draws the Color Line, 1887," *National Pastime: A Review of Baseball History* (Fall 1983): 14–29; Bond, "Jim Crow at Play," 272–76.
14. *Toronto Globe*, September 19 and September 20, 1887; Toronto Daily Mail, September 21, 1887; *Rochester Democrat and Chronicle*, September 21, 1887.
15. Emslie, Memoir.
16. Emslie, Memoir; *Buffalo Times*, August 1, 1887; *Buffalo Morning Express*, December 23, 1888.
17. *Rochester Democrat and Chronicle*, April 19, 1888.
18. *Rochester Democrat and Chronicle*, May 12, 1888; *St. Louis Globe-Democrat*, November 27, 1888; *Buffalo Courier*, December 1, 1888; *Spalding Guide* (1889), 112.
19. *Buffalo Morning Express*, May 13, 1888; *Rochester Democrat and Chronicle*, June 9, and July 10, 1888.
20. *Sporting Life*, August 8, 1888; *Buffalo Evening News*, July 2, August 8 and August 15, 1888.
21. *Sporting Life*, June 13, 1888; *Rochester Democrat and Chronicle*, May 9, 1888; *Sporting Life*, May 16, 1888 *Buffalo Evening News*, July 5, 1888.
22. *Buffalo Evening News*, May 12, 1888; *Buffalo Morning Express*, May 13, July 3, August 20, and September 16, 1888; *Buffalo Courier*, July 28 and August 19, 1888.
23. *Buffalo Morning Express*, November 20, 1887 and January 22, 1888.
24. *Buffalo Courier*, August 1 and August 3, 1888; *Rochester Democrat and Chronicle*, July 31 and August 3, 1888; *Sporting Life*, August 8, 1888.
25. *Rochester Democrat and Chronicle*, August 5, August 12, August 19, and August 22, 1888.
26. *Rochester Democrat and Chronicle*, June 25, 1888.
27. *Rochester Democrat and Chronicle*, June 27, July 20, August 9, September 9, and September 10, 1888.
28. *St. Thomas Times*, January 10, 1889.
29. *Hamilton Spectator*, April 19, 1889; *Toronto World*, April 22, 1889; Bond, "Jim Crow at Play," 272–76.
30. *Rochester Democrat and Chronicle*, June 2 and July 28, 1889; *Sporting Life*, July 3 and July 24, 1889.
31. *Rochester Democrat and Chronicle*, May 23, 1889; *Detroit Free Press*, May 24, 1889.
32. *Buffalo Commercial Advertiser*, August 28, 1889; *Buffalo Courier*, August 16, 1889; *Rochester Democrat and Chronicle*, May 15, June 9, and August 15, 1889; *Detroit Free Press*, July 7, 1889.

33. *Detroit Free Press*, August 22, 1889.
34. *Detroit Free Press*, August 14, 1889.
35. *Detroit Free Press*, September 22 and September 24, 1889; *Rochester Democrat and Chronicle*, August 25, 1889.
36. *Buffalo Commercial Advertiser*, November 13, 1889.
37. *Buffalo Commercial Advertiser*, November 13, 1889.

7. REACHING THE MAJORS

1. *Brooklyn Daily Eagle*, July 15, 1890. When two crews showed up at Eastern Park, Bob Ferguson umpired home plate in the first inning with Lon Knight at first, Charley Jones at second, and Bill Holbert at third; thereafter the umpires rotated positions each inning.
2. Robert B. Ross, *The Great Baseball Revolt: The Rise and Fall of the 1890 Players League* (Lincoln: University of Nebraska Press, 2016); Ed Koszarek, *The Players League: History, Clubs, Ballplayers and Statistics*. (Jefferson NC: McFarland, 2006); Daniel M. Pearson, *Baseball in 1889: Players vs. Owners* (Bowling Green OH: Popular Press, 1993).
3. *Louisville Courier-Journal* January 26, 1890; *Reach's Official American Association Base Ball Guide 1890* (Philadelphia: A. J. Reach, 1890), 124; Emslie, Memoir.
4. *Louisville Courier-Journal* January 24, February 10, February 11, and February 14, 1890; *Rochester Democrat and Chronicle*, January 7 and February 9, 1890.
5. *Louisville Courier-Journal*, January 26 and February 11, 1890.
6. *London Advertiser*, March 10 and March 12, 1890; *Guelph Mercury*, March 8, March 10, and March 11, 1890; *Guelph Herald*, March 11, 1890. *Bronchitis* was often used as a generic term for respiratory illness marked by coughing spells. It is likely she suffered from bronchiectasis, which could cause cardiac failure or consumption (tuberculosis) as reported in the *Guelph Mercury*, March 11, 1886. Respiratory illness, common among her sons, may have been genetic.
7. *Buffalo Courier*, *Brooklyn Daily Eagle*, *Philadelphia Inquirer* and *Rochester Democrat and Chronicle*, January 7 and March 12, 1890; *Louisville Courier-Journal*, January 19, 1890. Like the NL, the AA experimented a bit with the double-umpire system, thirty-two games pairing a regular umpire with a newcomer.
8. Londoners Tom Gillean umpired twenty-nine games in 1879 and two in 1880, Billy Reid, six in 1882. Subsequently five other native-born Canadians were appointed regular staff: Fred McCrum, (1892), Jim McKean (1971–2001), Paul Runge (1973–97), Ian Lamplugh (1999–2002), and Stuart "Stu" Scheurwater (2014–24).
9. *St. Louis Globe-Democrat*, April 22, 1890; *Louisville Courier-Journal*, June 23, 1890; *Ohio State Journal*, September 7, 1890; *Spalding Guide* (1891), 26–30.

10. *Louisville Courier-Journal* January 28, 1890; *Ohio State Journal*, June 7, 1890; *St. Louis Globe-Democrat*, July 9 and 14, 1890; *Louisville Courier-Journal*, July 9, 1890.
11. *St. Louis Globe-Democrat*, July 11 and October 8, 1890.
12. *Ohio State Journal*, September 4, September 12, and September 13, 1890; *Rochester Democrat and Chronicle*, May 16, 1890. Jennifer Mooney, *Irish Stereotypes in Vaudeville, 1865–1905* (New York: Palgrave Macmillan, 2015) and *Flora Moore's Irish Songster* (New York: Popular Publishing, 1880).
13. *St. Louis Globe-Democrat*, August 15, 1890; *St. Louis Post-Dispatch*, August 15, 1890.
14. *St. Louis Globe-Democrat*, August 17, 1890; *St. Louis Post-Dispatch*, August 17, 1890; *Philadelphia Times*, August 18, 1890; *Philadelphia Inquirer*, August 18, 1890.
15. *St. Louis Globe-Democrat*, August 18, 1890; *St. Louis Post-Dispatch*, August 18, 1890; *Philadelphia Inquirer*, August 18, 1890.
16. *Louisville Courier-Journal*, July 9, 1890.
17. *St. Louis Globe-Democrat*, *St. Louis Post-Dispatch*, and *Philadelphia Times*, July 14, 1890.
18. *Rochester Democrat and Chronicle*, May 16 and August 4, 1890; *St. Louis Globe-Democrat*, August 3, 1890.
19. *Baltimore Sun*, August 28 and September 1, 1890; *St. Louis Globe-Democrat*, July 14 and August 28, 1890.
20. *Baltimore Sun*, September 1, 1890.
21. *Ohio State Journal*, *Philadelphia Times*, and *Philadelphia Inquirer*, June 2, 1890.
22. *St. Louis Globe-Democrat*, September 17 and September 18, 1890; *Ohio State Journal*, September 18, 1890.
23. Bob lived in London. *Ohio State Journal*, September 20 to 22, 1890; *Baltimore Sun*, September 20, 1890.
24. *Sporting Life*, February 5 and February 12, 1890; *St. Louis Globe-Democrat*, July 14, 1890; Louisville *Courier-Journal*, September 21, 1890.
25. The three New England teams were the Lebanon Cedars, New Haven Nutmegs, and Providence Clamdiggers. The other five were Albany, Buffalo, Rochester, Syracuse, and Troy.

8. TO THE BUSHES AND BACK

1. The Sioux City team was sometimes written as "Cornhuskers," as it would be later for University of Nebraska sports teams, but the *Sioux City Journal* spelled it with two words.
2. *Kansas City Times*, April 15, 1891; *Sporting Life*, August 22, 1891. On the con-

fusion between the Western Association and the contemporaneous Western League see the SABR *Minor League Newsletter*, June 2002. For the league history see Bill Bryson and Leighton Housh, eds., *Through the Years with the Western League since 1885* (n.p., The Western League, 1951); for the experience of a WA city see Stew Thornley, *On to Nicollet: The Glory and Fame of the Minneapolis Millers* (Minneapolis MN: Nodin, 1988), and Dennis Pajot, *The Rise of Milwaukee Baseball: The Cream City from Midwestern Outpost to the Major Leagues, 1859–1901* (Jefferson NC: McFarland, 2009).

3. *Nebraska State Journal* (Lincoln), March 3, 1891; *Kansas City Star*, March 3, March 9, March 21, and April 7, 1891.
4. *Kansas City Times*, April 15, 1891; *Sporting News*, April 25, 1891.
5. *Kansas City Star*, April 14, 1891; *Nebraska State Journal*, April 16. 1891.
6. *Lincoln Daily Call*, April 17, 1891; *Nebraska State Journal*, April 16 to 18, April 20 to 21, and April 24, 1891.
7. San Francisco, with 298,997 residents, was the largest Western city and the eighth largest in the country. The next-largest Western city was Los Angeles, number fifty-seven, with a population of 50,395.
8. *Sioux City Journal*, May 6, May 8, and May 12, 1891.
9. *Guelph Mercury*, May 16 and May 18, 1891; *London Advertiser*, May 19, 1891. Several WA newspapers noted Alexander's death, including *Rocky Mountain News*, May 16, 1891; *Chicago Tribune*, May 25, 1891; *St. Paul Daily Globe*, June 1, 1891.
10. *Sporting Life*, October 20, 1906.
11. *Sioux City Journal*, June 8, July 16, and July 17, 1891; *Nebraska State Journal*, July 17, 1891.
12. *Sioux City Journal*, May 12 and June 10, 1891; *Kansas City Star*, June 3, 1891; *St. Paul Globe*, July 22, 1891.
13. *Rocky Mountain News*, May 1, 1891; *Sioux City Journal*, June 5, June 8, June 10, June 11, June 13, and July 12, 1891; *Nebraska State Journal*, August 10, 1891.
14. *Sioux City Journal*, May 8, 1891; *Rocky Mountain News*, June 22 and July 25, 1891; *Nebraska State Journal*, July 31, 1891; *Minneapolis Tribune*, July 5, 1891.
15. *Sporting Life*, August 15, 1891.
16. *Sioux City Journal*, August 15, 1891; *Sporting Life*, August 22, 1891; Emslie, Memoir.
17. *Cincinnati Enquirer*, August 20, 1891.
18. *Cincinnati Enquirer*, August 24, 1891.
19. Umpire Rule 55 provided for the game to be called "in case rain falls so heavily that the spectators are compelled by the severity of the storm, to seek shelter. In which case he shall note the time of suspension, and should such rain con-

tinue to fall thirty minutes thereafter, he shall terminate the game." The rule emphasized play should be suspended when spectators had to find cover, not for "an ordinary drizzle or a slight shower." *Spalding Guide* (1891), 205.

20. *Boston Globe*, September 25, 1891.
21. *Chicago Tribune*, August 28, 1891; *Inter Ocean*, August 29, 1891.
22. *Cincinnati Enquirer*, *Chicago Tribune*, and *Inter Ocean*, September 22, 1891; *Sporting News*, September 26, 1891; *Sporting Life*, October 3, 1891.

9. THE NOT-SO-GAY NINETIES

Epigraph by C. P. McDonald, Chicago Tribune, April 24, 1910, reprinted in David W. Anderson, "Deadball Era Umpires: What They Did for Baseball," in Gerlach and Nowlin, SABR *Book of Umpires, 409.*

1. *Sporting Life*, January 23, February 27, 1892. Charles C. Alexander, *Turbulent Seasons: Baseball in 1890–1891* (Dallas: Southern Methodist University Press, 2011), ix, and Rich Eldred, "Umpiring in the 1890s," in Mark Alvarez, ed., *The Perfect Game* (Dallas: Taylor, 1993), 226–33. There were 154 games in 1892, 132 from 1893 to 1897, 154 in 1898–99, and 140 in 1900. For annual schedules see Ronald G. Liebman, "Schedule Changes Since 1876," SABR Research Journals Archive, http://research.sabr.org/journals/schedule-changes-since-1876.
2. *Sporting Life*, April 2 and May 7, 1892; *Louisville Courier-Journal*, April 13, 1892; *Cincinnati Enquirer*, April 23 and 25, 1892.
3. *Cincinnati Enquirer*, April 23 and April 25, 1892; *Boston Globe*, June 12 and August 2, 1892.
4. *Sporting Life*, October 29 and November 5, 1892.
5. William Chase Temple, former president and part owner of the Pittsburg Pirates, initiated the playoffs between the teams that had finished first and second during the regular season, and donated the $800, thirty-inch-high silver Temple Cup to be awarded to the winner. See Jerry Lansche, *The Forgotten Championships: Postseason Baseball, 1882–1981* (Jefferson NC: McFarland, 1989), 49–61.
6. *Inter Ocean*, October 9, 1986.
7. 1897 *Boston Herald*, Emslie scrapbook, Elgin County Museum; *Baltimore Sun*, October 2, 1897.
8. *New York Clipper*, September 19, 1896; *Sporting Life*, January 25, 1896.
9. *Sporting Life*, September 16, 1893.
10. Pete Sheridan, St. Thomas historian, to Larry Gerlach, email, March 15, 2022. Pete may be right, as her family was working class, her father a railroad worker.
11. *Sporting News*, January 4, 1923; Seymour, *Early Years*, 289.
12. *Brooklyn Eagle*, July 26, 1890.

13. *Sporting Life*, October 28, 1893; Seymour, *Early Years*, 290; Fred Lieb, *The Baltimore Orioles* (New York: Putnam's, 1955), 90; *Brooklyn Daily Eagle*, April 21, 1898; Nemec, *Encyclopedia of 19th-Century*, 580.
14. *Atchison Daily Globe*, August 18, 1894; *Brooklyn Daily Eagle*, February 28, 1899.
15. *Washington Evening Star*, March 26, 1896; *Boston Globe*, March 27, 1896; *St. Louis Globe-Democrat*, May 17, 1892; *Sporting Life*, May 23, 1892.
16. *Boston Globe*, June 27, 1893; *Sporting Life*, April 15, 1899 and September 12, 1896.
17. *Washington Evening Star*, June 4, 1897 and March 26, 1896; *Boston Globe*, March 27, 1896.
18. Among them were James "Pud" Galvin; Hardie Henderson, Emslie's Orioles pitching partner; Tim Keefe; Jim McDonald; Jeremiah Murray; "Orator Jim" O'Rourke; Charles "Pop" Snyder; and George "Stump" Weidman.
19. *Chicago Chronicle*, July 14, 1895; *Boston Post*, April 4, 1896; *Sporting Life*, December 5, 1896; *Sporting News*, May 21, 1898.
20. *Chicago Chronicle* and *Inter Ocean*, July 8, 1895. O'Day, home in Chicago, was summoned to substitute for Ed Andrews, who had been injured by a foul ball, not because Lynch's train had been delayed. Addie Joss's recollection in the *Pittsburgh Press*, January 7, 1910, is incorrect. See Bingham, "Hank O'Day," note 25.
21. Sullivan, *Early Innings*, 219.
22. 1894 clipping, Emslie scrapbook; *St. Louis Post-Dispatch*, May 14, and July 25, 1895.
23. 1897 *Boston Herald*, Emslie scrapbook.
24. *Boston Globe*, August 22, 1893; *Pittsburgh Post*, September 15, 1893; *Baltimore Sun*, September 25 to September 28, 1897; *Boston Globe*, October 1,1897.
25. *New York Times*, July 4 and July 5, 1895; *Baltimore Sun*, July 4 and July 5, 1895; *St. Louis Post-Dispatch*, July 10, 1895.
26. Related by Guy M. Smith, "He Could Catch Anything," typescript in McGuire's Hall of Fame file, reprinted in John Thorn and David Reuther, eds., *The Complete Armchair Book of Baseball* (New York: Galahad Books, 1997), 769; also retold in Bruce Anderson, "A Former Foundry Worker Forged a Record by Playing for 26 Seasons," *Sports Illustrated*, August 13, 1984. No such incident occurred in any Washington games Emslie umpired in 1898. On August 20, 1901, McGuire did incur "a finger split" on a Donovan pitch in the first game of a doubleheader in Philadelphia. Emslie, suffering from heat exhaustion, did not "feel physically able" to umpire the second game, so was replaced by McGuire and the Phillies' Al Orth. Donovan and McGuire were then playing for Brooklyn and newspapers did not mention Emslie fainting.

27. *Cincinnati Enquirer*, August 16 and August 17, 1900. The condition, often stress-related, results from pressure of the blood vessel on the trigeminal nerve located at the base of the brain.
28. As told by John Heydler, *Cincinnati Enquirer*, January 7, 1933, and *Camden Courier-Post*, January 6, 1934, the latter with a cartoon illustration.
29. *Washington Evening Star*, June 26, 1895.
30. *New York Times*, September 30, 1892; *Boston Globe*, July 21, 1899; *Philadelphia Inquirer*, August 17, 1900.
31. *Inter Ocean*, September 2, 1892; *Chicago Tribune*, September 17, 1896; *St. Louis Post-Dispatch*, August 8, 1900; *Pittsburgh Commercial Gazette*, October 10, 1900, and May 24, 1894; *New York Times*, September 30, 1892; *Boston Globe*, July 21, 1899; *Philadelphia Inquirer*, August 17, 1900; *St. Louis Globe-Democrat*, May 16 and July 25, 1892; *St. Louis Post-Dispatch*, July 25, 1892.
32. *Sporting Life*, October 24, 1896.
33. *Boston Globe*, September 1, 1895; *Washington Evening Star*, June 23, 1897; *Brooklyn Citizen*, May 7, 1900; *St. Louis Globe-Democrat*, July 25, 1896; *St. Louis Post-Dispatch*, July 25, 1896; *Baltimore Sun*, July 25, 1896; *Cincinnati Enquirer*, July 25, 1896; *Brooklyn Times*, September 8, 1899; *New York Tribune*, September 8, 1899.
34. *Washington Times*, June 20, 1897; *Washington Evening Star*, June 21, 1897.
35. *Sporting Life*, September 16, 1893; *Sporting News*, May 2, 1896; *Cincinnati Enquirer*, May 10, 1896; *Cleveland Leader*, September 16, 1896; *Washington Times*, June 20, 1897; *Washington Evening Star*, June 21, 1897.
36. *Atchison Daily Globe*, August 18, 1894, and January 25, 1896; *Philadelphia Times*, June 29, 1897; *Cincinnati Enquirer*, May 10, 1896; *Sporting Life*, July 20, 1895, and June 9, 1900.
37. *Atchison Daily Globe*, August 18, 1894; *Sporting Life*, January 25, 1896.
38. *Sporting Life*, January 2, 1896; *Dayton (OH) Herald*, January 29, 1896; Undated 1897 *Boston Herald*; Emslie scrapbook.
39. *Louisville Courier-Journal*, May 25, 1899; Brooklyn *Times*, May 25, 1899; *Brooklyn Daily Eagle*, May 25, 1899. The new balk rule provided sending the batter to first and runners advancing a base if the catcher received a pitch outside the catcher's box.
40. *Cincinnati Enquirer*, April 28 and May 2, 1893; *Inter Ocean*, April 28, 1893; *Sporting Life*, May 27 and June 3, 1893.
41. Joe Dittmar, "A Shocking Discovery," *Baseball Research Journal* (Cleveland OH: Society for American Baseball Research, 1991), 52–53.
42. Unidentified newspaper, Emslie scrapbook.

43. *Sporting Life*, July 23, 1892 and September 16, 1893; *New York Clipper*, September 19, 1896.
44. *Sporting Life*, April 2, 1892 and October 28, 1893; *Spalding Guide* (1894), 106–7; William J. Klem and William J. Slocum, "I Never Missed One in My Heart," *Collier's* (March 31, 1951): 61.
45. *Sporting Life*, April 15,1899; *St. Louis Post-Dispatch*, July 25, 1896; Undated 1897 *Boston Herald*; Emslie scrapbook.
46. *St. Louis Globe Democrat*, April 1, 1897; *Sporting Life*, July 6, 1895; *St. Louis Post-Dispatch*, July 6, 1895; *Washington Evening Star*, July 6, 1895.
47. "A Story and Interview of Louis Sockalexis," *Did the Tribe Win Last Night?* (blog), April 2014.
48. *Chicago Chronicle*, August 9, 1896; *Sporting Life*, November 18, 1893; *Washington Evening Star*, March 26, 1896.
49. *Brooklyn Citizen*, August 8, 1894; *St. Louis Post-Dispatch*, May 18, 1895; *Chicago Tribune*, July 28, 1896; *St. Louis Globe-Democrat*, May 21, 1906.
50. *Sporting Life*, September 26, 1896.
51. *Spalding Guide* (1896), 170; *Spalding Guide* (1899), 176. Years later, Clark Griffith erroneously claimed he was the one who had taken the field in a bathrobe. *New York Times*, April 20, 1940.
52. *New York Tribune*, June 16, 1894; *New York Sun*, June 16, 1894; *New York World*, June 16, 1894.
53. Nervous stress, a common affliction for umpires, may have exacerbated the condition. Lynch and Heydler acknowledged having frequent nightmares about their umpiring days, Silk O'Loughlin was "a bundle of nerves," and Bill Klem experienced a skin condition related to nerves.
54. *Cincinnati Enquirer*, May 10, 1896; *Boston Globe*, March 21, 1897; *Baltimore Sun*, July 30, 1897; *Washington Evening Star*, July 30, 1897; Eddie Mitchell, *Baseball Rowdies of the 19th Century* (Jefferson NC: McFarland, 2018), 160.
55. For a survey of the more than three thousand instances of violence, see Larry R. Gerlach, "'Batter Ump'—Basebrawls" in Gerlach and Nowlin, SABR *Book of Umpires*, 388–94.
56. The following account of the incident is drawn from the extensive but varying accounts of the incident in the *Brooklyn Daily Eagle*, *Brooklyn Citizen*, *Brooklyn Times*, *New York Times*, *New York Tribune*, *New York Sun*, *New York World*, and *Boston Globe*, September 8 and 9, 1899; *Sporting News*, September 9; 1899; *Sporting Life*, September 16, 1899.
57. Undated article, Emslie scrapbook, and *Windsor (Ontario) Border Citizens Star*, April 27, 1943. Joe Corbett pitched in the NL in four seasons. Emslie called

twelve games Joe pitched, four Temple Cup games in 1896 and 1897 along with eight regular-season games in 1897 and three in 1904.

58. *Brooklyn Times*, September 8, 1899; *New York Tribune*, September 8, 1899.
59. *Brooklyn Daily Eagle*, September 8, 1899.
60. *Brooklyn Daily Eagle*, September 8, 1899.

10. STANDING THE GAFF

Epigraph from Grantland Rice, Base-Ball Ballads (Nashville: Tennesseean, 1910), 114.

1. *Base Ball Guide and Official League Book for 1895* (New York: American Sports, 1895), 119–20; *Spalding Guide* (1894), 106–7.
2. *Boston Globe*, August 15,1894; Mitchell, *Baseball Rowdies*, 160; *Sporting Life*, June 10, 1893.
3. *Sporting News*, August 24, 1895; *Spalding Guide* (1896), 19.
4. He ejected three in 1894, four in 1895, six in 1896, eight in 1897, six in 1898, three in 1899, and five in 1900. I have found nine more ejections than the twenty-six recorded in Retrosheet.
5. 1891 *Spalding Guide* (1891), 67; *Sporting Life*, November 21, 1896; *Boston Globe*, June 28, 1896; *Cincinnati Enquirer*, August 9, 1896; *St. Louis Globe-Democrat*, January 26, 1897; *Sporting Life*, January 30, 1897.
6. *Sporting News*, December 12, 1896; *Boston Globe*, December 14 and December 20, 1896; *Spalding Guide* (1899), 5.
7. *Boston Globe*, January 15, 1897; *Baltimore Sun*, January 21, 1897; *Sporting Life*, March 6, 1897; *Washington Evening Star*, March 11, 1897; *Cincinnati Enquirer*, March 12, 1897; *Boston Globe*, August 9, 1897.
8. *Boston Globe*, November 15, 1895.
9. *Sporting Life*, December 5, 1896; *Sporting News*, December 15, 1896; *Boston Globe*, February 26 and February 28, 1896; *New York Times*, February 28 and March 1, 1897; *Chicago Tribune*, February 28 and March 1, 1897; *Sporting Life*, August 7, 1897.
10. *Philadelphia Inquirer*, November 14 and November 17, 1897; *Boston Globe*, November 17, 1897; *Sporting Life*, November 20, 1897; *Washington Evening Star*, December 18, 1897.
11. *St. Louis Globe-Democrat* and *St. Louis Post-Dispatch*, March 2, 1896; *Philadelphia Inquirer*, March 2, and March 3, 1898; *Sporting Life*, March 12 and March 25, 1898.
12. *Sporting Life*, April 6, 1898. The other examples cited were "You cock-sucking son of a bitch!" "You prick-eating bastard!" "You cunt-lapping dog!" "A dog must have fucked your mother when she made you!" "I fucked your mother, your sister, your wife!" "I'll make you suck my ass!"

13. *Washington Times*, July 25, 1898; *Sporting Life*, March 12 and April 23, 1898.
14. *Sporting News*, November 5, November 12, and November 19, 1898; *New York Times*, March 3, 1898; *Sporting Life*, March 11, 1898. For a full account of the Brush Resolution see Larry R. Gerlach, "Much Ado About Profanity: The 1898 Brush Resolution," *NINE: A Journal of Baseball History and Culture* 32, no.1 (Fall 2023): 34–47.
15. *Sporting Life*, March 11, 1898; *Sporting News*, March 11, 1898.
16. *New York Sun*, March 19, 1900.
17. Of the umpires who worked more than three thousand games through 2022, ten of the twelve with the highest ejection rates are from the Deadball Era, all but two in the National League. David W. Smith, "Ejections through the Years and the Impact of Expanded Replay," table 5, https://www.retrosheet.org/Research/SmithD/EjectionsThroughTheYears.pdf.
18. *Sporting Life*, October 28, 1893.
19. *Boston Globe*, August 2 and August 15, 1894; *Brooklyn Times*, August 4, 1894; *New York Sun*, August 4, 1894; *Boston Globe*, August 15 and August 16, 1895.
20. *Washington Evening Star*, August 31, 1895; *Spalding Guide* (1896), 19; *Sporting News*, July 6, 1895, and December 12, 1896; *Sporting Life*, May 15, 1897; *Philadelphia Times*, December 25, 1895.
21. *Spalding Guide* (1898), 22–23; *Chicago Chronicle*, August 8, 1897.
22. *Cincinnati Enquirer*, August 5, 1897; *Pittsburgh Commercial Gazette*, August 5, 1897; Bill Felber, *A Game of Brawl: The Orioles, the Beaneaters, and the Battle for the 1897 Pennant* (Lincoln: University of Nebraska Press, 2007), 165–68.
23. *St. Louis Globe-Democrat*, July 21, 1897; *New York Times*, August 22, 1897; *Chicago Tribune*, August 29, 1897.
24. *Boston Globe*, August 8, 1897; *Washington Evening Times*, August 4, 1897.
25. *Sporting News*, December 4, 1897.
26. *Sporting News*, December 11, 1897, and January 1, 1898.
27. *Cincinnati Enquirer*, November 14, 1897; *Sporting News*, January 1, 1898; *St. Louis Globe-Democrat*, March 1 and March 6, 1898; *Boston Globe*, December 12 and December 13, 1898.
28. *Cincinnati Enquirer*, November 14; *Washington Evening Star*, November 20, 1897.
29. *Brooklyn Times*, January 8, 1898; *New York World*, January 9, 1898; *St. Louis Globe-Democrat*, March 3, 1898; *Philadelphia Inquirer*, March 3, 1898; *Sporting News*, May 7, 1898.
30. *Sporting News*, May 21, 1898; *Boston Globe*, October 12, 1899.
31. *Sporting Life*, June 18, 1898; *New York Sun*, July 5, and July 7, 1898; *Washington Times*, July 7, 1898; *Pittsburgh Press*, July 7 and July 8, 1898; *New York Times*, July 10, 1898; *Wilkes-Barre Record*, July 27, 1898.

32. *Brooklyn Daily Eagle*, October 9, 1898; *Boston Globe*, January 8, March 10, and April 16, 1900.
33. *Brooklyn Citizen*, August 28, 1900; *St. Louis Globe-Democrat*, May 15, 1900.
34. *Boston Globe*, March 18, April 16, and May 13, 1900; *Chicago Tribune*, April 19, 1900.
35. *New York Sun*, March 19, 1900; *Chicago Tribune*, March 19, 1900; *Boston Globe*, May 13, 1900.
36. *St. Louis Globe-Democrat*, July 20, 1900.
37. *St. Louis Globe-Democrat*, June 8 and September 27, 1900.
38. According to Irish folklore, two Kilkenny male cats fought so fiercely that they literally destroyed each other, only their tails remaining at the end of the fight.
39. *Cincinnati Enquirer*, July 5 and July 6, 1900; *New York Sun*, July 5, 1900; *New York Times*, July 5, 1900; *Sporting News*, July 7 and July 14, 1900; *Sporting Life*, July 14, 1900.
40. *Sporting News*, July 14 and August 4, 1900; *New York Sun*, July 6, 1900; *Washington Evening Star*, July 6, 1900; *Sporting Life*, July 21, 1900.
41. *New York Sun*, July 6, 1900; *Sporting News*, July 14, 1900; *Brooklyn Citizen*, August 17, 1900.
42. *New York Sun*, July 6, 1900; *Brooklyn Daily Eagle*, July 14, 1900; *Sporting News*, March 28 and August 25, 1900; *Sporting Life*, July 21 and July 25, 1900.
43. *Sporting News*, July 7, July 14, and August 4, 1900; *Boston Globe*, July 8, 1900.
44. *St. Louis Globe-Democrat*, *St. Louis Post-Dispatch*, *Pittsburgh Press*, October 8, 1900.
45. Hurst and Swartwood umpired as Brooklyn won four straight.
46. "Steamboat" Johnson, *Standing the Gaff: The Life and Hard Times of a Minor League Umpire* (Nashville: Parthenon Press, 1935, repr. Lincoln: University of Nebraska Press, 1994).
47. Tommy Connolly was born in Manchester, England, and Jim Johnstone in Ireland, perhaps in Cork, where he died.
48. See Cyril S. Adams, *Live Pigeon Trap Shooting* (Grantham ON: Sporting Library, 2017) and D. H. Eaton, *Trapshooting: The Patriotic Sport*, third ed. (Cincinnati: Sportsmen's Review, 1921).
49. In a trapshooting with pigeons, the birds are held in a box or "trap" sunk into the ground with the top at ground level. When the shooter, standing sixteen to twenty-seven yards behind the trap (depending on skill) calls for the bird, the trap lid springs open and various mechanisms launch the bird, which flies away in erratic directions and elevations. With clay targets, the trap machine oscillates left to right, randomly flinging the disc-shaped targets at various angles down range. With either birds or clay discs the shooter has less than a

second to point, rather than aim, at the target moving speedily and randomly away from him and shoot five times from at each of five stations spaced at intervals along the trap field.

50. *Rod and Gun in Canada* 1, no. 7 (December 1899): 137; *Montreal Gazette*, December 6. 1889; *Sporting Life*, December 9, 1899, and January 27, 1900; *London Advertiser*, December 13, 1900.
51. *London Advertiser*, January 4, 1899.
52. John A. Stevenson, *Curling in Ontario, 1846–1946* (Toronto: Ontario Curling Association, 1950). Excelling in all kinds of throws, the skip throws the final two granite stones (rocks), the last one (hammer) often deciding the result. When not throwing, he usually does not sweep, but instead stands at the end of the sheet behind the house (target) and determines strategy—force and direction—for throwers and sweepers.
53. *Brooklyn Daily Eagle*, April 21, 1898; *New York Sun*, March 19, July 10, July 11, and September 11, 1898; *Philadelphia Inquirer*, January 30, 1898; *Brooklyn Daily Eagle*, February 28, 1899.
54. *Boston Globe*, March 18, 1900; *Sporting Life*, May 26, 1900; *Brooklyn Citizen*, August 6, 1900.

11. DEADBALL VETERAN

Epigraph "This You Should Know" in a 1959 PONY *League pamphlet, courtesy of Lee Lowenfish.*

1. *Atchison (*KS*) Daily Globe*, April 27, 1901; *Pittsburgh Post*, July 14, 1901 and May 22, 1902; *Boston Globe* May 17, 1903; *Baseball Magazine* quoted in the *Evening Record (Windsor* ON*)*, July 27,1908.
2. *St. Louis Republic*, May 3, 1903.
3. "The Rulers of The Game: Some Famous Baseball Umpires and Their Ways," *Harper's Weekly*, July 3, 1909, 14.
4. *St. Louis Republic*, May 3, 1903; *Washington Post*, July 6, 1907; *St. Louis Post-Dispatch*, July 22, 1909; *Sporting Life*, September 21, 1907.
5. *Brooklyn Daily Eagle*, August 30, 1905.
6. *Sporting Life*, May 11, 1901.
7. *New York World*, July 1, 1905; *Philadelphia Press*, July 9, 1902.
8. Billy Evans, "Repartee on the Ball Field," *Washington Evening Star*, November 8, 1908.
9. Evans, "The Fan and the Umpire," *Pearson's Magazine*, July 1911, 50.
10. McGraw, with 121 career ejections, is second to Bobby Cox, with 165. Smith, table 3, https://www.retrosheet.org/Research/SmithD/EjectionsThroughTheYears.pdf.

11. *New York Sun*, May 20, 1903; Lou Hernández, *Manager of Giants: The Tactics, Temper and True Record of John McGraw* (Jefferson NC: McFarland, 2018), 33.
12. *New York Sun*, December 11, 1907; *Brooklyn Daily Eagle*, December 12, 1907. Pulliam reported 112 ejections and 12 suspensions: New York 25; Philadelphia 18; St. Louis 13; Chicago and Cincinnati 12; Brooklyn and Pittsburg 11; and Boston 10.
13. *Cincinnati Enquirer*, August 14, 1904.
14. *New York World*, August 15, 1904; *New York Times*, August 16, 1904; *Cincinnati Enquirer*, August 16, 1904.
15. *St. Louis Republic*, February 6, 1905; *Washington Evening Star*, February 8 and February 16, 1905; *New York Tribune*, February 14, 1905; *New York Times*, February 15 and February 16, 1905.
16. *St. Louis Post-Dispatch*, March 14, 1909; *New York Times*, September 2, 1909; *Inter Ocean*, September 24, 1905; *Mansfield (OH) News*, June 8, 1904; *Brooklyn Standard Union*, May 5, 1910; *Brooklyn Daily Eagle*, May 5, 1910.
17. *New York American* and *New York Sun*, May 22, 1902.
18. *New York Tribune*, May 26, 1908; *New York Times*, May 26; 1908; Allen Sangree, "As the Umpire Sees Them," *Collier's*, September 19, 1908, 23; Patten and McSpadden, *Book of Baseball*, 110.
19. *Washington Post*, July 6, 1907.
20. *Cincinnati Post*, August 16, 1904.
21. *Pittsburgh Press*, July 14 and July 20, 1901; *Pittsburgh Commercial Gazette*, July 15, 1901; *Pittsburgh Post*, July 20, 1901; *Brooklyn Times*, July 20, 1901.
22. *New York World*, May 23, 1907; *Sporting Life*, June 1, 1907.
23. *Brooklyn Daily Eagle*, August 12, 1897.
24. *Boston Globe*, June 29 and June 30, 1901; *Boston Post*, June 29, 1901; *St. Louis Republic*, June 29, 1901. Heatstroke was a serious affliction. AL umpire Jack Sheridan never "fully recovered" from "sunstroke" in August 1914, perhaps contributing to his death shortly after the season on November 2.
25. *Atchison Daily Globe*, April 27, 1901.
26. *Cincinnati Post*, September 23, 1904. In the second game of doubleheaders, Emslie worked two games at first, Hank one at home.
27. *Brooklyn Daily Eagle*, July 9, 1907; *Philadelphia Inquirer*, August 25, 1907; *Chicago Tribune*, September 12 and September 16, 1907; *London Advertiser*, September 18, 1907.
28. *New York Tribune*, May 3, 1908; *Sporting Life*, May 30, 1908.
29. *Sporting Life*, December 15, 1906, and April 13, 1907; *Wilmington (DE) Evening Journal*, March 6, 1907; Mathewson, *Pitching in a Pinch*, 175.

30. *St. Louis Post-Dispatch*, November 26, 1905; *London Advertiser*, December 16, 1905.
31. *New York Sun*, August 26, 1906; *Cincinnati Enquirer*, August 26, 1906. The most extensive account is in the *Wilmington Evening Journal*, March 6, 1907.
32. Mathewson, *Pitching in a Pinch*, 177–78.
33. *Inter Ocean*, April 11, 1902; *Chicago Tribune*, March 23, 1902; *Boston Globe*, January 26, 1902, and July 15, 1901; *Sporting News*, June 15 and June 29, 1901.
34. *Cincinnati Enquirer*, April 20, 1902; *Sporting Life*, April 26, 1902.
35. *Chicago Tribune*, January 27, 1902; *Inter Ocean*, January 28, January 30, and February 1, 1902; *Brooklyn Daily Eagle*, February 2 1902.
36. *Brooklyn Daily Eagle*, February 5, 1902; *Philadelphia Inquirer*, February 5, 1902.
37. *Sporting Life*, March 14,1903; *Spalding Guide* (1904), 266–67.
38. *Sporting Life*, May 30, 1903.
39. *Boston Globe*, July 2, July 5, and July 6, 1905; *New York Tribune*, June 13, July 3, July 6, and July 8, 1905; *Sporting Life*, June 10, 1905; Mark Peavey, *Take Nothing for Granted in Baseball: The Harry Pulliam Story* (Jefferson NC: McFarland, 2018), 183–86.
40. *Spalding Guide* (1907), 118, 127, 136, 138, 142, 146, 148,152.
41. David J. Gordon, "The Rise and Fall of the Deadball Era," *Baseball Research Journal* 47, no, 2 (2018): 92–102; David W. Anderson, *You Can't Beat the Hours: Umpires in the Deadball Era from 1901–1909* (Scotts Valley CA: CreateSpace, 2013); *Wright & Ditson Base Ball Guide* (Boston: Wright & Ditson, 1911), 21–33.
42. Peter Morris, *A Game of Inches* (Chicago: Ivan Dee, 2006), 256, 391–93; Jonathan Fraser Light, *The Cultural Encyclopedia of Baseball*, second ed. (Jefferson NC: McFarland, 2005), 970–71; *Sporting News*, June 15, 1912.
43. *Brooklyn Daily Eagle*, May 15, 1902; *Sporting Life*, November 26, 1904.
44. At the same meeting, Ban Johnson suggested installing scoreboards operated electronically, a la football, to show pitch counts and outs as well as runs. In the American, the installation of electronic scoreboards as planned by Charles Comiskey was left to the preference of individual owners; National owners voted down electronic scoreboards. Newspapers had already installed large scoreboards outside their office buildings that showed game progress to fans gathered outside.
45. *Cincinnati Enquirer*, May 22, 1908; T. H. Murnane, ed., *How to Umpire, How to Captain a Team, How to Manage a Team, How to Coach* (New York: American Sports, 1905), 22–25; Morris, *Game of Inches*, 385–91; Paul Dickson, *The Hidden Language of Baseball: How Signs and Sign-Stealing Have Influenced the Course of Our National Pastime* (New York: Walker, 2019), 33–36. For the myth

of Dummy Hoy being responsible for signals see Bill Deane, *Baseball Myths: Debating, Debunking, and Disproving Tales from the Diamond* (Lanham MD: Scarecrow Press, 2012), 17–21.

46. *Detroit Free Press*, October 14, 1908; *Sporting Life*, October 24, 1908; Emslie, "Ramblings,"18.
47. *Chicago Tribune*, November 17, 1908; *Boston Globe*, December 7, 1908; *Sporting Life*, January 29, 1909; *Cincinnati Enquirer*, April 15, 1909.
48. *Sporting Life* from 1895 to 1916 featured both baseball and trapshooting, and *Baseball Magazine* for several years included articles about the sport. Among the prominent Major Leaguers who took up the sport were Chief Bender, Ty Cobb, Fred Clarke, Gavvy Cravath, Doc Crandall, Joe Jackson, Walter Johnson, Dutch Leonard, Christy Mathewson, Carl Mays, and Tris Speaker. *St. Charles Herald* (Hahnville LA), February 14, 1920.
49. *American Rifleman*, October 24, 1901, 37; *Rod and Gun in Canada* (May 1904): xxii; *Forest and Stream*, January 13, 1906, 71.
50. John Kerr, *Curling in Canada and the United States: A Record of the Tour of the Scottish Team, 1902–3* (Edinburgh: Morton, 1904), 303–12 and Stevenson, *Curling in Ontario*, 100–102.
51. *St. Thomas Evening Journal*, February 18, 1908; *Sporting Life*, February 29, 1908.
52. When New Orleans in 1949 held an appreciation night for legendary Southern League umpire Harry "Steamboat" Johnson, the "Steamer," who always carried an oculist's certificate attesting to his 20–20 eyesight, emerged from the dugout wearing dark glasses, led by a seeing-eye dog and handcuffed to a policeman as the former umpires in attendance booed the fans. *New Orleans Times Picayune*, July 29, 1949.
53. *St. Louis Post-Dispatch*, April 29, 1903. The apple-orange story circulated for years. *Sporting News*, July 22, 1905; Mathewson, *Pitching in a Pinch*, 175; *Brooklyn Daily Eagle*, May 1, 1942.
54. *Cincinnati Post*, July 30, 1906, and July 26, 1907; *Cincinnati Enquirer*, May 15, 1904; *New York Sun*, July 4, 1905; *St. Louis Star*, February 8, 1913; *Sporting Life*, July 14, 1906; *Brooklyn Standard Union*, September 29, 1906; *Pittsburgh Press*, June 3, June 9, June 19, and June 21, 1907.
55. *Inter Ocean*, June 21, 1907; *Washington Post*, July 22, 1907; *Sporting Life*, October 19 and December 21, 1907; *Allentown (PA) Democrat*, December 18, 1913.
56. *Brooklyn Times*, June 12, 1908; *Sporting Life*, July 25, 1908.
57. For views on the game see SABR Deadball Committee newsletter, "The Inside Game," September 23, 1908.
58. The batter-runner touching first base is not a given; "Steamboat" Johnson tells

of the time a batter hit what appeared to be a game-winning triple, only to be put out when he failed to touch first base. *Standing the Gaff*, 44.

59. *Sporting Life*, October 17 and October 24, 1908; William Phelon, "The Opening Broadsides," *Baseball Magazine*, June 1915, 118; *Sporting News*, April 29, 1943; *Chicago Tribune*, September 6, 1908.
60. *Inter Ocean*, July 27, 1909; Kahn, *Umpire Story*, 39.
61. Raymond Schuessler, "You Can't Kill the Umpire," *American Legion Magazine* 102, no. 4, April 1976, 26; "Robert Emslie," Guelph Sports Hall of Fame, https://www.guelphsportshalloffame.com/athletes/robert-emslie; *St. Louis Star*, February 8, 1913.
62. Certainly erroneous were rumors of Emslie and Hurst collaborating on an article titled "Short Cuts to Well-Known Despots" castigating contentious players and managers. *Washington Post*, February 9, 1906.
63. Emslie, "Ramblings," 17–19, reprinted in *Sporting Life*, December 31.
64. *St. Louis Post-Dispatch*, May 20, 1909; *Philadelphia Inquirer*, July 15, 1909; *New York Times*, July 13, 1909.
65. *Atchison Daily Globe*, July 3, 1908, May 7, May 8, and May 28, 1909; *Atchison Daily Champion*, July 3, 1908 May 7, May 8, May 14, and May 28, 1909.
66. *London Advertiser*, December 21, 1909; *Sporting Life*, December 25, 1909.
67. *Sporting Life*, January 1, 1910; *New York Times*, January 18 and January 26, 1910.
68. *New York Times*, April 5, 1910; *Sporting Life*, April 9, 1810; *Washington Post*, April 24, 1910.
69. Kahn, *Umpire Story*, 87, said, "Emslie, getting older and his nerves having been badly shaken, could not stand the strain required in calling balls and strikes and running a ball game as umpire-in-chief from behind the plate." Charlie Grimm's recollection that because Emslie wore a toupee and the plate umpire had to remove his cap so often he "usually demanded a base line station" is nonsense; Jolly Cholly, who reached the National in 1918, never saw Bob behind the plate. *Chicago Tribune*, May 11, 1943.
70. *Mansfield News*, May 23, 1903; *St. Thomas Evening Journal*, September 21, 1905; *Washington Post*, September 23, 1905; *Brooklyn Citizen*, October 15, 1908; *Sporting Life*, January 30, 1909.
71. *New York Times*, *New York Tribune*, and *Brooklyn Daily Eagle*, December 16 and December 17, 1910; *Inter Ocean*, December 18, 1910; *Washington Post*, December 18, 1910; *Boston Globe*, December 21, 1910; *Sporting News*, December 21, 1910; *Sporting Life*, December 24, 1910.
72. *New York Times*, June 30, 1910; *Washington Evening Star*, July 14, July 29, and August 22, 1910; *Chicago Tribune*, June 30 and July 29, 1910; *Washington Post*,

August 21, 1910; *Inter Ocean*, October 25, 1910. See also Stephen V. Rice, "Jack Sheridan," https://sabr.org/bioproj/person/jack-sheridan/.

73. Frank Umont (thirty-nine), who wore glasses on April 24 in Kansas City, is credited as the pioneer, although later Eddie Rommel (fifty-eight) said he wore them on April 18 and Larry Goetz (sixty-one) claimed he did so on April 22 that same year. Bill Francis, "Umpires Break Through Glass Ceiling," https: /baseballhall.or/discover-more/stories/short-stops/umpires-break-throuigh -glass-ceiling.
74. *Washington Evening Star*, December 18, 1910; *Boston Globe*, December 21 and December 22, 1910; *Brooklyn Citizen*, December 23, 1910; *Sporting Life*, December 31, 1910; Brennan, "Confessions of an Umpire," unidentified newspaper dated 1916, Emslie scrapbook; *St. Louis Post-Dispatch*, December 30, 1910.
75. *Sporting News*, December 25, 1910; *Brooklyn Daily Eagle*, January 8, 1911.
76. *Brooklyn Daily Eagle*, December 20, 1910; *Sporting Life*, January 28, 1911.
77. He was five months older than O'Day but senior to Johnson by fifteen years, Klem by seventeen, and Rigler by twenty-five. In the American, Sheridan was forty-eight, Connolly forty, and Silk O'Loughlin thirty-eight. In their last regular season, Ferguson and Snyder were forty-six, Gaffney forty-five, Hurst forty-four, Kelly forty-one, Lynch forty, and Keefe thirty-nine. Billy McLean umpired twenty-two games as a substitute in 1885 at age fifty-two. Life expectancy for males, which in the United States was forty-eight years in 1910 and fifty-one in 1911, was similar in Canada.
78. *Washington Evening Star*, June 4, 1905.
79. *Washington Post*, July 6, 1907; *Boston Globe*, June 3, 1904.
80. *New York Tribune*, July 22, 1915.
81. *Brooklyn Citizen*, September 16 , 1907; *Washington Evening Star*, September 30, 1907.
82. *Sporting Life*, September 28, 1907.
83. A Major League Umpire [Billy Evans], "Call 'Em as You See 'Em," *Saturday Evening Post*, October 15, 1921, 30.
84. *Saturday Evening Post*, October 15, 1921, 30.

12. DEAN OF UMPIRES

Epigraph Shakespeare, Henry IV, Act 4.

1. *Allentown Democrat*, January 19, 1911; *London Advertiser*, January 30, 1911.
2. *London Advertiser*, February 2, 1911; *Washington Evening Star*, February 6, 1911; *St. Louis Star*, February 16, 1911; *Sporting News*, February 25 and August 12, 1911; *Boston Globe*, February 16, 1911.
3. Cormack, vice president of the St. Thomas Medical Association, received his

medical degree from Queen's University, Kingston, Ontario, in 1894. *Journal of the American Medical Association* (January-June 1909): 1191; *Polk's Medical Register and Directory of North America 1910* (Chicago: Polk, 1910), 2037.

4. *St. Thomas City Directory* (1911), 134; *New York Times*, April 2, 1911; *St. Louis Star*, November 30, 1915; *Sporting News*, December 25, 1910.
5. *Washington Post*, April 2, 1911; *New York Times*, April 2, 1911; *Sporting Life*, April 8, 1911.
6. *Sporting News*, August 10, 1939, May 7, 1942, August 4, 1946, and September 2, 1949; *New York Times*, May 15, 1941; *Brooklyn Daily Eagle*, May 1, 1942. Klem also told Parrott a questionable story about Emslie's frugality and insecurity. "I used to get these mileage tickets on the railroads. They'd save you $60 or so over the course of a season—a book of tickets, you know. Well, Emslie was traveling with me and I said, 'Bob, why don't you buy a book of tickets like this?' I'll never forget, he said to a me. 'I might never be around the National League long enough to use 'em up , Bill. You never can tell about your job in this business.'" *Brooklyn Daily Eagle*, May 27, 1938.
7. William J. Klem and William J. Slocum, "I Never Missed One in My Heart," *Collier's Weekly*, March 31, 1951, 31–32, 59–65; "Umpire Bill Klem's Own Story," April 7, 1951, 30–31, 50–52; "Diamond Rhubarbs," April 14, 1951, 30–31, 68–70, and "My Last Big League Game," April 21, 1951, 30–31, 73–74.
8. Mathewson, *Pitching in a Pinch*, 177.
9. *St. Louis Post-Dispatch*, May 7, 1911; *Sporting Life*, August 12, 1911; *St. Louis Star*, August 19, 1911; *Literary Digest*, June 17, 1911, 1216.
10. *New York Times*, February 15, 1911; *Brooklyn Daily Eagle*, July 9, 1911; *Pittsburgh Gazette Times*, July 9, 1911.
11. Retrosheet has Emlie umpiring home plate in the second game, but Philadelphia and St. Louis box scores on August 20 list O'Day behind the plate for both games, as do *Sporting Life* and *Sporting News*.
12. *St. Thomas Evening Journal*, February 12, 1912.
13. *Sporting Life*, October 5, 1912; *Spalding Guide* (1912), 125; *Spalding Guide* (1913), 11, 32, 34; *Official Handbook of the National League of Professional Base Ball Clubs 1913* (New York: American Sports, 1913), 15.
14. *Sporting News*, August 11, 1906; *Sporting News*, May 8 and May 15, 1913; *Chicago Tribune*, May 7, 1913; *New York Times*, May 7, 1913; *Sporting Life*, May 17, 1913; Ronald T. Waldo, *Baseball's Roaring Twenties: A Decade of Legends, Characters, and Diamond Adventures* (Lanham MD: Rowman & Littlefield, 2017), 92–93.
15. *Pittsburgh Post*, October 14, 1913; *Pittsburgh Gazette Times*, October 14, 1913; Eric Sallee, Vean Gregg, SABR biopic.
16. *Baltimore Sun*, June 9, 1885.

17. *Allentown Democrat*, December 18, 1913; *Sporting Life*, December 20, 1913.
18. *Sporting Life*, August 8, 1914; *Brooklyn Times*, July 29, 1916; *Cincinnati Post*, July 24, 1919; *New York Tribune*, June 19, 1914; *New York Sun*, June 19, 1914; F. C. Lane, "Getting the Straight Dope," *Baseball Magazine*, August 1917, 415–19; *Pittsburgh Gazette Times*, January 28, 1924.
19. *Philadelphia Inquirer* July 23, 1916; *Brooklyn Times*, July 29, 1916; *Washington Evening Star*, December 24, 1923; *Boston Globe*, August 17, 1920.
20. Larry R. Gerlach, "Ernie Quigley: An Official for All Seasons" *Kansas History* 33, no. 4 (Winter 2010–11), 232.
21. Retrosheet lists him at the plate on April 17, 1917, but the *Cincinnati Enquirer* specifically mentions him calling a play at first base.
22. *New York Times*, April 9, 1914; *Sporting News*, March 20, 1915; *Sporting Life*, August 8, 1914, and March 20, 1915; *St. Louis Star*, May 13, 1915; *New York Tribune*, July 30, 1918.
23. *New York Tribune*, March 16, 1919.
24. *Honolulu Star-Bulletin*, May 12, 1914.
25. *Washington Post*, July 6, 1914.
26. *New York Times*, July 27, 1919; *Boston Globe*, August 4, 1920; *Boston Globe* and *Boston Post*, April 28, 1916.
27. Undated Pittsburgh newspapers, Emslie scrapbook.
28. *Honolulu Star-Bulletin*, May 12, 1914; *Boston Globe*, February 1, 1917; *St. Louis Republic*, March 20, 1904; *New York Times*, June 12, 1918; Mathewson, *Pitching in a Pinch*, 175.
29. Brennan, "Confessions of an Umpire," unidentified 1916 newspaper, Emslie scrapbook; *St. Louis Star*, February 8, 1913; *New York World*, July 10, 1915; *St. Louis Post-Dispatch*, July 13, 1915; *Boston Globe*, January 22, 1916.
30. *New York Tribune*, June 14, 1918; *Pittsburgh Gazette Times*, August 4, 1915; *St. Louis Post-Dispatch*, August 13, 1915; W. R. Hoefer, "Cutting the Corners," *Baseball Magazine*, October 1916, 72; *St. Louis Star*, July 24 , 1914; *Sporting Life*, November 7, 1914.
31. *Ottawa Journal*, July 19, 1916; *New York Times*, August 30, 1919; *Brooklyn Times*, August 30, 1919; *New York Times*, August 9, 1920.
32. *Calgary (AL) Herald*, May 6, 1910; Ronald T. Waldo, https://www.facebook.com/.../photos/...story...umpiring.../1083320721833841/
33. *Mansfield News*, October 23, 1914.
34. *Mansfield News*, October 23, 1914; *St. Louis Post-Dispatch*, July 19, 1916.
35. *New York Sun*, July 15, 1912; *St. Louis Star*, May 4, 1916; *St. Louis Post-Dispatch*, May 15, 1916; *St. Louis Star*, February 8, 1913; Mathewson, *Pitching in a Pinch*,

176; *Pittsburgh Gazette Times*, January 28, 1924; *Winnipeg (Manitoba) Free Press*, December 9, 1911; *Los Angeles Herald*, August 14, 1916.

36. *Wilmington Evening Journal*, September 21, 1904; *Dayton Daily News*, October 20, 1904; unidentified clipping, October 14, 1904, Emslie scrapbook; *Boston Globe*, June 14, 1904.
37. *Honolulu Star-Bulletin*, May 12, 1914; *Washington Post*, December 26, 1909.
38. *Boston Globe*, January 22, 1916; *Wilmington Evening Journal*, April 6, 1916; *Philadelphia Inquirer*, July 23 1916; *Port Huron Times Herald*, October 11, 1916; *Sporting Life*, August 19, 1916. The information was not always correct. The basis for many reports, columns by Seattle's R. W. Kent in the *Honolulu Star-Bulletin*, May 12, 1914, and Charles Chester in *Sporting Life*, February 26, 1916, incorrectly say Emslie's birth date was January 21, 1861, and his playing career ended pitching for Memphis in 1887.
39. *New York Times*, August 10 and August 13, 1916; *New York Tribune*, August 10 and August 13, 1916; *Brooklyn Daily Eagle*, August 13, 1916; *Times and Star* (St. John NB), August 16, 1916; *Sporting News*, August 17, 1916.
40. Letter from John A. Crawford, August 11, 1916, Emslie scrapbook.
41. *Boston Globe*, August 14, 1916; Grantland Rice, *Songs of the Stalwart* (New York: Appleton, 1917), 152–53.
42. *Boston Globe*, January 22, 1916; *Philadelphia Inquirer*, July 23, 1916; *Brooklyn Times*, July 29, 1916. Umpires who worked the World Series received $400, increased to $500 in 1910. Bill Klem demanded and received $650 in 1917; the next year Klem received $1,000 for the Fall Classic. Beginning in 1921 the four umpires divided a sum equal to one winning and one losing player's share instead of a flat fee of $1,000. Kahn, *Umpire Story*, 120–21; *Boston Globe*, January 13, 1921; *Chicago Tribune*, January 14, 1921.
43. Brian Douglas Tennyson, *Canada's Great War, 1914–1918: How Canada Helped Save the British Empire and Became a North American Nation* (Lanham MD: Rowan and Littlefield, 2015); Barbara M. Wilson, ed., *Ontario and the First World War, 1914–1918* (Toronto: Champlain Society and the University of Toronto Press, 1977); Edward Butts, *Wartime: The First World War in a Canadian Town* (Toronto: Lorimer, 2017).
44. For baseball's response to subsequent epidemics, see Emma Baccellieri, "Masks, Fundraisers and Smallpox-Only Teams: How Baseball Has Dealt with Infectious Diseases Before," *Sports Illustrated*, March 9, 1920, and Bill Nowlin, "Major-League Umpiring during the Pandemic of 2020," Baseball Prospectus, April 8, 2021, https://www.baseballprospectus.com/news/article/66026/major-league-umpiring-during-the-pandemic-of-2020/.

45. *New York Times*, August 7 and December 11, 1918; Stephen V. Rice, "John Heydler," SABR biopic.
46. Prior to "The Star-Spangled Banner" becoming the official U.S. national anthem in 1931, "My Country, 'Tis of Thee" was the de facto national anthem with "America the Beautiful" and "Hail Columbia" also frequently sung at public events.
47. Randy Roberts and Johnny Smith, *War Fever: Boston, Baseball, and America in the Shadow of the Great War* (New York: Basic Books, 2020); Skip Desjardin, *September 1918: War, Plague, and the World Series* (Washington DC: Regnery, 2018); Marc Ferris, *Star-Spangled Banner: The Unlikely Story of America's National Anthem* (Baltimore: Johns Hopkins University Press, 2014).
48. Bill Francis, "1918 Pandemic Did Not Spare Baseball," National Baseball Hall of Fame, baseballhall.org/discover/1918-flu-pandemic-didnt-spare-baseball.
49. In Canada there were about 55,000 deaths in a population of 8.7 million. Mark Osborne Humphries, *The Last Plague: Spanish Influenza and the Politics of Public Health in Canada* (Toronto: University of Toronto Press, 2013).
50. *St. Louis Post-Dispatch*, January 9, 1919; *Popular Mechanics*, May 1919: 730.
51. *Chicago Eagle*, April 26, 1919; unidentified 1919 Lieb column, Emslie scrapbook.
52. The fastest professional baseball game occurred on August 30, 1916 in Asheville, North Carolina, when the Class D Winston-Salem Twins beat the hometown Tourists 3–1 in 31 minutes. Wynn Montgomery, "Quicker than Quick: A 31-Minute Professional Game," *Baseball Research Journal* 40. no. 2 (Fall 2011): 104–6.
53. *Saskatoon (SA) Daily Star*, March 29, and *Border Citizens Star* (Windsor ON), August 19, 1920.
54. Gene Carney, *Burying the Black Sox: How Baseball's Cover-Up of the 1919 World Series Fix Almost Succeeded* (Washington DC: Potomac Books, 2007), 25.
55. *Wilmington Evening Journal*, April 6, 1916; *Port Huron (MI) Times Herald*, October 11, 1916; undated St. Thomas newspaper, Emslie scrapbook.
56. *London Advertiser*, February 2 and December 2, 1911; *Winnipeg Free Press*, December 9, 1911; *Sporting Life*, January 20 and February 24, 1912; *St. Thomas Journal*, February 12, 1912; *Toronto World*, December 4, 1915; *Brooklyn Citizen*, November 26, 1916; *Day Book* (Chicago), November 26, 1916; *Montreal Gazette*, December 8, 1916; Uy Barnes and William Slaney, "Trap Shooting in Canada: The Growth of the Recreation, Its Past, Present and Future," *Rod and Gun in Canada*, December 13, 1911, 877.
57. Club records for early years are not extant. Darlene Morphy, St. Thomas Gun Club secretary-treasurer, email to Larry Gerlach, March 16, 1920.
58. Ed Banks, "Sidelights on the Traps and Shooters," *Baseball Magazine*, June 1920: 354–56.

59. *Buffalo Morning Express*, January 31, 1913; *Wilmington Evening Journal*, April 6, 1916.
60. *Boston Globe*, September 5, 1915.
61. Cameron McWhirter, *Red Summer: The Summer of 1919 and the Awakening of Black America* (New York: St. Martin's Press, 2011) and Jan Voogd, *Race Riots and Resistance: The Red Summer of 1919* (New York: Peter Lang, 2008).
62. For the United States see Elaine Weiss, *The Woman's Hour: The Great Fight to Win the Vote* (New York: Random House, 2018); for Canada, Catherine L. Cleverdon, *The Woman Suffrage Movement in Canada*, 2nd ed. (Toronto: University of Toronto Press, 1974) and Tarah Brookfield, *Our Voices Must Be Heard: Women and the Vote in Ontario* (Vancouver: University of British Columbia Press, 2018).
63. Daniel Okrent, *Last Call: The Rise and Fall of Prohibition* (New York: Scribner's, 2010); Gerald A. Hallowell, "Prohibition in Ontario, 1919–23," (MA thesis, Carleton University, 1966).
64. Anderson, *You Can't Beat the Hours* and "Deadball Era Umpires: What They Did for Baseball," in Gerlach and Nowlin, *SABR Book of Umpires*, 408–14.
65. *New York Tribune*, March 29, 1919.

13. UMPIRE SUPERVISOR

1. Two decades later Grimm said the wild throw "caught Emslie at the base of the spine, knocking him flat on his face. Although he was suffering great pain, the first thing he did was to grab his toupee, which had been knocked loose, and replace it." Grimm's account, which he erroneously said happened in 1922, is a tall tale at variance with the newspaper reports. *Chicago Tribune*, May 11, 1943.
2. Retrosheet has Emslie behind the plate and Klem at first base on June 17 in Chicago, but the *Chicago Tribune*, June 18, specifically mentions Klem calling pitches.
3. Brennan and Emslie followed the Giants across the river for a single game against the Robins; since Bob Hart and Barry McCormick, en route from Boston to Philadelphia, were in town, Heydler assigned them as well to the battle between the cross-town rivals then in a virtual tie for second place.
4. *Chicago Eagle*, June 25, 1921; David Nemec and Eric Miklich, *Forfeits and Successfully Protested Games in Major League Baseball* (Jefferson NC: McFarland, 2014), 212.
5. *New York World*, December 14, 1922; *Battle Creek (MI) Enquirer*, December 21, 1922. Klem and Evans had been umpiring eighteen and seventeen years, respectively.

6. Bob Hart, Bill Klem, and Paul Sentell were the only ones never on a three-man crew.
7. For a history of Old Timers' games see Keith Spalding Robbins, "Old Timers' Games: A Transformation from Player Benefits Events to Clubs' Historical Celebrations and the Rise of a Baseball Goodwill Communion," *Nine: A Journal of Baseball History and Culture* 25, no. 1–2 (Fall 2016–Spring 2017): 26–47.
8. Evans, "Twenty Years a Big League Umpire," *Liberty*, July 25, 1925, 35. Between 1904 and 1941, Conlon, an New York City photographer, produced at least thirty thousand images, most no longer extant. The iconic picture of Emslie in 1922, used for the *Sporting News* Conlan card collection, was taken either when he umpired two games in New York or ten games in Brooklyn. Neal McCabe and Constance McCabe, *Baseball's Golden Age: The Photographs of Charles M. Conlon* (New York: Harry N. Abrams, 1997) and *The Big Show: Charles M. Conlon's Golden Age Baseball Photographs* (New York: Harry N. Abrams, 2011).
9. *Sporting News*, January 4, 1923.
10. *New York Times*, December 14, 1922; *Sporting News*, December 21, 1922, and January 4, 1923; *Washington Herald*, December 27, 1922.
11. *Chicago Eagle*, June 23, 1917; *Brooklyn Citizen*, June 24, 1917.
12. *Cincinnati Enquirer*, April 4, 1924; *St. Louis Star*, January 9, 1923.
13. *Sporting News*, January 4, 1923.
14. In 1906 Chicago owner Charles Murphy, inspired by numbered football and hockey jerseys, proposed numerals be affixed to the sleeve or back of uniforms, and in 1916 Cleveland briefly experimented with a sleeve number, but it was not until 1929 that the Indians and Yankees regularly wore numbers on their jerseys. Cleveland was the first on opening day, April 16, as New York was rained out.
15. Umpire John McSherry died on April 1, 1996, of a heart attack after calling four pitches on opening day in Cincinnati.
16. *Washington Evening Star*, May 3, 1923; *Sporting News*, January 4 and May 10, 1923. Retrosheet's listing of 4,230 games omits a 1921 game.
17. Bob LeMoine, "Golden Jubilee Game" in Bill Nowlin and Bob Brady, eds., *Braves Field: Memorable Moments at Boston's Lost Diamond* (Phoenix AZ: SABR, 2015), 74–76. Emslie may have been present for jubilee celebrations in Philadelphia on May 18, Brooklyn on May 19, or Chicago on June 9, but certainly not in St. Louis on June 18.
18. *Boston Globe*, April 6, 1924.
19. *Brooklyn Daily Eagle*, March 24, 1924.
20. *Brooklyn Times*, February 4, 1925; *Boston Globe*, February 6, 1925.
21. *Boston Globe*, February 10, 1926; *New York Times*, April 3, 1926.

22. Emslie, Memoir.
23. *New York Times*, April 5, 1925; *Saskatoon Phoenix*, April 8, 1925. Johnstone's Original Full Vision Mask, used by catchers and umpires, would remain largely unchanged until the development of the hockey-style mask in the twenty-first century. David W. Anderson, "Jim Johnstone," sabr.org/bioproj/person/jim-johnstone.
24. *New York Times*, April 2, 1963.
25. O'Day was notoriously reticent about his age. His birth certificate is lost, but census records say he was born on July 9, 1859. Upon his death in 1935, the *Chicago Tribune* said, on July 3, "Authoritative records give the date of his birth as 1861 making him 73 years old"; obituary notices in the paper, submitted by either Edward Rice, a close friend, or his nephew and lone relative, Henry McNamara, also cite 1861. The birth year 1861 on his *Sporting News* umpire card has been crossed off and replaced with July 8, 1862; one might assume the handwritten change is the more accurate as his headstone in Calvary Cemetery, Evanston, Illinois, also reads "born July 8, 1962." See Dennis Bingham, "Hank O'Day," sabr.org/bioproj/person/hank-oday.
26. *Chicago Tribune*, December 15, 1928. A "designated hitter" was suggested as early as 1891. See John Thorn, "The Origins of the Designated Hitter," March 7, 2016, https://ourgame.mlblogs.com/the-origins-of-the-designated-hitter-7608dcc4bbf9.
27. *London (ON) Free Press*, December 3, 1925; *Sporting News*, November 16, 1933; *Border Citizens Star*, August 31, 1933.
28. Pierre Berton, *The Great Depression: 1929–1939* (Toronto: Anchor Canada, 2001); H. Blair Neatby, H. Blair; *The Politics of Chaos: Canada in the Thirties* (Toronto: Macmillan of Canada, 1972).
29. *Toronto Telegram*, undated 1927 issues, Emslie scrapbook; *Border Citizens Star*, January 25, 1927.
30. *Border Citizens Star*, August 22, 1930 and September 30, 1931; *Cincinnati Enquirer*, October 9, 1932; Emslie scrapbook.
31. *Cincinnati Enquirer*, October 9, 1932.
32. Gerlach, "Ernie Quigley," 218–39; Anderson, *You Can't Beat the Hours*, 78; William J. Klem and William J. Slocum, "I Never Missed One in My Heart," *Collier's*, March 31, 1951, 59; *Sporting News*, July 11, 1935; Bingham, "Hank O'Day."
33. *St. Louis Star*, June 24, 1930; *Cincinnati Enquirer*, January 7, 1933; *Brooklyn Daily Eagle*, January 30, 1934; *Sporting News*, February 8, 1934; *Boston Globe*, July 20 and August 1, 1927.
34. His ranked order: Evans, Emslie, O'Day, Klem, and Rigler. *Washington Evening Star*, December 24, 1923. John B. Kennedy, "The Flying Dutchman," *Collier's*,

April 12, 1930, 81; *New York Times*, April 4, 1930; *Brooklyn Times*, April 4, 1930; *St. Louis Globe-Democrat*, May 29, 1927; Harold "Speed" Johnson, comp., *Who's Who in Major League Baseball* (Chicago: Buxton Publishing, 1933), 448–49.

14. LATE INNINGS

Epigraph: With apologies to William Shakespeare for reworking the king's St. Crispin's Day speech given on the eve of the battle of Agincourt, October 25, 1415, Henry V, Act IV, Scene III.

1. Unidentified newspaper article, Emslie scrapbook. Every newspaper mentioning the pension program identified Rigler as the first recipient; none mentioned Emslie.
2. Rigler was an appropriate successor to Emslie, but his tenure was short-lived as he died at age fifty-three on December 21 following an operation in Philadelphia for a brain tumor. The position then went to Ernie Quigley when he retired in 1936.
3. Undated 1943 *St. Thomas Times-Journal* clipping, Emslie scrapbook; Glen Curnoe emails to Larry Gerlach, November 22 and 23, 2019. Kitty, mentioned as a survivor in Bob's obituaries, may have been too ill to attend. She died in January 1987 in Detroit. Jack, who died July 25, 1960, and wife Velma, who died March 11, 1992, are buried in Elmdale Memorial Park, St. Thomas. After Jack's death Velma married William Victor Parsons on July 20, 1970; she died in St. Thomas on March 11, 1992.
4. Using a hand-size hard rubber ball, the bowler has three attempts in each of ten frames to knock over five pins, three-quarter the size of regular tenpins, arranged in a triangle at the bottom of the bowling lane.
5. *St. Thomas Times-Journal*, April 27, 1843.
6. *Sporting News*, October 9, 1941. The other members: Yankee president Ed Barrow, former NL president John Heydler, Senators owner Clark Griffith, A's owner-manager Connie Mack, and Braves president Bob Quinn.
7. Founded in 1919 the Intercounty League, composed of teams in Ontario, continues today as the top amateur circuit in Canada and the fifth oldest continuously operating baseball league. Among its alums are Ferguson Jenkins, Jesse Orosco, Chris Speier, John Axford, and Rob Ducey.
8. *St. Thomas Times-Journal*, February 5, 1938 and April 26, 1943; undated 1939 *Niagara Falls Review*, Emslie scrapbook.
9. *St. Thomas Times-Journal*, January 26, 1937.
10. *St. Thomas Times-Journal*, April 26, 1943.
11. *St. Thomas Times-Journal*, April 26, 1943.

12. *St. Thomas Times-Journal*, April 26, 1943; undated 1939 article, *Niagara Falls Review*, Emslie scrapbook.
13. The year of death and age of umpires from the 1890s: 1895 Jack McQuaid 36; 1913 John Gaffney 58; 1915 Tim Hurst 50; 1924 Tom Lynch 65 and Ed Swartwood 65. From the Deadball Era: 1915 Steve Kane 46; 1920 Peter Harrison, 35; 1923 Paul Sentell 44; 1927 Jim Johnstone 55 and Tom Brown 68; 1928 Frank Wilson 41; 1929 Billy Nash 65; 1933 Bill Brennan 53; 1935 Hank O'Day 73 or 75 and Cy Rigler 53; 1937 Bob Hart 58 and Cy Pfirman 49; 1943 Frank Dwyer 75. NL Deadball stalwarts who died after Emslie: 1948 Al Orth 76; 1955 Bill Byron 83; 1960 Ernie Quigley 81; 1970 Mal Eason 91.
14. White and Watkins died in 1937, Atlantics teammates Jim Tray 1905, Charles "Chub" Collins 1914, Billy Hunter 1918, Jacob "Jay" Faatz 1923, and Billy Reid 1940; Orioles stalwarts Hardie Henderson 1903, Bill Traffley 1908, Jimmy Clinton 1921, Jimmy Macullar 1924, Tim Manning 1934, and Joe Sommer 1938.
15. *Sporting News*, December 19, 1940. Only James "Doc" Prothro's .301 winning percentage (138-320) with the Phillies 1939–41 is worse than McCloskey's .313 (190-417).
16. *Sporting News*, February 6, 1941; *Border Citizens Star*, May 24, 1939.
17. *St. Thomas Times-Journal*, January 26, 1939.
18. *St. Thomas Times-Journal*, April 26; *London Advertiser*, April 27, 1943; Robert Emslie death certificate.
19. *St. Thomas Times-Journal*, April 26 to April 29, 1943.
20. *Buffalo Courier-Express*, April 27, 1943; *Detroit Free Press*, April 27, 1943; *New York Times*, April 27, 1943; *Sporting News*, April 29, and May 6, 1943. *TSN* incorrectly says that Bob's birth date is January 21, he pitched for Guelph in 1880–81, and his playing career ended with Memphis in 1887. The *Times* also mistakenly said he developed a "bad arm" pitching for Memphis.
21. *St. Thomas Times-Journal*, April 27, 1943; *Niagara Falls Review*, April 30, 1943; *Montreal Gazette*, April 29, 1943; *Buffalo Courier-Express*, April 27, 1943; *Niagara Falls Review*, April 30, 1943.
22. *Toronto Telegram*, April 29, 1943; *Sporting News*, May 6, 1943; unidentified article, Emslie scrapbook.
23. David Fleitz, "The Forgotten Honor Rolls of the National Baseball Hall of Fame," *Baseball Research Journal* (Cleveland OH: Society for American Baseball Research, 2005), 53–59, and Bill James, *Whatever Happened to the Hall of Fame? Baseball, Cooperstown, and the Politics of Glory* (New York: Simon and Schuster, 1995). The other umpires selected were Bill Klem, Tommy Connolly, Bill Dinneen, Billy Evans, John Gaffney, Tim Hurst, "Honest John" Kelly, Francis

"Silk" O'Loughlin, Tom Lynch, and Jack Sheridan. Surprisingly, Hank O'Day was not included in the honor roll.

24. The other umpires with their dates of election: John "Jocko" Conlan 1974, Cal Hubbard 1976, Al Barlick 1989, Bill McGowan 1992, Nestor Chylack Jr. 1999; Doug Harvey 2010, and Hank O'Day 2013.
25. *Montreal Gazette*, June 4, 1955; Stephen J. Gamester, "You Can't Tell the Canadian Big-League Heroes without a Program," *Maclean's*, August 22, 1964, 22.

EPILOGUE

Epigraph: Published on February 20, 1951, by Memphis Press-Scimitar sports editor George Bugbee upon the death of umpire Harry "Steamboat" Johnson, "Emslie" inserted in place of "the Steamer."

1. He played and umpired in 1887 and as supervisor umpired in 1923 and 1924.
2. *St. Thomas Times-Journal*, April 27, 1843.
3. *Boston Globe*, August 17, 1920.
4. The others: O'Day, thirty-five and 3,983; Sheridan, nineteen and 2,177; Hurst, fifteen and 1548; Gaffney, fourteen and 1,107; and Lynch, thirteen and 1,325. Retrosheet's listing of 4,231 for Emslie omits a game on August 5, 1921. Connolly umpired for thirty-four years as a regular, in retirement calling one game in 1932 as a ceremonial substitute. O'Day actually umpired thirty years as a regular, as he worked seven games in four years (1884–90) as a player substitute and one game in 1896 as a civilian sub.
5. John M. Gruber, *Buffalo Morning Express*, January 11, 1914.
6. The two non-Deadball Era umpires with the most ejections through 2017 are Joe West, 27.4, and Bob Davidson, 22.3. David W. Smith, "Ejections through the Years and the Impact of Expanded Replay," table 5, https://www.retrosheet.org/Research/SmithD/EjectionsThroughTheYears.pdf.
7. Emslie began playing Minor League ball in 1883 and reached the Majors in 1884, while Connie Mack started in the Minors in 1884 and the Majors in 1886.
8. In 1946 Bill McKinley became the first graduate of a training school to reach the Majors. By the mid-1950s attending a training school was common, and by the 1960s it was a requirement. Bill Pruden, "Umpiring Schools: Training Grounds for the Guardians of the Game," in Gerlach and Nowlin, *SABR Book of Umpires*, 235–44.
9. See Chris Williams, "Major League Umpires and Unionization," Gerlach and Nowlin, *SABR Book of Umpires*, 415–20.
10. Not until 1966, twenty years after Jackie Robinson broke the modern color line, did Emmett Ashford join the AL to become the first Black Major League

umpire; in 1973 Art William became the NL's first African American arbiter. Despite the prominence of Latino players since the 1940s, Cuban-born Armando Rodriguez (1974) and American-born Rich Garcia (1975), both AL, were the first Hispanic umpires. Major League baseball, unlike professional football and basketball, has yet to hire women officials. For Negro League and women umpires see Leslie Heaphy, "Umpires in the Negro Leagues," and "Professional Women Umpires," Gerlach and Nowlin, *SABR Book of Umpires*, 170–76, 213–20.

11. David Vincent "Replay As An Umpiring Tool," Gerlach and Nowlin, *SABR Book of Umpires*, 306–18.
12. Eventually Bill Klem would become the oldest umpire, at sixty-seven, to call a game, and Tommy Connolly and Connie Mack would hold the consecutive league and overall service records. Connolly tallied fifty-six years, umpiring from 1898 to 1931 then serving as American League supervisor until 1954. Mack, who retired at age eighty-seven, logged sixty-one years, eleven as player (1886–96) and fifty as manager of the Philadelphia A's (1901–50), his tenure with the A's surely owing to being owner of the club.
13. Ernie Quigley also became significantly bald but did not wear a toupee while umpiring. *Chicago Daily News*, October 7, 1935.
14. Thomas P. Simon, ed., *Deadball Stars of the National League* (Cleveland OH: Society for American Baseball Research, 2004), 20, 21.
15. His ranking: Evans, Emslie, O'Day, Klem, and Rigler. *Washington Evening Star*, December 24, 1923; John B. Kennedy, "The Flying Dutchman," *Collier's*, April 12, 1930, 81.
16. *Pittsburgh Gazette Times*, January 28, 1924; *Sporting News*, March 17, 1954; *Wilmington News Journal*, March 17, 1954.
17. *Boston Globe*, July 8, 1900, and March 6, 1915; *Pittsburgh Gazette Times*, December 14. 1927; *New York Times*, July 31 and August 1, 1941.
18. For biographical sketches of Hall of Fame umpires see Gerlach and Nowlin, *SABR Book of Umpires*, 3–72.
19. *St. Louis Post-Dispatch*, August 12, 1974. The others were Francis "Silk" O'Loughlin, Hank O'Day, Tim Hurst, John "Beans" Reardon, Larry Goetz, and Cal Hubbard.
20. The University of Kansas named its baseball field after Ernie Quigley, National League umpire, 1913–38, who also served 1944–50 as the school's athletics director. John Ducey Park in Edmonton, Alberta, Canada, honored an Edmonton baseball executive who had previously umpired amateur and Minor League ball (1931–45). Unfortunately, money has trumped tradition, and both facilities have been renamed to recognize financial donors.

Index